Video Field Production and Editing

Video Field Production and Editing

Fifth Edition

Ronald J. Compesi

San Francisco State University

Allyn and Bacon

Boston   London   Toronto   Sydney   Tokyo   Singapore

Vice President and Editor-in-Chief: Paul A. Smith
Editor: Karon Bowers
Series Editorial Assistant: Jennifer Becker
Marketing Manager: Jackie Aaron
Composition/Prepress Buyer: Linda Cox
Production Administrator: Deborah Brown
Production Coordinator: Susan McNally
Copyeditor: Tammy Zambo
Text Design and Electronic Composition: Denise Hoffman
Manufacturing Buyer: Megan Cochran
Cover Administrator: Linda Knowles

Copyright © 2000, 1997, 1994, 1990, 1985 by Allyn & Bacon
A Pearson Education Company
160 Gould Street
Needham Heights, MA 02494

Internet: www.abacon.com

Library of Congress Cataloging-in-Publication Data

Compesi, Ronald J., 1949–
    Video field production and editing / Ronald J. Compesi. — 5th ed.
        p.   cm.
    Includes bibliographical references and index.
    ISBN 0-205-29556-8
    1. Television—Production and direction.   2. Video recordings—
Production and direction.   3. Video recordings—Equipment and
supplies.   I. Title.
    PN1992.75.C59   1999
    778.59'4 21—dc21   99-026738
                                                          CIP

Printed in the United States of America

10 9 8 7 6 5 4 3 2 1   04 03 02 01 00 99

Photo credits begin on page 459.

In Memory of Glenn Starlin

Contents

6 Lighting 149

7 Sound 193

Contents

VIDEO EDITING 4

Digital Nonlinear Video Editing 315

Graphics and Design 331

Production Planning 355

APPENDIX ONE

Production Projects 401

APPENDIX TWO

Development of Videotape Recording 409

Preface

As we enter the new millennium, a seemingly endless stream of technological developments continues to change the field of video production. The introduction of lightweight, portable video field production equipment has moved video production out of the studio and into the field, and the development and refinement of reliable, inexpensive editing systems has made postproduction editing more important then ever in the video production process.

Today the personal computer is well established as a video production tool and as a means both of displaying multimedia programs that integrate video with sound and text and of accessing live or recorded audio and video on the World Wide Web. The development of a variety of digital video recording formats, aimed at both the consumer and professional markets, and the adoption by the Federal Communications Commision of a new set of standards for advanced television services promise to usher in a new age of digital media production and distribution.

When the first edition of this book appeared in 1985, single-camera video field production represented a relatively new approach to video production. Most college and university courses in video production were taught in the context of multicamera studio production, and even in the world of professional broadcasting, one-piece camcorders were still a relatively new and expensive form of technology.

The world of video production has changed significantly since then. Field production is now one of the three major modes of video production (studio production and computer-generated imagery are the other two), and since the publication of the first edition of this book, video has become an increasingly important part of American life. Video camcorders and VCRs have become almost omnipresent in American homes and offices. Video is widely used in education, business, medicine, and law, as well as in the traditional broadcast arena.

This new edition of *Video Field Production and Editing* reflects the changes in technology and production processes that have taken place since the publication of the fourth edition. However, the central purpose of this book remains the same: to provide a text for students involved in video field production, concentrating on production techniques and technology appropriate to single-camera electronic field production (EFP) and electronic news gathering (ENG). The principal features of the book are as follows:

1. A focus on the single-camera or camcorder video field production process, with an emphasis on portable video (8mm/Hi8, VHS/S-VHS, Betacam SP, and 1/4" Digital Video Cassette [DV]) equipment. This new edition includes more than 100 new photographs and illustrations of contemporary video field production practices and equipment. A section of color plates (CP) illustrates basic principles of the color video system and production techniques dependent on color signal processing.

2. A fusion of aesthetic and technical concerns. The book discusses production strategies and processes, as well as principles of equipment operation. Material has been reorganized and updated throughout the text. Chapter 2 has been refocused on how the video camera creates the electronic video signal, and Chapter 5 now deals with camcorder operation. The text and illustrations in Chapter 12 (on graphics and design) have been thoroughly revised, and Chapter 13 (on production planning) has been expanded to include updated material on copyright issues, as well as a discussion of ethics and video production.

3. A full discussion of the elements and techniques of video recording and postproduction editing, including editing aesthetics; linear, cuts-only editing; and A/B-roll and digital nonlinear editing. The material on editing aesthetics has been expanded, and new sections on digital recording and the new ATSC digital television standards have been added. A new Chapter 11 focuses exclusively on digital nonlinear editing.

4. The appendixes contain a series of production exercises designed to help the potential producer develop production competence, as well as additional information on lighting, videotape recording, digital media and the metric system, and remote production planning.

5. As in the previous editions, key words are identified in boldface throughout the text. The book contains a comprehensive glossary of terms and a bibliography of books and periodicals of interest to the video field producer.

The organization of the book reflects my concern with providing a discussion of the production techniques and organization that are commonly used in video field production, as well as the technology that makes this kind of production possible. As a result, most chapters are divided into two parts: one section deals with the technical aspects of production, and the other deals with production techniques or aesthetics.

Throughout the book I have attempted to aim the technical discussion at the general reader who has little or no technical background in video or electronics. I hope that you will let me know whether, through your experience with the text, I have hit or missed the mark.

Each chapter is a self-contained unit, and the chapters may be read out of sequence without causing problems. For example, the material in Chapter 13 may serve well as an introduction to the book, as it provides an overview of the major components of the field production planning process. In the classroom I have had success assigning that chapter early on in the semester and then reassigning it as a refresher near the middle or end of the course.

One other comment deserves to be made here. The focus of the book is on video field production, but this needs to be qualified. I have concentrated primarily on what some writers have called "small-scale" field production, because this is the type of production that most student and home video producers (as well as many independent and broadcast producers) are most often engaged in. These productions typically involve a minimum amount of field equipment and a small crew. The book is thus most informative for the video producer who has access to a camcorder, a few microphones, a small lighting kit, and a simple linear or nonlinear editing system. Although the text does provide some descriptions of larger-scale productions and production equipment, this is not the primary focus of the book. I should note, however, that small-scale production does not mean amateur production. Because the line between broadcast-quality production and equipment and nonbroadcast production is a thin one indeed, professional standards of production are stressed throughout the book.

Acknowledgments

I owe a great debt of gratitude to the many people who have contributed to the making of this book. My colleague and former coauthor, Ronald E. Sherriffs of the University of Oregon, made significant contributions to the book as it evolved through its first four editions, and his influence is still strongly felt in this edition. My colleagues in the Department of Broadcast and Electronic Communication Arts at San Francisco State University have provided invaluable assistance as the book has evolved through five editions. In particular I thank Larry Whitney, Vinay Shrivastava, Herb Zettl, Josh Hecht, Lena Zhang, and John Hewitt. Thanks are also due to my many students at San Francisco State University.

Winston Tharp, Jerry Higgins, Peter Maravelias and Kim Foscato, all of San Francisco State University, deserve special thanks for the guidance they provided on technical matters. Phil Arnone, Rosy Chu, Michael Krajac, Steve Shlisky, Robert Erdiakoff, and Steele Douglas, all of KTVU-TV in Oakland, California, provided a wealth of information on field production techniques and technologies.

I also thank those people who provided new photographs for the fifth edition: Jason Pavelko (De Sisti Lighting), Jan Biles (Digidesign), Rebecca Waters and John Tariot (FOOTAGE.net), Tasha Campos (Kino Flo, Inc.), Patrice Jackson and Gregg Perry (Mackie Designs), Jim Wickizer and Tina Dobra (Panasonic Broadcast and Digital Systems Company), Jason Frenchman (Quantel, Inc.), Lori Vanicek, Carol Ann Whisker, Robert Ott, and Alex Johnson (Sony Electronics, Inc.), Frank Logan (Tektronix), Bill Stickney (Videomedia), Brett Kotheimer, Marlon Quintero, and in particular, Larry Whitney and Jedidiah Gildersleeve (San Francisco State University). Thanks are also due to the following people who appear in the photographs in this edition: Michael Bellew, Tim Burby, Matt Chan, Cara and Marisa Compesi, Alan DeDeaux, Arthur France, Joshua Haworth, Monique Hedrick, Delicia Hegwood, Jamie Holthouse, Deana Igelsrud, Wa'el Kassis, Dennis Kellett, Megan Kling, Sindia Massis, Pedro Moreno-Carrascal, Andy Sandeen, Parul Shah, Ron Sherriffs, Dawn Smith, Frank Somerville, Andrew Tsonis, and Jane Veeder.

Thanks also to those individuals who read earlier drafts of the manuscript and whose comments made it a better book, including Ralph Carmode (Jacksonville State University), Greg Durbin (San Diego State University), Joel Fowler (California State University at Fresno), Slawomir Grunberg (Ithaca College), Susan Kehoe (George Mason University), John MacKerron (Towson State University), Nikos Metallinos (Concordia University), Warren Pease (University of Oregon), Louis Pullano (Brookdale Community College), Michael Real (San Diego State University), Michael Schoonmaker (Syracuse University), Pete Seel (Colorado State University), Sharon Sandeen (McGeorge School of Law), C. John Sincell (University of Maryland), and Larry Whitney (San Francisco State University). I would like to thank my editor, Karon Bowers, and the members of the design and production team at Allyn and Bacon for their enthusiasm and attention to detail: production administrator Deborah Brown, production coordinator Susan McNally, copyeditor Tammy Zambo, and text designer Denise Hoffman.

Finally, special thanks are due to Cathy Sandeen for her encouragement and constructive criticism through five editions of this book and to Marisa and Cara for being cooperative models and for giving up their time on the computer while Dad was using it to revise the manuscript.

1 Introduction

In the Field with *Evening Magazine*

The clock on the train platform reads 6:30 A.M. as I climb aboard the train and head for the city. The sun is not yet up and the usual bay fog hangs over the water as the train pulls out of the station. Today is a big day. In a few hours, I will be on the road with the crew from *Evening Magazine,* accompanying them on a remote shoot to see how things are done in the real world of video field production.

In less than 30 minutes, the train reaches the downtown station and I hop off and head for the escalator to street level. The sky has brightened considerably as I join the other morning commuters in their trek to the office. The fog has left the pavement slick, and I walk carefully as I thread my way through the downtown streets to the television station where I am scheduled to meet the field producer who has invited me along for the morning shoot. I arrive at the station at 7:30 and Mike, the producer, arrives moments later. We are not scheduled to leave until 8:30, so we duck into a restaurant across the street for a quick breakfast and some strong coffee.

Today's shoot centers on Tom K., a 24-year-old patient at a nearby medical center. Several months ago, Tom was stricken by a virus that seriously damaged his heart. Today, his heart is working at only 15 percent of its normal capacity—the damage done by the virus is severe and irreparable. He has been on the waiting list for a heart transplant for over a month.

The story being planned by *Evening Magazine* focuses on Tom and on a fund-raising effort that has been organized by some of his friends. They plan to waterski over 70 miles in the ocean to publicize Tom's case and to solicit funds to help pay his medical bills. The story will consist of interviews with his friends, actual footage of the open-ocean waterskiing, and interviews with Tom and his doctor. The latter interviews are scheduled to be recorded today. We have a 9:30 A.M. appointment with Tom at the medical center.

Mike and I finish breakfast and walk the short block and a half back to the station and go up to the *Evening Magazine* offices. There's not much activity at this time of the morning. The office occupies one corner of the floor of the building. Sections of the office have been partitioned off into small cubicle-like offices for the staff members. Two permanent rooms off to one side house the video editing equipment and serve as work stations for the two video editors. Several other offices have been assigned to the show's producer and associate producer. Large windows face out into the city and toward the bridge across the bay.

Mike makes a few last-minute phone calls as we prepare to leave the station. Rita, the camera operator, or "shooter," has arrived. We're waiting for Don, the production assistant. It's Don's job to drive the van that will carry us to the medical center, which is about an hour's drive south. At 8:30, there's still no sign of Don, and Mike begins to get a bit agitated. It's crucial that the interview be completed today, as Tom could receive the transplant at any time and the interview must be finished before the operation. Mike is getting more anxious. Finally, Don arrives.

The van is parked in the basement garage, along with other station vehicles and the employees' cars. The sides and rear are decorated with the distinctive logo that identifies *Evening Magazine*. I notice an electrical extension cord trailing out a window into a wall socket. This connection to power is being used to charge up the extra batteries carried inside the van that will power the video equipment in the field.

We all pile into the van and head toward the freeway through the early morning traffic. Three bucket seats hold the driver and two regular passengers. I get to sit on a milk carton next to the sliding door. The interior of the van is paneled and carpeted, and shows the effects of plenty of wear.

Against one wall of the van is a metal cart. On it are various pieces of video equipment: a color monitor, a portable videocassette recorder (VCR), and a forest of cables. Next to this, against the same wall, is a shelf holding half a dozen or so batteries, all locked into the charging unit. Above them is a shelf of videocassettes. On the floor at the rear of the van, on a small rectangular piece of carpet, lies the camcorder. The body of the camcorder shows signs of wear. It's scratched and dented in the places that are not covered over with decals. The *Evening Magazine* logo is evident. One side of the camera carries a decal of Chinese ideographs—a souvenir from a recent trip to the People's Republic of China.

We arrive at the medical center at 9:30 A.M. and, after some negotiation with a traffic guard, manage to park the van in a red zone near the main entrance to the hospital. Mike goes inside to confirm the interview arrangements with the publicity director of the hospital, and Rita and Don begin to take equipment out of the van.

While Mike is inside, Rita and Don talk about whether today will be a two-tape or a three-tape day. The discussion is important from a planning standpoint because Don has responsibility for bringing along enough blank tape to record the interviews. If he brings only two tapes and they need a third, he will have to return to the van. However, more important than the planning considerations is what a two-tape or a three-tape day means in terms of the amount of work the crew will be required to perform. On a two-tape day, they finish work earlier than on a three-tape day.

A few minutes later, Mike returns and indicates that everything is set—the interviews can go on as planned. For the next 10 minutes or so, he gives a quick overview of the story as he sees it. He indicates that when the story is edited, it will begin with a montage sequence built out of the waterskiing shots, and then the piece will establish the main theme—that this is a benefit for Tom. Mike talks briefly about the interview segments with Tom and his doctor and mentions some specific shots he would like to have: a shot of Tom walking down a hallway to establish him and the location, shots of Tom being examined by his doctor, and so on. At 9:45, we head into the hospital. Rita carries the camcorder and a tripod. Don has a shotgun microphone and some headphones. I'm carrying a canvas bag filled with tape, cables, batteries, extra microphones, and other miscellaneous equipment, and Mike has a large soft light and stand in hand.

We set up the equipment in a hallway and Mike introduces us to Tom. He's extremely personable and jokes about his health and his role in this program. "I've never been on TV before," he deadpans. "I feel like one of Jerry's kids."

Between 10:00 and 10:45 A.M., the crew shoots at least six different situations with Tom. The establishing shot Mike called for is staged in the hallway. Two takes are recorded, since Tom looked at the camera and laughed in the first one. The camera is moved outside, and we record several takes of Tom entering and exiting the hospital. Then it's back inside the building to record him as he is weighed on a scale in the hall, as his blood pressure is taken in an examining room, and as he talks with the nurse who has been supervising this activity. The entrance of the doctor into the examining room is staged and recorded, then his actions in the room are recorded without any rehearsal or guidance from the crew.

Throughout most of the taping, the crew members ask the nurse, the doctor, and Tom to go about their normal business and not pay any special attention to the camera. Rita, the camera operator, busily focuses on different elements of the activity. I notice on several occasions that she appears to reshoot something she has just shot; for example, at one point she starts a shot on a close-up of the nurse and then pans across to Tom. Apparently unhappy with the way the shot came out, she refocuses on the nurse and repeats the shot.

At 10:45, Mike interviews Tom's doctor in the hall outside the examination room. The light is set up, a small microphone is pinned onto the doctor, and the interview is completed in about 10 minutes. Hospital personnel freely move through the hall as the interview takes place. Once again, Don and Rita tell the hospital personnel not to worry about interfering with the crew's work.

At 11:10, we move upstairs to the Cardiac Echo Lab, where a sonar device will be used to show what the inside of Tom's heart looks like. The output of the device is displayed on a small television monitor. It's eerie to watch Tom lying on the examination table and to see his heart beating on the nearby television screen. Rita records the image on the screen and also records the doctor as he traces over Tom's chest with the sonar device. Don uses a shotgun microphone on an extendable fishpole boom to record the sound.

We move back downstairs and out to an exterior courtyard to set up for the interview with Tom. The fog has reappeared and the day is a bit gloomy. Rita finds a bench for Tom to sit on and decides she will need to use the soft light to add some brightness to the picture. We find some exterior electrical outlets to plug in the light. A large piece of blue plastic, a conversion filter, is clipped onto the front of the lighting instrument so that its light matches the color of daylight.

Don worries about the noise being generated by air conditioners protruding from the building walls into the courtyard. He conducts an audio test and decides together with Mike that the sound is acceptable. At 11:25, Tom joins us outside and Mike conducts the interview. He has some questions written down in a reporter's notebook and asks the questions from off-camera. The interview is short—approximately 10 minutes. We thank Tom for his help and he heads back inside to wait for the day when a heart is available for transplant. We dismantle the equipment and return it to the van. Rita pops one of the videotapes into the VCR on the rack inside the van and checks the picture quality and sound on the monitor. Everything is OK. My watch reads 11:48 as we climb into the van to head back to the station. It is a two-tape day.

During the next week, two events occur that have significance to the story. First, the crew goes out in the middle of the week and shoots the ocean waterskiing footage. Unfortunately, the weather is bad and the sea is rough, and the skiers are unable to complete the planned 70-mile event. Then, one week after our interview with Tom, a compatible heart becomes available for transplantation. The operation is completed without complications. About three weeks after the interview with Tom was shot, the story is broadcast on *Evening Magazine*. It appears as a hopeful story of a young man's fight to win back the life that once hung so precariously in the balance.

The kind of production typified by *Evening Magazine* represents an approach that has become one of the dominant modes of video production. Shooting with a single camcorder, which combines a high-quality video camera and videocassette recorder into one easily carried unit, and a relatively small crew by traditional television standards, organizations like

Figure 1.1
Television News
Photographers
Equipped with
Professional
Camcorders
Cover the Arrival
of the President

Evening Magazine have revolutionized the concept of video production. Increasingly, video production is **field production;** it takes place in the outside world, rather than in a studio inside a television station or video production facility (see Figure 1.1).

This type of production depends on reliable, portable video production equipment and on the ability of skilled production personnel to use it. The focus of this book is on such single-camera video field production—on the equipment that makes it possible and on the production techniques and strategies that can be used to create effective messages through the use of this technology.

 # The Changing Nature of Video Production

When television was introduced to the U.S. public at the 1939 World's Fair in New York, it thrilled those who saw it. The display was impressive: Technicians, cameras, lights, and the instantaneous transmission of a televised image and sound were all part of the event. Not only was the demonstration impressive but so was the equipment, particularly its size. Television cameras and television lights were very large and complicated pieces of equipment. Indeed, during the first several decades of its existence, television production was characterized by the large size of the equipment needed to produce those images.

In the early days of television (and even today for large-scale remote sports productions), a **remote production**—one staged outside a studio—was an incredibly complicated event, involving scores of technicians and an armada of equipment. When one went on a *remote*, essentially one took the television studio along and set it up at the remote location. The same equipment used in the studio was often rolled into a truck and used for a remote broadcast.

For many years, only two alternatives were available to a producer who wished to incorporate remote material into a production. The first alternative was a live electronic remote broadcast, with the attendant problems inherent in transporting huge amounts of television equipment to the remote location. The other possibility was to cover the event on film. And so, for many years, film had an important place in television production primarily because it was portable. Until the mid-1970s, film was used extensively in television for news and documentary production, largely because of the portability of 16mm film equipment. However, a revolution was brewing in television that would change remote production. It started quietly enough, but by the 1980s, the use of film for remote television production was largely replaced by the use of portable video equipment.

In many ways, the development of television paralleled the development of film. Just as film depended on a studio setting for recording in its early decades, so did television. Television of the 1940s, 1950s, and 1960s was essentially studio production. Live television was studio television (unless it was a sports event). The teleplays of the *Golden Age of Television* (the mid-1950s) were live television studio productions. When the first videotape recorders were introduced by Ampex in 1956, at the annual convention of the National Association of Broadcasters (NAB), they also followed the large format of studio television cameras. The videotape recorders were behemoths, weighing hundreds of pounds. Even though they came equipped with wheels, they could hardly be characterized as portable.

However, in 1965, Sony introduced the first "small-format" recording system to the market, and the video revolution began. This black and white videotape recorder used a $1/2$"-wide tape format (compared to the 2" broadcast format then in use) and an extremely small camera pickup tube. Although the signal quality was not technically of broadcast quality, the introduction of the equipment was a boon for people interested in video equipment and production. Video production equipment, previously accessible only to those with a large amount of capital to invest, was now available to almost anyone who wanted it. In addition, whereas television had largely been a studio enterprise prior to the introduction of portable small-format equipment, videomakers now could venture into the field with their electronic equipment. In 1970, $1/2$" video formats were standardized, $1/2$" videotape editors were introduced, and the revolution was truly under way. Table 1.1 chronicles some of the highlights in the development of video technology.

The introduction of portable $3/4$" VCRs and automated editing systems in the early 1970s was of great importance because the $3/4$" format was

Table 1.1 Video Technology Marches On

1939	Television introduced at New York World's Fair. Black and white only; no videotape recording.
1941	Federal Communications Commission (FCC) accepts National Television System Committee (NTSC) standards for black-and-white broadcast television.
1953	FCC accepts NTSC standards for color television.
1956	Ampex introduces black-and-white 2″ quadruplex videotape recorder (VTR) at annual National Association of Broadcasters (NAB) convention and receives 1,000 orders for machines before the convention ends.
1956	First use of videotape on network television. On November 30, CBS uses Ampex VR 1000 to rebroadcast *Douglas Edwards and the News* to the West Coast.
1965	Sony introduces first ½″ portable VTR system, including portable camera and recorder.
1966	Commercial television networks achieve full-color, prime-time schedules.
1968	Ampex introduces first color VTR.
1970	½″ formats are standardized, and ½″ editors are introduced.
1971	Sony introduces the ¾″ videocassette recorder (VCR).
1972	Consolidated Video Systems introduces the first time-base corrector.
1974	CBS begins electronic news gathering with Ikegami cameras and IVC 1″ VTR.
1974	Sony introduces portable ¾″ VCR and automated ¾″ editing system.
1975	Betamax (½″ cassette format) is introduced by Sony.
1976	VHS (½″ cassette format) is introduced.
1981	One-piece Betacam (Sony) and M-format camcorders (RCA Hawkeye and Panasonic RECAM) are introduced.
1983	Beta HiFi is introduced to consumer market. VHS HiFi follows the next year.
1983	United States Supreme Court decides that use of VCRs for off-air recording at home does not violate the Copyright Act (*Disney* v. *Sony Corporation of America*). Sales of home VCRs boom.
1984	FCC approves stereo television broadcasting. First stereo broadcasts of *The Tonight Show* and the Olympics.
1984	RCA and NEC introduce broadcast-quality CCD (charge-coupled device) cameras in which vacuum-type pickup tubes are replaced with silicon chips.
1985	Sony 8mm camcorder is introduced.
1986	Introduction of ½″ Betacam SP format.
1987	S-VHS (Super VHS) ½″ tape format introduced.
1989	First successful experimental broadcast of HDTV (high-definition television) in the United States.
1990	Introduction of NewTek Video Toaster.
1991	Panasonic introduces portable ½″ D3 digital tape format camcorder.
1995	Ikegami and Avid Technologies introduce "Camcutter," a docking camcorder that records a digital video signal on magnetic disks instead of conventional videotape.
1995	Sony and Panasonic introduce DV (digital videocassette) format camcorders. Most major video equipment manufacturers join in accepting the DV format standards.
1996	FCC adopts Advanced Television System Committee standards for digital HDTV.
1998	First regularly scheduled network HDTV broadcast on November 1 as ABC broadcasts the Disney film *101 Dalmations*. Digital television transmission begins at more than 40 local stations by the end of November.
2003	(May) Target date for all United States television stations to convert to digital broadcasting.
2006	Target date to phase out analog televison broadcasting in the United States.

suitable for use by both broadcasters and other videomakers interested in nonbroadcast remote production. The portable $^3/_4''$ recorder-camera-editing systems, along with the newly developed **time base correctors (TBCs)** that stabilized the video signal, paved the way for the full development of broadcast electronic news gathering and the acceptance of portable video equipment by the broadcast community. Today a large variety of small tape formats offer video producers a wide range of production choices.

Portable video systems have been significantly refined in the three decades since their introduction. Portable systems composed of a separate camera tethered by cable to a portable VCR have been replaced by one-piece camcorders, and video editing systems have become smaller, less expensive, and more precise. While much of the equipment used in video field production and editing today is based upon conventional analog signal processing and recording, a whole new generation of digital camcorders and nonlinear digital editing systems is poised to take their place as the current analog systems wear out and are replaced and as the U.S. broadcast system converts to a new, federally mandated digital standard.

Production Uses of Portable Video Equipment

It is important to note that video production no longer is an expensive, labor-intensive activity available only to federally licensed television broadcasters. As a result of the portability and accessibility of this new technology, video has found a host of new uses. Portable video is increasingly being used for personal expression, for independent production, in educational institutions and corporations, and in the arena of broadcast and cable television.

Personal Video

Because of its relatively low cost, portable video equipment has made video accessible to individuals in much greater numbers than ever before. VCRs can be found in almost 90 percent of all U.S. homes and camcorders in about half. VCRs and camcorders are among the most popular consumer electronics items introduced in recent years.

Personal uses of portable video equipment vary. Some people buy player-recorders for use primarily in their home entertainment systems. These machines are used to record programs that have been broadcast or cablecast, or they are used to play back owned or rented videocassettes. A growing segment of users have purchased portable video camcorders in addition to their home player-recorders. These low-cost camcorders have the

Figure 1.2
Hi8 Camcorder—
A Popular Portable
Video Recording
Format

advantage of producing electronic recordings that are available for imme-
diate playback. They are used extensively to record family events such as
birthdays, special parties, and weddings. Sports enthusiasts use them to record and then criticize their own sports performances, such as golf swings,
swimming strokes, and tennis serves. In addition, they are convenient for
making visual and sound messages to send to friends or relatives who live
far away (see Figure 1.2).

Independent Video Production

Independent video production refers to those organizations and individuals who use video to make their own programs or who make their production skills and facilities available to others who want to produce and distribute messages via video. A large group of independents have used video
to produce television documentaries. Almost any large or medium-sized
community contains individuals who are working on video documentaries
that focus on various community-oriented social, economic, and political
problems. These independents may have a number of goals in mind. Some
may try to gain access to their local cable company or television station
with their finished program, whereas others may try to distribute their material regionally or nationally. Whatever the distribution aim, the availability of relatively inexpensive equipment and facilities provides an opportunity for video production independents to express alternative viewpoints
on community and national problems.

9

Independent artists have been using video for some time. Video has become popular as a medium for artistic expression, and numerous video experimenters have gained access to the medium through the use of portable equipment. Whether the artistic statement is dramatic or experimental, whether it involves the manipulation of content or formal properties of the medium (such as lighting, editing, or sound), access to the medium has been facilitated by the introduction and use of this equipment.

Many independent producers produce videotapes for clients. These may range from producing a videotape for a couple who want to record their wedding, to producing tapes for a small company that does not have its own video production facility but that wants a tape that introduces a new product to a client or trains employees in new sales techniques, new methods of product maintenance, and so on.

Educational Uses

In the past decade, numerous educational institutions have turned to video, primarily for nonbroadcast, in-house uses. For example, video is often used in schools as a supplement to instruction. Indeed, some actual instruction may be done via televised lectures live or on videotape. Speeches in public-speaking classes are taped and then played back for a critique by the instructor or class. Teacher-training programs often videotape student teachers to provide a record of their classroom performance. Colleges and universities with programs in the broadcast or electronic media most frequently use portable, small-format equipment in their laboratories and cable television facilities.

Medical Video

Many hospitals have their own video staffs and put video to a variety of uses. It is used for the distribution of in-house information or for instruction in new medical techniques as a part of an ongoing program of continuing education. It is also sometimes used to provide information to patients on various health problems and their treatment. Institutions involved in providing therapeutic treatment, such as counseling or other forms of therapy, to patients with speech defects or mental or emotional problems often use video as part of therapy or to record therapy sessions.

Legal Video

Video is finding increasing use in legal settings. The broadcast of President Bill Clinton's August 17, 1998, videotaped grand jury testimony brought worldwide attention to this specialized use of video technology.

Professional guidelines have been established in most states for the recording of legal depositions. Legal video producers are in demand to produce video reenactments of accidents and crime scenes as well as to design effective video presentations of critical exhibits of evidence, such as photographs, maps, time lines, and so on, for use in courtroom presentations.

Corporate Video

Many large corporations use videotape to distribute electronic corporate newsletters to their employees, particularly if corporate offices are widely distributed. In-house training or staff development is another common use, as are videotapes for use at the point of sale. You have probably seen product demonstrations on cassettes being played in department stores.

Government Uses

Local, county, state, and federal government agencies also are significant users of video. Many government agencies produce videotapes to inform their constituents of new programs, policies, regulations, or accomplishments (see Figure 1.3). In some cases, these tapes may be cablecast or broadcast via local media outlets.

Figure 1.3
Portable Video on
the Moon

11

Public Access

Similarly, portable video has proved invaluable for local media access groups. Many cable systems operate public access centers in which studio or remote equipment is available to community members. A provision for community access may be included in the franchise agreement for the cable company that operates in the town or city where you live.

Broadcast and Cable Television

The move toward the miniaturization of professional-quality equipment is a strong and continuous process. Broadcast and cable television uses of portable video equipment have centered in two areas: **electronic news gathering (ENG)** and **electronic field production (EFP)**. It was in the area of ENG that portable video equipment first made a significant impact in broadcasting. Prior to its introduction, broadcasters relied on film for stories that took place in the field, or on the placement of live remote television cameras. The difficulty with film recording was the time delay involved in returning the film to the station or network and in processing and editing the film.

The introduction of lightweight, portable video recording systems changed the face of television news. Most local television stations, as well as the major broadcast networks, made the transition from film to portable video for electronic news gathering in the mid-1970s. The creation of 24-hour cable news channels like CNN and MSNBC was made possible by portable video production equipment and the microwave and satellite transmission links that are used to instantaneously transmit pictures and sound of news events as they occur anywhere in the world.

Similarly, the existence of portable broadcast-quality video recorders and cameras made possible the growth of EFP. Before the introduction of this equipment, much local television programming had been based in the studio or shot on film by those few stations with a commitment to remote production. The introduction of portable professional-quality equipment made it much easier for producers to get out of the studio. Nationally syndicated television magazine feature programs, such as *Hard Copy, A Current Affair,* and *Entertainment Tonight,* rely on remote production crews using portable video camcorders. Programs such as *48 Hours, 60 Minutes, Dateline,* and *20/20* are examples of network television programs that make extensive use of portable video technology. A host of "reality-based" programs, such as *Real World, Cops,* and *America's Most Wanted,* rely as well on portable video technology for field production and editing. These programs reflect the fact that quality production no longer depends on studio-based equipment. Portable video production equipment has proven itself to be a reliable and cost-effective part of the professional video production process.

Multimedia/CD-ROM Production and the World Wide Web

Not all video is destined to be viewed on a conventional television set. With the increasing popularity of personal computers for the home, there is a growing demand for the skills professional video producers can bring to multimedia production. **Multimedia** programs incorporate animation, sound, text, illustrations, and video. Frequently produced for distribution on **CD-ROMs** (compact disc read-only memory), these programs are viewed on a computer screen and allow the viewer to interact with the program material (see Figure 1.4).

In addition, viewers have increasing access to video that is distributed via the Internet from a wide variety of World Wide Web (WWW) sites. Although the limited bandwidth of the typical telephone modem link to the Internet does not yet allow for full-screen, full-motion video displays on home computer screens, new developments in video compression and transmission technologies, and more powerful home computers, will continue to improve the quality of video and sound distributed through the Internet.

Figure 1.4
Multimedia
Incorporates Video
and Sound

Sony Prosumer Digital Video Cassette (DV)
Camcorder (DCR-VX 1000)

JVC Professional S-VHS Camcorder
(GY-X2 BU)

Panasonic Professional DVCPRO
Camcorder (AJ-D200)

Figure 1.5
Prosumer and
Professional
Camcorders

Consumer, Industrial, and Broadcast Equipment

Manufacturers of video equipment are sensitive to the fact that equipment capabilities and cost need to be matched to the needs and budgets of different kinds of equipment users. As a result, equipment is designed and marketed to serve distinct segments of video users: *consumer (or home) video users,* the *professional corporate/ industrial* market of largely nonbroadcast producers, and the *broadcast* market. A fourth market niche, often called *prosumer,* falls between consumer video and professional/industrial video. Generally speaking, as you move up the scale from one category of equipment to the next, the range of features, performance characteristics, and cost of the equipment all increase significantly (see Figure 1.5).

 ## Video as a Medium of Communication

Video is both a medium of communication and a type of technology. The successful producer must understand not only the components and operation of the technology of video communication but also the elements of the process of communication via video. As we view the process of video field production, five elements characterize this particular communication situation:

1. The unique elements of the production organization (*source*)
2. The fundamental importance of *message* design
3. The importance of the video medium as a *channel* of communication
4. The particular nature of the *audience*
5. Audience *feedback* to the program producer

Figure 1.6 graphically displays this communication process.

Production Organization

The video field production group is often significantly smaller than the studio production organization. Typically, the principal roles involved in producing single-camera remote productions are the **producer,** who is responsible for the overall organization of a production and for delegating responsibility to the other members of the production team; the *camera operator,* or **videographer** (sometimes called the **shooter**), who is responsible for the visual treatment of the subject matter as well as for the physical operation of the camera; the **production assistant,** who is responsible for monitoring audio, helping to set up the lights, and providing other general production support; and the **video editor,** who is responsible for executing the producer's vision in the process of postproduction editing. The editor has primary responsibility for physically performing the edits, and, depending on the role of the producer, the editor may have much or little responsibility for actually making editing decisions. In many cases, work roles overlap. An entire production may be produced by two or three people, with each assuming several responsibilities during the production.

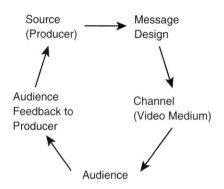

Figure 1.6 Communication Process via Television and Video

15

The nature of single-camera field production and the small production crew it involves often create a sense of excitement and responsibility that studio productions lack. Each person's contribution counts. There is often intense involvement by the crew on the production, and those involved exercise greater control over the final product than do their counterparts in studio production. The challenge of recording in the field, the excitement of instantly playing back images that were recorded only minutes ago, and the intense involvement demanded by the editing process all characterize video field production (see Table 1.2).

Message Design

Message design is a critical part of the telecommunication process. Ironically, one of the first elements that should be considered is the desired *effect* of the message. Who is to do what with this information? Because the goal of most commercial television programming is to maximize the size of the viewing audience at a given time, many program producers and station program directors desire to design and distribute entertaining and infor-

Table 1.2   Multiple-Camera Studio and Single-Camera
Video Field Production Characteristics

	Studio	Field
Number of cameras	Multiple cameras (usually 2 or 3)	Single camera

Size of crew	Large (often 8 or more)
	    Producer
	    Director
	    Audio
	    Camera operators (2 or 3)
	    Floor director
	    Technical director
	    VTR operator
		Small (usually 2 or 3)
		    Producer
		    Camera operator
		    Production assistant

Recording method	Usually live or live on tape; a complete program or large segments	Individual segments or shots to be edited or inserted into a larger program

Amount of control over environment	Controlled studio
	    Studio lighting
	    Sound (acoustics) controlled
	    Assured source of power
	    Availabe technical support staff
		Uncontrolled remote location
		    Available light
		    Ambient, location sound
		    Must provide own power
		    No technical support

Type of script	Usually fully or semiscripted	May be fully scripted, often semiscripted

mative programs that will appeal to the largest cross-section of the general viewing audience. Success is typically measured in terms of program ratings, which provide an estimate of the size of the audience and determine how much money advertisers can be charged to place their commercials on the air.

Producers of educational and industrial video programs frequently begin the design stage of their productions by thinking in terms of a list of specific objectives—things they hope the audience will be able to understand or do after viewing a particular program. Whether you are producing a program designed to teach language or computational skills to children or new safety procedures to employees in your manufacturing facility, you must have a clear understanding of the effects you expect your program to have on the viewer before you begin to produce it. Naturally, you will also need to consider your target audience as well. A program aimed at children will be approached differently from one aimed at adults, even if the subject matter is similar. Message design is therefore concerned with the basic idea, which involves the choice of subject; a decision about how that subject will be treated as it is presented through the video medium; and an understanding of how to control the treatment of the subject to achieve maximum impact on the target audience.

The Video Medium

Perhaps more than anything else, the small screen characterizes television and video. Unlike theatrical motion pictures, for which the screen may be 30 feet high and 100 feet wide, in most home, school, and institutional viewing situations television is most often watched on screens measuring 27 inches or less in diagonal. Until larger-screen "home theater" and HDTV (high-definition television) television sets become the standard, television programs will continue to be designed in close-up detail for viewing on small screens.

The audience has learned to expect close-ups and reaction shots, and the successful producer will give the audience what it expects with respect to these conventions. Close-ups provide the magnification often necessary for small-screen use. Magnification, a key to visibility, is central to most video production. Close-ups are also important because they are a means of focusing audience attention on a specific detail or relationship by eliminating all other parts of the picture.

Reaction shots are important to messages designed to persuade or to generate an emotional response. The use of reaction shots evolved as media practitioners learned that the effect of a statement or action is determined by the receiver, not the sender. The quick cut to the face of a person listening to a speaker reveals how the speech is being received, whether it is being accepted or rejected. In seeing how this person reacts, the audience is told how to react in turn.

The Audience

The dictum "know your audience" is just as important for video producers as it is for public speakers. Producers of corporate and instructional video always include a description of the characteristics of the program's target audience in their preproduction planning material and use their knowledge of the target audience to guide production decisions at each step of the production process. Even though broadcast and cable television are often thought of as forms of mass communication, the successful video producer realizes that communication takes place between the message and an *individual* in the audience. Even though someone may be part of a very large audience, the individual's response to a program is always an important one. For a message or program to be effective, it must communicate individually to each person in the audience. This is no easy task, given the variations that may exist among different audience members.

Feedback

Feedback is that part of the communication process in which audience responses to the production are transmitted to the producers. The nature and extent of feedback are related to the type of production and the way in which it is distributed to and received by the audience. In commercial broadcast and cable television, program ratings—a measure of the size of the audience—provide one indication of the audience response to a program. Telephone calls and letters from audience members to stations and networks are also an important part of the feedback process. For the home video producer, feedback might take the form of comments by family members on the quality of the videotape documenting a family celebration. Feedback is extremely useful to the video producer because it provides important information about the audience's response to the program or videotape—information that the producer needs to have in order to make subsequent productions more effective.

Technical Factors and Aesthetic Factors

Video field production combines an understanding of the technical factors of production with the aesthetic factors of production. **Technical factors** relate to developing an operational understanding of the way in which equipment functions. To work successfully with portable video equipment, you must understand how the equipment works. This does not mean that you need to be an engineer or understand all of the electronic and physical principles that govern the operations of the equipment. What it does mean is that you must have an understanding of the way in which the system operates—the way in which different technical elements interrelate and the way in which you can control the technical components of production. It does mean that you need to have a basic understanding of what the video signal is and how it can be controlled. All video equipment operates on similar principles; this book stresses fundamental underlying principles of operation. Because underlying operational principles vary little among brands of equipment, you should have little difficulty in adapting the general principles discussed here to the specific requirements of a particular system.

Many handbooks on video production are nothing more than manuals of equipment operation. However, it is our position that one must know not only how to manipulate the equipment but also how to manipulate the medium in which one is working: video. This brings us to the area of media aesthetics. **Aesthetic factors**, throughout this text, refer to production variables and the ways in which they can be manipulated to affect audience response to the video message.[1]

The process of video field production is a combination of technical factors and aesthetic factors. Whether you are engaged in video production for personal, artistic, educational, or broadcast uses, the requirements of the technology and the medium must be considered. The fundamentals of production and the production processes discussed in this book will be helpful to you, no matter what type of video production you are engaged in.

Creative Problem Solving

If there is one phrase that expresses what is at the center of video field production, it is *creative problem solving.* Communication via video means that the producer/writer/director must understand the medium and how to use it. Finding the appropriate techniques to effectively express the idea and content of a program presents problems that must be solved creatively.

Video field production also presents a unique set of logistical problems. No two days of shooting in the field are ever quite the same, because no two locations are ever the same. The ability to deal with the range of problems encountered on location is the mark of the successful field production person.

Finally, video field production presents a set of unique technical problems. People involved in field production simply must know more about the technical side of video production than must their studio counterparts. All manner of technical problems arise in the field, and field producers must be able to anticipate and avoid them or correct them when they arise.

Teamwork and Control

Control.   One of the most important challenges in video field production is to take control of the location in order to maximize the chances of completing a successful production. Unlike the studio video producer who works in an environment with controlled lighting, acoustics, and sound, the video field producer works in remote locations where these elements may vary greatly from location to location and from one time of day to another. The ability to effectively control these elements is an essential characteristic of the effective field producer.

Teamwork.   Video production is a group activity. No one individual can do everything that needs to be done on a production. Successful producers and crew members need to remember at all times that they are part of a production team focused on a common goal—the creation of an effective video production. To achieve this goal, all team members should have a clear idea of their responsibilities, and they should strive to communicate clearly with each other at all times.

NOTE

1. For a full discussion of media aesthetics, see Zettl, Herbert, *Sight Sound Motion: Applied Media Aesthetics,* 3rd ed., Belmont, CA: Wadsworth, 1999; and Dondis, Donis A., *A Primer of Visual Literacy,* Cambridge, MA: MIT Press, 1973.

2

The Portable Video Camera

At the center of all video field production systems is the portable video camera. A marvel of modern electronics, the video camera produces the electronic video signal.

Whether configured as a stand-alone camera or as the camera section of a camcorder, all video cameras have a number of standard components, including an image sensor, viewfinder, camera control unit, and lens assembly (see Figure 2.1). This chapter will focus on portable video cameras and on the way the electronic image is generated and displayed. Lenses will be discussed in Chapter 3.

Microphone

Electronic Eyepiece Viewfinder

Electric Zoom Lens

Shoulder Brace

Camera Controls

Figure 2.1
Parts of a Portable Video Camera

Electronic Image Reproduction

The Camera Image Sensor

The most important component of the video camera is its image sensor. Its function is to change light into electrical energy. Technically speaking, the camera image sensor is an **optical-video transducer**, which simply means that it changes incoming light (physical input) into an electrical video signal (electrical output). By way of comparison, microphones are also transducers—they change incoming sound waves (physical input) into an electrical audio signal (electrical output). All video cameras manufactured today use one or more charge-coupled devices as image sensors.

CCD (Charge-Coupled Device) Principles

A **charge-coupled device (CCD)** image sensor is a solid-state semiconductor that converts incoming light into a video signal. (See Figure 2.2.) The surface of the CCD contains a grid of **pixels**, or picture elements, arranged in a precise series of horizontal rows, or lines, and vertical columns. The camera lens focuses the scene before it on this array of pixels, each of which is responsible for reproducing one tiny part of the picture. Each pixel contains a metal oxide or silicon semiconductor that converts the incoming light into an electrical charge. The strength of the electrical charge is proportional to the brightness of the light hitting the pixel, and the amount of exposure time.

After the incoming light is converted into an electrical charge, it is transferred and stored in another layer of the chip, and then the information is read out one pixel at a time in a line-by-line sequence in conformity with normal television scanning rates. An analogy frequently used to describe this process is that it is like an old-fashioned bucket brigade, except that instead of containing water, each of the buckets—or in this case each of the pixels—contains an electrical charge.

First demonstrated by Bell Laboratories in 1969, the CCDs designed for use in video cameras today are very small (the image-sensing area is $1/3''$, $1/2''$, or $2/3''$ measured diagonally) and very rugged, and they consume very little electrical energy. For these reasons, CCDs have effectively replaced the old-style vacuum pickup tubes previously used as image sensors in video cameras.

All CCD cameras are equipped with an electronic shutter. The electronic shutter controls the amount of time that the incoming light hits the photosensitive layer of the chip. In recording situations in which the re-

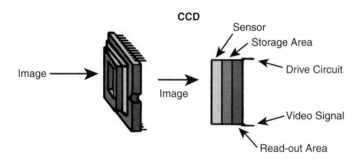

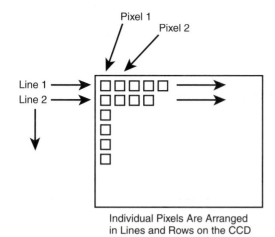

Individual Pixels Are Arranged
in Lines and Rows on the CCD

Figure 2.2
CCD Image Sensor

corded image tends to flicker or become blurred because of high-speed movement of the subject in front of the camera, shutter speed can be increased to reduce these picture artifacts and improve the sharpness of the image.

Shutter speeds commonly range from 1/60 to 1/10,000 of a second, with incremental settings of 1/100, 1/250, 1/1,000, 1/2,000, 1/4,000 and 1/8,000, even on some of the least expensive consumer camcorders. In addition, some cameras feature a variable shutter speed, which can be adjusted to eliminate the screen flicker that becomes visible when a computer screen or video monitor appears in a video shot.

Video Display

Your home television set works in much the same way as the camera image sensor, except it reverses the process. That is, instead of turning light into electrical energy as the CCD does, your receiver turns electrical energy into light. This is accomplished by scanning the television picture tube with an electron beam. At the back of the picture tube in your television is an electron gun, which shoots an electron beam at the inside of the face of the picture tube. The picture tube is coated with a photosensitive material that glows (becomes brighter) when it is hit by the beam of electrons. A large blast of electrons causes it to glow a lot; a small blast causes little action.

 # Television Scanning: The NTSC and ATSC Standards

Television and video in the United States are now operating under two different sets of technical standards that govern how the video signal is scanned and displayed: the original NTSC (National Television System Committee) standards adopted for analog television by the Federal Communications Commission (FCC) in 1941, and the ATSC (Advanced Television System Committee) standards for digital television adopted by the FCC in December of 1996. These standards cover a wide range of technical specifications for how the video signal is constructed and transmitted. For the purpose of our discussion, the important elements of the standards that need to be considered are the aspect ratio of the image, frame and line rates, and scanning patterns.

NTSC Video

The **NTSC standard** is the dominant system in use throughout the United States and Canada today. In this system the video picture is transmitted and displayed as an analog signal, as opposed to a digital signal (more on the differences between analog and digital signals in Chapter 4). The **aspect ratio**, or shape, of the screen is always expressed as a ratio of 4:3 (width:height). No matter how large or small the screen is, it will retain these standard rectangular proportions. (See Figure 2.3.)

The video image is composed of a number of **frames** and **lines**. Because we normally think of the television process as existing in time, we can measure the frame rate of television rather easily. In the NTSC system, there are 30 frames of video information per second, and each one of those frames is composed of 525 lines of information.

In actuality, the precise frame rate for NTSC video is 29.97 frames per second, and of the 525 actual scanning lines, only 480 are actively used to transmit picture information. However, this text follows the widely adopted convention of referring to the NTSC standard as 30 frames per second and 525 lines per frame.

Conventional Screen

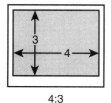

4:3

Wide Screen

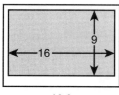

16:9

Figure 2.3
Conventional-Screen
and Wide-Screen Shapes

Starting with line number 1, the beam in a television receiver moves across the picture tube until it gets to the end of that line. Then the beam automatically shuts off, returns to the other side of the picture tube, drops down to line number 3, and scans across that. When it reaches the end of the line, it automatically shuts off, drops down to line number 5, and repeats the process all over again. When it gets down to the bottom of the frame (line 525), it shuts off, returns to the top of the picture, and scans the even-numbered lines (2, 4, 6, 8, and so on). This process is known as **2:1 interlaced scanning.** First the odd-numbered lines are scanned and then the even ones. Each time the gun reaches the bottom of the picture, it has completed one **field**, or 262.5 lines, of information. A complete frame of information (525 lines) is composed of two individual fields: one field of odd-numbered lines and one field of even-numbered lines (see Figure 2.4). With a frame rate of 30 frames per second (actually 29.97) and two fields per frame, NTSC video runs at 60 fields per second (actually 59.94).

There are two reasons for this interlaced system of scanning. First, in the early days of television the phosphorescent materials used to coat the inside of the picture tube had a tendency to fade out before the picture was complete. The photosensitive surface on the picture tube glowed for a very short time when the electron beam hit it. If the beam scanned every line beginning at the top of the frame, by the time it got down to the bottom, the top of the picture had faded to black. By breaking each frame into two

25

INTERLACED SCANNING

Each Television Frame Is Composed of Two Fields

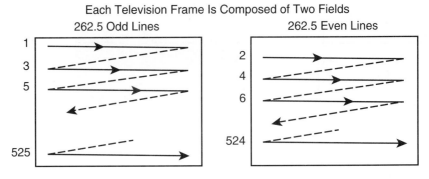

262.5 Odd Lines   262.5 Even Lines

The Odd Lines are Scanned First   Then the Even Lines are Scanned

PROGRESSIVE SCANNING

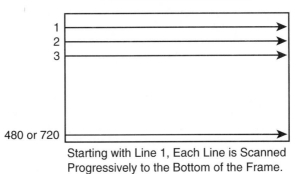

Figure 2.4
Interlaced and
Progressive Scanning

Starting with Line 1, Each Line is Scanned
Progressively to the Bottom of the Frame.

fields and interlacing the lines as the picture was reassembled on the screen, this problem of flickering was solved and the picture maintained its brightness throughout the program.

The second reason for the use of interlaced scanning was the limited amount of information that could be transmitted through the typical television channel. A signal transmitted at the rate of 60 fields of 262.5 lines per field could be accommodated within the 6 MHz bandwidth assigned to each television station to transmit its signal. A signal transmitted at 60 frames per second with 525 lines per frame contained twice as much information as the interlaced signal but exceeded the capacity of the channel to transmit it. By interlacing the fields, this problem was solved as well—although at the expense of the sharpness of the picture.

Incidentally, the 525-lines-per-frame standard characteristic of NTSC television in the United States is an arbitrary standard. That is, the system

Table 2.1 Varying Television System Standards
throughout the World

Country	Frames per Second	Lines per Frame
United States, Canada, Japan, Latin America	30	525
Europe (most systems), China, Commonwealth of Independent States	25	625

could have more or fewer lines and still function. Indeed, many other
countries use 625-line systems, which actually provide greater picture detail than 525 lines (see Table 2.1).

ATSC Video

Because of the limitations inherent in the picture and color quality of
NTSC television, and because of a desire to move from an analog system of
broadcasting to a digital system, over the past decade a considerable
amount of effort has been invested in developing a new U.S. television
standard, culminating with the adoption of the **ATSC standards** in 1996.
Initially, the goal was to develop a set of standards for **high-definition
television (HDTV)**, based on a 16:9 aspect ratio (see Figure 2.3) and an increased line rate to improve picture quality. However, as the standards debate dragged on, great advances were being made in digital recording and
transmission technologies.

Finally, at the insistence of the FCC, a "Grand Alliance" of major U.S.
electronic manufacturing companies were encouraged to work together to
develop a set of digital standards for advanced television services in the
United States. The standards that were finally adopted by the FCC allow
digital television to be produced and distributed in a variety of scanning
formats (see Table 2.2). To receive these signals, consumers will need to
buy new digital television receivers or set-top boxes that will convert the
incoming digital signal into an analog signal for display on conventional
television receivers.

The new standards contain several variants of HDTV, but all include
pictures in a 16:9 aspect ratio with more scanning lines and pixels per
line than conventional NTSC. Several of the U.S. broadcast networks
have adopted the 720-line-by-1,280-pixel-per-line HDTV format, scanned
progressively.

Table 2.2 The ATSC Digital Television Scanning Formats

Vertical Lines	Horizontal Pixels	Aspect Ratio	Picture Rate	HDTV/SDTV
1,080	1,920	16:9	60I 30P 24P	HDTV
720	1,280	16:9	60P 30P 24P	HDTV
480	704	16:9 and 4:3	60I 60P 30P 24P	SDTV
480	640	4:3	60I 60P 30P 24P	SDTV

In the "Picture Rate" Column, "I" Means Interlaced Scan and "P" Means Progressive Scan.
HDTV = High-Definition Television
SDTV = Standard-Definition Television

Source: Advanced Television System Committee

In **progressive scanning**, each of the lines in the frame is scanned successively. Thus, in the 720-line system, scanning would begin with line 1 and continue to line 720 (see Figure 2.4). The next frame would begin again at line 1, and there would be no "fields" as there are in the NTSC system. The standard allows the picture to be transmitted at 60, 30, or 24 frames per second. (Twenty-four frames per second is the standard frame rate for theatrical feature films and for television programs produced on film. Currently almost half of the programs seen on prime-time television are produced on film.)

The 1,080-line-by-1,920-pixel-per-line HDTV standard has been adopted by several of the U.S. networks as well. However, because of limitations in the channel capacity of the digital channels that have been assigned to U.S. broadcasters, current technology can accommodate only the 1,080-line interlaced variant, and not the 30-frame progressive scan variant. Undoubtedly this will change as more sophisticated methods of processing and compressing the video signal emerge.

The new ATSC standards also contain 480-line-by-704-pixel-per-line wide-screen (16:9) and traditional (4:3) versions of the old NTSC system (now referred to as **standard definition television**, or **SDTV**), as well as a 480-line-by-640-pixel variant that is equivalent to the Super VGA standard used to display graphics on computer screens.

Production equipment has been produced to accommodate some of these new standards, and more is in development. Some inexpensive camcorders produced in the NTSC standard already allow the operator to record in either a 4:3 or a 16:9 aspect ratio, and this feature is likely to be found on increasing numbers of cameras and camcorders, even if they are not truly capable of generating HDTV pictures with their higher line and pixel rates.

Video Signal
Control

Horizontal and Vertical Sync

Regardless of whether the video signal is produced within the NTSC or ATSC standards, each frame of video information is constructed by combining picture information and synchronizing information. Among the most important synchronizing control pulses are horizontal and vertical sync and blanking pulses. These pulses are generated by a sync generator that can be located as an integral component inside the camera or as a separate component outside the camera.

The **horizontal sync** and blanking pulses control the timing of each line of video information; the **vertical sync** and blanking pulses control the timing of each field and frame of information. Essentially, each line of information begins with a horizontal sync pulse and ends with a horizontal blanking pulse. Similarly, each field begins with a vertical sync pulse and ends with a vertical blanking pulse.

Thus, you can see that for each frame of NTSC video information there are 525 lines of information and 525 horizontal blanking and sync pulses. These 525 lines are arranged in two fields of information along with two vertical blanking and sync pulses. In the ATSC system the number of sync and blanking pulses per frame will vary depending on which one of the 18 possible scanning patterns is used.

Internal and External Sync

When sync pulses are generated within the camera, we refer to the sync as **internal sync**. When sync pulses are generated outside the camera, we refer to the sync as **external sync**.

When a single camcorder is used for video field production, the horizontal and vertical sync pulses are produced internally in the camcorder itself. Most single-camera field production units fall into this category.

In more complex multiple-camera field production systems, which include a video switcher and several cameras operating simultaneously, all cameras must scan synchronously. To accomplish this, they all must have the same reference to horizontal and vertical sync. In such a situation, an external sync generator is used to regulate the timing of all the camera sources.

Sometimes, the sync pulses generated by one camera can be used to "drive" the signal of another camera through a process called **gen-lock**. In

29

this process, the second camera senses the incoming sync pulses from the first camera and then creates its own video signal synchronously with the other camera.

The Video Waveform

As this discussion has already indicated, the video signal is somewhat complex because it contains not only picture information but also synchronizing information. The picture information alone is referred to as a **noncomposite signal**. When video information and sync are both present in a signal, it is referred to as a **composite signal**.

Let's continue our discussion of the video signal by talking more specifically about the black-and-white picture signal. Black-and-white television presents a range of **brightness** only; elements in the picture are somewhere between white and black. This range of variation between white and black, or between the brightest and darkest parts of a scene, can be seen in the video waveform, which shows us what the video signal actually looks like. Figure 2.5 shows the components of one line of information of a typical video waveform.

Figure 2.5
Video Waveform

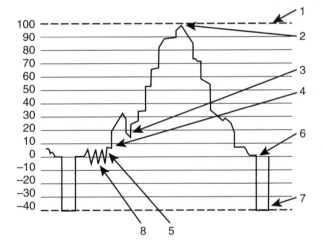

(1) Reference White—Brightest Point TV System Will Produce
(2) Peak White—Actual Brightest Point in the Scene
(3) Peak Black—Actual Darkest Point
(4) Reference Black—Darkest (Black) Possible Point TV System Will Produce
(5) Setup (Pedestal)—Determines the Point at Which Reference Black Is Set
(6) Blanking Level—Turns Off Beam of Electrons
(7) Horizontal Sync Pulse—Turns On Electron Beam
(8) Color Burst—Controls the Phasing of the Color Signal

Camera Control Unit

Control over the video signal is the function of the **camera control unit**
(**CCU**). Camera control units contain components that regulate the sensitivity of the image sensor, the size of the iris opening of the lens (described
in Chapter 3), and the level of the gain and pedestal of the video signal,
which we will discuss in a moment.

CCUs can be of two types: external or internal. External CCUs are
completely separate from the camera. Studio video cameras frequently utilize external CCUs. Portable video cameras almost always contain an internal CCU, which is one that is built into the camera. On some portable
cameras, the functions of the CCU are fully automatic; on others, some
manual adjustment of the signal is possible.

The adjustment that allows you to amplify the level of the video signal is called the **gain**. Just as you can turn up the level of sound on your car
radio or home stereo, so can you turn up the level of the video signal. Increasing the gain usually has the effect of making the picture brighter. However, it may also have some negative effects. When you amplify any electronic signal, you also increase the **noise** inherent in the system. If you
increase the gain of the video signal too much, the picture will become
"noisy," or grainy. Picture noise is sometimes also called *snow*. This is the visual equivalent of the static or white noise that you hear when you turn up
the volume on your home stereo too high. Increasing the gain on a video
signal may also affect the contrast and make the picture look washed out.

The other important element of video picture signal control is the
pedestal. **Pedestal** controls the black level of a picture. Every black-and-white picture reproduces a number of shades of black and white. These
range from the brightest or whitest white, through several shades of gray,
to black. The deepest black that is reproduced is controlled by the pedestal
control.

The Waveform Monitor

To set pedestal and gain levels, video engineers use what is called a *waveform monitor* (see Figure CP-9). This monitoring equipment shows the form
of the video signal (the **waveform**). If you look at the waveform in Figure
2.5, you can see a number of the things we have discussed so far. The highest part of the wave is the **peak white**; it is equivalent to the brightest part
of the scene that the camera is shooting. Peak white should not exceed 100
percent (**reference white**) on the waveform. The pedestal, or black level, is
always set at 7.5 percent on the waveform monitor. An engineer will usually make the pedestal adjustment and then increase the gain until the
peak white level reaches 100 percent, unless this makes the picture too
noisy. The horizontal sync pulse is also visible in the waveform display.

In most portable cameras, the adjustments for pedestal and gain are controlled automatically within the camera. You do not have to adjust them at all. But occasionally you may have the opportunity to manually adjust these controls yourself. It is therefore important to know what they do.

 # The Color Signal

Luminance and Chrominance

Up to this point, we have been talking about a black-and-white video signal. Today, most video programs, and therefore most video cameras, are color. Color video cameras work under the same principles as black-and-white cameras, but they are a little bit more complex. The two principal components of the color video signal are luminance and chrominance. **Luminance** refers to the black-and-white brightness information that we have already discussed. Every color video signal contains a luminance signal as well as the color information. **Chrominance** is the color information and includes two components: hue and saturation. **Hue** refers to the color itself: red, green, blue, and so on. **Saturation** refers to the amount or intensity of the color. For example, a very light pink and a very vivid or deep red both have the same hue (red), but differ in terms of how saturated they are. Pink is a very lightly saturated red, whereas the deep red is a highly saturated red.

Additive Primary Colors of Light

Color video systems work with the **additive primary colors** of light: red, green, and blue (see Figure CP-3). Do not confuse these with the subtractive primaries—the type you use when you are working with paint: red, blue, and yellow. Red, green, and blue are called primary colors of light because they can be combined to form white light, as well as any other color of the spectrum. No other three colors can do this.

Color video systems take the light that enters the lens and break it into its red, green, and blue components. There are two different ways this is done (see Figures 2.6 and CP-1):

1. Incoming light can be passed through a small prism block.
2. A stripe filter can be attached to the face of the image sensor to break the light into its primary colors there.

Prism Block Camera Systems

The most sophisticated color video cameras use a **prism block** to break the incoming light into its red, green, and blue components. Light is reflected off the object or person being videotaped. This light is captured by the lens of the video camera and directed into the camera itself. Inside the camera, the light goes through a prism block coated with a series of dichroic filters, where it is separated into its red, green, and blue components. Each color is then directed to its own CCD. So, for each color, we have a separate signal. The gain and pedestal can be adjusted individually for each. It would be possible to take only the output of the red channel and send it to a video monitor, but all we would see would be red. Similarly, we could take the output of the green channel or the blue channel. Again, all we would see would be green or blue. In this state, the signal is called the **RGB signal**.

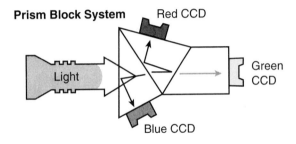

Prism Block System   Red CCD

Light

Green CCD

Blue CCD

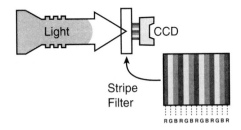

Stripe Filter System

Light

CCD

Stripe Filter

RGBRGBRGBRGBR

Figure 2.6   Two Common Color Video Camera Systems

However, within the camera is a device called the **color encoder**. This device takes the output of each of the three color channels (red, green, and blue) and recombines them into one color signal, including both chrominance and luminance. This is the **encoded color signal**, and when it is displayed on a video monitor, we see the scene as the camera saw it, in full color. In addition, the presence of the luminance signal ensures that the picture is seen in black and white on black-and-white receivers.

All of the highest-quality color cameras use three image sensors. These cameras produce the best pictures because each color is assigned to its own CCD, thereby ensuring the highest amount of control over the signal of each. Prism blocks with dichroic filters are used in these high-quality cameras because the prism is the most efficient way of splitting the light into its red, green, and blue components without interfering with the signal of each.

Stripe Filters

The other type of color camera uses only one CCD and a device known as a **stripe filter**. The stripe filter, which consists of extremely thin stripes of red, blue, and green filter material, is applied to the face of the CCD. Incoming light goes through the lens and strikes the stripe filter, which sequentially breaks it into its red, blue, and green components. The single-chip camera can produce all three channels of chrominance as well as luminance. This system sacrifices picture sharpness and individual color control for decreased cost, weight, and technical complexity. For this reason, most color camcorders designed for home use rely on a single CCD as the image sensor.

Color Burst and Vectorscopes

To keep the color information in proper synchronization, a special control pulse called **color burst** is used. The color burst signal ensures that the three color signals begin at the right time at the beginning of each line of video information, and the pulse can be seen on the video waveform immediately after the horizontal sync pulse. If you are not sure whether you have a color signal, and if you have access to a waveform monitor, you can simply look to see if color burst is present in the waveform. Figure 2.5 shows what the color burst pulse looks like.

Although color burst tells you if color is present, it does not tell you *which* colors are present. This is the function of a piece of monitoring equipment known as the **vectorscope** (see Figure CP-9). Each of the three primary colors of light (red, green, and blue) and their complements (cyan, magenta, and yellow) are marked on the face of the vectorscope. By look-

Figure 2.7   Areas of Color Display on a Vectorscope

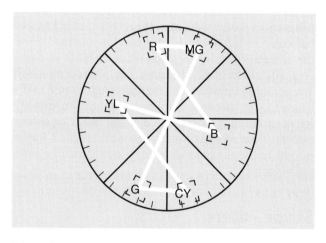

Primary Colors	Complementary Colors
R — Red	MG — Magenta
B — Blue	CY — Cyan
G — Green	YL — Yellow

ing at the vectorscope, you can determine which colors are present in the signal and how much of each one is present (see Figure 2.7).

Since the vectorscope provides critical information about the color information in the video signal, it is an essential component of the monitoring system that is used by video engineers when color adjustments are made to cameras and VCRs. In multiple-camera shooting situations, the vectorscope is used to help match the color quality of the cameras so that the color values they reproduce are the same for each camera. In single- or multiple-camera operations, a vectorscope can assist in gauging whether the camera is properly white-balanced, that is, adjusted to reproduce colors correctly in the lighting conditions that exist at the recording location.

Color Reproduction

The color picture that you see on a home television receiver is recreated in a way that is similar to the camera color process. The picture tube in your television set is covered with a series of phosphorescent dots. In black-and-white television, these dots are capable only of growing brighter or darker. In the color set, these dots are arranged in groups of three: one red, one blue, one green (see Figures 2.8 and CP-2). The color video signal, as we have seen, is composed of varying amounts of these three colors, depending on the scene that is being shot. When the color video signal is fed into a monitor, it triggers an electron gun to scan the face of the picture tube, and it activates the red, blue, and green dots on the screen in relation to their relative strength in the signal. What you see as you watch the screen is a full-color picture. Actually, if you get close enough to the screen of your television and stare at it, you can see there are really only three colors present: red, blue, and green. When you move away from the set, these three primary colors combine to form the other colors of the spectrum. Color mixing, therefore, is really subjective. It takes place in your head, not in the television system itself.

World Color Television Standards

Just as there are several different television frame scanning rates and line standards in operation throughout the world, so are there differences in

Figure 2.8   Color Television Display (Picture Tube System)

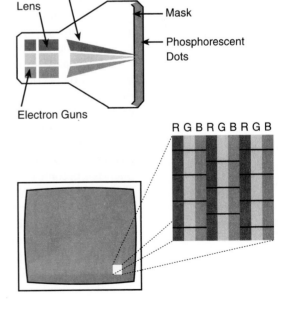

35

the way the color signal is produced and recorded. The U.S. system, established by the National Television System Committee, is *NTSC* color. Critics suggest that NTSC stands for "never twice the same color," because the NTSC system allows for adjustment of color, hue, and saturation at the point of reception, with the result that color values may vary greatly from receiver to receiver. The NTSC system is used throughout North and Central America as well as in parts of the Far East.

In other parts of the world, two other color systems are also used: *PAL* (Phase Alternation by Line), designed by the Germans and the British and found in England, Western Europe, and throughout Africa and the Middle East; and *SECAM* (Système Électronique pour Couleur avec Mémoire), designed by the French and widely used in Eastern Europe and parts of Africa as well as in France and Russia. SECAM is generally regarded as the best of color systems, followed by PAL and then NTSC.

As you might imagine, these different color television standards present problems when a program produced in one format is scheduled to be shown in a country that operates in another, incompatible format. Fortunately for video producers, electronic standards converters are widely available.

Broadcast Quality

Technical standards exist by which engineers can determine whether a particular video signal is of **broadcast quality**. All broadcast signals fall under the jurisdiction of the FCC, which publishes specifications that all broadcast signals must meet. Of particular importance to the video field producer is the size of the horizontal and vertical blanking intervals and the pedestal or setup level. Cameras that rely on their own internal sync generators should be periodically checked to ensure that they are operating properly, especially if the tape will be distributed to broadcast outlets.

The standards of broadcast quality for different organizations often involve variables other than these technical qualities. Program content and overall production values are as much a part of broadcast quality as technical elements. The proliferation of consumer-quality camcorders provides an interesting perspective on this issue. Although inexpensive home video camcorders are generally not considered to produce broadcast-quality recorded images, videotape of news events recorded by amateur videographers has become commonplace. One broadcast news operation, the Cable News Network (CNN), actively solicited videotapes of newsworthy events recorded by amateur videographers. CNN called this its News Hound service. Interestingly, when the News Hound service was announced, CNN executives expressed more concern about the quality of the techniques of the camera operator than about the quality of the video signal produced by home video camcorders. In addition, concerns about technical problems such as color quality and image stability may be overlooked if the content of the videotape has extremely significant news value.

The relative importance of interesting content versus technical quality extends to entertainment programs as well. One of the most popular programs on U.S. commercial television in the 1990s has been *America's Funniest Home Videos*. Viewers submit homemade videotapes of people and animals in funny, unusual, or embarrassing situations, which are then edited for broadcast and embellished with sound effects and narration by the program's producers. As is the case with amateur news videotapes, interesting content overrides concerns about the technical quality of images recorded on consumer-level video equipment.

Although it is always a good idea to try to achieve the highest possible technical production standards, we should note that not all media outlets require that the signal be broadcast-quality. Tapes produced for home viewing or for other kinds of closed-circuit distribution may deviate from the technical standard of broadcast quality, but the signal should still produce a clear, stable picture.

 # Camera Performance Characteristics

Not all cameras perform at the same level. Depending on the number and size of CCDs, the internal electronics of the camera, and the type of lens attached to the camera, picture quality may vary significantly from one camera to another.

One, Two, or Three CCDs

Most modern video cameras contain either three CCDs or one CCD. Cameras with three CCDs are known for their excellent color reproduction and detail resolution and are almost always used in broadcast situations. However, they are not without their disadvantages. They are larger and heavier than their single-CCD counterparts and, of course, they are more expensive.

Camcorders with a single CCD have become the standard in consumer-quality video equipment. Single-CCD camcorders are known for their portability and low cost. However, one does sacrifice some quality when using a camera with a single-image sensor. Usually, both resolution and color quality are not as good as they are in a three-CCD counterpart. Two-CCD cameras (one for chrominance and one for luminance) offer a compromise in cost and quality but are not in wide use.

37

CCD Size

As noted above, CCDs are extremely small, typically $1/3''$, $1/2''$, or $2/3''$ in diameter. Generally speaking, larger CCDs produce better image quality than smaller CCDs; however, image quality is also dependent on the number of pixels in the array. The more pixels in a particular CCD, the smaller each pixel will become, resulting in an increase in the overall resolution that that CCD will reproduce.

Resolution

Resolution is a term used to describe the amount of detail that a camera is able to reproduce. It is always reported in terms of lines of *horizontal resolution*. Think of a series of extremely narrow vertical lines. If the lines are very narrow and very close together, they will be more difficult for the camera to "see" than if they are thicker and farther apart. High-quality cameras have much greater horizontal resolution than low-quality cameras have. For example, an inexpensive single-chip camera may provide only 250 lines of horizontal resolution, whereas a high-quality camera equipped with three CCDs may provide 600 to 700 lines. This figure is a measure of the camera's ability to reproduce fine detail in a picture. The higher the number, the greater the detail the camera can reproduce.

Figure 2.9
Video Resolution
Chart

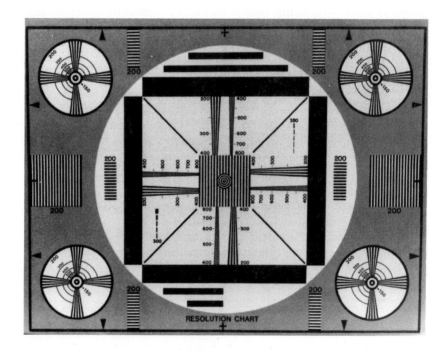

Video engineers use a standard resolution chart to determine how much resolution, or detail, a camera is able to produce (see Figure 2.9). High-quality cameras are generally able to reproduce much greater fine detail in a picture than do low-quality cameras.

Do not confuse this measure of a camera's resolution ability with the number of scanning lines in the picture. All cameras operating in the NTSC system will produce pictures using the 525-line scanning standard; however, some cameras will produce pictures that are sharper or clearer than others. This difference in sharpness or clarity results from differences in the resolution ability of various cameras.

No matter how good the camera is, the amount of resolution, or detail, apparent in the image at its final display point will be only as good as the weakest link in the recording and transmission system. Most home television receivers produce an image with approximately 300 lines of horizontal resolution; VHS VCRs record the signal with 250 to 300 lines of resolution. This may increase to 400 lines when DV, S-VHS, or Hi8 VCRs are used with compatible monitors. High-quality television studio monitors may be able to resolve 600 to 800 lines.

One of the principal picture advantages of HDTV is its ability to reproduce greater image detail than conventional NTSC video. This is the result of the greater number of pixels available in HDTV systems. For example, a traditional NTSC CCD array in the 704-pixel-per-line-by-480-line format contains 337,920 pixels per chip, whereas HDTV arrays in the 1,920-pixel-per-line-by-1,080-line format contain 2,073,600 pixels per chip, and those in the 1,280-pixel-per-line-by-720-line format contain 921,600 pixels! Cameras and monitors built to the HDTV standards are capable of delivering resolution in excess of 1,000 lines, so it's not hard to understand why HDTV pictures are often described in terms of their sharpness and lifelike detail.

Color Reproduction

The quality of color produced by the camera varies depending on the number and type of CCDs used and the lighting conditions. Color reproduction by high-quality CCDs is exceptional, although three-CCD cameras generally produce pictures with better color than their single-chip counterparts. In both systems, the amount and quality of the light falling on the subject make a critical difference in the quality of the final picture.

Sensitivity to Light and Operating Light Level

The operating light level of a camera varies with the number and size of image sensors in the camera, the type of lens, and the type of system used to break incoming light into its components for color processing. Not long ago, the operating light level for color cameras was in the range of 400 foot-candles. Today, the highest-quality cameras can produce excellent pictures with 150 to 200 foot-candles of light, and many cameras provide excellent color with low noise at 50 foot-candles and less. (Foot-candles will be discussed in more detail in Chapter 6.)

Most CCD-type cameras and camcorders can produce excellent color pictures in extremely low light. Two guidelines should always be followed with respect to the amount of light required for the optimum performance of your camera system. First, read the camera operation manual, if available, to learn the manufacturer's recommendation. Second, check with your engineering staff (if you have one!) for their recommendations.

Signal-to-Noise Ratio

The **signal-to-noise ratio (S/N)** is the ratio of the total signal to the electronic noise produced by the camera. It shows how much higher the signal level is than the level of noise. Expressed in decibels (dB), the larger the value is, the crisper and clearer the picture will be during playback. For example, a camera with an S/N ratio of 62 produces a much better picture with less electronic noise than a camera with an S/N of 54.

CCD Image Problems: Smear and Moiré

Pickup-tube-type video cameras exhibited a number of problems that have been eliminated by the use of CCDs with electronic shutters. Gone are problems such as **image lag** or **image retention** (a double-image effect caused by insufficient light), **comet tail** (a bright flare following an object, caused by too much contrast or light reflecting off a highly reflective surface), and **burn-in** (damage to the photosensitive surface of the pickup tube, resulting in a permanent dark mark or streak in all images subsequently produced by the camera).

CCDs do not suffer from burn-in and are relatively free from lag and image-sticking problems. However, CCDs are susceptible to smear and moiré effects. **Smear** is a unique type of image distortion caused by very bright illumination in which a bright vertical band appears above and below the bright object in the picture. Automobile headlights and high-intensity streetlights frequently produce CCD smear effects. **Moiré** is caused by photographing subjects that have high-contrast fine detail—for example, a shirt with a light and dark pinstripe pattern or a herringbone fabric pattern. The resulting image created will appear to vibrate on the screen.

Camera Viewfinder Systems

The camera **viewfinder** is the part of the camera that the camera operator looks into to see what is being shot. *Electronic viewfinders* are found on all high-quality video cameras. The viewfinder is actually a small video screen. When you look into it, you see what the image sensor sees. Usually, viewfinders display only a black-and-white picture, even on most color cameras. However, an increasing number of color cameras incorporate color viewfinders. Camera viewfinders come in two configurations: studio and remote (eyepiece) (see Figure 2.10).

A studio viewfinder is mounted on top of the camera. Usually, it produces an image that is approximately 5″ in diagonal. Studio viewfinders allow the camera operator to stand behind the camera as shots are composed and focused.

The remote **eyepiece viewfinder** is usually mounted on the side of the camera. It contains an eyepiece that allows the videographer's eye to be put firmly against the camera. This prevents natural light from hitting the small screen inside the eyepiece and washing out the picture. Viewfinders of this type are usually

Figure 2.10   Camera Viewfinder Systems

Portable Video Camera with Studio Viewfinder

Portable Video Camera with Eyepiece Viewfinder

Portable Video Camera with Studio Viewfinder and Large Studio/Field Zoom Lens

41

Figure 2.11 Camcorder with
Large LCD Viewfinder

quite small, often approximately $1^1/_2''$ in diagonal. More expensive eye-piece viewfinders can be rotated in numerous directions so that the camera can be held in positions other than on the shoulder.

An increasing number of consumer camcorders replace the small-eyepiece viewfinder with a larger color *LCD* (*liquid crystal display*) view-finder. This viewfinder system not only makes it easier to view the image as it is played back through the camcorder but also allows the videographer to see the viewfinder image while the camcorder is held at arm's length, making it possible to record from difficult or unusual angles (for example, overhead) that might not have been possible with a conventional-eyepiece viewfinder system (see Figure 2.11).

Camcorder viewfinders usually contain electronic displays that indi-cate whether the lens aperture setting is correct. They also contain indica-tors that monitor the status of the VCR: record mode, play mode, the amount of battery power remaining, the tape counter number, and so on.

Finally, on most portable cameras, a scene that has just been re-corded can be played back and viewed in the eyepiece viewfinder in order to check the quality of the recording. Some cameras and camcorders con-tain a small audio speaker that allows you to monitor the sound as well.

 **Camera
Configurations**

Modern video cameras are available in a number of different configura-tions. These include camcorders (in either a one-piece unit or a dockable system) and convertible cameras that may be used in either a studio setting or a remote field production setting. A third group of cameras include large-scale models designed primarily for in-studio use.

Camcorders

A combination camera and VCR, or **camcorder**, combines the camera and recorder into one easily carried unit (see Figure 2.12). This gives the camera operator much greater mobility than with a recording system composed of a separate camera and VCR, which relies on a cable connection between the two pieces of equipment.

Panasonic DVC Pro Camcorder (AJ-D800)

Figure 2.12   Professional One-Piece Camcorder

Camcorder systems designed for broadcast applications use high-quality three-CCD cameras. These professional-quality camcorders may be one-piece systems or dockable systems. Dockable cameras are designed to be connected to a special docking VCR to create a camcorder unit. High-quality docking VCRs are available in a variety of professional tape-recording formats.

One-piece camcorders in the VHS/S-VHS, 8mm/Hi8, and DV formats have become immensely popular and are widely used by home video producers and other producers not requiring the quality of the most expensive broadcast-quality camcorder systems. The camera portion of these consumer-level camcorders almost always utilizes a single CCD as the image sensor (see Figure 2.13).

Figure 2.13
Recording With a
One-Piece Portable
S-VHS Camcorder

Most one-piece consumer-level camcorders are designed to operate independently from other cameras or camcorders in a field recording situation. These portable camcorders are equipped either with eyepiece-type viewfinders or fold-out LCD viewfinders.

The second characteristic of these consumer camcorders is that they cannot be operated synchronously with other cameras. That is, they are usually incapable of accepting an external sync signal and, therefore, operate independently of other cameras. The video signal is recorded directly on the camcorder's own VCR.

Convertible Studio/ Field Cameras

Convertible cameras are designed to be used either in the studio or in the field with several others in a typical multiple-camera configuration or as single-camera portable units in the field. In a typical field situation, the camera is connected to the recorder by a long or short cable. In other situations, the camera output can be sent via microwave either to the recorder or back to the station for broadcast.

Two main characteristics distinguish these convertible cameras from others. First, they have the capability to be outfitted with either a studio viewfinder or a small-eyepiece viewfinder. In the studio configuration (see Figures 2.11 and 2.14), the camera operator stands behind the camera, which is usually mounted on a tripod or camera pedestal. Because the operator stands behind the camera, the camera viewfinder must be mounted on top of the camera. Usually, the viewfinder has a fairly large (approximately 5″ in diagonal) viewfinder screen, so the camera operator can easily see the image. In addition, convertible cameras can easily be adapted so that the zoom lens controls and lens focus controls are removed from the lens itself and are instead mounted on *panning handles* that protrude from either side of the rear of the camera. As a result, the camera operator can easily see the viewfinder image and make zoom lens and focus changes while standing behind the camera.

The second characteristic of convertible cameras is that they are capable of being operated synchronously with the other cameras. In order to be able to do this, the camera must be able to accept an external sync signal. Usually, the camera has a small input through which the sync generator can be connected.

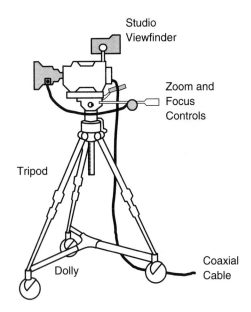

Figure 2.14 Convertible Camera in Studio Configuration with Tripod and Dolly

The sync generator provides the composite sync pulses (horizontal and vertical) simultaneously to all the cameras. In addition, when the camera is used in a multicamera production (studio or field), the camera output is fed into a video switcher rather than into its own VCR.

Studio Cameras

Some video cameras are designed primarily for use in studios. They tend to be much larger than their field production counterparts, are equipped with large studio-type zoom lenses, have highly developed internal signal adjustment circuitry, and usually do not have the capability to be operated by battery power.

CP-1 Color Video Camera Systems

Color video systems work with the **additive primary colors** of light—red, green, and blue. As light enters the lens, the color video system breaks the light into red, green, and blue components. This can be done in two different ways. Incoming light can be passed through a **prism block** (see left below) or a **stripe filter** can be attached to the face of the image sensor to break the light into its color components (see right below).

Prism Block System

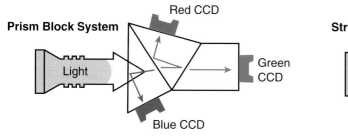

Stripe Filter System

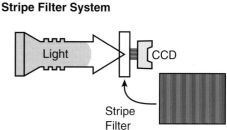

CP-2 Color Reproduction

The color picture on a home television receiver is created in a way similar to the camera color process. The picture tube in a television set is covered with a series of phosphorescent dots arranged in groups that consist of one red, one green, and one blue dot. The color television signal is composed of varying amounts of these three colors, depending on the scene that is being shot. When the color video signal is fed into a monitor, it triggers the electron gun(s) to scan the face of the picture tube, and it activates the red, green, and blue dots on the screen in relation to their relative strength in the signal. What you see when watching the screen is a full-color picture.

Three-Electron Gun System

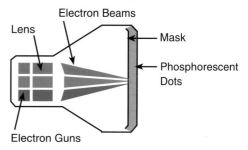

Color Television Display

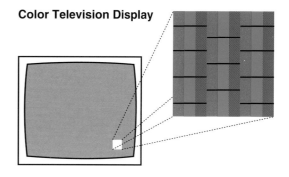

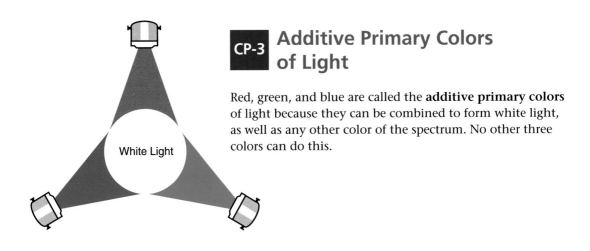

CP-3 Additive Primary Colors of Light

Red, green, and blue are called the **additive primary colors** of light because they can be combined to form white light, as well as any other color of the spectrum. No other three colors can do this.

White Light

CP-4 White Balance

White balance adjusts the relative intensity of the red, green, and blue camera color channels to allow the camera to produce an accurate picture in the particular light in which the subject is placed. If the principle illumination is daylight (5,600°K) and the camera white balance controls are incorrectly set on the indoor setting (3,200°K), the resulting picture will be too blue.

Correct

Incorrect

Foreground subject is recorded against a blue or green background.

CP-5 Image Compositing

Multi-layered images can be constructed by using **chroma key** effects. The foreground subject is recorded against a blue or green backdrop. A different background image is recorded separately. The two images are combined electronically by subtracting the blue or green background from the foreground picture.

Background image is recorded separately.

Green background is subtracted and foreground image is combined with background image.

CP-6 Fluorescent lighting instruments are ideally suited for lighting chroma key backgrounds because they provide uniform distribution of light at a precisely controlled color temperature.

CP-7 Nonlinear Video Editing

This nonlinear video editing system screen display provides information for each of the video shots stored in the system and produces a color coded timeline for the audio, video, graphics, and special effects components of the edited program.

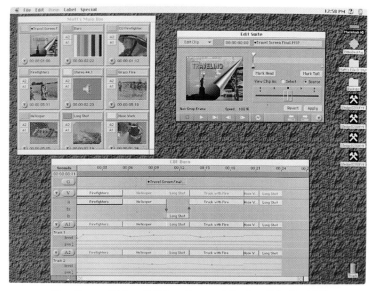

Nonlinear Video Editing Screen Display (Media 100)

CP-8 Contrasting Colors

Lettering that constrasts with the background is easier to read than lettering that is similar in color to the background.

CP-9 Monitoring the Signal

A portable waveform/picture monitor and vectorscope is used to monitor the video signal (Tektronix WFM90).

3 Lenses and Visualization

PART ONE
Lenses

Chapter 2 concentrated on the role the camera plays in producing an electronic image. This chapter will look at the function of the lens and the way manipulation of the camera and lens functions as a part of the process of visualization. We are concerned here with the technical elements of lens operation and manipulation as well as with the aesthetic impact that results from that manipulation. Video is not only an electronic phenomenon that produces an electronic signal, it is also an artistic or aesthetic phenomenon that produces images that audiences respond to. Any discussion of lenses, therefore, should contain a discussion of these complementary components.

Lenses: Functions and Types

The lens is the camera's eye. What it sees and how it sees it form the basis of the visual element of video. The camera **lens** gathers light that is reflected off the scene being recorded and directs an image onto the pickup device within the camera.

Focal Length

Camera lenses are often described by their **focal length,** which is defined as the distance from the optical center of the lens to the point where the image is in focus (the surface of the CCD). When we talk about lenses, we usually describe them in terms of how long or short they are. *Long* and *short* refer both to the focal length of the lenses and to their relative physical length, since long-focal-length lenses are actually longer than short-focal-length lenses.

The focal length of the lens determines the angle of view of a scene that the lens will reproduce. Short-focal-length lenses have a wide angle of view (they show you a wide expanse of a scene) and therefore are referred to as **wide-angle lenses.** Long-focal-length lenses have a narrow angle of view; they magnify a scene by making distant objects appear large and close, and they are often referred to as *narrow-angle* lenses or, more commonly, **telephoto lenses** (see Figure 3.1). The focal length of the lens also affects depth of field. We will talk about this a little later in this chapter.

Figure 3.1 Lens Focal Length
and Angle of View

Short Focal Length; Wide Angle of View

Medium Focal Length; Medium Angle of View

Long Focal Length; Narrow Angle of View

Types of Lenses

Two basic types of lenses are found on video cameras: zoom lenses and fixed-focal-length lenses. Portable color video cameras typically come equipped with a zoom lens. A **zoom lens** is a lens that has a variable focal length. That is, by making an adjustment on the lens, you can vary the focal length, thereby changing the magnifying power of the lens. By adjusting the zoom control, you can *zoom in* (make an object appear larger and closer) or *zoom out* (make the object seem to decrease in size or move farther away). (See Figure 3.2.)

The focal length of a lens is generally measured in millimeters (mm). At the wide-angle setting, the zoom lens on most portable video cameras has a focal length of 8 to 10mm or less. The focal length of the lens when it is zoomed

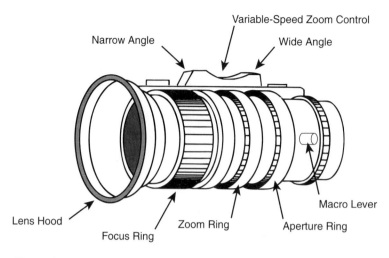

Variable-Speed Zoom Control

Narrow Angle   Wide Angle

Lens Hood

Focus Ring   Zoom Ring   Aperture Ring

Macro Lever

Figure 3.2   Zoom Lens Components

in—that is, when it is in its narrow angle or telephoto setting—depends on the **zoom ratio**, or zoom range, of the lens. For example, a zoom lens with a wide-angle focal length of 8mm and a zoom ratio of 10:1 has an effective focal length of 80mm (10 × 8mm) when it is zoomed in all the way. However, a lens with the same wide-angle focal length of 8mm but a zoom range of 20:1 has an effective focal length of 160mm (20 × 8mm) when it is zoomed in all the way. This provides greater magnification than the 10:1 lens; small objects appear larger and objects that are far away appear closer when they are shot with the 20:1 lens zoomed all the way in to its 160mm narrow-angle position.

A zoom lens with a zoom ratio of 20:1 or higher is particularly useful for outdoor shooting. Distant objects can be magnified simply by zooming in to them. Similarly, a lens with a 10:1 ratio may be suitable for indoor shooting. Because the optical system in the 10:1 lens is less complex than the 20:1 lens, it requires less light. And because the camera is always held relatively close to the subject indoors, the 10:1 lens provides adequate magnification.

Most high-quality video field production cameras are equipped with zoom lenses with a minimum zoom ratio between 10:1 and 15:1, and lenses with zoom ratios of 20:1 and 30:1 are readily available for most professional cameras and camcorders. Even consumer-quality camcorders are typically equipped with lenses with a zoom ratio of 20:1 or 30:1.

The other basic type of lens is the *fixed-focal-length* lens. This kind of lens, which is found on most still-photography cameras, does not have a zoom control. If you want to make an object appear larger or smaller by changing from a close-up to a wide-angle shot, you must either change the

49

lens or physically move the camera closer to or farther away from the object being photographed.

A number of different kinds of fixed-focal-length lenses are available for use in special situations. Extreme wide-angle lenses, or *fish-eye lenses,* produce a 180-degree angle of view of a scene as well as extremely dramatic distortion of objects (or faces) positioned close to the lens. Special *periscope lenses,* or *snorkel lenses,* allow the camera operator to move the camera lens around small objects and are used extensively to photograph products for television commercials.

Lens Mounts

The lens is attached to a professional ENG/EFP camcorder with a **bayonet mount.** The lens is inserted into the lens mount opening in the camera head and turned until it locks into place. Because different cameras use image sensors of different sizes (typically $1/3''$, $1/2''$, or $2/3''$ CCDs), bayonet mounts and lenses are designed in all three formats. On most consumer-level camcorders, the lens is integrated with the camera housing and is not designed to be easily removed or interchanged with another lens.

# Zoom Lens Components

How a Zoom Lens Works

A zoom lens is a variable-focal-length lens. The focal length of the lens can be changed by adjusting the zoom control, which moves the internal elements of the lens. The advantage to a zoom lens is that it combines the benefits of a short-focal-length lens and a long-focal-length lens. By adjusting the zoom control, you effectively change the lens from a wide to a narrow angle of view. This is accomplished in a smooth, continuous action and produces the sensation of zooming in or out, continuously magnifying or decreasing the size of the image. The ability to change the angle of view without moving the camera or changing lenses makes the zoom lens extremely versatile, and for that reason it is widely used in video production.

If you look at the zoom lens on a portable video camera, you can see its three major components: the focus ring, the zoom ring, and the aperture control. Each of these components plays a major role in controlling the quality of the image delivered to the camera's image sensor (see Figure 3.2).

The Focus Ring

The **focus ring** is at the far end of the lens. By turning the focus ring clockwise or counterclockwise, you can focus the image that the lens is capturing. An image is *in focus* when the important parts of the image are seen in sharp detail, and *out of focus* when it is seen as fuzzy and unclear. The correct focus depends on what it is you are trying to communicate. This is what dictates which part of the picture is most important and must be kept in focus. If you are shooting an interview, you usually want the person who is talking to be seen in focus. If you are shooting a sporting event, you usually want the large area of action to be in focus. You can tell whether something is in focus or not simply by looking at the image in the viewfinder of the camera to see if the focus is sharp, and by adjusting the focus ring if it is not.

The focus ring on all professional camera lenses is operated manually. Most consumer-grade camcorders, however, are equipped with **automatic focus (auto-focus)** mechanisms. These auto-focus systems work by emitting a beam of infrared (invisible) light or ultrasound (inaudible sound). The beam bounces off the object being videotaped and travels back to the camcorder, which calculates the distance from the camcorder to the object. A **servomechanism** then automatically adjusts the focus ring for correct focus.

Although use of auto-focus lenses often carries the stigma associated with nonprofessional camera work, they can be helpful, particularly for inexperienced camera operators. Auto-focus guarantees sharp focus in shooting situations that may be difficult for novice camera operators. For example, the continuously emitted focusing beam keeps the subject in focus, even if it or the camera moves, or if the lens is zoomed in or out. In extremely low-light conditions, when it is difficult to see the image on the camera viewfinder, auto-focus often provides more reliable focus than manual focus.

These benefits notwithstanding, some serious disadvantages are associated with the use of auto-focus lenses. Most auto-focus devices tend to focus on large objects located centrally in the frame. This is fine if you are shooting Grandpa as he tells ribald stories at the dinner table. However, if your subject is small or not centrally located in the frame, the lens will probably focus on some other part of the picture. If there are two similar-sized objects at different distances from the camera and both are positioned in the center of the frame, the auto-focus device will not know which one to focus on. If the auto-focus device is ultrasonic and the object you want to focus on is behind a glass window, the ultrasonic beam will be reflected back from the glass and will focus on the window rather than on the object behind it.

For these and other reasons, a lens that allows you to focus automatically and manually is preferable to one that works only in the auto-focus mode. Manual focus gives the camera operator more control over the lens, and in situations in which it is important to focus only part of the picture, manual focus is essential.

The Zoom Ring

The middle part of the lens contains the **zoom ring**, which can usually be controlled either manually or automatically. When the control is manual, you turn the zoom ring by hand to zoom in or out. Manual control gives you very good control over the zoom speed. You can go as fast or as slow as you want.

Automatic zoom lens controls are motor driven. A small motor drives the lens elements when you activate it. Some automatic zoom lens controls have one or two preset speeds that allow you to set the speed selector switch for a fast or slow zoom. Depending on the preset speed setting, you automatically zoom in or out at a fast or slow speed when you push the button that activates the zoom lens. More sophisticated automatic zoom lenses have continuous variable-speed motors hooked up to the lens. With these devices, a control switch is mounted on the zoom lens itself. The control has a *zoom in* position at one end and a *zoom out* position at the other end. The ends of this control are often respectively labeled "T," to indicate the tight, zoomed-in position, and "W," for the wide, zoomed-out position. The lens zooms in or out when you depress the appropriate side of the control. In addition, the zoom speed is controlled by the amount of pressure put on the control—the zoom speed increases with increased pressure and decreases with decreased pressure. This guarantees extremely smooth zooming over the whole zoom range of the lens.

The Aperture Ring

The **aperture ring** is mounted at the end of the lens next to the camera. The aperture ring controls the size of the **iris** opening of the lens. The iris of the lens works like the iris of your eye. In low-light situations, the iris needs to be opened up to allow more light to hit the image sensor. In bright situations, the iris needs to be closed, or shut down, to reduce the amount of light hitting the sensor.

Technically speaking, the aperture ring controls the size of the f-stop of the lens. **F-stops** are a standard calibration of the size of the aperture opening. F-stop numbers are printed on the lens itself, and usually vary from about 1.4 to 22 (see Figure 3.3). Small f-stop numbers correspond to large aperture openings. Therefore, a lens that is set at f-l.4 (a small f-stop number) is one in which the aperture is open very wide. A lens that is set at f-22 (a large f-stop number) is one in which the aperture is extremely small. This inverse relationship is one that you should memorize. Though this

Figure 3.3
F-Stop Numbers
and Aperture Size

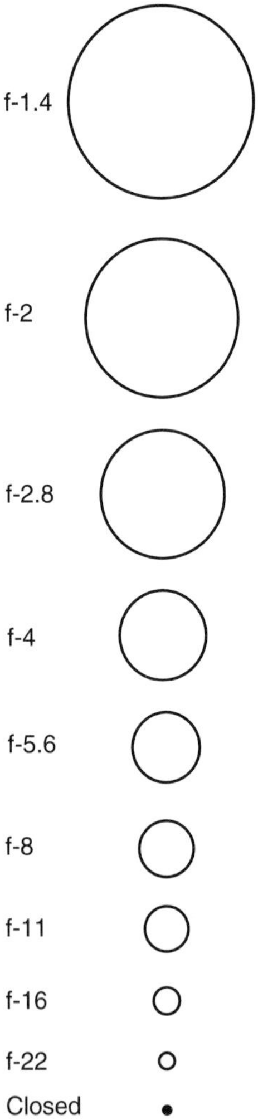

f-1.4

f-2

f-2.8

f-4

f-5.6

f-8

f-11

f-16

f-22

Closed

52

may seem confusing at first, the relationship between f-stop numbers and aperture size should become clear as soon as you take your camera in hand and work with it for a few minutes.

The f-stop settings on most high-quality lenses are a series of **click stops.** As you change from one f-stop to another, the lens clicks into place at the new setting. This helps you to determine how many stops you have opened or closed the lens. Typical f-stop settings on a lens are f-1.4, f-2, f-2.8, f-4, f-5.6, f-8, f-11, f-16, f-22, and closed. It is not necessary to set the aperture precisely at one of the click stops. You may set it at any position on or between f-stops because the aperture size varies continuously as the aperture ring is turned.

In addition, most lenses have an iris setting in which the aperture can be completely closed. Normally, the iris is left in the closed position when the camera is not in use. The closed iris setting can also be used for aperture **fades,** in which an image is faded up from black by opening the aperture or faded out to black by gradually closing it.

Many consumer-quality camcorders eliminate manually operated apertures and f-stop settings in favor of an automatic iris system. In some cases, the automatic system can be overridden by using the "backlight" control, which opens up the aperture one or two additional stops to correct lighting problems when the background light is brighter than the subject you are trying to photograph. An additional manual override for the automatic iris may also be present, but on inexpensive camcorders the range of possible adjustments to the iris is often limited. Both the backlight and manual iris controls are usually found on the side of the camcorder housing rather than on the lens assembly.

Other Lens Components

Before beginning a discussion of the control of the aesthetics of the image, several other lens components ought to be mentioned. The **lens hood,** attached to the end of the lens, works like the visor on a hat to prevent unwanted light from hitting the lens and causing lens flare. A **lens flare** is an optical aberration that is caused when light bounces off the elements within a lens. Most often, it is caused by pointing the camera directly at the sun or other light source with the effect of causing a glaring point of light to appear in the picture. The **lens cap** is a covering that can be attached to the end of the lens. The lens cap has two functions: it protects the glass in the lens from damage when the camera is not in operation, and it prevents any light from hitting the image sensor. The lens cap should *always* be used when the camera is not in operation. It should be used when transporting the camera and when the camera is turned off between shots. It is the single most important safety feature on a portable camera. A **macro lever** is a device that converts the lens to a **macro lens,** which allows you to take extreme close-up shots of very small objects. In the normal zoom lens mode, most lenses are not capable of focusing on objects closer than two or three feet from the end of the lens. When the macro lens switch is activated, you can focus the camera on objects that are only inches away from the lens and magnify their size so that they fill the video frame. A macro lens is extremely useful if you plan to shoot a large number of small objects.

Lens Filters and Extenders

A variety of lens filters and range extenders are available for use with existing lens systems. Many camera operators attach a clear filter to the front of the lens to protect the outside lens element from physical damage such as scratching or chipping. Other special-effects filters are used to change the quality or amount of light passing through the lens, allowing the camera operator to manipulate the incoming light in a number of ways. Among the most commonly used special-effects filters are *fog filters* and *star filters*.

Range extenders that double the magnifying power of the lens (2×
extenders) are built into many ENG/EFP camcorder zoom lenses. If they aren't built in, they may be available as an attachment to be screwed onto the front of the lens. Remember, however, that if you use an extender, you double the magnification of the lens throughout the entire zoom range. The focal-length range of a lens with a zoom range from 8mm to 160mm becomes a range from 16mm to 320mm when a 2× extender is engaged. Thus, not only is the narrow-angle shot twice as narrow (320mm vs. 160mm), but the wide-angle shot becomes narrower as well (16mm vs. 8mm).

Aspect Ratio Converter

An increasing number of professional-quality ENG/EFP lenses now come equipped with an **aspect ratio converter**, a two-position switch with which the videographer can select either the traditional NTSC 4:3 ratio or the wide-screen 16:9 ratio.

Lens Care

In addition to placing the lens cap on the lens for protection when the camera is not in use, care should be taken not to damage the face of the lens. In some shooting conditions, the lens may get wet or dirty; if by looking through the viewfinder and closely examining the lens it becomes apparent that dust or dirt is present, the lens should be cleaned. Special lens-cleaning solutions are available from photographic or video supply houses.

The solution can be sprayed onto the lens and then removed with special nonabrasive lens paper. Common tissue paper should not be used to clean the lens. It usually leaves some lint residue behind and, depending on the quality of the paper, may be abrasive as well.

Zoom Lens Operation

Zoom Lens Focus

Presetting the focus on a zoom lens is a fairly simple matter. Turn on the power to the camera (so that an image is visible in the viewfinder) and, with the camera in the automatic aperture mode, zoom in as close as possible to the object you plan to shoot. Turn the focus ring until the image appears to be in focus. Then zoom out and frame up your shot. Do *not* adjust the focus ring again. You can now zoom in and out on the subject, and it will remain in focus as long as its position remains constant in relation to the camera. If you move the camera or if the subject moves, you must reset the zoom focus.

Correct Exposure

Because the aperture setting affects not only the quality of the image but also the level of the video signal, it is extremely important to set the aperture accurately by finding the correct exposure for a scene. Opening the aperture too wide and letting too much light hit the image sensor washes out the details in the picture and causes extreme color distortion. In addition, overexposure often produces very bright, glowing spots, known as **hot spots**, in the picture. Image detail and correct color are lost in hot spots.

Hot spots are unacceptable for several reasons. First, the loss of image detail (unless this is a desired special effect) is extremely distracting to the viewer and unflattering to the subject. Second, in terms of the video signal, hot spots represent places in which the video signal is driven far above the maximum point for the peak white. Therefore, the video signal, as well as the image, is somewhat distorted. Conversely, if the exposure is too low, it will produce a picture with a lot of electronic noise, muddy or gray colors, and an inadequate video signal.

How can you know which aperture setting is correct? There are a number of approaches you can take. Perhaps the most commonly used method is eyeballing. With this method, you literally look at the viewfinder image to see what the scene looks like. With the lighting you will use in place, open the aperture until the viewfinder produces the best picture, one with good contrast between the bright and dark areas, and without any hot spots. If you have a color monitor, it is extremely helpful to look at the color picture to see whether the colors are reproduced accurately. Slight corrections in the aperture setting often make dramatic changes in color reproduction.

Most cameras are equipped with a **light meter** built into the camera viewfinder (see Figure 3.4). The light meter tells you whether the scene is too bright, too dark, or just about right. However, remember that the light meter usually works as an averaging meter. The light meter senses the brightest and darkest parts of the image and sets the exposure at a middle point. The average brightness on the scene may or may not give the correct exposure for the most important part of the scene, that is, the center of interest you are shooting. Usually, the light meter tells you if you are in the ballpark as far as exposure goes, and then you can make minor adjustments for the correct aperture setting.

Some camera viewfinders contain a **zebra-stripe** exposure indicator. In this system, a series of black-and-white lines appears over the brightest portion of the picture when the maximum video level has been reached. In some camera viewfinders, the zebra stripes are set to appear when correct exposure for skin tone is achieved.

The most accurate way to set the aperture is to use a waveform monitor in conjunction with a good camera monitor. This allows you to monitor the parameters of the video signal. Some camera viewfinders produce a waveform display superimposed over the viewfinder image. However, remember that the way the image looks is every bit as important as how good the waveform looks. You do not want to adjust every scene so that

Figure 3.4 Camcorder
Viewfinder Display

the peak white is at 100 percent if you have some scenes that are indeed darker than others. A scene shot in outdoor daylight looks different (aesthetically and technically) from a scene shot in a candlelit room. The waveform monitor is extremely useful, however, in determining whether you are exceeding the 100 percent video level. Exceeding this level distorts the picture, and the waveform monitor can help you avoid this distortion and keep the signal within its normal limits.

 # Aperture Control and Depth of Field

Aperture Control

The lens iris, like the zoom lens control, can be operated manually or automatically. With manual aperture (or manual iris) control, the camera operator looks into the viewfinder and manually adjusts the aperture until a good picture appears in the viewfinder. In a lens equipped with an **automatic aperture** (or automatic iris), a small light meter in the camera controls the size of the aperture opening. The picture area is sampled for brightness and an average brightness is calculated. The iris opening is then adjusted automatically for this scene. If the lighting changes, the lens automatically responds and makes the appropriate iris correction. Camera operators often use the automatic aperture feature of the lens to establish a preliminary exposure for a shot, and then shift to the manual aperture mode to make fine adjustments in the exposure.

Automatic aperture can be a helpful feature to have, but the videographer should always keep two things in mind: contrast range and center of interest. **Contrast range**, expressed as a ratio of brightness to darkness, refers to the video system's ability to reproduce a range of different values of brightness. A contrast ratio of between 30:1 and 40:1 is normal for most portable color video cameras. That is, the brightest part of the scene must not be any more than 30 to 40 times brighter than the darkest part of the scene. If the ratio is greater than 40:1, the camera is not able to handle it, and the very bright parts of the scene will wash out or turn into glowing hot spots. Compare the video contrast ratio with the contrast ratio possible with the human eye (100:1). The eye is significantly better able to handle extreme contrast than is a video camera.

Contrast ratio is mentioned here (as well as when lighting is discussed) because it is very important when one is trying to find the correct aperture setting. When the camera is set on automatic aperture, it samples the picture for brightness and, as stated earlier, averages these brightness values to set the correct iris setting. The automatic iris, however, cannot determine the brightness only for the part of the frame most important to

Figure 3.5 Silhouetting Caused by Bright Background

Silhouetting Evident on the Wide Shot Can Be Controlled by Zooming in to a Tighter Shot.

you. It simply takes an average reading. Sometimes a particular spot or point in the frame is important in terms of what you are trying to communicate; it is the **center of interest** in the frame. To correctly expose for it, you may have to set the aperture manually. Subjects photographed against a very bright background may appear in silhouette with the lens in the automatic iris mode. This exposure problem can often be corrected simply by zooming in to a tighter shot of the subject and eliminating as much of the bright background from the picture as possible. (See Figure 3.5.)

When the aperture is set on automatic, the camera compensates for any change in the lighting or brightness of the image. Suppose you are shooting an interview outdoors with the lens on automatic aperture, when a large white truck drives by in the background. The automatic aperture responds to the increased brightness caused by the presence of the truck and closes down the iris accordingly. When the truck disappears from the frame, the aperture adjusts again and reopens to the previous setting. The effect of the aperture closing and opening is that the face of the person being interviewed gets darker when the truck enters the frame and then brighter again when the truck leaves the frame. At best, this is very distracting to the viewer.

Some lenses have a feature called **automatic aperture lock.** This locks in the setting first calculated by the automatic aperture and prevents the camera from responding to any subsequent changes in brightness. Going back to our example, with the camera in the automatic aperture mode, you prepare your shot of the person to be interviewed. You focus the shot and then engage the aperture lock. This holds the facial exposure that has been automatically set. When the white truck drives by in the background, the camera does not respond to it, and the exposure on the subject's face remains constant.

A word of caution is necessary at this point. If the lighting changes radically while the camera is in the aperture lock mode, picture quality will suffer greatly. The camera operator must constantly monitor the image and make aperture corrections when necessary.

Depth of Field

Depth of field refers to the portion of the scene that is in focus in front of the camera (see Figure 3.6). Depth of field can be very long or very short, depending on the aperture setting, the distance between the subject and camera, and the zoom lens setting. Table 3.1 shows these relationships.

Short Depth of Field

Longer Depth of Field

Very Long Depth of Field

Figure 3.6
Depth of Field:
Area in Focus in
Front of Camera

Table 3.1 Depth-of-Field Relationships

+ amount of available light + f-stop number (– aperture size) – focal length of the lens + distance from camera to subject	Depth of field *increases*[a]
– amount of available light – f-stop number (+ aperture size) + focal length of the lens – distance from camera to subject	Depth of field *decreases*[b]

[a]Read as: With increase in amount of available light, f-stop number also increases (aperture size decreases) and depth of field increases. With decrease in focal length of lens, depth of field increases. With increase in distance from camera to subject, depth of field increases.

[b]Read as: With decrease in amount of available light, f-stop number also decreases (aperture size increases) and depth of field decreases. With increase in focal length of lens, depth of field decreases. With decrease in distance from camera to subject, depth of field decreases.

Perhaps the easiest way to explain these depth-of-field relationships is through the use of examples. We will consider two different lighting situations: one outdoors, in which the depth of field is long, and one indoors, in which the depth of field is shallow.

Example 1: Daylight Outdoors.   Let's briefly discuss the way the elements of aperture, focal length of the lens, and distance from camera to subject affect the depth of field. Let's assume that you plan to videotape a football game. You take the camcorder to the field and are given a camera position on the 50-yard line at the top of the grandstand. This puts you and your camera at a considerable distance from the action. It is a bright, beautiful autumn day.

Now, let's analyze each of the variables that affects the depth of field. First, let's consider the amount of light falling on the scene. Because it is early afternoon on a beautiful, cloudless day and you are shooting in full sunlight, we can assume you have more than enough light to shoot your video. Because you have a lot of light, you set your camera iris at f-16, a fairly normal setting for a bright day. This aperture setting (with a high f-stop number) gives you a fairly small aperture opening. This makes sense because on a very bright day you want to limit the amount of light hitting the camera image sensor so that you do not overexpose the scene (see Table 3.1). The first rule of the relationship among amount of available light, f-stop number, and depth of field tells us that as the amount of available light increases, the f-stop number increases, aperture size decreases, and, as a result, depth of field increases. These relationships are apparent in the example, and you will discover that your depth of field under these conditions is quite long.

Next, let's consider the focal length of the lens. From your vantage point, you are able to zoom in or out on the scene below. To provide a cover shot of the action, you can zoom out the lens to its widest possible shot. This effectively sets the zoom lens on its shortest focal length and enables you to cover a great deal of the field. In this position, the second rule of relationship becomes apparent: as focal length of the lens decreases (as the lens is zoomed out to a wide shot), depth of field increases. In the light described, all of the action below is in focus with the wide-angle lens setting. As a matter of fact, everything from about three feet in front of the lens to infinity in the distance is in focus. You are shooting in a situation that gives you virtually the greatest possible depth of field.

Depth of field is enhanced because the camera is positioned a considerable distance from the action. Again, as distance from the subject to the camera increases, so does depth of field. All of these factors contribute to great depth of field as you shoot this football game.

Now let's consider changing one variable: the focal length of the lens. At times during the game you want to zoom in on the action, thereby effectively increasing the focal length of the lens. The zoom in makes the lens act like a long-focal-length telephoto lens. It magnifies the scene, and instead of showing you all the action in a long shot, it shows only a part of it in close-up detail. As you zoom in, you notice that the depth of field decreases significantly. On the long shot, you were able to keep all the action across the field in focus. Now as you shoot while zoomed in, you find that some of the field and players in the foreground (closer to the camera) are out of focus, as are some of the players in the background. You have to work the focus ring to keep the center of interest—the player with the ball—in focus, particularly if the player runs toward either side of the field (toward or away from the camera) rather than in a straight line toward the end zone.

Example 2: Low Light Indoors.

Let's contrast the brightly lit outdoor scene with another scene in which all the elements contribute to give you very short depth of field. Let's assume that you are now recording an evening scene indoors, using only the light available in the room. The room in which you are to record is dimly lit. To produce an acceptable picture with your camera, you are forced to open the aperture as wide as it will go, in this case to f-1.4. In addition, since you are working in a small room, your camera is significantly closer to the action than it was at the football game, when you were positioned high in the grandstand.

All these elements produce a situation in which the depth of field is extremely short. There is very little available light, and to compensate for this and give the camera enough light to make an acceptable picture, you have opened up the aperture (large aperture = small f-stop number). In addition, the distance from the camera to the subject is short. As you look through the viewfinder, you find that if you focus on one person, the background and foreground go out of focus. It is very difficult to keep in focus all the people standing at different distances in front of the camera. This becomes even more apparent when you zoom in (increase the focal length of the lens) on the scene. The only way to improve the situation— to increase the depth of field—is to increase the amount of available light, which allows you to shut down the lens slightly (decrease the aperture size).

PART TWO
Visualization and Composition

Aesthetics of
Visual Composition

Have you ever noticed that not all television programs look alike? Different programs and different movies often have a particular look or style that results from the way that particular program or film was visualized by the camera operator. The most significant elements of visualization include the impact of lighting and editing (to be discussed in later chapters) and the way in which the camera and its lens are used to create the visual images to which we respond. The rest of this chapter will concentrate on this last element.

How does the camera operator decide whether or not a shot is good? We have standards that determine whether something is *technically* good (Is the color accurate? Is the video signal adequate? Is the contrast range accurate?), but we seldom talk about the *aesthetics* of visual composition. At a seminar given several years ago, a leading Hollywood camera operator said that he trained his eye for composition by going to art museums and looking at the paintings. (We should note here that he was a fan of portraits, not modern art.) His point was an interesting one: How do you know how to shoot a scene? What should it look like? Some people seem to know intuitively, and we often say that a good photographer has a "good eye." But how does someone get a good eye? Is it something that you are born with? Or is it something that is learned? It is probably a combination of both.

This discussion will examine some of the factors you should take into consideration when composing images for video, including screen size and aspect ratio, focus, field of view, framing and balance, the rule of thirds, and camera movement. This is not a comprehensive list, but it will help you get started in thinking about the ways to structure the composition of the individual images in your production.

Screen Size and Aspect Ratio

Two primary considerations for anyone working with video images are the size and aspect ratio of the television screen. There are two inescapable constants: most television screens are small, and they all have the same aspect ratio. By **aspect ratio**, we mean relationship of the width to the height of the screen. For television, this is a fixed ratio of 4:3 (four units high by three units wide) or 16:9.

Let's talk about size first. The screen size of most television sets in use in the United States today is approximately 27 inches or less in diagonal. Although large-screen systems have become more popular in recent years, they constitute a small percentage of the actual number of television display systems at use in home, office, and school settings. For now, when you think of a television screen, think small.

What does this mean in terms of the composition of images? For one thing, it means that close-ups are important. Since the screen is so small, a long shot cannot provide a lot of detail. Therefore, if detail is important to your production, it usually must be shown in close-up. If you are producing a tape about a new medical procedure or a new type of electronic component, to present your subject matter to the audience effectively you are going to have to shoot it in close-up detail. A long shot of the operating room or manufacturing facility may help establish the location, but a transition to a close-up of the event is essential to communicate your subject matter effectively to your audience.

The lens plays some important functions with respect to image size; the zoom lens or a fixed-focal-length macro lens can be used to magnify objects. This magnification is important because it makes elements of the scene more visible by magnifying them. It also eliminates or reduces other visual distractions because a close-up often eliminates the other elements in the frame from the field of view.

The fixed 4:3 or 16:9 aspect ratio of the television screen is important in defining the visual potential of the medium because the screen is always wider than it is tall. The screen has a basic stable, horizontal orientation that approximates the normal field of vision produced by our eyes. However, this horizontal screen orientation makes it somewhat difficult to accurately shoot extremely vertical subjects such as buildings, tall people,

Vertically Oriented Shot Not
in TV/Video Aspect Ratio

A Portion of the Same Shot Framed
Tighter in 4:3 Aspect Ratio

Long Shot in 4:3 Aspect Ratio

Figure 3.7
Aspect Ratio

Long Shot in 16:9 Aspect Ratio

and so on. In using the camera to frame something that is taller than it is wide, we either have to cut off part of the object or person to make it fit into the aspect ratio of the screen (see Figure 3.7) or pull out to a wider shot.

The 4:3 and 16:9 aspect ratios of video provide static rectangular frames in which to compose the picture. Videographers have learned to create more dynamic frames within the boundaries of the screen by using silhouettes, doorways, or crowds of people in the extreme foreground (see Figure 3.8).

Figure 3.8
Creating a Frame within
a Frame

Focus

The use of the lens **focus** is important in directing the audience's attention to what is important in a shot. If everything in a shot is relatively the same size and everything is in focus, all parts of the shot appear to be of equal importance to the viewer. Focus can be used to isolate the more important parts of a shot from those less important or to direct the audience's attention to one part of the shot.

Focus and Depth

We see the world in three dimensions when we look at it through our eyes. However, the world as it is presented on the television screen has only two dimensions: height and width. The third dimension, depth, is really an illusion because the television screen surface is actually flat. Because our normal experience of the world is in three dimensions, video images seem more realistic when they also appear to be three-dimensional. To create the sense of depth on the television screen, it is important to construct images that are divided into distinct foreground, middleground, and background areas. Focus is one technique that can be used to separate these three planes. The technique through which the camera focuses on one of these planes and lets the others go out of focus is known as **selective focus** (see Figure 3.6). Selective focus is most commonly used with a short depth of field created through the use of a telephoto lens (or a zoom lens zoomed in to the telephoto position).

Field of View

A basic terminology is used to describe the types of shots found in video production. The following shot descriptions refer to the field of view apparent in the shot (how much of the scene the shot shows) and to the number of people visible in the shot. It is important to have a terminology for shots because these shot descriptions are used by writers to describe shots in written scripts and by directors or videographers to communicate to the other crew members how they want a shot or scene to look. (See Figure 3.9.)

Extreme Long Shot.   The **extreme long shot (XLS)** gives the audience an overall view of the large scene. It provides a panorama of the elements of the scene or shot. Although we may not be able to see all of the significant individual details in the shot, the XLS is nevertheless important for establishing the relationship between the parts and the whole or creating impact through the use of wide-open spaces.

Long Shot.   The **long shot (LS)** is not as wide as the extreme long shot. When people are involved in an LS, it shows us the positional relationship between the actors and their setting. Extreme long shots and long shots are often referred to as **establishing shots**, because they establish locale and the relationships between the individual parts of the shot.

Medium Shot.   The **medium shot (MS)** is tighter (closer) than the long shot but not as tight as a close-up. The medium shot is used to show the relationship between people in a shot or scene but generally does not present as much information about the setting as a long shot. When people are shown in a medium shot, they are usually cut off somewhere between the knees and the waist.

Medium Close-Up.   The **medium close-up (MCU)** is one of the most frequently used shots in video production. It consists of a head-and-shoulders shot that ends at the chest of the subject. The medium close-up gives full-face detail on the subject but without the extreme impact of the close-up.

Close-Up.   The **close-up (CU)** is an extremely powerful shot that gives an extremely tight shot of the subject's head. A close-up of an object practically fills the screen. The close-up is one of the most effective shots available for providing a close view of the details of a face or object.

Extreme Close-Up or Tight Close-Up.   The **extreme close-up (ECU)** or **tight close-up (TCU)** is the tightest shot possible for your subject. On a person, the extreme close-up frames the subject's eyes and nose or mouth. If both the eyes and mouth will not fit in the frame, it is usually better to frame the shot to include the eyes and nose rather than the nose and mouth.

Figure 3.9 Fields-of-View Terminology

Extreme Long Shot (XLS)

Medium Close-Up (MCU)

Long Shot (LS)

Close-Up (CU)

Medium Shot (MS)

Extreme Close-Up (ECU)

67

1-Shot, 2-Shot, and 3-Shot.   This terminology refers to the number of people seen in a shot. Thus, a medium 2-shot is a medium shot that includes two people; a long 3-shot is a long shot that includes three people; and so on.

Composition through Framing

Framing refers to the placement of a person or object within the video frame. When a person is the subject of a shot, two compositional elements related to framing are headroom and noseroom. **Headroom** refers to the distance between the top of the person's head and the top edge of the frame. In gauging the correct amount of headroom, the camera operator usually tries not to leave too much or too little space at the top of the frame. With too little headroom, the person appears to stick to the top of the frame. This simply looks wrong to the viewer. (See Figure 3.10.) Simi-

No Headroom

Too Much Headroom

Figure 3.10   Headroom

Comfortable Headroom

larly, if the subject is placed too low in the frame, the person appears to be sinking out of the frame. There is no formula for determining how much headroom is correct, although more headroom is appropriate on longer shots, and less headroom works better on close-ups.

You should pay particular attention to headroom whenever you zoom in or out on a subject. Typically, as you zoom out and the subject becomes smaller, headroom will increase. Therefore, you will need to tilt the camera down to compensate for this. On the other hand, as you zoom in and the subject becomes larger, the amount of headroom will decrease. In this situation you may need to tilt up to correct the framing.

The concept of noseroom is similar to the concept of headroom. (See Figure 3.11.) **Noseroom** refers to the distance between the edge of the nose of the person in the shot and the edge of the video frame. In reality, **eyeroom** might be a better term than *noseroom,* because it is the person's eyes, not the nose, that create a powerful force within the frame. Correct framing is based on the direction of the eyes (where they are focused), the dynamics of the story being told, and the graphic composition of the picture.

Figure 3.11
Eyeroom (Noseroom)

Attention Focused in Front of Subject

Attention Focused behind Subject

For example, if the subject looks to one side of the frame, the rules of normal composition dictate that the camera pans slightly to allow sufficient eyeroom (or noseroom) so that the person does not appear glued to the frame's side. If, however, within the context of the story we know that the subject is being pursued and is about to be overtaken, framing the person without sufficient eyeroom reinforces the idea that this person is trapped. This technique is commonly used in horror films and television programs of that genre; when the picture cuts to a close-up as the subject struggles to escape, the end is near. Similarly, if the camera pans to create space *behind* the subject, rather than in front, the audience knows something is going to happen in the space behind the subject.

Finally, the camera operator should pay attention to the outlines of people or objects in a shot. Because most shots commonly have a background with detail in it, the outline of foreground objects should *overlap,* rather than *coincide,* with the outline of background objects. For example, consider a shot of someone sitting in a chair with a painting on the wall in

BAD: Coincident Lines Are Distracting

Figure 3.12   Foreground/Background Coincident Lines

BETTER: But Does Not Express Depth

BEST: Overlap Expresses Depth

the background. It is best to frame the shot so that the outline of the head either does not reach up to the bottom of the painting or instead blocks part of the painting from view. If the outline of the top of the head touches the outline of the bottom of the painting, the resulting image will be distracting, if not comical (see Figure 3.12). Trees and poles in the background that appear to grow out of someone's head should also be avoided for similar reasons.

Framing and Balance

The way in which a shot is framed and composed affects the viewer's perception of the balance of the shot. **Balance** refers to the relative weight created by objects or people in the frame. These weights may be distributed evenly (*symmetrical balance*) or unevenly (*asymmetrical balance*). (See Figure 3.13.) Symmetrical framing, in which the graphic weight of objects in the

Figure 3.13   Symmetrical and Asymmetrical Balance

Symmetrical Balance

Asymmetrical Balance

frame is symmetrically balanced, is very stable and tells the viewer that the situation is at rest or under control. Asymmetrical framing, in which the graphic masses are asymmetrically balanced, creates a sense of imbalance and instability. It produces tension and suggests that something is about to happen.

The Rule of Thirds

There are few lasting "rules of composition" because story context and audience expectations constantly change. "Rules" reflect current practices and change as audiences become too familiar with them and they lose their effectiveness. One such formerly common practice was called the *rule of thirds* because the screen area was divided into three equal parts both horizontally and vertically (see Figure 3.14). The four points located one-third of the distance from the four parts of the frame were considered to be

Figure 3.14
Rule of Thirds

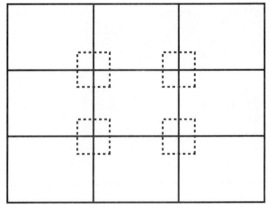

the optimum location for objects and persons of importance to the story. In practice, this type of composition offers an unobstructed view of the objects or persons central to the story but with a relatively neutral treatment. No particular tension, movement, or progression of the story is suggested by this composition.

Camera Movement

Camera Head and Zoom Lens Movement

There are two basic types of camera movements: (1) movements of the camera head or zoom lens, with the camera itself in a fixed position; and (2) movements of the entire camera and its support system. The two most common camera head movements are panning and tilting. A **pan** is a horizontal movement of the camera head only. The word *pan* is short for *panorama,* and the purpose of the pan is to reveal a scene with a sweeping horizontal motion of the camera head. A **tilt** is a vertical (up-and-down) movement of the camera head. Again, it is usually accomplished with the camera in a fixed position. The **zoom** is accomplished by simply moving the zoom lens assembly, causing the lens to zoom in or zoom out. The effect of the zoom is to bring the scene closer to the viewer or to move it farther away from the viewer.

Zoom lenses were developed to allow the camera operator to change the field of view without changing lenses. Thus, technically speaking, the zoom lens made production more efficient because the camera operator could get new shots set up quickly. Beyond this, however, the zoom movement itself has found considerable popularity in video productions and is particularly useful when shooting with a single camera.

A word of caution is in order here: Do not overuse the zoom. The zoom can be extremely effective when it is used properly, but the zoom must have a reason for its existence. The scene must call for it—it must be motivated or introduced to present new information in a shot. It is extremely bad practice to simply zoom in and out to add movement to a scene. Not only will constant zooming nauseate your audience but it will also create difficulty when editing the videotape because it is usually easier to cut between two still shots than between two moving shots.

Zoom speed is also an important variable. A fast zoom draws attention to the zoom and the image, whereas a slow zoom may hardly be noticed, as it subtly directs the viewer's attention to the content of the shot.

Movement of the Camera
and Its Support Unit

Movement of the camera and its support unit (often a tripod with a three-wheel dolly attached to the legs) produces the movement of dolly, truck, and arc. A **dolly in** or **out** is the movement of the entire camera and its support toward or away from the scene. A **truck left** or **right** is the horizontal movement of the camera and its support in front of the scene. An **arc** is a semicircular movement of the camera and its support around the scene. These terms can also be used if the camera is handheld, although the movements will not be as smooth because the up-and-down walking motion of the camera operator will be visible in the shot.

Trucking shots are also sometimes called **tracking shots**, in reference to the practice of constructing a set of rigid tracks for a camera dolly to roll on in locations where the ground or floor is not smooth enough to allow the use of a wheeled dolly. The technique of constructing tracks for camera movement is frequently used in the production of television commercials, dramas, and music video productions when smooth, level movement of the camera in a field location is required.

Smooth, effective camera motion can also be achieved by using some rather untraditional methods of moving the camera. Grocery carts, wheelchairs, and bicycles can provide steady support for moving camera shots, as can shooting out of the window or sunroof of an automobile.

Handheld versus Tripod-Mounted
Camera Movement

There are differences between movements accomplished with a handheld or shoulder-mounted camera and those done with a camera mounted on a tripod dolly or other stable yet movable mounting device. The differences are both physical and psychological. A camera mounted on a tripod is extremely stable. Because it is so stable, the camera becomes an invisible, objective observer of the scene. The purpose of the camera in television studio presentations such as news programs and interviews is to record what happens, not to participate in the event. For this reason, tripod- or pedestal-mounted cameras are almost always used for these kinds of programs.

If the lens is zoomed out all the way, it is easier to control the perceived effect of camera movement than if it is zoomed in. Nevertheless, when the camera is handheld, it becomes significantly less stable. As a result, the viewer becomes aware of the movement of the camera and consequently also becomes aware of the presence of the camera. The camera participates significantly more in the event because its presence is apparent. It is no longer an invisible observer without an effect on the scene. The effect of the camera is now visible and the viewer can see how it responds to the scene. Thus, the decision to mount a camera on a tripod or to hold it should be made with a great amount of forethought.

Shooting to Edit

In almost all single-camera video field productions, the camera operator shoots material that will be edited together in postproduction. The camera operator has a responsibility to give the editor material that can be coherently assembled. The following guidelines should be considered when shooting material that is going to be edited in postproduction.

Shoot Establishing Shots

The function of the establishing shot is to set the scene; it tells the viewer where the action is happening. Establishing shots, most often in the form of extreme long shots or long shots, show the relationship of the parts to each other and to the scene as a whole. An establishing shot is essential if the viewer, who otherwise has no knowledge of the scene or setting, is to make sense of the scene.

Cover the Action

When you look at a situation or scene, try to identify the principal action or event. Break scenes or events down into their principal components and then try to cover them. For example, if you are commissioned to videotape a friend's wedding, you could break that event into components like these:

1. Prewedding activities—bride dressing, arrival of groom at church, bride's drive to church, and so on
2. Ceremony—arrival of bride, walk down the aisle into church, ceremony including exchange of rings and traditional kiss, and so on
3. After ceremony—walk down the aisle and out of church, throwing rice or birdseed at bride and groom, drive to reception, reception line, cutting the cake, and so on

By breaking the event into component parts, you can determine what you need to cover to faithfully capture the essence of the event. Breaking an event into components also tells you whether you need one camera or more. If you have only one camera, you can decide which parts of the event are most important and plan to cover these.

Repeat the Action If Possible

If you have only one camera to shoot an event and the participants are willing and able to repeat the action, you can shoot the same event from different angles. In traditional Hollywood-film-style shooting, the director provides a master shot of the entire scene, shot on a wide-angle lens. Then the scene is repeated from several additional angles to provide close-up detail of the major characters or actions in the scene. In a television studio program utilizing multiple cameras, one camera usually holds a wide shot and the others are set on close-ups of the details of the action. The director then cuts from one camera to another as the scene unfolds.

Because you typically have only one camera for shooting in the field, it is helpful to shoot multiple takes. This is often easy to arrange. For example, if you are recording a musical group, you can do one take of a song on a wide shot, then shoot a close-up of the lead singer, and then perhaps do a third take, shooting each of the instrumentalists during his or her solo segment. For editing, this provides a cover shot (the long shot of the whole group) plus repeated action of the significant details from which to assemble your segment.

Whether your subject can repeat the action depends to a certain extent on the nature of the action. Product demonstrations and dramatic scenes lend themselves quite readily to multiple takes of repeated action. You will most likely have more success in arranging multiple takes with the music recording session just described than with your local hockey team's score of a game-winning goal. Instant replays, unfortunately, are not a characteristic of real life.

If you are shooting a program from a script that involves dialogue or action, then the technique of **overlapping** should be used. Begin each new shot by repeating the action or dialogue that ended the previous shot. This technique of shooting overlapping action and dialogue greatly simplifies the editor's task.

Shoot Essential Details

In addition to the overall action or principal elements of a scene, what are the essential details? Shoot close-up shots of essential details of the event to be used as **cut-ins**, and shoot other related details that are not parts of the scene itself to be used as **cutaways.** For example, if you are shooting an interview with a painter who is discussing current projects, you might also shoot some footage of the artist at work. Shots at work might include wide shots of the painter in the studio as well as close-ups of the brush moving against the canvas. A cut from a shot of the painter talking on camera during the interview to a shot of the painter at work is a cutaway. A cut from the wide shot of the artist in the studio to a close-up of the brush moving is a cut-in.

Another common type of cutaway shot in an interview scene is the **reaction shot.** Shoot some footage of the interviewer responding to the painter. A cutaway from the painter to the reaction shot will show the audience how the interviewer is responding to what is being said.

If the artist demonstrates the techniques used, you should shoot some close-ups of this activity. You can then cut in from a wide or medium shot of the artist in the studio to a close-up shot of the artist's hands at work.

Another term frequently used to describe cutaway shots in interview sequences is **B-roll.** The term is also widely used in news production to describe the visual footage that covers the reporter's voice-over. Cutaway, or B-roll, footage is used extensively in video production to enhance the interview or news-story voice information (the **A-roll**) with appropriate visual sequences. Cutaways provide a visual alternative to "talking heads."

When working with interview-based material, it is generally preferable to record the interviews first and then to use the subjects' answers to questions to identify appropriate B-roll footage to shoot to be used as cutaways. This cutaway material should allow the editor to create appropriate shot sequences. It's not sufficient to shoot only one long shot or close-up of the projected B-roll material. Rather, you should change angles and record a variety of shots so that they can be edited together into a sequence to tell a part of the story visually.

Shoot Material for Transitions

You should have a good idea of the way in which you are going to achieve your transitions from one segment or scene to another when you go into the field to shoot. Let's assume that you are constructing a program out of interviews of people involved in the debate over the safety of nuclear energy. You shoot a series of interviews in two towns that are several hundred miles apart. The people in town A are almost unanimously opposed to nuclear energy because there have been several accidents at the reactor in their community, and they fear for their own safety and the safety of their children. The people in town B get most of their electrical energy from the plant but live far enough away to not have to worry about radiation leaks. They are almost unanimously in favor of nuclear energy and the continued operation of the plant in question.

When you assemble your program, how will you make the transition from the antinuclear interviews to the pronuclear interviews? This is the function of transitional material. Perhaps you will use an on-camera narrator to bridge the gap. Or you might use a cover or establishing shot of the locale or a shot taken from the window of a car driving down the main street of the town. Whatever device you use, you should have an idea of what it is going to be before you go out to shoot so that you can be sure to get the appropriate footage on tape.

Shoot Segments Long Enough for Editing

The mechanics of most video editing systems require that any segment of tape to be used during editing must have *at least* five seconds of preroll material. This means that you must focus your camera and begin recording for a minimum of five seconds before you will have usable video. This is necessary for several reasons. When a videotape is played back in a VCR, it usually takes about five seconds for the tape to get up to speed and for the image to stabilize. If you are using a videotape-based linear editing system, the edit control units that govern the playback and editing VCRs need this preroll time to cue up the tapes and execute edits. If you are using a digital nonlinear editing system, you will want to have at least five additional seconds of material at the head and tail of each shot, not only to allow the playback VCR to get up to speed before you transfer your footage into the computer in which you will perform the edits, but also to provide additional shot material in case you want to add transition effects (e.g., dissolves or wipes [discussed in Chapter 8]) to the beginning or end of a shot as you are editing. All shots should therefore be 10 seconds and preferably much longer to ensure that you have enough usable video to edit.

Shoot Shots That Utilize Matched Camera Movements

If, for example, you are shooting a series of still photographs to be incorporated into a profile of a local photographer, start with a long shot of the first photograph and hold it for 10 or 15 seconds. Then zoom in slowly to the important detail in the picture and hold that; then zoom out slowly at the same rate you used to zoom in to your original wide shot, and hold that again. Repeat the procedure with all the photographs you record. Your editor can then choose from a series of long shots, slow zooms, and close-ups of all the relevant photographs.

Similarly, if you are shooting landscapes, you may want to use the same technique of holding the long shot and then zooming in. Or you may want to record a series of pans across significant details of the land-scape, all shot at the same panning speed. These shots can then be cut together into the most effective sequence of shots with matched camera action.

Specific Suggestions for Shooting Interviews

One of the most common single-camera situations is the on-site or remote interview. Some specific camera blocking (position) setups are discussed in the next few pages, but here the focus is on some basic strategic decisions that should be made before you begin shooting. First, decide whether the interviewer is going to be seen on camera. Also, decide whether the questions are going to be heard on camera or whether you plan to edit them out and allow your audience to hear only the subject's answers. If the questions are to be heard on the tape, will the interviewer be seen?

Let's assume that you want to show the interviewer asking the questions and that you plan to edit the questions and answers together into a continuous sequence. Shoot the interview with the camera focused on the subject and with the background slightly out of focus. This forces the viewer's attention to the subject.

Background details that are visible should be arranged to provide pleasing picture composition and, if possible, to provide additional environmental information about the subject. For example, in an interview with a biologist you might place a microscope on a table in the background and light it to make it visible. If the interview subject is a judge, state and national flags in the background will lend an additional air of authority to the scene. A hard light (spotlight) focused across the flags will bring out the texture in them and give the shot more depth. Make sure that whatever is visible in the frame supports the interview subject, and remember that if the background focus is too sharp, your audience's attention may wander.

Vary the lens angle (zoom in and out) at appropriate points in the interview. For example, you might want to pull out a little when a question is asked and then zoom in as the question is answered. Or, if the subject makes a startling or personal revelation, you might want to slowly zoom in for emphasis.

79

Because you have kept the camera focused on the subject during the interview, you will need to shoot some additional material for cutaways. After the interview is over, shoot several **over-the-shoulder shots** (also called *reverse shots* or *reversals*) of the interviewer and interviewee. You do not even need to record sound. Just shoot both people from several different angles (see Figure 3.15). After the interview is over, you can shoot the interviewer asking the questions. This technique of **question re-ask** is frequently used in television news and documentary production. Make sure the questions are re-asked in the same location and with the same background as the original interview. Also make sure that the re-asked questions are the same as the original questions! If the questions are in a script, the interviewer can simply re-ask them into the camera after the real interview has been completed. If the questions are ad-libbed, a production assis-

Figure 3.15   Over-the-Shoulder-Shot Interview

2-Shot

Close-Up

2-Shot

Close-Up

tant should make a record of the questions while the interview is in progress. If there is any doubt about what actually was asked, you can always refer to the video itself, because the subject's microphone will have picked up the questions even if the interviewer did not wear a microphone. News producers have an ethical and legal responsibility to make sure that the questions that are re-asked and the answers that are given in the edited version of the program correspond to what was actually asked and answered in the original interview.

Subject–Camera Relationships

Above-, at-, and below-Eye-Level Positions

Because camera position has a profound impact on the audience's perception of the subject, determining the position of the camera in relation to the subject is extremely important. So-called objective videography places the camera at the eye level of the subject. **At-eye-level camera position** makes the viewer and the subject equal in terms of their relative height. The viewer looks directly at the subject rather than up or down. At-eye-level camera position is probably the most commonly used camera position. Almost all studio presentations shoot at eye level, and most typical kinds of remote footage—such as news, documentaries, and on-site interviews—place the camera in this neutral, objective position.

When the camera is positioned above or below the eye level of the subject, the dynamics of the audience's perception of the subject change radically. When the camera is placed in the **above-eye-level camera position**, it shoots down at the subject. Because the audience views the shot from the perspective of the camera, the audience assumes a position of superiority over the subject. If you want to make someone seem smaller, less significant, or less important, shoot from above the eye level of the subject.

Conversely, when the camera is placed in the **below-eye-level camera position**, it shoots up at the subject. Again, the audience views the shot from the perspective of the camera, which now places the viewer below the subject. The viewer looks up at the subject, who now towers over the camera. Below-eye-level camera position increases the power, significance, and perceived size of the subject. The effect is almost the exact opposite of shooting from above eye level.

Objective and Subjective Cameras

The camera can either observe an event or participate in it. When the function of the camera is simply to observe an event, we classify it as an **objective camera**. The perspective of the objective camera viewpoint is from outside the scene. The camera acts as an unseen observer, and the participants within the scene seem unaware of its presence. Two examples of the use of the objective camera are a documentary in which the camera records an event, and a dramatic program such as a soap opera in which the characters play to each other and are oblivious to the camera. Most programs are shot from this perspective.

Subjective camera refers to the use of the camera as a participant in the scene. This may take a number of forms. The camera may act as the eyes of a person in a scene, or the characters may talk directly into the camera. A classic episode of the television series *M*A*S*H* used the subjective camera technique quite effectively. The entire episode was shot from the point of view of a wounded soldier who was brought to the medical unit for treatment. The audience saw everything through the eyes of the wounded soldier, from the time he arrived via helicopter at the beginning of the episode to the time he left the hospital at the episode's conclusion. Throughout the episode, the camera acted as the soldier's eyes and made the audience experience the scene through its (the camera's) and his (the soldier's) point of view.

When used appropriately, the subjective camera is an extremely powerful production technique. The portable video camera has the mobility demanded by the subjective camera technique and is therefore easily used in this context. However, care must be exercised so that the technique is not overused, as overuse may well diminish its effectiveness.

Many programs use a combination of both objective and subjective camera viewpoints. An easily understood example of programming that frequently combines these techniques is the on-site television news report. Typically, at the beginning of the report, the reporter introduces the story by speaking directly to the camera and the audience. This is a classic example of the use of subjective camera. Then, a voice-over accompanies shots of the event that is being reported. Here, the camera assumes the position of the objective observer. The techniques complement each other to present a news report that is both personal and informative.

Principal Action Axis

When shooting any type of dramatic scene, interview, or event that will be edited in postproduction, the videographer must determine the position of the **principal action axis**. The camera must be kept on one side of the principal action axis while recording the scene to maintain continuity in the direction of action and position of the scene. This principal action axis is sometimes referred to as the *principal vector line,* and keeping the camera to one side of the axis is sometimes called the *180-degree rule.* These three terms are interchangeable.

To identify the principal action axis, look at the direction of the action in a scene and draw a line tracing it. For example, in a football or basketball game, the principal action moves the ball and the players from one end of the field or court to the other. This motion to one end and back again creates the principal action axis (see Figure 3.16). To position your camera correctly and to maintain continuity of direction from shot to shot, the camera must shoot all coverage of the action from one side of the action axis. The camera may be positioned on either side of the action axis, and as long as all action is shot from the same side of the line, directional continuity will be maintained. If, however, the camera moves to the other side of the line, the action will appear to be reversed (see Figure 3.16).

Figure 3.16   Principal Action Axis—Football Game

Principal Action Axis

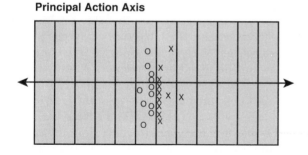

Possible Camera Positions: Side A or Side B

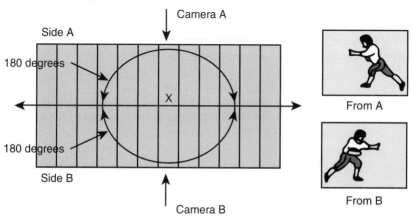

On-Site Interview Setup

One of the most common remote shooting situations is the on-site interview. Since video equipment has become so portable, it is a rather simple operation to travel to the home or office of the person you want to interview and shoot the interview in the subject's normal environment, rather than in the artificial studio environment. Almost all on-site interviews are shot with a single camera, and as a result, the videographer must shoot all the angles needed to edit the interview into a coherent sequence. The interview must have both content and visual continuity. The remainder of our discussion here will focus on visual continuity.

The following factors should be considered when setting up an on-site interview.

1. Position of the subject
2. Position of the interviewer
3. Position of the camera
4. Principal action axis

Position of the Subject.   When you travel to the home or office of the subject of your interview, you are able to show the subject in his or her normal working or living environment. The subject should be placed comfortably, facing the camera, where you can take advantage of the surroundings to provide rich background detail to the interview. In many cases, particularly when the interview takes place in an office, your subject will be sitting behind a desk. In the home, the subject will normally be sitting in a chair or on a couch. With your subject in position for the interview, examine the background to be sure that it does not detract from the subject. Lamps and pictures on the wall often provide unwanted distractions. If they interfere with the composition of your shot, move them into a more favorable position.

Be careful not to position the subject in front of a window. If there is a window in the background and you cannot move the subject so that the window is out of the shot, close the window blinds or draperies when shooting during the day to avoid silhouetting the subject.

Position of the Interviewer.   There are two possible positions in which to place the interviewer—next to the subject or somewhat in front of the subject with the interviewer's back to the camera. The best place for the interviewer is in front of the subject, back to the camera (see Figure 3.17). Placement of the interviewer next to the subject may make the subject feel more comfortable, because this approximates a normal sitting position for conversations, but it will consistently present the camera with a poor view of the subject because he or she will have a tendency to turn toward the interviewer and away from the camera.

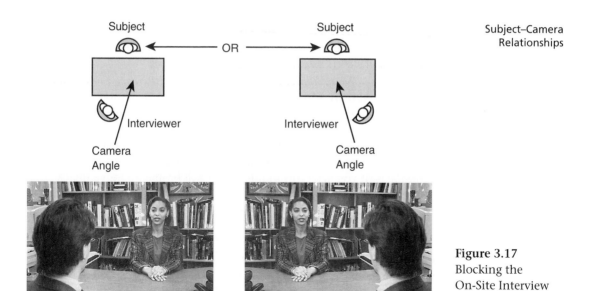

Figure 3.17
Blocking the
On-Site Interview
and Resulting Shots

Position of the Camera. The camera should be positioned behind
the interviewer and slightly off to one side. In this position, the camera can
easily shoot a three-quarter profile of the subject as well as an over-the-
shoulder shot of the interviewer and subject. From this position, the subject will always be able to maintain easy eye contact with the interviewer
and will present the camera with an almost full-face shot.

Figure 3.18 Good and Bad Interview Camera Angles

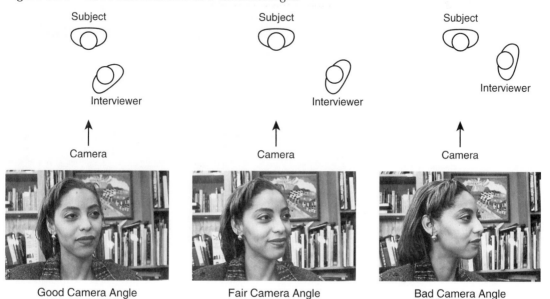

Be careful to keep the interviewer close to the camera. The farther away from the side of camera the interviewer moves, the farther offscreen the subject will appear to be looking. (See Figure 3.18.)

Principal Action Axis.   A principal action axis is formed in an interview setting just as it is in an action-oriented scene. The principal action axis extends from the subject to the interviewer (see Figure 3.19). To maintain continuity when you shoot question re-asks or reaction shots, the camera must remain in the 180-degree semicircle formed by the principal action axis. If you keep this in mind, you will be able to move the camera during or after the interview to shoot additional material of your subjects from different angles and still present your editor with material that retains continuity when edited.

Figure 3.20 presents another blocking diagram of an interview; however, this one is not arranged as well as the previous examples. In news or on-the-street interviews, where the interviewer is forced to hold the microphone that is recording the sound, or when the interviewer must face the

Figure 3.19   Principal Action Axis—On-Site Interview

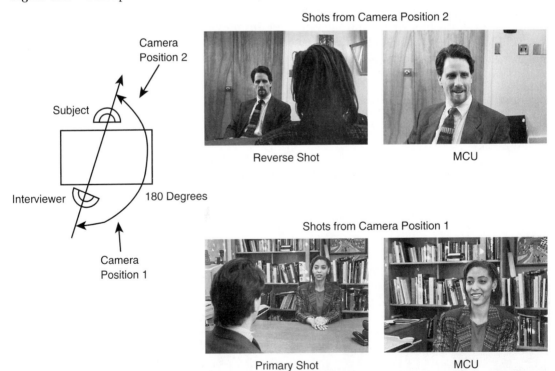

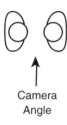

Camera
Angle

2-Shot

Ear Centered, One Eye Visible

Figure 3.20   Poor Composition (The Great American Ear Shot)

camera directly to introduce the subject, it is common for the interviewer to stand next to the subject. The difficulty with this blocking arrangement is that it is natural for the subject to talk to the interviewer rather than to the camera when answering the questions. As a result, the camera is left with a poor shot of the subject—the infamous **ear shot**—in which any zoom in to a close-up reveals the subject's face in profile rather than from the front. Because the eyes of the subject convey significantly more information to the audience than does an ear, try to avoid this situation whenever possible.

Shooting for Depth

As mentioned earlier, we try to increase the sensation of depth in video images to make them seem more realistic because we know that objects in the real world are three-dimensional rather than flat. Following three simple shooting rules can increase the sense of depth in television images. First, always try to compose images that have a distinct foreground, middleground, and background. Place objects between the camera and your subject, as well as behind your subject, to draw attention to depth. Second, when staging a scene, or even when simply setting up the position of interviewer and subject, try to stage for depth by placing the subjects at different distances away from the camera. And third, whenever possible, bring action toward or away from the camera rather than moving it horizontally in front of the camera. Although it is not possible (or advisable) to adhere to these rules all of the time, you can improve the look of your video presentations by using them in situations that call for them.

4 Video Recording

In the early days of television, all programs originated from one of two sources: they were live broadcasts or they were broadcasts of programs that had originally been produced on film. Initially, there was no electronic means of storing the television image, and those programs that were aired live often disappeared forever—they were seen once at the time of the broadcast and then they were gone for good. The only way to save a live broadcast was to record the picture and sound by pointing a film camera at a television monitor during the live broadcast. Today, such film recordings of television programs, called **kinescopes,** provide the only record of many early television broadcasts.

Although kinescope recordings were useful in providing a historical record of what had been broadcast, they were less useful as a production device because their picture and sound quality were greatly inferior to that of the television system. What was needed was a means of electronically recording and editing the television signal. Such a system would preserve the electronic character of the television image and not distort it the way kinescope recording did. However, it was not until 1956 that the Ampex Corporation, then a small electronics company in Redwood City, California, introduced the first practical videotape recorder, which provided the first all-electronic storage and production medium for video programs. All of today's VCRs are derived from the basic recording principles pioneered by Ampex. (See Appendix 2 for a discussion of the development of videotape recording.)

Helical Scan Recording

The Magnetic Recording Process

Modern videotape recording systems work by passing the video signal through two or more rotating video heads, which then encode the signal onto a piece of videotape. A video recording **head** is really a small electromagnet. Both sides of the head are wrapped with a coil of wire, and a current passing through the wire causes an electromagnetic charge to be emitted at the **gap**—the space between the two sides of the head (see Figure 4.1).

The video heads are mounted on a bar that spins inside the **head drum**—a stainless steel cylinder inside the VCR. The heads protrude from a slot cut in the drum. This is where they make contact with the **videotape**—plastic tape coated with metal particles that stores the charge emitted by the head as it passes over the tape.

During playback, the process is reversed. The magnetic charge on the tape is converted back into electrical energy—the video signal—by the video heads as they pass over the tape.

The way in which the head encodes the signal onto a piece of magnetic tape can be explained fairly easily using a simple scientific experiment on magnetism. You probably remember conducting this experiment as a child. You place a pile of iron filings or small pieces of metal shavings on a piece of paper and then pass a magnet under the paper. This results in

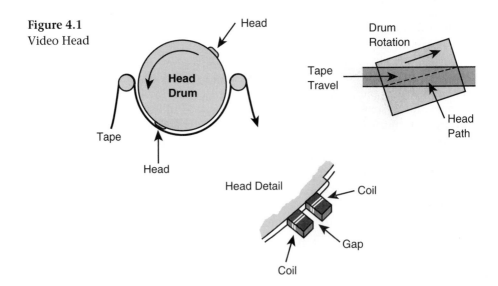

Figure 4.1
Video Head

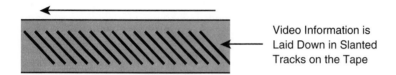

Video Information is
Laid Down in Slanted
Tracks on the Tape

Figure 4.2   Helical Scan Tracks

the metal filings arranging themselves in a pattern that corresponds to the movement of the magnet under the paper. If the magnet is moved in a straight line, it creates a straight line of iron filings; if it is moved in a circle, it creates a circular pattern of iron filings. The process of recording on audiotape or videotape works on the same principle of the magnetism of metal particles.

Helical Scan Recording

All modern VCRs use the **helical scan** method of recording the video signal. This name is used because the videotape is wrapped around the head drum inside the machine in the form of a helix. Sometimes, this type of recording is called **slant-track** recording, as this describes the angle of the video information on the tape (see Figure 4.2). By recording the video tracks at an angle on the tape instead of straight up and down, the width of the recording tape can be reduced. The initial format developed by Ampex used tape that was 2″ wide, whereas today the most popular videotape recording formats are $1/4$″ (6.35mm) and $1/2$″ wide.

Number of Video Heads

VCRs may have two, four, or more video heads, depending on whether the video signal is analog or digital, and to accommodate different tape playback and recording speeds.

Analog VCRs.   Most analog helical scan systems use two rotating heads in a head bar that rotates at 1,800 revolutions per minute (or 30 revolutions per second). Since the head bar contains two heads, and the bar rotates at 30 revolutions per second, you can see that the heads come into contact with the tape 60 times per second (two heads per revolution multiplied by 30 revolutions per second). These 60 contacts per second correspond to the 60 fields of information displayed in one second of NTSC video information. (See Figure 4.3.)

91

S-VHS and 8mm/Hi8: Two Video Tracks per Frame

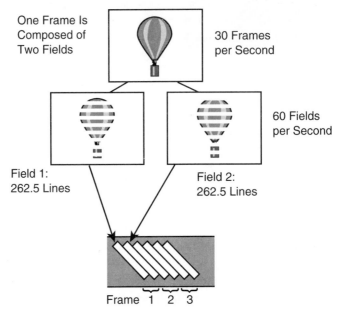

One Frame Is
Composed of
Two Fields

30 Frames
per Second

60 Fields
per Second

Field 1:
262.5 Lines

Field 2:
262.5 Lines

Frame 1 2 3

Each Track on Tape Contains One Field (262.5 Lines) of Video Information.

DV/DVCAM/DVCPRO: Ten Video Tracks per Frame

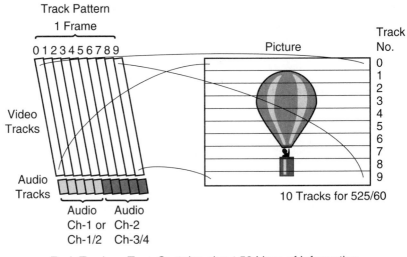

Track Pattern
1 Frame

0 1 2 3 4 5 6 7 8 9

Picture

Track
No.

0
1
2
3
4
5
6
7
8
9

Video
Tracks

Audio
Tracks

10 Tracks for 525/60

Audio
Ch-1 or
Ch-1/2

Audio
Ch-2
Ch-3/4

Figure 4.3
Analog and
Digital Video
Track Patterns

Each Track on Tape Contains about 52 Lines of Information.

Digital VCRs. VCRs that record the signal digitally are much more complex than analog VCRs. Some digital systems utilize more than two video heads (DVCPRO machines use six: two record, two erase, and two play back, rotating in a head drum at 9,000 rpm), and rather than recording the information onto the videotape one field at a time, they may use multiple tracks to record the information for each video frame. For example, the popular DV formats (DV, DVCAM, and DVCPRO) use 10 video tracks on the tape to record one frame of information. (See Figure 4.3.)

Multispeed VCRs. Some VHS machines on the market contain four video heads to maximize the quality of the signal at different playback and recording speeds. Standard play (**SP**) is the two-hour mode; long play (**LP**) is the four-hour mode; and standard long play/extended play (**SLP/EP**) is the six-hour mode. Increases in playing or recording time are achieved by slowing the speed at which the tape runs through the machine. Changing the tape speed also changes the **track pitch**, or width of the track available for each track or field of video information. The track pitch (width) in SP is three times greater than in SLP/EP. Because of these differences in track width, the heads designed to record and play back the signal at one speed will not work properly at other speeds. This is because the width of the head gap does not match the width of the track of video information. Four-head machines, therefore, contain one pair of heads maximized for record and playback in the SP mode, and another pair maximized for the SLP/EP mode. Only one pair of heads is used at a time, and which pair is used depends on the mode in which the machine is operating.

In early models of VHS machines with multispeed capability, the heads were maximized for the SP mode. As a result, the quality of the recording and playback image in the SLP/EP mode was significantly lower than in the SP mode. Four-head machines have greatly improved the quality of the image in the longer-play modes, but SP still gives the highest-quality recording because tape speed is higher than in the other modes, thereby providing the greatest frequency response in the recording.

Control Track

As discussed in Chapter 2, the stability of the video signal produced by the camera is related to a series of sync pulses controlling the timing of the horizontal and vertical scanning of the images. As long as we are dealing with a live system, these horizontal and vertical timing controls are sufficient to ensure that the image seen by the camera is reproduced correctly by the home receiver. The horizontal and vertical sync pulses that drive the camera are encoded into the video signal and transmitted to the home receiver, where they also drive the scanning beam in the television receiver. But what happens when a signal is recorded onto videotape? How can we guarantee that the speed of the videotape will be precisely controlled so that it plays back at precisely 30 frames per second? And how can we guarantee that the playback heads precisely trace over the tracks of recorded information on the videotape and faithfully play back the recorded signal?

The problem of precisely controlling the speed of the playback medium is one that plagues anyone who works with the recorded image or sound. Film, of course, solves the problem through the use of sprocket holes. These sprocket holes guide the speed of the film and regulate the action of the camera or projector shutter. But in audio and video recording, there are no sprocket holes in the tape. How, then, can the system be regulated?

Controlling Tape Speed— The Capstan

In an audiotape system, the tape moves but the heads do not, so the problem is relatively simple. All one has to do is control the speed of the movement of the tape. If the record and playback speeds are the same, the system will work. Since no sprocket holes are used on the tape itself, how does it move through the machine? The solution is simple—the tape is driven by the **capstan**, a rotating shaft driven by the recorder's motor. The tape is sandwiched between the capstan and a rubber pinch roller, and the friction of the two against the audiotape literally pulls the tape through the machine. The speed of the capstan is regulated so that the speed of the audiotape is correct for the system: $1^7/_8''$ per second for audiocassettes and $3^3/_4''$, $7^1/_2''$, or 15" per second for reel-to-reel machines.

In video, however, the problem is more complex. Not only must the movement of the tape be controlled but also the movement of the video heads must be precisely synchronized so that they accurately hit the tape on the tracks of video information. Any change in tape speed must also be reflected in a change of the movement of the heads, or the recording will not play back correctly.

The Function of Control Track Pulses

Some way had to be found to synchronize the movement of the head assembly with the movement of the capstan. This is the function of the control track. The **control track**, a series of electronic impulses recorded directly onto the videotape, regulates the playback timing of the system.

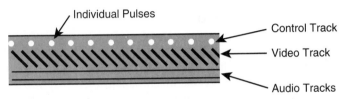

Figure 4.4   Control Track Pulses

In most helical scan systems, there are 30 control track pulses per second. One control track pulse is recorded for each frame of video information. In the record mode, these control track pulses are timed off the vertical sync pulses of the video signal as it enters the VCR. Because there are 60 vertical sync pulses per second, every other one causes a control track pulse to be recorded. These control track pulses are recorded onto the videotape in their own track, separate from the audio and video signals (see Figure 4.4).

Do not confuse control track with horizontal or vertical sync. Horizontal and vertical sync regulate the timing of the lines, fields, and frames of video and are part of the video signal. They are recorded in the slanted tracks of information along with the picture information. Control track pulses, on the other hand, are found only on videotape, where they function to regulate the playback of the signal by controlling the movement of the capstan and the heads. There are no control track pulses in the video signal produced by the camera.

Capstan and Head Drum Servos

The playback speed and scanning of the video information are controlled by the capstan and head drum servos. The capstan is driven by a motor connected to a servo (an abbreviation for *servomechanism*). The **capstan servo** senses the control track pulses on the tape and adjusts the speed of the motor that turns the capstan to maintain the correct tape speed.

The **head drum servo** then adjusts the position of the video heads so that they rotate in phase with the tracks of video information on the tape. Not only must the heads be positioned directly over the tracks of information on the tape but also they must spin in such a way that they begin and end their movement across the tracks in precise synchronization with the actual beginning and end of each track. Some VCRs contain a **servo-lock indicator** (usually a small light) that illuminates steadily when the VCR has reached its proper recording or playback speed and the picture has stabilized.

Poor Tracking

Poor Signal

Heads Not in Line
with Video Tracks

Good Tracking

Good Signal

Heads in Line
with Video Tracks

Figure 4.5   Tracking

Tracking Control

Normally, any tape will play back correctly on the machine on which it was recorded. However, when you record a tape on one machine and then play it back on another, you sometimes run into problems caused by small differences in the machine speeds. This results in slight differences in the way the heads hit the tape. To ensure that the video heads are correctly in line with the tracks of information on the tape, many machines contain a **tracking control.** The tracking control adjusts the relationship between the heads and tracks of video information on the tape to optimize the level of the playback signal (see Figure 4.5).

You can tell if a VCR is tracking properly simply by looking at the picture on a monitor. If the tracking is correct, the picture will be clear and stable. If the tracking is not correct, the picture will contain a large band of noise running through it. This band of noise indicates that the heads are not in proper alignment with the video information tracks.

Many machines incorporate a **tracking meter.** By twisting the tracking control until the meter reaches its maximum point, you can adjust the machine for the best playback of the signal. An exception to this is found in the 8mm/Hi8 format, which substitutes automatic track finding (ATF) for the traditional control track pulses. The ATF signal is recorded in the tracks of video information on the videotape. During playback, the VCR automatically senses the ATF signal and adjusts the VCR for the best playback of the video information recorded on the tape. Similarly, DV- and DVCAM format tapes record pilot tones in one of the tape's data tracks. These pilot tones regulate the speed of the capstan during playback.

Some machines have the capability to perform **dynamic tracking.** That is, the heads remain in proper contact with the tape at a variety of slow and fast playback speeds. Slow-motion and fast-motion playback effects can be achieved on VCRs that have this feature.

Videotape Recording Formats

Since the introduction of the first practical videotape recording system in 1956, more than 50 different videotape recording formats have been developed. Today about 20 different tape formats are in use in a wide variety of production applications. The principal formats in use for the acquisition of video in small- to medium-scale field recording situations are shown in Table 4.1.

Table 4.1 Popular Video Field Acquisition Formats

Format	Year Introduced	Tape Width	Analog or Digital	Composite, Y/C, or Component	Notes (Manufacturer)
VHS	1976	½"	Analog	Composite	Consumer-quality home video. (JVC)
S-VHS	1987	½"	Analog	Y/C	Prosumer and professional; very good quality first-generation field acquisition. (JVC)
Digital S	1995	½"	Digital 4:2:2	Component No Compression	Professional quality; moderately priced; S-VHS is upwardly compatible with some Digital S machines. (JVC)
8mm	1981	8mm	Analog	Composite	Popular consumer camcorder format. (Sony)
Hi8	1989	8mm	Analog	Y/C	Prosumer and professional; very good quality first-generation field acquisition. Metal tape can be fragile. (Sony)
Betacam	1982	½"	Analog	Component	Professional quality; uses conventional oxide tape. (Sony)
Betacam SP	1986	½"	Analog	Component	Professional quality; uses metal particle tape. (Sony)
Digital Betacam	1993	½"	Digital 4:2:2	Component Compressed	Professional quality; very expensive. (Sony)
Betacam SX	1996	½"	Digital 4:2:2	Component Compressed	Professional quality; targeted at ENG users, less expensive than Digital Betacam. (Sony)
M-II	1986	½"	Analog	Component	Quality equivalent to Betacam SP but a distant second in the marketplace (and fading). (Panasonic)
DV	1995	6.35mm (¼")	Digital 4:1:1	Component Compressed	Consumer and prosumer quality; expensive in comparison with S-VHS and Hi8 but with higher quality. (Most major manufacturers)
DVCAM	1995	6.35mm (¼")	Digital 4:1:1	Component Compressed	Professional quality; moderately priced; cannot play back DVCPRO tapes. (Sony)
DVCPRO	1995	6.35mm (¼")	Digital 4:1:1	Component Compressed	Professional quality; moderately priced; can play back DV and DVCAM tapes. (Panasonic)

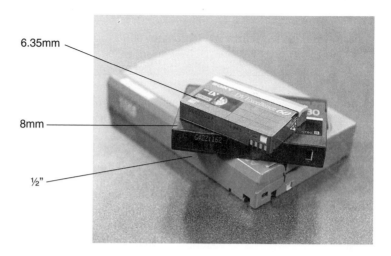

6.35mm

8mm

½"

Figure 4.6
6.35mm, 8mm, and
½" Videocassettes

Tape format is determined by the width of the videotape; its configuration (reel-to-reel or cassette); the arrangement of the tracks of audio, video, and control track information on the tape; and the speed at which the tape moves through the recorder. Several different tape widths are widely used in a variety of professional, industrial, and consumer VCRs (see Figure 4.6). All of these tapes are housed in videocassettes, which greatly simplify the tape-loading process in comparison to reel-to-reel machines. Additional variables to consider are how the color information is processed when it is recorded onto videotape (is it composite, S-Video, or component?) and whether the recorded signal is analog or digital.

Location of Signals on Videotape

All videotapes contain the following tracks of information: the video track, control track, and one or more audio tracks for SMPTE time code. In addition, some videotape formats also include a special cue or address track, and some of the digital formats include data tracks (called **insert and track information [ITI]** in the DV/DVCAM/DVCPRO system). The placement of these tracks of information varies from one tape format to another. Figure 4.7 illustrates the location of each of these tracks of information for some of the most popular field tape formats.

The Video Track.   Video information is always centrally located on the tape, and the tracks of video information occupy most of the tape surface. Differences in formats are found in the width of the tracks of video information and the angle at which the tracks lie on the tape. In addition,

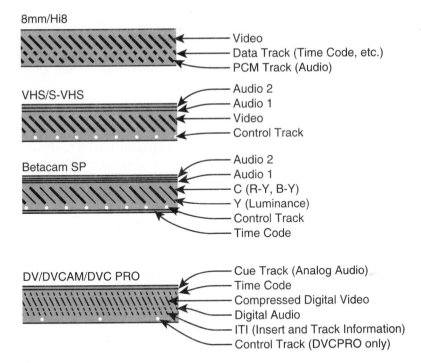

8mm/Hi8
- Video
- Data Track (Time Code, etc.)
- PCM Track (Audio)

VHS/S-VHS
- Audio 2
- Audio 1
- Video
- Control Track

Betacam SP
- Audio 2
- Audio 1
- C (R-Y, B-Y)
- Y (Luminance)
- Control Track
- Time Code

DV/DVCAM/DVC PRO
- Cue Track (Analog Audio)
- Time Code
- Compressed Digital Video
- Digital Audio
- ITI (Insert and Track Information)
- Control Track (DVCPRO only)

Figure 4.7
Location of Tracks
on Videotape

formats differ with respect to the number of video tracks used to record each frame of information. For example, in analog formats like VHS/S-VHS and 8mm/Hi8, each video track contains one field of video information, and two tracks constitute a frame. In the DV/DVCAM/DVCPRO formats the digital signal recording process is more complex, and 10 individual video tracks are needed to record each frame of the picture. (See Figures 4.3 and 4.7.)

The Control Track.   Control track information in most formats is recorded at or near the edge of the videotape by a stationary control track head. Although it is easier to record the control track at the edge than in the interior of the tape, edge recording presents a problem because the tape edge sometimes wrinkles in the machine. If the tape sustains any damage to the edge and the damage extends into the area where the control track has been recorded, the tape may be unstable when played. Great care should be taken to protect the tape edge from damage. In the 8mm and Hi8 formats, a control signal (automatic track finding) recorded in the tracks of video information by the rotary video heads replaces the traditional control track pulses. In the DV formats, only DVCPRO records control track; DV and DVCAM use pilot tones in one of the data tracks to control the rotating heads during tape playback.

Audio Tracks.   Audio information can be recorded in three ways, depending on the tape format: one or more stationary audio heads can record sound in the longitudinal audio track(s), rotary heads can record analog high-fidelity audio along with the video information in the video tracks, or rotary heads can record digital audio.

The Cue or Address Track.   Some tape formats contain an additional cue or address track that is used to record a longitudinal audio track or SMPTE (Society of Motion Picture and Television Engineers) time code information. Time code information provides an accurate identification code for each frame of video information and is widely used for logging tapes and in video editing. This is discussed in greater detail in Chapter 10.

Data Tracks.   Digital tape formats may make use of one or more data tracks. For example, in the DV/DVCAM/DVCPRO formats a special subcode track area contains SMPTE time code information, and a separate ITI area contains additional information about the track (e.g., whether it is consumer DV or DVCPRO) as well as the pilot tones that control DV and DVCAM playback. Figure 4.7 shows how this information is laid out in the tracks on the tape.

Composite and Component Recording

The color video signal can be processed and recorded onto videotape in a number of different ways.

Composite Recording.   The conventional way to record the signal is to record a **composite**, NTSC-encoded video signal. Each track of video information on the tape (the equivalent of one field of video information) contains the luminance (Y) and chrominance (C) parts of the signal mixed together with all the synchronizing information: color burst and horizontal and vertical sync. This type of recording is used in the conventional $1/_2''$ VHS, 8mm, and $3/_4''$ U-Matic and U-Matic SP formats.

Y/C Signal Processing (S-Video).   Another term used to describe the way in which the video signal may be processed within a VCR is **Y/C signal processing**. In the Hi8 and S-VHS formats, luminance (Y) and chrominance (C) channels of information are processed separately within the VCR in order to achieve better color purity and image detail than is possible in conventional composite recording systems. The luminance and chrominance signals may actually be output from the VCR as two separate signals and displayed on special video monitors equipped with an "S-Video" input connector. However, insofar as the videotape recording process is concerned, Y/C signals in Hi8 and S-VHS VCRs are recorded as composite signals with luminance and chrominance recorded together in the same track of video information on the tape, not on separate tracks as is the case with true component systems.

Component Recording. The highest-quality color recordings are made in professional systems (e.g., Betacam SP) that record the signal through the color difference process. This is often simply referred to as **component recording**. Almost all of the new videotape recording formats developed in the past 10 years use the component recording process.

Like the S-Video process described in the preceding section, the luminance signal (Y) is processed and recorded separately from the color components. However, in component recording, the process is carried further, resulting in a recording composed of the luminance signal (Y) and two color difference signals: red minus luminance (R – Y) and blue minus luminance (B – Y). Because the composition of the luminance channel is based on a fixed formula (Y = 30% red, 59% green, and 11% blue), there is no need to create the green minus luminance (G – Y) component because it can be reconstructed from the other three signals.

By processing and recording the luminance and chrominance signals separately on the videotape, component VCRs produce pictures with superior picture quality—the images are sharper (a function of processing the luminance signal independently) and the colors are purer than those obtained in composite or Y/C recordings.

As is noted earlier, in analog component recording systems the color components are referred to as R – Y and B – Y. In digital systems the color components are Cr and Cb. In both systems, the luminance signal is Y.

One drawback of component processing and recording is that the component signal is incompatible with conventional video distribution and display equipment and requires special monitors and processing equipment. Although they record a component signal, consumer DV-format VCRs and camcorders have both S-Video and standard NTSC composite video outputs, which allow the tapes to be dubbed to conventional VCRs and viewed on conventional video monitors.

Analog and Digital Recording

Analog Recording. Another difference in the way in which the video signal is processed and recorded is reflected in whether the signal is analog or digital. An **analog signal** is one in which the recorded signal (audio or video) varies continuously in relation to the sound or light that produced it. The electrical video signal produced through the analog process, for example, varies in direct proportion to the light entering the camera lens, and the video waveform that is produced is continuous. When that signal is stored on videotape, the electrical signal is stored as a continuous variation in voltage as well.

Digital Recording.   In the **digital recording process**, the incoming analog signal (audio or video) is converted into a **digital signal** composed of series of on/off pulses, or bits. The conversion occurs first by sampling various points of the signal and then by converting that information into a numerical code for storage and replay. When the signal is replayed, the process is reversed and the digital information is converted back to an analog representation of the appropriate sound or picture.

Two important variables that affect the quality of the digital signal are the sampling rate and compression.

Sampling Rate.   The **sampling rate** describes how often the luminance and chrominance elements of the analog video signal are sampled for conversion into packets of digital information. Three sampling rates are frequently used in digital video: 4:2:2, 4:1:1, and 4:2:0.

In 4:2:2 sampling, each pixel in each line of video is sampled for luminance information (Y), whereas the chrominance values (Cr and Cb) are sampled only for every other pixel. Thus, in a string of four pixels there will be four luminance samples (one for each pixel) and two each of the chrominance samples (see Figure 4.8).

In 4:1:1 sampling, the luminance sampling rate is the same, but chrominance is sampled only once, instead of twice, for each set of four pixels.

In 4:2:0 sampling, luminance is again sampled for each pixel. However, the Cr color component is sampled at every other pixel only in the odd numbered scan lines, while the Cb color component is sampled at every other pixel only in the even numbered scan lines.

Because 4:2:2 sampling provides twice as many chrominance samples as either of the other two sampling methods, it produces a higher quality signal.

Compression Ratio.   Many digital video systems use **compression** to reduce the amount of data they produce. Compression makes it easier to store and transmit digital information. When compression is employed, each frame of information is analyzed to identify which information in the frame is repetitive and which information is new.

For example, imagine a video shot in which the camera is held still as an automobile drives into the frame and toward the camera. In each frame the foreground and background information (trees, street, houses, etc.) remains the same. What changes is the position of the car in the frame and its relative size as it gets closer to the camera. When the video signal is compressed, the background information is encoded once for the entire sequence of frames in which the car appears, but the car needs to be encoded continuously for each frame in which it appears, in order to capture its movement.

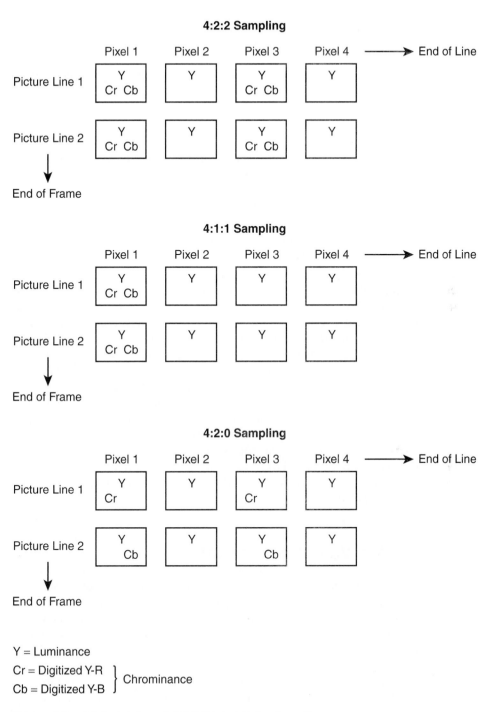

Figure 4.8 4:2:2, 4:1:1, and 4:2:0 Digital Color Sampling

Compression is expressed as a ratio; higher numbers indicate greater compression, and lower numbers indicate lesser compression. So you can see that the 5:1 compression ratio used in the DV formats is higher than the approximately 3:1 compression ratio used in Digital-S. Signals recorded with less compression generally produce better pictures than those recorded with more compression.

Types of Compression.   Several different compression methods are widely used in video systems. **JPEG (Joint Photographic Experts Group)** compression was originally designed for use in digital still photography and has been adapted for use with video (motion JPEG). **MPEG-1 (Motion Picture Experts Group) compression** is designed for use in CD-ROMs, and **MPEG-2** is the standard for broadcast television. Although a discussion of the technical differences between these compression methods is beyond the scope of this book, you should at least be familiar with them by name.

Digital Advantages.   There are several advantages to digital signal recording. First, because the digital signal is stored as a group of numbers, rather than as a varying electrical current, it can be recorded, replayed, and copied with greater accuracy and less noise than can an analog signal. This is very important in videotape recording and editing because it allows a tape to be copied many times without the loss of picture or sound quality or the introduction of noise. In fact, copies made in digital tape formats may be virtually indistinguishable from the originals. In addition, digital signals can be processed by a computer and manipulated in ways simply not possible with an analog signal. Most of the striking visual effects now seen on television are digital effects. Because many of these effects are accomplished by adding layer after layer of visual effects to the original recording, they take advantage of the multigenerational copying capabilities of the digital signal.

Analog Videotape Formats

8mm and Hi8.   The 8mm/Hi8 video systems feature one of the smallest videocassette sizes currently available. Because the tape is only approximately $1/4''$ wide, camcorders and VCRs can be made quite small. As a result, 8mm/Hi8 has become quite popular as a home video recording format. These systems achieve high-quality recording by using metal particle tape. High-fidelity audio is recorded by the rotating video heads.

Hi8 format equipment, introduced by Sony in 1989, incorporates the capability to record time code (see Chapter 10) along with resolution and color that exceed the standard 8mm format. The availability of up to two high-fidelity (AFM) and two digital (PCM) audio tracks allows for very high quality recording (see Figure 4.7). Hi8 is popular in the consumer and pro-sumer markets because of its low cost, extreme portability, and very high quality of first-generation recordings.

$1/_2''$ VHS and S-VHS.

VHS (video home system) emerged as the dom-inant format for home video recording in the early 1980s. Most VCRs in the United States that are used in the home to play back rented movies available on videocassette are in the VHS format.

S-VHS (Super-VHS) was introduced by Victor Company of Japan (JVC) in 1987 and is marketed by several manufacturers. Although not a true component recording system like Betacam SP and the DV formats, S-VHS VCRs process the luminance and chrominance signals independently within the system and improve the resolution (approximately 400 lines versus 240) and color recording relative to conventional VHS systems. High-quality VHS/S-VHS VCRs offer two channels of longitudinal audio as well as two channels of high-fidelity audio. A limitation of this format is the lack of a dedicated address track for time code that is separate from the two available longitudinal audio channels (see Figure 4.7). Whereas VHS is classified as a consumer video format, S-VHS appeals to industrial and pro-fessional users as well.

Betacam SP and M-II ($1/_2''$ Component Video Recording).

Beta-cam SP (Superior Performance) and M-II are professional, broadcast-quality $1/_2''$ recording formats. Because of the small size of the videocassettes and the VCRs that are used for recording, they have found very wide use in camcorders used for video field production. In both of these formats, the video signal is recorded onto $1/_2''$ videocassettes using the component recording process (see Figure 4.7).

Four audio tracks are available in the Betacam SP and M-II formats: two longitudinal tracks and two high-fidelity tracks. In addition to provid-ing broadcast-quality field tapes, Betacam SP and M-II perform extremely well as editing formats where multiple-generation recording is necessary.

Betacam SP represents the second generation of development of this format, succeeding the original Betacam format (both developed by Sony). Similarly, M-II is the second generation of the original M format developed by Matsushita. Whereas Betacam and Betacam SP remain compatible with each other, M and M-II are incompatible. And because the position of the tracks of information on the videotape as well as the tape speed differs be-tween the Betacam/Betacam SP and M/M-II formats, the Betacam formats are incompatible with the M formats. M-II format machines require the use of a special metal particle videotape; Betacam SP can record with either conventional metal oxide or special metal particle tape, but the highest-quality recordings are achieved with the special tape. Betacam/Betacam SP has been the de facto standard for field recording in electronic news gathering (ENG) and EFP in professional broadcast operations in the United States for the past decade, although today its primacy is being seriously challenged by several of the new digital tape formats.

$3/_4$" **U-Matic.** The $3/_4$" U-Matic tape was the format that initially made possible broadcast-quality video field production. This format is still used in some broadcast applications as well as in educational and industrial/corporate video applications. An improved version of this format developed by Sony, $3/_4$" U-Matic SP (Superior Performance), records the signal with more resolution than does the conventional $3/_4$" format and is fully compatible with it.

Due to the width of the tape and the size of the cassettes used in the $3/_4$" format, it was not possible to develop a practical camcorder. Given the development of lightweight camcorders in a number of other formats, many of which record a higher-quality signal with smaller tape, use of the $3/_4$" format for field recording has all but disappeared.

1" (Type C). The 1" (Type C) reel-to-reel format replaced 2" tape as the broadcast standard in the early 1970s. One-inch tape records a high-quality, composite NTSC video signal. Although 1" tape continues to be used in some television studio operations and on-line videotape editing, the format has largely been replaced by higher-quality digital tape formats and by tapeless, digital, nonlinear editing systems.

Digital Videotape Formats

Thus far, all of the videotape recording formats that have been discussed are analog formats. In addition to these formats, several high-quality digital recording formats are currently available. Digital VCRs are found where the highest-quality editing is needed, as they produce the least amount of quality loss in the editing process. Several of the digital formats feature portable camcorders as well, and these are finding increasing use as the formats of choice for the acquisition of video material in the field.

D-1 and D-2. Utilizing special 19mm (approximately $3/_4$") videocassettes, D-1 format machines record a component digital signal, and D-2 machines record a composite digital signal. Neither format provides a portable camcorder.

D-3, D-5, and HD-D5. D-3 (composite) and D-5 (component) digital VCRs record four channels of digital audio in addition to video on small $1/_2$" cassettes. The small size of the tape has allowed development of relatively lightweight camcorders in both formats in addition to the larger studio-type recording and editing VCRs. D-5 is particularly well suited to postproduction applications that require complex layering of digital effects. HD-D5, a high-definition version of the D-5 format, is one of the principal formats used for recording the HDTV signal in the 1080i or 720p variants.

D-6. Developed by Toshiba/BTS, this system uses 19mm cassettes and was designed primarily as an HDTV recorder.

Digital Betacam and Betacam SX.

Digital Betacam records a component digital signal with four digital audio tracks onto $1/2''$ tape. An advantage to this format is that it is capable of playing back analog Betacam and Betacam SP tapes, making it particularly attractive in those production facilities that have a large inventory of analog Betacam equipment and tapes. A portable camcorder and the standard array of players, recorders, and editors are available. In addition, the Betacam SX format features a battery-powered, compact portable laptop editing system designed for editing ENG tapes in the field. (See Figure 4.9.) Betacam SX uses 9:1 MPEG compression.

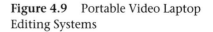

Figure 4.9 Portable Video Laptop Editing Systems

Sony DSR-70 DVCAM™ Laptop Editor

Digital Videocassette (DV).

The digital formats described above are very expensive in comparison with one of the newest and smallest digital tape formats: DV. DV systems record four digital audio tracks and a digital component video signal with over 500 lines of horizontal resolution on a small 6.35mm ($1/4''$) cassette $1/12$ the size of a standard VHS cassette.

Sony Betacam SX™

Panasonic DVCPRO (AJ-LT75)

107

Image and sound quality rival the professional Betacam SP format. Three variants of the format exist:

DV (digital video) is targeted at the consumer and prosumer markets. Most of the major electronics manufacturers participated in the development of the specifications for this format, which was approved in 1994, with the first equipment arriving on the market in 1995.

DVCAM is manufactured by Sony and is targeted at industrial and professional users.

DVCPRO (D7) was developed by Panasonic and BTS/Philips and is targeted at the professional and broadcast market (see Figure 4.10).

Major differences between the variants of the DV format include the width of the video tracks (10 microns for DV, 15 microns for DVCAM, and 18 microns for DVCPRO), tape speed, and the type of videotape used (DV

Figure 4.10 Digital Videocassette-Format Camcorders

Panasonic AG-EZ30 (DV Format)

Panasonic AJ-D700 DVCPRO (DVCPRO Format)

Sony DSR-PD1 DVCAM™ Mini-Camcorder
(DVCAM Format)

Sony DSR-200A DVCAM™ Digital Camcorder
(DVCAM Format)

and DVCAM record on metal evaporated tape, DVCPRO uses metal particle tape). As a result of these differences, not all of the variants are compatible with each other: While DV tapes will play back in DVCAM and DVCPRO equipment, Sony's DVCAM format machines cannot play back DVCPRO tapes, and neither DVCPRO nor DVCAM tapes can be played back in DV machines.

Tape-to-tape editing can be done in the DVCPRO format using a very portable laptop editing system developed by Panasonic (see Figure 4.9). On equipment with a FireWire connector (a standardized six-pin connector developed by Apple Computer carrying digital video, audio, and time code), VCR output can be connected directly to a personal computer for digital desktop video production.

Digital-S (D-9).   Yet another of the recently developed "affordable" digital video formats is Digital-S, developed by JVC. Digital-S records a component digital signal and four audio channels (two linear analog tracks and two digital tracks that may be edited independently) onto $1/2''$ metal particle tape. Available equipment includes dockable and one piece camcorders for field acquisition, as well as a variety of players, recorders, and editing VCRs. Some of the machines accept standard analog S-VHS cassettes for playback. High-end Digital-S editing VCRs equipped with a "pre-read" feature can play back and simultaneously record new information, making it possible to create multiple layers of images for special effects and transitions without the use of a sophisticated editing system and video switcher.

Other Formats.   Several other videotape formats are also in use and/or development. W-VHS (wide-screen VHS) is a $1/2''$ analog high-definition television recording format. D-VHS (digital VHS) is designed for off-air recording of digital television broadcasts. VCRs use a set-top decoder to pick up the broadcast signal. Traditional video inputs and outputs are replaced with a FireWire connector. Both formats are manufactured by JVC.

Sony's HDW-500 is a $1/2''$ HDTV recorder, and Panasonic's DVCPRO 50 is also designed for HDTV production. It is a modified version of DVCPRO that features 4:2:2 sampling instead of the 4:1:1 rate characteristic of the other DV formats. (See Figure 4.11.)

Figure 4.11   Panasonic DVCPRO 50 HDTV VCR

AJ-D2000HD

Choosing a Tape Format

As the preceding discussion has indicated, there has been a large growth of tape formats, particularly in the past few years. This can be very confusing to the video producer who is trying to make an informed decision about which format to use. Although the student producer may not have a choice to make because laboratory equipment has been purchased and assigned for student use, other producers can benefit by considering what their production needs are and how much they can afford to spend to buy or lease equipment. Generally speaking, tape use falls into three large applications: acquisition (field or studio production), postproduction (editing), and distribution. Different tape formats present different advantages and disadvantages.

Because of the extremely low cost of tape and VCRs and the remarkably good quality of first-generation recordings, the consumer-level VHS and 8mm formats are widely used in camcorders and VCRs dedicated to home video use. VHS is the standard in the United States for movies that are rented for home use. Because VHS VCRs are almost omnipresent, VHS is an excellent format for distributing tapes for viewing in the home or workplace.

S-VHS and Hi8, by virtue of their Y/C signal processing and high-quality tape, are excellent low-cost acquisition formats. Tapes and camcorders are extremely small and portable. Relatively high-quality editing is available, and the final product is usually acceptable up to the third or fourth generation, after which signal loss begins to become noticeable.

Betacam SP and M-II are extremely high-quality analog acquisition formats (camcorders and portable VCRs are both available). Betacam SP is the more popular of the formats.

The highest-quality original recordings can be made in the digital formats. Portable camcorders are available in a variety of digital formats (DV/DVCAM/DVCPRO, Digital Betacam/Betacam SX, D-3, and D-5) at greatly varying cost. Digital tape formats (particularly D-1, D-2, D-3, D-5, and Digital Betacam) excel in the areas of editing and dubbing, where little or no signal loss will be apparent, even when the final tape is many generations removed from the original. When complex, multilayered special effects are required, the digital formats will provide superior performance over the analog formats.

 ## Compatibility

Upward and Downward Compatibility

Compatibility refers to the capability of a given VCR to play back a particular videotape. If a videotape can be played back on a VCR, the two are compatible; if it cannot be played back, the two are incompatible. Compatibility is determined by the format of the videotape recording and the playback machine. Tapes recorded on any Hi8 VCR should be compatible with all other Hi8 VCRs. Similarly, any VHS tape should play back on any other VHS machine. However, remember that a tape must be played back at the same speed at which it was recorded. A tape recorded in the six-hour SLP/EP mode will not play back on a machine equipped with only two-hour (SP) and four-hour (LP) record/playback speed modes.

Tapes may be incompatible with certain VCRs for two reasons. First, the physical configuration of the tape may not be acceptable to the VCR. Second, the tape format may be incompatible with the VCR. The question of compatible physical configuration is easy to understand. For obvious reasons, a Hi8 cassette will play back on another Hi8 VCR but not on a $1/_2''$ VHS VCR. However, Betacam SP and M-II cassettes, which are both in the $1/_2''$ cassette configuration, are incompatible because of differences in the format. The location of the video tracks and the speed at which the tapes move through the VCRs are different in each format.

The terms *upward compatibility* and *downward compatibility* are used to describe compatibility issues that arise between conventional tape formats and their improved-performance successors. For example, conventional $1/_2''$ VHS has been modified to create a higher-resolution Super-VHS tape format. Conventional VHS recordings can be played back in S-VHS machines; thus, they are upwardly compatible. However, S-VHS tapes cannot be played back in conventional VHS machines; thus, we can say that S-VHS is not downwardly compatible with conventional VHS. DV tapes are upwardly compatible with DVCAM and DVCPRO, and DVCAM is upwardly compatible with DVCPRO (DV → DVCAM → DVCPRO). However, neither DVCAM nor DVCPRO is downwardly compatible: DVCAM can't be played back on DV machines, and DVCPRO can't be played back on DVCAM or DV equipment.

Dubbing

What, then, do you do if you have a tape in one format but have a machine in another, incompatible format? The answer is to make a dub. A **dub** is simply a copy of a tape. Because all VCRs have a series of standard video and audio inputs and outputs, it is possible to take a tape in one format and make a copy of it in another format. For example, you can dub a Hi8 tape to VHS, S-VHS to Betacam or vice versa, and so on. To make a dub, you need the original tape and a machine capable of playing it back. In addition, you need another machine in the format you want to dub to, and a blank tape. Put the original tape into the machine that will play it back, and connect the video and audio outputs of that machine to the video and audio inputs of the other machine. The machine with the original tape in it is called the **source VCR**, and the machine on which the information will be rerecorded is the **record VCR**.

Through the process of dubbing, copies of any tape can be made in any other format. However, there is always some quality loss in the copy.

This quality loss appears first as noise in the video picture. The copy may appear a little grainy and fuzzy. If a copy is made of the copy, the signal will continue to degrade, losing definition and color values. The further away from the original your copy is, the poorer the quality of the tape.

The original tape is referred to as a first-**generation** tape. The first copy made from the original is a second-generation tape; a copy made of the second-generation tape is a third-generation tape; and so on. VHS and 8mm systems are capable of producing good-quality copies only up to the second, and sometimes the third, generation. After that, the quality of the signal becomes noticeably poorer, and by the fourth or fifth generation, even the color of the original may be unrecognizable. Green faces and red grass hint at how many generations away from the original the copy may be.

One of the principal motivations for developing improved-resolution recording formats such as S-VHS and Hi8 has been to improve the ability of those formats to produce higher-quality images in terms of detail and color reproduction, even when they are several generations removed from the master tape. Indeed, one of the reasons that the digital tape formats are used so extensively in videotape editing is their ability to produce high-quality copies of the original tape, even when the copy is many generations removed from the original. Digital video VCRs that have digital video inputs and outputs (e.g., a FireWire connector) allow the signals to be transferred from one VCR to another with no noticeable loss in quality.

 # Types of Videocassette Recorders

Some VCRs are portable; others are not. The difference is primarily one of size. There are three types of full-sized VCRs: video players, player-recorders, and editing VCRs. (Portable VCRs are discussed in the next chapter.)

Video Players

Video players are VCRs incapable of recording—they can be used only to play back a videotape. The principal reason for buying a playback-only VCR lies in its cost. They are considerably cheaper than player-recorders because they do not contain the extra circuitry that makes recording possible.

Video players are used wherever it is not important to have recording capability. For example, if a VCR is going to be used only to play back a videotape demonstrating a particular product in a department store, a player, rather than a recorder, would be appropriate. Similarly, video players are sometimes used as source machines in videotape editing systems.

Video Player-Recorders

Probably the most common type of VCR is the **video player-recorder.** Any VCR with the capability to record and play back a videotape is a player-recorder. These machines are extremely versatile. They can record signals from video cameras and switchers. If they are equipped with a television tuner—the device that picks up broadcast or cablecast television signals—they can also record programs off the air or cable.

Editing Videocassette Recorders

The third type of machine is the **editing VCR.** It is equipped with special electronic circuitry that enables it to edit the video signal. We will discuss how this works in considerable detail in Chapter 9.

 # Videotape

The storage medium employed in most video recording systems is videotape. **Videotape** is simply a very thin strip of plastic (polyester or mylar) that is coated with metal oxide particles. Videotape works in the same way as audiotape. The picture and sound received by the camera and microphone are generated in the form of electrical impulses. These electrical impulses are directed to the videotape, where they are stored magnetically. A series of video and audio **heads,** which in effect are very small electromagnets, magnetize the metal particles (usually iron oxide or chromium dioxide) on the tape in a pattern that corresponds to the electrical input signals. Once these particles have been magnetized by the heads in the correct pattern, the signal is safely stored on the tape. Playback of the stored signal simply reverses the process. As the tape is played back, the video and audio heads read the information recorded on the tape. If the VCR is connected to a monitor, you see the image and hear the sound.

Improvements in tape quality have been a significant factor in the development of recording formats with enhanced detail and color qualities (S-VHS, Betacam SP, Hi8, and so on). High-quality recordings are obtained in these formats by using special metal tapes. These tapes feature higher-quality recording particles than do conventional tapes. The particles tend to be smaller and more uniform in size than those on conventional tapes. The orientation of the particles on the tape (that is, the direction in which the particles face on the tape) is more regular and more highly controlled. All of these factors create a recording surface that is much more densely coated with recording material and capable of recording a broader range of frequencies (and consequently better picture detail and color) than conventional videotape.The *metal evaporated tape (ME)* used in Hi8 and consumer DV recording systems is fragile and, at least with respect to Hi8, has earned a bad reputation for having a lot of dropouts. The *metal particle tape (MP)* used in many of the digital formats is more durable and less prone to dropouts (discussed later in this chapter).

Size

The size of a videotape refers to its width. Videotape comes in a number of different widths. The most common portable field production systems use tape that is either 6.35mm, 8mm, or $1/_2''$ wide (see Figure 4.12). The trend is toward smaller tape size for a number of reasons: it is more economical to use because it costs less money to produce; the machines used to record and play back the video signal can be made smaller because narrower-width tapes do not require the massive head drum assemblies that the older, large-format tapes required; and the tape is smaller and requires less space to store.

Figure 4.12 Tape Size Varies by Format

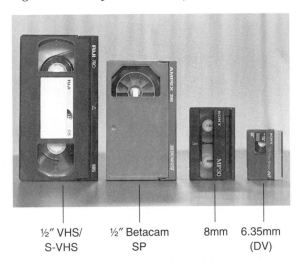

½″ VHS/   ½″ Betacam   8mm   6.35mm
S-VHS   SP   (DV)

In many cases, due to improvements in the way in which the signal is recorded, smaller-format tapes provide better-quality recordings than do their larger-format predecessors. So, the proliferation of formats should not be read only as the difference between less expensive and more expensive systems, or high-quality and poor-quality systems. In many ways, the development of these smaller-tape formats reflects significant advances in electronic technology. The move toward miniaturization in all other areas of electronic technology has also had a dramatic impact on the design of video gear.

Configuration

The other important aspect of videotape is its configuration. Configuration refers to the physical design of the tape. Is it an **open-reel** tape? or is it a **cassette?** The 1″ systems were the last to use open-reel tapes.

8mm/Hi8 Cassette Format

All the other contemporary formats use cassette tapes. The principal advantage to the use of a cassette tape is that the machine automatically threads the tape into the machine; reel-to-reel systems require that the tape be manually threaded into the machine.

If you are working with a portable video system, you are working with videotape in the cassette configuration. That is why you will find two different terms used to refer to video recorders. Some people call them *videotape* recorders, or *VTRs*, which simply indicates that videotape is used to record the video signal. Others will make a point of referring to their *videocassette* recorder, or *VCR*. Although *VCR* is more precise than *VTR*, the two terms are used interchangeably.

Mini-Cassettes

Many portable field recording systems use smaller videocassettes than are normally used in full-size VCRs of the same format (e.g., VHS/S-VHS type C [compact], Betacam SP, Mini-DV). The tape width in these compact cassettes is the same as in their full-size relatives, but the tape housing is smaller because the cassettes contain less tape, and consequently have a shorter recording time, than do the cassettes used in the full-size VCRs (see Figure 4.13). If the cassettes are smaller, portable camcorders can be made smaller as well.

The 8mm and Hi8 cassettes offer standard tape lengths of 30, 60, 90, and 120 minutes. Regardless of tape length, all 8mm and Hi8 tapes use the same size housing—there are no mini-cassettes in this format.

Figure 4.13
Comparison of Standard VHS and VHS-C Mini-Cassettes

Tape Thickness

One other factor to consider with regard to videotape is the thickness of the tape. Tape thickness is one of the elements that manufacturers vary to be able to fit more tape onto a reel or into a cassette. The other factor that is varied is simply the amount (length) of the tape on the reel or in the cassette. For example, in the $1/2$" VHS/S-VHS formats, the tape in a 120-minute cassette is simply twice as long as the tape in a 60-minute cassette. Longer-playing full-size cassettes with up to 180 minutes of tape are available. However, in these long-playing cassettes, the tape is actually thinner than the tape used in the 60- and 120-minute cassettes. The thinner tape takes up less space on the reels inside the cassette, and so more of it can fit into the cassette.

You should be very careful when working with videotape that is thinner than normal. Thinner tape is not as strong and more likely to stretch or break than normal tape, particularly if it is subjected to heavy stress. These thin tapes will not stand up to the pressure put on them by an editing system or still framing and should therefore not be used if you plan to edit your field tapes. Use only tapes with extended still-framing capability that have been designed for use in editing VCRs and that are capable of withstanding the pressure of fast- and reverse-motion tape shuttling and still framing.

Record Safety Devices

Because information is stored on videotape as magnetic impulses, the videotapes can be used over and over. It is quite simple to erase an entire tape by exposing it to a **bulk eraser**, a powerful electromagnet that randomizes the arrangement of the particles on the tape, thus eliminating the recorded signal.

In addition, all VCRs contain several **erase heads**. When a machine is put into the record mode, the erase heads engage and erase the previously recorded signal before the record heads pass over the tape to lay down the new signal. Because accidental erasure of material is something that everyone wants to avoid, all cassette tapes contain a **record safety** (see Figure 4.14). When the record safety device is removed from the tape housing, it is impossible to record over the material on a tape. Depending on the tape format, the record safety may be a small plastic tab (VHS/S-VHS) or switch (8mm/Hi8, Betacam SP, and DV/DVCAM/DVPRO) on the side of the tape housing. In each of these tape configurations, you can record when the record safety device is in place, but not if it has been removed or set.

A bulk eraser will erase a tape whether or not the record safety has been removed. Tapes can be bulk-erased, or

Figure 4.14 Videocassette Record Safety Devices

8mm/Hi8

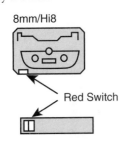

Red Switch

VHS/S-VHS

Plastic Tab

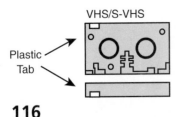

bulked, simply by passing the tape over the surface of the bulk eraser. There is no way to prevent the bulk eraser from doing its job. The best protection against accidental bulk erasure of tapes is through correct, clear labeling of tapes. If you know what is on the tape and clearly mark it "DO NOT ERASE," you stand a greater chance of preventing accidental erasure than if the tape does not carry such a warning. Finally, because any electromagnet can act as a bulk eraser, it pays to store tapes away from telephones, fan motors, and so on.

Care of Videotape

Videotape should be handled and stored with care. The surface of the tape can easily be damaged, so videotape should never be touched with bare hands. Fingers leave an oily deposit that can damage the tape. If you must touch the tape, wear cotton gloves.

Videotape should be stored under conditions similar to those comfortable for people. Temperature should not vary excessively, as extreme heat and cold will damage the tape. Similarly, extreme humidity can cause great problems by making the tape sticky. This may cause it to bind together within the cassette or cause excessive friction against the head drum of the VCR, making tape playback and recording impossible.

Protection from dust and smoke is also important. Both of these elements can seriously damage the recording surface of the tape as well as the video heads within the VCR.

Videotapes should be stored on end, rather than on their side. Do not lay them down flat and stack them up one on top of another; instead, stand them up side by side. Also make sure that tapes are wound to the beginning or end of the spools for storage.

Dropouts

Videotape begins to wear out as it gets old. One sign of wear is the dropping out of information in the picture. **Dropouts** occur when parts of the magnetic coating that hold the signal information fall off the tape, leaving a hole in the picture. These can easily be seen on a monitor, where they appear as small black specks in the picture. Tape with a lot of dropouts should be discarded. Excessive dropouts not only affect the picture quality but may also affect picture stability and sound quality.

Many high-quality VCRs contain dropout compensators. A **dropout compensator** detects the loss of information caused by tape dropouts and corrects the problem by replacing the lost information with the line of information that immediately preceded it.

Excessive dropouts can cause the video heads to clog. If there is **head clog,** the heads do not record or play back, and need to be cleaned. The VCR heads may become clogged if the videotape is old or if the VCR is left

117

in the pause mode for an excessive period. If the latter happens, the heads are in continual contact with one spot on the tape. This tends to damage the tape by wearing off the magnetic particles at that point, leaving a blank spot that will no longer hold signal information.

Cleaning the Heads

As the video heads come in constant contact with videotape during record and playback, they tend to get clogged with oxide particles that drop off the tape. Consequently, the heads must be cleaned regularly to guarantee high-quality signal recording and playback.

You can tell when the video heads are getting dirty simply by looking at the picture produced by the VCR on a monitor. Clean heads produce a clear, sharp picture. When the heads are dirty, the picture looks fuzzy or noisy. In extreme cases, the heads become completely clogged, and the machine may fail to play back or record anything. All you see on the screen is *snow,* or electronic noise.

Heads should therefore be cleaned regularly, depending on use. If you use your VCR infrequently, you may need to clean the heads only every month or two. If you use the machine heavily, or if you are using old tape stock, you will certainly need to clean them more often—perhaps weekly, if not daily.

Many video service centers provide a head-cleaning service, or you may have technical staff on hand who can perform the job. The heads may be cleaned by applying commercially available head-cleaning fluid to the video heads, head drum, and pinch rollers and guides within the VCR, or by using a wet or dry head-cleaning cassette. Be sure to follow the manufacturer's guidelines in choosing the appropriate head-cleaning method so you do not damage the delicate head assembly or void the equipment warranty.

Other Video Recording Devices

Although videotape has been the principal medium for recording the electronic video signal for more than 40 years, new technologies are evolving that will ultimately replace videotape as the recording medium of choice. A number of these technologies are in use now.

Computer Hard Disks and Video Systems

A **hard disk** is a magnetic storage system for a computer. Information is stored on a series of round magnetic platters within the computer's disk drive system. Because computers work with digital rather than analog signals, the video and audio signals are converted from analog to digital before they are recorded. All modern computers come with built-in hard disk drives. However, full-color moving video with sound takes up a large amount of storage area and can easily overwhelm the capacity of most hard drives. Using up the available hard drive storage is a problem when more than one project needs to be completed using one available computer. A solution to both problems is found in removable hard drives. Individual projects can be stored on separate removable hard disks, freeing up the computer's main drive for other uses.

Figure 4.15   Ikegami Digital Disk Camcorder

One professional camcorder system is now available that uses specially designed removable computer hard disks for field recording (see Figure 4.15). The system is capable of 15 to 20 minutes of recording time and allows random access to the recorded material.

Video servers are computers equipped with hard disk storage systems that can record and play back video. In editing applications, servers are often used to store video footage in a central location, which can then be accessed from individual editing workstations. A producer in need of file footage of a presidential press conference, for example, could locate that footage in the central server and transfer a copy of it to his/her workstation, where it could then be edited into the news story.

In broadcast and cable stations, video servers are increasingly used in place of VCRs to store commercials and programs. When the server is connected to the central computer, which contains the day's program log, commercials and programs can be replayed automatically.

Jaz and Zip Disks

Two popular magnetic recording disks are Iomega's Jaz™ and Zip™ disks. Like other computer peripherals, Jaz and Zip drives can be connected to a computer through its **SCSI** (pronounced "scuzzy"[**small computer system interface**]) port. Zip disks hold 100 MB of data and are most useful for text, data (e.g., edit decision lists and footage logs), small audio files, and still image files. Jaz drives and disks are available in one- and two-gigabyte versions. Because of their larger size, they are useful for storing large amounts of audio and small video files.

CD-ROM and DVD

CD-ROM.   CD-ROM technology has become more pervasive as a result of the increased distribution of multimedia programs for home computers in this format. While most CDs are read- or playback-only devices, recordable CDs (CD-Rs) are available as well, but they are limited in how much information they can store and how fast they can play it back—both serious problems if the content is full-motion video. For example, a CD-ROM can hold 650 MB of information, equivalent to 74 minutes of recorded music or only a minute or so of high-quality video.

DVD.   In order to resolve these problems, major equipment manufacturers have agreed on a format for a CD standard identified as DVD (originally "digital video disc," but now called "digital versatile disc" to include music and computer content). DVDs containing popular movies are now available in most video movie rental stores, and the hope of the industry is that the public will abandon their VHS VCRs in favor of DVD machines, just as long-playing phonograph records were abandoned in favor of audio CDs. The new DVDs are the same size as CD-ROMs but hold up to 17 gigabytes of data—equivalent to several hours of high-quality video—making them a good choice for the distribution of video program material. CD-ROMs can be played back in DVD players, and increasingly personal computers are equipped with internal DVD drives rather than CD-ROM drives.

Optical Discs

Videodisc systems that can record and play back video signals are also finding increasing use in production situations (see Figure 4.16). Like the compact discs (CDs) that are widely used to distribute recorded music, these systems use a laser to read information from the disc. However, unlike audio CDs, which are a playback medium only, the videodisc systems can record information as well. Because no recording heads touch the disc, they are much more reliable than tape-based systems, and they also have the added advantage of allowing almost instantaneous random access to information anywhere on the disc. Current systems are capable of recording about 30 minutes of full-motion video on a single disc.

Figure 4.16   Videodisc Recording System (Sony LVS-5000)

Operating the Portable Video Camcorder

The Basic System

Today most small-scale EFP and ENG recording is done with a camcorder (see Figure 5.1). Camcorders contain two components: a video camera and a portable videocassette recorder. With these two components you can

Figure 5.1
Recording in the Field with Professional Camcorders

shoot and record electronic images. The camera section produces the basic video signal, which is then sent to the VCR section, where it is recorded. Videotape is the recording medium.

The camera and VCR sections of the camcorder may be manufactured as a single unit in which the camera and VCR components are inseparable, or the camera and VCR sections may be manufactured as separate, dockable units in which the camera outputs and VCR inputs can be directly connected together to create the camcorder unit (see Figure 5.2). Consumer-quality camcorders are typically one-piece systems, while professional quality camcorders may be either a one-piece or a dockable system.

Prior to the development of camcorder systems, single-camera video field production was accomplished using recording systems composed of a portable video camera tethered to a portable VCR with a camera cable. Although several manufacturers still produce stand-alone portable VCRs (see Figure 5.3), today the vast majority of single-camera field production work is recorded using one-piece or dockable camcorders.

In addition to these principal components, the camcorder system may have any number of auxiliary components. These auxiliary components may include power components (including both batteries and alternating current [AC] adapters), monitoring devices (equipment that lets you see the picture and hear the sound), lighting instruments, and additional audio equipment. Lighting and audio are the subjects of separate chapters. This chapter will focus on the typical operational controls of portable camcorders and the auxiliary field production components of power monitors and camera-mounting equipment such as tripods.

Figure 5.2   Dockable and One-Piece Camcorders

Dockable DVCAM™ VCR (Sony DSR-1)

One-Piece Betacam SP Camcorder

Dockable S-VHS Camcorder

Camcorder

Tape Carriage Mechanism

Common Camcorder
Camera Section
Controls

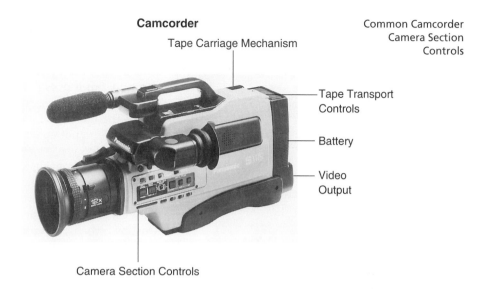

Tape Transport
Controls

Battery

Video
Output

Camera Section Controls

Portable VCR

Tape Carriage
Mechanism

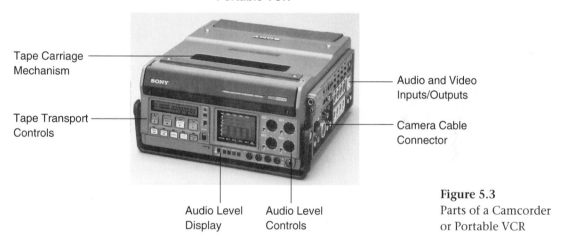

Audio and Video
Inputs/Outputs

Tape Transport
Controls

Camera Cable
Connector

Audio Level
Display

Audio Level
Controls

Figure 5.3
Parts of a Camcorder
or Portable VCR

Common Camcorder Camera Section Controls

Power Switch

All camcorders need to have a source of power supplied to them. Power can be supplied directly by a battery or by an alternating current (AC) adapter connected to wall current.

The power switch turns the camcorder on and off. Some camcorders include a standby switch, which allows the camera electronics and image sensor to warm up, but it does not cause the sensor to produce an image. In this way, it increases the life of the sensor and prolongs the life of the portable battery power system. It also lets you keep your camera ready to shoot without using as much power as in the "on" mode. Other switch configurations allow you to power up the camera and VCR sections independently for those situations when you want to use the camera section to produce an image without recording it, or conversely, when you want to use the VCR section to play back a tape for viewing without recording a signal from the camera. (See Figure 5.4.)

Figure 5.4   Camcorder Camera Section Controls

VCR Trigger

The **VCR trigger** is a small button, usually located at the back of the lens assembly, that is readily accessible by the camera operator's right thumb. The trigger gives the camera operator control over the recording process while operating the camcorder. Pushing the trigger and releasing it start and stop the VCR when it is in the ready-to-record mode.

Gain Boost/Sensitivity

The function of the **gain boost** switch is to amplify the video signal. This is most often used in low-light situations. Color cameras have a tendency to perform poorly when they do not have adequate light. The gain boost strengthens the signal and provides somewhat better color reproduction in these low-light situations. However, the benefit is not without a cost. As with any radical adjustment of the gain, the picture quality is usually somewhat degraded due to the increase in visual noise in the signal.

Indoor/Outdoor Filter

The **indoor/outdoor filter** allows the camera operator to compensate for changes in the color temperature of the light. As you may know, the actual color of white light varies. Some lighting instruments produce light that appears to be reddish or bluish, depending on the type of bulb used. The color of daylight varies from morning through evening. This is particularly apparent very early in the day and very late in the day. Color video cameras are extremely sensitive to these changes in the color temperature of light. (Color temperature is discussed in more detail in Chapter 6.) Consumer camcorders typically contain a two-position electronic filter with settings for indoor or outdoor light. Professional camcorders contain a *filter wheel* built into the camera between the lens and the prism block with positions for a variety of lighting conditions, as well as one or more *neutral density* filters that can be used to reduce the amount of light passing through the lens without affecting color temperature or the lens iris setting.

White Balance

Because the color temperature of light varies so much, all color video cameras contain electronic circuitry designed to correct the white balance of the camera. **White balance** adjusts the relative intensity of the red, green, and blue camera color channels to allow the camera to produce an accurate white signal in the particular light in which the camera is recording. Camera white balance is typically set manually by the videographer before recording begins by pressing the camera's white balance switch while focusing the camera on a white card in the light the subject will be recorded in. If the subject and camera move from one lighting condition to another (indoors to outdoors, for example), or if the lighting conditions change, the white balance procedure needs to be repeated. Many cameras with manual white balance also incorporate a memory system that is capable of retaining white balance settings for two different lighting conditions even if the camera power is turned off.

Some cameras contain a fully *automatic white balance* system that eliminates the need to set the white balance before each shot. In the "automatic" mode, the camera's electronic color correction circuitry automatically and continuously corrects the camera's white balance even if the color temperature of the light changes while the camera is recording the scene.

Yet another system is found on cameras with *preset white balance* controls that allow the videographer to manually choose either a tungsten (3,200°K) or daylight (5,600°K) lighting condition setting. (On consumer camcorders, this is usually represented as "indoor" and "outdoor.") As long as the color temperature of the ambient light is close to one of these standards, the color quality will be reasonably good.

Color Bars

Most professional and industrial-quality camcorders now available have a color bar switch. This switch causes the camera to generate a standard NTSC color bar output. These **color bars** are a standard pattern of yellow, cyan, green, magenta, red, and blue bars and are used as a standard color reference by video engineers. It is a good idea to record some color bars generated by your camera at the head of each field tape. This can be used as a color reference when it is time to play back your tape.

Automatic Camera Setup

Many of the professional-quality camcorders now on the market have a full set of controls that allow the camera operator to quickly set the correct electronic parameters for proper signal recording within the camera. Automatic white balance (auto-white) is a standard feature on these cameras, as is automatic **black balance** (auto-black), which automatically sets the black level of the picture. In addition, many cameras now have a microcomputer memory system to retain this information, even when the camera is turned off. This eliminates the need to reset the camera each time it is turned on.

Camcorder Special Effects and Image Stabilizers

An increasing number of camcorders have the ability to record a variety of special effects produced digitally within the camcorder. These may include a *still picture* effect, which freezes the moving video image and records it as a still image; a *strobe* effect, which breaks the incoming video signal into a series of still images to create a stroboscopic motion effect; and a *time-lapse recording* effect, in which the camera can be set to record one or more frames of video at predetermined intervals.

Digital zoom effects can be used to enlarge an image significantly beyond the magnification possible with the zoom lens. This has the effect of producing even closer close-ups, but it also increases the graininess of the picture and often results in unnatural color shifts in the picture.

Although it is not a special effect, camcorders equipped with a *digital image stabilizer* process the incoming signal to reduce the motion artifacts created when the camera operator shakes the camera—a problem that is particularly evident when the lens is zoomed in on very tight close-up shots. One unfortunate side effect of this feature is that if the stabilizer is left on while shooting a stationary subject with a steady camera, the image stabilizer may actually introduce motion into the image and cause it to appear to be out of focus.

VCR Section Controls and Inputs/Outputs

The four important parts of any portable VCR, whether the VCR is config-ured as part of a one-piece or dockable camcorder system or as a separate component, are the following:

1. Tape transport controls
2. Audio and video inputs and outputs
3. Power inputs
4. Meters, warning lights, and tape counters

Tape Transport Controls

The tape transport controls regulate the movement of the videotape within the VCR and are arranged like the tape transport controls on most audio-cassette recorders. The following controls are found on most portable camcorders.

Eject.   This button is used to eject the tape from the machine or to insert a tape into the machine. Most VCRs have a safety device to prevent you from ejecting the tape while the machine is running, but it is nevertheless a good idea never to eject the tape unless the machine has been stopped.

▲ Eject

Play.   This causes the tape to move forward at a normal speed; it is used to play back a tape. When the play button is used in conjunction with the record button, it allows you to record on a tape.

▶ Play

Slow-Speed Playback.   When the tape is in the play mode, pressing this button reduces the tape playback speed to a preset slow speed.

▍▶ Slow-Speed Playback

Stop.   To stop the movement of the tape in any mode, press STOP.

■ Stop

Fast Forward.   Pushing this button with the VCR in the stop mode causes the tape to move forward at a fast rate of speed. You do not see the picture or hear the sound when the VCR is engaged in fast forward because the tape is not in contact with the heads. Use the fast forward button when you want to find a spot that is a considerable distance into the tape.

▶▶ Fast Forward

Rewind.   This functions the same as the fast forward except that it moves the tape in the opposite direction.

◀◀ Rewind

Pause.   When the tape is in the play mode, pressing the pause button will stop the movement of the tape and give you a still frame. The tape re-mains engaged against the heads so that you can still see the picture. Do

▍▍ Pause

127

not leave the tape in the pause mode for more than a few minutes, as this may damage the tape by subjecting it to excessive wear. Many machines will automatically stop and release the tape from the heads if the machine is left in the pause mode for more than a few minutes.

▐▐▶ Forward Frame
by Frame

◀▐▐ Reverse Frame
by Frame

Forward/Reverse Frame by Frame.   With the VCR in the pause mode, this control advances or reverses the tape one frame at a time.

▶▶ Forward Search

◀◀ Reverse Search

Forward Search and Reverse Search.   Many machines incorporate forward- and reverse-search controls. These allow you to forward or reverse the image at a high speed when the VCR is in the play mode. Unlike the fast forward and rewind controls, the tape is not released from the head drum. As a rule of thumb, this mode should be used only to move the tape relatively short distances in either direction. If more than a few minutes of forward or reverse movement are necessary, use the fast forward or rewind button.

● Record

Record.   The record button is used to record new audio and video onto videotape. To go into the record mode, first press the record button, which engages the recording circuits. Then push the play button while continuing to hold in the record button. When the tape is engaged by the machine, you can release both buttons, and the tape will now be locked into the record mode.

⊖ Audio Dub

Audio Dub.   This is used to record new audio information onto a prerecorded tape without erasing the video information already recorded on it. It is engaged in the same way as the record button: press the audio dub button in conjunction with the play button.

Audio and Video Inputs and Outputs

Because VCRs record both picture and sound, there are a number of audio and video inputs and outputs on these machines (see Figure 5.5).

Audio Inputs and Outputs.   If audio is generated by a source other than the camera microphone, a number of additional inputs are available to route the signal into the VCR. Microphone-level inputs are used for unamplified sources, and line-level inputs are used for sources that have been amplified.

An external microphone can be connected to the **microphone in** connection; line-level audio signals from another VCR, audio tape recorder, and so on can be connected to the **audio in** (line) jack. Audio outputs can be used in conjunction with the video output or independent of

Figure 5.5
Camcorder Inputs
and Outputs

External Power Input   Audio Inputs

Video Outputs   Audio Outputs

it. The audio output signal, **audio out** (line), can be connected to a monitor so that the sound can be heard. Or it can be connected to another VCR or audio recorder to record the audio output signal. Professional-quality camcorders contain the normal series of audio and video inputs and outputs on the body of the camcorder. On consumer-quality camcorders, connectors for additional line-level audio and video inputs and outputs are frequently found on the AC power adapter.

Video Inputs and Outputs.   Sometimes a video source other than the camera provides the video signal to the VCR. For example, the signal from another VCR may be transferred to your camcorder and recorded on it. In this case, the auxiliary video input (also called **video in**) would be used. The video output (**video out**) can be used to connect the output signal of the camcorder to a monitor or to send the signal to another VCR. In addition to conventional video inputs and outputs, S-VHS VCRs have **S-Video connectors**, where the luminance and chrominance signals are kept separate.

129

Camera Output to VCR.   Most portable video field recording systems consist of one-piece or dockable camcorders in which the camera output is delivered directly to the VCR's input. In one-piece systems, the camera output is wired directly to the VCR input within the camcorder unit. In dockable systems, the camera/VCR connection is automatically made when the camera and VCR units are docked together.

In two-piece systems with a separate camera and VCR, a multipin camera cable connects the camera to the VCR input. If the portable camera is equipped with a built-in microphone, the camera cable will deliver audio as well as video to the portable VCR.

Radio Frequency Output.   Some systems contain a **radio frequency (RF)** output. The RF signal mixes the picture and sound together and makes it possible to see and hear your recording on a regular television set. To do so, you must tune the television to the channel to which the RF converter has been preset (usually channel 3 or 4). On consumer-quality camcorders, the RF output is usually found on the AC power adapter.

Power Inputs

All portable VCRs are powered by a 12-volt **direct current (DC)** power source rather than by standard household 110-volt **alternating current (AC)**. If AC current is used, a special AC adapter that converts household current to 12-volt DC is needed. AC adapters usually connect to a special four-pin connector on the outside of the VCR case.

Because the batteries used with portable VCRs all deliver 12-volt DC, no special adapters are needed for their use. The electrical contact points on the battery are exposed, and the proper connection is made by correctly inserting the battery into the camcorder's battery holder.

Meters, Warning Lights, and Tape Counters

All high-quality VCRs contain a series of meters for monitoring different machine functions. In many camcorder systems, even the most inexpensive consumer-level systems, displays for many of these metering functions (with the exception of audio levels) are shown in the camera's viewfinder while recording.

Battery Meter.   The **battery meter** is used to monitor the level of power in the battery. Typically, this is a viewfinder display.

Volume Unit Meters.   All professional equipment contains a **volume unit (VU) meter** to monitor the level of the audio and/or video input. A VU meter contains a scale that is a standard calibration of signal strength used in all broadcast and nonbroadcast media facilities. A small needle or LED display indicates how high or low the signal is.

There is only one rule of thumb to be observed when reading a VU meter: Keep the signal level high but out of the red zone. For example, if the audio level consistently peaks in the red, the sound will be distorted and scratchy. If the video level peaks in the red, colors will be distorted. If you can manually control the input signal level, check to make sure that it falls within the acceptable range on the VU meter. (See Chapter 7 for a more detailed discussion.)

Warning Lights. Many VCRs come equipped with a variety of warning lights that tell you if something is wrong. The **dew lamp** warns you that moisture or condensation has formed on the head drum. Because the videotape must glide smoothly over the head drum and moisture can make the tape sticky, the dew indicator is extremely important. If it comes on, it means the head drum is damp and the VCR will not make a satisfactory recording. Sometimes this happens if the camcorder has been stored in a damp place or if it has been moved from outdoors to indoors. If the dew warning lamp comes on, push the eject button, remove the tape, and allow air to circulate inside the VCR. The problem will usually correct itself in a few minutes. Many viewfinder displays also contain a *tape end warning* that lets you know when you are a minute or two from the end of the tape.

Tape Counters. Three types of tape counters are found on portable VCRs. The most common is the simple *numerical counter* that begins running when the tape is moving and stops when the tape is stopped. The counter numbers generally have no relationship to minutes or seconds of tape and are useful only in providing a rough estimate of the location of shots on a tape. There are usually differences in the calibration of counters from one machine to another. Thus, it is often difficult to find a specific place on the tape when you play it back on another VCR, even when you know the recording VCR's counter number associated with the visual event on the tape.

Another type of counter is the *real-time frame* counter. This type of counter displays a readout in hours, minutes, and seconds, and works by counting off the control track pulses on the videotape. Real-time frame counters are accurate so long as you remember to reset the counter to zero at the beginning of the tape. Also, you must be careful not to hit the reset button while you are playing a tape, because this will return the readout to zero. The counter will then begin counting in time from that new zero point.

The most accurate type of counter is the **SMPTE time code counter.** With this system, each frame of video information is assigned its own unique time code number in hours, minutes, seconds, and frames. Because this information is actually encoded onto the videotape, you can always find the precise frame of information you are looking for and hitting the

131

reset button does not affect the readout. The meter will always display the actual time code number for the particular frame of information that is being played back. Time code counters are available only on professional-quality machines.

Other Controls

Video Input Selector.   The video input selector switch tells the VCR where the input video signal is coming from. The switch typically has two positions: camera and VCR/line. To record a video signal from the camera, the input switch must be in the camera position. When using the VCR to record a video signal from another VCR or to play back a tape through the camcorder without engaging the camera section, the VCR/line position is used.

On some one-piece consumer-level camcorders, a sliding plastic plate on top of the camcorder housing controls the signal flow to the VCR section of the camcorder. In other systems this control may be integrated with the camcorder's power switch, which may have "camera" and "VCR" positions. In the "camera" position, the VCR section records the video signal that the camera section of the camcorder is generating. Recording is stopped and started by using the stop/start button located on the zoom lens assembly. When the selector plate or power switch is in the "VCR" position, the camcorder can be used to play back a recorded tape or record a video signal from another VCR.

S-VHS Record Mode Selector.   S-VHS VCRs are capable of recording in either the conventional VHS mode or in the S-VHS mode. In order for an S-VHS recording to be made, the S-VHS selector switch must be properly set and an S-VHS tape, rather than a conventional VHS tape, must be used in the VCR. With the S-VHS selector switch in the "on" position and with an S-VHS videotape in the VCR, an S-VHS recording will be made. If the selector switch is in the "off" position, the recording will be made as conventional VHS, regardless of the type of tape used. Some selector switches contain an "auto" position. When this is selected, the recording will be S-VHS when an S-VHS tape is used, and conventional VHS when a conventional VHS tape is used.

Audio Input Selector.   This control tells the VCR where the audio signal is coming from—microphone, camera, or line.

Audio Mode Selector.   The audio mode selector can usually be set to "normal" or "high fidelity" on S-VHS VCRs and to "AFM" or stereo "PCM" on 8mm/Hi8 VCRs. This selector controls the audio record and playback functions of the VCR and the VU meter display on VCRs that are capable of recording and playing back normal and high-fidelity (or digital) audio signals.

Audio Monitor Control.   On VCRs with two audio channels, the audio monitor control determines which audio channel is heard in the earphones or camcorder audio monitor speaker. In the channel 1 position, only audio channel 1 is heard; in the channel 2 position, only channel 2 is heard. In the mix position, both channels are heard simultaneously. The audio monitor control does not affect the way the audio signals are recorded; it only affects what you hear when you are monitoring the audio during recording or playback.

Tracking Control.   The tracking control is used in the playback mode to maximize the quality of the playback image by compensating for slight differences in the way different VCRs record and play back a signal. Without adjusting the tracking control, something recorded on one machine may not play back correctly on another machine due to the slight mechanical differences between the VCRs.

The tracking control should always be set in the fixed position when recording. This position is usually marked on the control, and there is a small notch in the fixed position where the control clicks into place.

Remote Controls.   Some VCRs contain a remote control input that allows the operator to control the tape transport system with a remote control unit. The remote controls duplicate the standard tape transport controls.

Other Features of
Videocassette Recorders

Most camcorders' VCR sections contain several other features that deserve at least brief mention.

Automatic backspace editing gives clean cuts from shot to shot when you are recording and using the camera trigger at the beginning and end of each shot. When you push the record trigger at the end of a shot or sequence, the VCR stops and then automatically backs the tape up a few frames. When you push the trigger to begin recording the next shot, the tape rolls and then begins the new recording in sync with the previously recorded material. The effect is that of a clean cut, or edit, from one shot to the next, without any blank tape or image break between the two shots.

Video insert (called *video dub* or *video add* on some machines) allows you to insert new video into a previously recorded segment. This feature gives a clean entrance to and exit from newly inserted video.

133

Power and Videotape

Power for the Camcorder

All portable camcorders can be powered by a battery or by standard AC power through the use of a special AC adapter. Your choice of power source depends on the recording situation and the available equipment. If you are using a consumer-quality camcorder to record your grandmother's 80th birthday party indoors at home, you can choose between an internal camcorder battery or external AC power because of its availability. However, if you're recording an interview with a geologist who is surveying an earthquake fault at a remote mountain site, you will probably have to rely on batteries. Most camcorders use internal batteries that are inserted into the camcorder or clip-on battery packs that attach to the back of the camcorder with a special adapter.

As mentioned earlier, AC adapters convert 110-volt household alternating current into the 12-volt direct current that video recorders and cameras run on (see Figure 5.6). They can also be used to charge spare camcorder batteries. One end of the AC adapter plugs directly into a wall outlet and is equipped with a standard three-pronged AC connector. The other side of the AC adapter is equipped with a connector that attaches to the camcorder.

The external power (DC) input usually is either a multipin Deutsche–Industrie-Norm **(DIN) connector** or a four-pin **XLR connector** (also called a Cannon connector). The XLR connector is slightly more rugged than the DIN connector, and for that reason XLR connectors are typically found on

Figure 5.6
AC Adapter /Battery
Charger

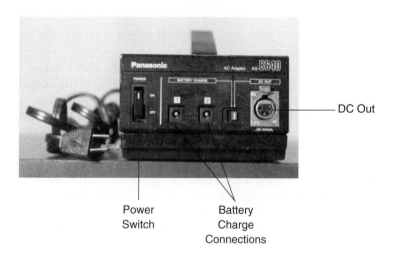

DC Out

Power
Switch

Battery
Charge
Connections

professional-quality machines. DIN connectors are used most often on consumer and industrial machines.

The AC adapter also has an on/off switch. Two cautions should be observed when connecting the AC adapter to a camcorder:

1. Make sure that the AC adapter is turned off when you plug it into the wall and the camcorder. Do not turn it on until you have made all connections correctly.
2. When you connect the AC adapter to the camcorder, make sure you make the connection correctly.

If the pins of the AC adapter are not inserted into the correct holes on the camcorder, you might blow a fuse in the deck and will be unable to operate the machine until the fuse is replaced. The pins are arranged so that you can insert the connector correctly in only one way.

At this point, a suggestion with respect to making connections is in order: *don't force anything.* Many of the receptacles (and some of the plugs) found in portable equipment are made of plastic. If forced into an incorrect connection, they will break. Always examine the pin configuration before you attempt to connect a piece of equipment.

Inserting the Videocassette

All videocassettes have a top and a bottom. The top of the cassette is a smooth piece of plastic; the bottom contains the recessed portion of the tape spools. In addition, each tape has a front and a back. The back of the cassette is a solid piece of plastic and the front has a small metal or plastic door.

In order to insert the tape into the machine, push the eject button on the camcorder. This will cause the tape carriage (the part of the machine that holds the tape) to pop open. (*Note:* In most portable systems, the eject button will not work unless the camcorder has been connected to battery or AC power.) Carefully insert the tape into the carriage with the door away from you and the open spools to the bottom, and then insert the tape as far as it will go. Then push down on the carriage assembly to close the door and lock the tape into position.

If you are using a new videotape for recording, it is a good idea to fast forward the tape to the end and then rewind it before recording. This process, known as *repacking the tape,* loosens up the tape within the cassette and allows the tape to move through the VCR at a uniform speed when you begin to record. Because videotape sometimes has a tendency to bind or stick to itself when it is stored, this is a good practice to adopt before recording with any tape. It also makes sense to do this when you have access to AC power so that you do not waste valuable battery power.

135

Tape Movement inside the Camcorder

What happens to the videotape when you insert it into the tape carriage and push it down into the VCR? Several things happen inside the camcorder. First, as the tape carriage is depressed, the small door on the front of the videocassette opens automatically. The door acts as a shield to protect the tape when it is outside the machine. But, for the tape to operate within the machine, the tape must be withdrawn from the cassette and brought into contact with the video heads. So, a small device triggers the door to release, and the door pops open. (If you want to see how this works, you can manually trigger the door to release. Take a blank videocassette and hold it with the door facing you and the open part of the spools facing the floor. Slightly off to the side of the door you will see a small rectangular opening, and immediately inside the opening you will see a small piece of metal or plastic. Carefully take a pencil or other small object, insert it into the opening, and press down on the release. The door should pop open and reveal the videotape to you. Be careful not to touch the tape with your fingers, as this may damage the magnetic coating. Also make sure that you close the door completely before you attempt to insert the cassette into the camcorder.)

What happens after the tape is inserted into the camcorder and the door is opened depends on the mode or function selected for the VCR section. In the stop mode, the tape stays within the cassette and does not move. In the fast forward and rewind modes, the tape is driven forward or in reverse at a high speed. Again, the tape remains entirely within the cassette housing.

However, in the record and play modes (including forward and reverse search, pause, single-frame advance and reverse, and slow-speed playback), something very different happens. In order for a VCR to play back a

Figure 5.7
Tape-Loading
Schematics

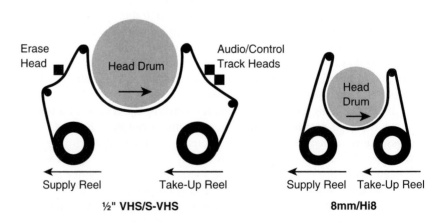

tape or record onto a tape, the videotape must be brought into contact with the video heads. As we have already mentioned, the video heads lay down the signal in the record mode and read the signal on the tape in the play mode. The video heads are located within the **head drum**—a stainless steel cylinder inside the VCR. In order for the tape to make contact with the heads, a mechanical arm reaches inside the cassette, physically pulls the tape out of the cassette, and wraps it around the head drum. This is a complicated mechanical operation and demands that the mechanical arm and tape guides be precisely adjusted and aligned (see Figure 5.7).

This mechanical method of extracting the tape from the cassette housing is one of the greatest trouble areas with portable equipment, particularly older VCRs. When the mechanism malfunctions, the tape gets "eaten" by the machine. Anyone who has ever worked with portable equipment for any amount of time has seen a tape chewed by a VCR.

Camcorder System Setup

Let's assume that you simply want to record some video and audio information onto videotape with your portable camcorder. To make matters even simpler, we will assume that you plan to use the microphone that is built into your camcorder. How to proceed varies slightly, depending on the particular features of your camcorder. In general, the following steps apply to the setup of most simple one-piece camcorder systems.

Step 1. With the power switch off, make sure the camcorder is secure (either mounted on a tripod or resting safely on a hard surface).

Step 2. Connect the camcorder to power by inserting the internal battery into the camcorder.

Step 3. Turn on the power to the camcorder. The power light should illuminate.

Step 4. Open the tape carriage door by pushing the eject button. Insert the videocassette carefully and correctly. Lower the tape carriage. Rewind the tape to the beginning.

Step 5. Set the filter and white balance controls to their proper positions for the lighting conditions in which you will be recording. Set the gain boost to normal.

Step 6. Uncap the camcorder lens. An image should be visible in the viewfinder.

Step 7. Look through the viewfinder. Frame up and manually focus the image (or set to auto-focus). Set the iris to automatic (or manually adjust the aperture for correct exposure).

Step 8. Push the record trigger button to begin recording. Make a brief test recording.

Step 9. Push the record trigger button to stop the recording. Rewind the tape to the beginning, and check your recording by watching it in the viewfinder. Use an earphone to monitor the recorded audio, or listen to it through the earspeaker if your camcorder is so equipped.

Audio and Video Connectors

Quite often in field production, you need to go beyond the simple setup described above. Most camcorders contain a series of auxiliary audio and video inputs and outputs. These additional inputs and outputs are used when you want to record from a video or audio source other than the camera or camera microphone into the VCR section, when you want to monitor the output of the VCR section, or when you simply want to play back a tape into a monitor to check its quality.

A big problem with auxiliary inputs and outputs on portable equipment is that the connectors used have not been standardized. As a result, you need to become familiar with the range of video and audio connectors in use, and in particular, you need to know which specific connectors are used on your equipment. Figures 5.8 and 5.9 illustrate the most common audio and video connectors found on portable video equipment.

Audio Connectors

The most common use of additional inputs is for recording audio. The quality of the audio recording can almost always be enhanced by using an external microphone rather than the camera microphone.

The variety of audio connectors in use in portable equipment is guaranteed to drive you crazy. Professional equipment uses a three-pin **XLR** (Cannon) **connector** for all audio inputs and outputs. (See Figure 5.8.) Consumer-quality $1/2''$, DV, and 8mm equipment utilizes the **RCA/phono connector**, a small pin surrounded by a metal sheath, for line-level audio inputs and outputs. (Line-level signals will be discussed further in Chapter 7.) Microphone inputs are typically **mini-plugs**, small single-pin connectors. Mini-plugs are also used for the earphone jack, which is used to

Figure 5.8
Audio Connectors

Cannon (XLR)   Phone Plug   Mini-Plug   RCA/Phono
                                                       Connector

monitor the sound as it is being recorded. Once very popular, but now becoming less widely used, are **phone plugs.** These large pin-type plugs are sometimes used as headphone connectors and occasionally for microphone inputs.

Video Connectors

Many camcorders have a series of video inputs and outputs that are independent of the video input from the camera. For example, if you want to dub a videotape from one VCR to another, the video output from one machine can be connected to the video input on another machine. On high-quality VCRs, video inputs and outputs will be BNC connectors (see Figure 5.9). **Bayonet (BNC) connectors** are bayonet twist-lock connectors and are the type of connector used on almost all professional equipment.

And finally, DV (digital video) equipment may use a six-pin digital video connector known as **FireWire,** or IEEE 1394, to move digital video (as well as audio, time code, and machine control commands) from one

Another type of connector used for video is the RCA/phono connector. This type is most often found on consumer-quality DV, 8mm, and VHS machines; it is the same type of connector sometimes used for audio.

VCRs with **S-Video connectors** and outputs use a special four-pin connector that is used to make direct S-Video connections (separate luminance and chrominance signals) between VCRs, cameras, and monitors that are equipped with similar connectors.

And finally, DV (digital video) equipment may use a six-pin digital video connector known as **FireWire,** or IEEE 1394, to move digital video (as well as audio, time code, and machine control commands) from one

Figure 5.9
Video Connectors

| BNC | RCA | F-Connector | S-Video | FireWire |
| | | (RF) | | (IEEE 1394) |

DV VCR to another, or from a DV VCR directly into a computer equipped with a FireWire input.

One other type of connector deserves mention. The radio frequency (RF) output of home VCRs is carried by a coaxial cable with an **F-connector.** The RF output carries audio and video superimposed onto a carrier frequency, which allows you to play back a videotape and watch it on a conventional television. If you have cable television, you are already familiar with the F-connector—the cable ends in a small sleeve and a small, thin copper wire protrudes from the center of the cable. If your television has a female F-connector on the back, you can connect the cable (or VCR RF output) directly to the television.

Monitoring the Recording

Video field producers are always concerned that the scene being shot is actually being recorded on the videotape. What options are available to the field producer for monitoring the quality of the signal and recording? First, the visual quality of the image (usually only in black and white) can be monitored in the camcorder's viewfinder. This shows the camera operator what the picture that the camera section is sending to the VCR looks like. Second, the audio quality can also be monitored like the video. Headphones, or an earphone, can be connected to the camcorder, or the side panel of the camcorder may be equipped with a built-in **earspeaker**—a small speaker that allows the camera operator to hear the sound input directly without the use of headphones or an earphone.

Audio Meters and Gain Control

Audio can also be monitored through the use of the volume unit (VU) meter. This meter indicates the level of the signal going into the VCR section of the camcorder.

All high-quality VCRs contain VU meters for audio. The level of the audio input signal can be controlled automatically through the use of the audio automatic gain control (AGC). On many camcorders, the AGC can be overridden and switched to manual gain control. Usually, there is a small **potentiometer**, or pot, built into the VCR to allow the operator to increase or decrease the audio level. Because control of the audio is critical to good field production, manual control of the audio signal level is extremely valuable. It is unfortunate that most consumer DV, 8mm, and VHS camcorders do not contain either audio VU meters or manual audio gain controls, because this deprives the serious producer of an element of fundamental control over the signal.

Confidence Heads

Carefully monitoring the audio and video levels through the VCR meters and the quality of the picture and sound through the viewfinder and headphones tells you only what is coming from the camera and microphone and not what is actually being recorded. However, several professional models of camcorders incorporate what the manufacturers call video **confidence heads.** These are a second set of video heads positioned immediately behind the principal set of recording heads. As the record heads lay down the signal, they are immediately followed by the confidence heads, which can play back the signal while the machine is still in the record mode. Simply stated, this allows you to monitor the visual quality of the recording as it is being recorded.

Field Monitors

Since most machines do not have confidence heads, how can you actually monitor the quality of the recording? There is only one foolproof method of checking the quality of a recording, and that is to play back the videotape immediately after it has been recorded.

141

Most field producers will make a short test recording with the equipment at the beginning of the day and then immediately play it back to see that the equipment is working properly. The recording can be played back into the camera viewfinder, and audio can be monitored through the use of headphones or earspeaker. All you need do is rewind the tape to the beginning of the recorded test section and then play back the tape.

However, because most viewfinders on portable camcorders are black and white or low-quality color LCD displays, this method of monitoring does not allow you to check the quality of the color of your recording. To check the quality of the color that was recorded, as well as your recording's sound and image, you need to bring a portable color monitor into the field (see Figure 5.10). A portable color monitor is a small color video monitor. For field use, these monitors should be small (a 5″ diagonal screen is usually sufficient), lightweight, rugged, and capable of being operated via either AC or DC (battery) power. A monitor capable of operating only on AC wall current is not very useful out in the field, far from a source of AC power. As the previous discussion indicates, there are several different types of devices that can be used to view television programs or to display the output of a VCR. These devices include television receivers, video monitors, and combination monitor-receivers.

A television **receiver** is the type of television most common to all of us. Its function is to pick up a signal that is either **broadcast** (over the air) or **cablecast** (over a wire) and to display that signal as picture and sound.

Figure 5.10
Portable Field
Monitor

Television signals that are broadcast or cablecast are RF-modulated. That is, the actual video signal and audio signals are superimposed on a carrier that oscillates at a particular frequency. These different carrier frequencies correspond to different channels on home television receivers. For example, within your local community, you probably have access to several local television stations. Each station is assigned to a different channel, which in effect corresponds to the wavelength carrier that station uses to transmit its signal.

Video **monitors,** on the other hand, work by displaying video and audio signals that are not superimposed on a carrier. The outputs of all VCRs, when labeled *video line out* and *audio line out,* are straight video and audio outputs without the RF carrier currents. To monitor video and audio line outputs, you need a monitor—not a receiver—that is capable of displaying them.

Let's assume that you want to monitor what you are recording in the field through the use of a combination *monitor-receiver.* This type of equipment has the capability to act either as a receiver or a monitor. To operate it as a monitor, switch it to the monitor mode and connect it to power. Then connect the audio and video outputs on the camcorder to the audio and video inputs on the monitor. To make the connections correctly, you will need to pay attention to the types of connectors used on both the camcorder outputs and the monitor inputs. Once these connections have been made, you can simply insert a tape into the camcorder and play it back. Picture and sound should appear on the monitor.

In addition to monitoring picture and sound after they have been recorded, you can also use the monitor to display picture and sound while you are recording. The signal going into the VCR section from the camera section will automatically be routed through the monitor if you have made all the connections properly. In many portable systems, the VCR does not even have to be recording for you to monitor the camera output, as long as the power to the camera section of the camcorder is turned on. This is particularly useful if you want to warm up the camera or practice camera moves without actually engaging the tape around the head drum. It saves wear and tear on the video heads and the videotape.

One word of caution is needed here: remember to keep the audio speaker on the monitor turned down if you have a live microphone nearby. If the audio speaker is turned up too high, the audio components will begin to produce **feedback.** This is a loud, squealing audio noise that occurs when the microphone picks up its own sound from the speaker, which is then reamplified by the audio circuits in the VCR.

Some camcorders have an RF unit that allows the camcorder's output to be viewed on a regular television receiver. The RF output unit will contain a small switch that indicates which channel the output can be viewed on, usually channel 3 or 4. Switch the output to the channel that is *not* used by a local station in your area. If you have a local channel 3, switch

143

the VCR output to channel 4 so that the local station's signal does not interfere with the VCR output. If your area has a local channel 4, then switch the VCR RF output to channel 3 for the same reason.

On consumer-quality camcorders, line-level and RF video outputs can usually be found on the AC adapter rather than on the camcorder itself. These outputs can be used only when the AC adapter is being used to power the camcorder, either during the time the recording is being made or when the camcorder is being used to play back the tape.

Camera-Mounting Equipment

Perhaps the most common image that people have today of video cameras is the image of the electronic news gathering (ENG) crew on a remote shoot, with the camera held on the shoulder of the camera operator, and a news reporter chasing down a potential interviewee. This brings us to the area of camera-mounting equipment. What options are there for physically supporting a camera?

Shoulder Mount or Brace

One of the most common ways to support a portable camcorder is to carry it. Early portable camera designs were awkward and had to be held in front of the camera operator (usually because the viewfinder was mounted on the rear of the camera), but current models that have side-mounted viewfinders allow the camera to be carried on the shoulder of the camera operator. These cameras utilize a **shoulder mount** or brace to cushion the operator's shoulder from the weight of the camera. They consist of a contoured piece of metal with foam padding attached to the bottom of the camera. (See Figures 5.2 and 5.4.)

Some cameras contain braces that can be changed to accommodate right-handed and left-handed operators. In addition, well-designed camcorders take balance into account—the camcorder should rest evenly on the operator's shoulder. The weight of the lens at the front of the camcorder should be counterbalanced by the battery pack at the rear of the camcorder. The camcorder should not have a tendency to fall forward or back, but should rest squarely on the operator's shoulder.

The shoulder mount gives the camera operator the greatest amount of flexibility in the movement of the camcorder. The operator can walk easily with the camcorder, and all types of lateral or vertical camera movements are possible. However, even the strongest person can tire of holding a shoulder-mounted camcorder, and even the best camera operator will have trouble holding a steady close-up shot for any great amount of time. For these reasons, a tripod is used.

Tripod

Tripod mounts—or **sticks,** as they are often called because of the wooden legs on some models—are widely used in remote productions. If camera movement is not important (for example, in an interview with the subject remaining in one position), a tripod-mounted camcorder provides the greatest amount of control (see Figure 5.11).

The tripod provides a steady base for the camera. The shoulder brace is removed from the bottom of the camera, and the camera is then attached to the head of the tripod. Many tripods contain telescoping legs so that the height of the camera can be adjusted.

Tripod heads come in two types: friction heads and fluid heads. **Friction heads,** which are the less expensive of the two types, give fair control over camera panning (from left to right) and tilting (up and down). Smooth camera operation is achieved both by using a tripod head that is designed to accommodate the specific weight of the camera used and through practice on the part of the camera operator. Professional camera operators always use tripods with **fluid heads.** These are more expensive

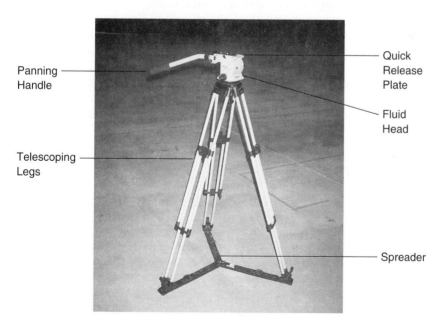

Figure 5.11
Camera Tripod

Panning Handle

Quick Release Plate

Fluid Head

Telescoping Legs

Spreader

than friction heads but are designed so that it is virtually impossible to make a jerky horizontal or vertical camera movement. For very smooth, solid camera operation, the tripod-mounted fluid head is the usual choice.

A **quick-release plate** may be attached to the tripod head to allow for quick mounting and release of the camcorder on the tripod. The plate is screwed onto the tripod head, and the camcorder then snaps into a locked position on the plate. A lever releases the camcorder from the plate. Quick-release systems eliminate the need to attach the camcorder to the tripod head with the mounting screw (the quick-release plate is attached instead). These systems reduce the amount of time it takes to attach and detach the camcorder from the tripod.

Two attachments for the legs of the tripod are often used. A *spreader* is used to spread the tripod legs out to their widest stance and hold them firmly in that position. A *tripod dolly* is a wheeled base that can be attached to the tripod legs if movement of the tripod is desired.

Monopods

While the shoulder brace method allows for maximum mobility of the camera, and the tripod gives maximum stability, the monopod provides a compromise between the two. A **monopod** is a telescoping rod that is attached to the base of the camcorder and is inserted into a special belt pouch. The monopod takes the weight of the camera off the shoulder of the camera operator but also allows for movement.

Monopods were originally designed for use with cameras with rear viewfinders, but they may be used on cameras with side-mounted viewfinders as well. The main disadvantage to the monopod is that some vertical camera movements are rather awkward to achieve. To tilt up, the camera operator must literally bend over backward. To tilt down, the operator must bend forward. Although these movements may have a yoga-like appeal, in practice they can be difficult and sometimes even dangerous.

Steadicam

An excellent compromise between mobility and stability appears to have been achieved by the mounting device known as the **Steadicam**®. This camera-mounting system, designed specifically for use with portable film and video cameras, won an Academy Award for its design when it was introduced. A number of different models of Steadicam are available, depending on the weight of your camera or camcorder. Models include an EFP model for use with professional video cameras and camcorders (see Figure 5.12), as well as others designed to be used with lightweight consumer camcorders.

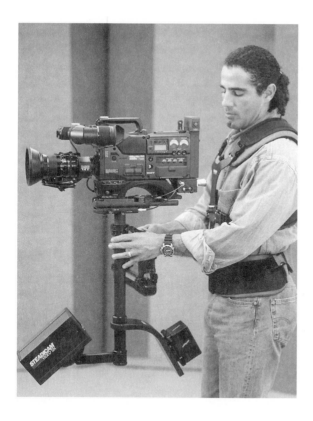

Figure 5.12 Steadicam® Camera
Mounting System

 **Carrying
the Equipment**

It should be apparent from the previous discussion that even a relatively
simple remote shoot involves the use of a significant amount of equipment. How does one carry all this gear around? A number of solutions are
readily available.

Carrying Case with Shoulder Strap

Most camcorders are equipped with a carrying case, a shoulder strap, and a
handle. Transport the camcorder from location to location in its case to
protect it from shock, moisture, and dust. Use the shoulder strap or camcorder handle to carry it when you reach your shooting location. Remember not to swing the camcorder by the strap or handle while you are
recording. Such motion can create a gyro effect, which may produce an unstable recording.

147

Carts

For an extremely complicated remote shoot, or in a situation where the camcorder will be augmented with the use of a field monitor, extra batteries, and additional audio or lighting equipment, *wheeled carts* (sometimes called *crash carts*) are frequently used. The carts are usually designed to hold the AC adapter, monitor, and other auxiliary equipment, and they provide convenient access to the operating controls of each piece of equipment. Some carts may even have a tripod head mounted directly onto them if stability, rather than mobility, is a primary concern.

Problems

Recordings made in the field will be more reliable and stable if the portable camcorder remains stationary while the recording is in progress. Obviously, this is not always possible. However, if you are carrying the camcorder or moving it around in a wheeled cart, try to minimize the amount of motion that the recorder is subjected to. If the camcorder is violently swung or bounced, this will almost certainly affect the speed at which the tape is moving through the VCR and introduce some instability into the recording.

6 Lighting

PART ONE
Physical Factors of Lighting

As cameras improve in their capacity to accommodate existing conditions, the pressure on the videographer to create high-impact, eye-catching pictures increases. The successful videographer must demonstrate the twin abilities to accommodate existing illumination in the field and to augment it for effect quickly, inexpensively, and without support from a large-scale production crew.

No matter what the content of the field-based video footage may be, the essential problem is that each story, program, or segment requires the integration of video materials with those gathered or produced elsewhere. From location to location, flesh tones must remain the same. They must not slip into the familiar blue/green/purple distortions caused by the failure to use light quality and color correction tools properly. Lighting for remote production, then, begins with avoiding such distractions and meeting audience expectations efficiently.

While the *craft* of lighting focuses on generating colors and visible detail acceptable to the viewing audience, the *art* of lighting involves controlling the aesthetic factors central to persuasive productions. Lighting for surveillance video is simple—you must provide sufficient illumination for sharp focus only at the prescribed distance from the lens. Lighting for persuasive video is more complex—to attract and maintain the attention of your viewers, you must help them see what they have not seen before. You do this by establishing expositional details of time and place, by expressing relationships among people or between people and objects, and by conveying senses of textures and atmospheres. This chapter will discuss how you achieve this in your video productions through the use of lighting.

Base Illumination

Baselight

As you remember from the discussion in Chapter 2, the camera CCD creates the television picture by changing light that is reflected off the scene into electrical energy—the video signal. For this process to take place, the camera requires that a certain minimum amount of light be present on the scene that is being recorded. The minimum amount of light that must be present for the camera to operate properly is called the **base illumination** level, or **baselight.** Baselight, then, refers to the amount, or intensity, of the light that is required to make the camera function properly.

Unfortunately, video cameras are not as efficient as the human eye when it comes to seeing the event in front of them. The human eye is much more sensitive than a video camera and requires less light to make a picture than does a camera. Similarly, some scenes that look fine to the eye may contain too much light/dark contrast for the camera to process without distortion.

Because the eye responds differently to light than does the camera, a mechanical way to measure the light present is needed to determine if it is

Figure 6.1
Incident Light Meter

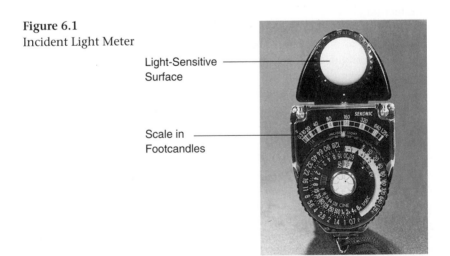

Light-Sensitive Surface

Scale in Footcandles

sufficient for the camera to make everything visible. The **light meter** does this (see Figure 6.1). The light meter provides a rough indication of the amount of light striking the photosensitive surface of the CCD and expresses the amount in **foot-candles (FC)**.

Increasingly, camera light-level requirements are expressed in **lux** instead of foot-candles. Lux are calculated in the same manner as foot-candles except that one meter replaces one foot in the formula. Because 1 foot-candle equals about 11 lux and because most of the world uses the metric system of measurement, manufacturers express the low-light capacity of their cameras in whole-number lux rather than in fractions of a foot-candle—for example, 3 lux instead of .27 foot-candles. (See Appendix 3 for a more thorough discussion of light measurement.)

Incident and Reflected Light

Light meters can be used to measure the amount of light falling on a scene, called **incident light**, or the amount of light reflected off a scene, called **reflected light** (see Figure 6.2). Incident light is measured by placing the light meter in the subject's position and pointing it at each lighting instrument. This results in a relatively high reading, which, although crude, is reliable. As long as subjects or materials of the same general reflectance are used, incident light can be used as the measure of the basic illumination on a scene. Some incident light meters have a light-sensitive area that is hemispherical rather than flat. The sphere approximates the shape of the human face and can be used to measure all the light falling on a subject from various directions.

A more precise method of measuring the intensity of the light present involves placing the light meter in the camera position and measuring the light reflected from the subject to the camera. This is called reflected light. Although both types of light meters are widely used in video production, incident light meters are probably the most common, largely because baselight requirements for cameras are most often reported in terms of the amount of incident light that they require.

Camcorder Baselight Requirements

In both the highest-quality cameras and camcorders designed for broadcast use with three-CCD arrays, and inexpensive single-chip camcorders designed for home or consumer use, the optimum lighting requirements are typically between 150 and 200 foot-

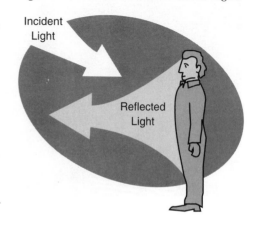

Figure 6.2 Incident and Reflected Light

Incident Light

Reflected Light

candles. This allows the lens aperture to be set at a midpoint in the range (usually f-5.6 or f-8.0) and produces reasonably long depth of field.

However, most CCD cameras can produce excellent pictures with significantly less light. With the lens aperture opened up, illumination levels of 30–50 foot-candles can yield excellent pictures, but with a shorter depth of field. In addition, most modern cameras now contain a low-lux or gain boost control that will allow the camera to produce acceptable images in as little as 2–3 lux.

 # Contrast Range

In spite of the technical improvements in cameras made in recent years, video systems are not able to match the **contrast range** capabilities of film, let alone those of the human eye. In this regard, the video camera cannot record reality as seen both in film and in our everyday experiences. As a rule of thumb, think of video as operating within a 30–40:1 ratio of light to dark. This can be understood as the difference between very light, highly reflective surfaces like a white wall and total darkness, or the lack of reflective light—black. The video camera's inability to process a full range of contrasts accurately is most often seen on tape as faces turning into silhouettes as the sky or wall behind them brightens (see Figure 6.3).

The technical term used to describe the camera's ability to reproduce the tonal gradations, or contrast range, of a scene is called **gamma.** Be-

Figure 6.3 As Background Becomes Brighter, Foreground Subject Becomes Silhouetted

cause gamma is constant in most inexpensive field cameras (no adjust-ment of this factor is possible), it is necessary to control the brightness of subjects within a scene to generate an acceptable picture. This control is next to impossible in some circumstances: moving from the interior of a dark chapel to a bright outdoor courtyard in a single shot, for example, ex-ceeds the capacity of most cameras. The camera automatically compresses part of the contrast range and loses something. If the scene is too bright, everything from middle gray to black is processed as black. This could in-clude the natural middle-brightness shadows on the face that combine to create a three-dimensional, or modeling, effect.

This is an area of great concern to video camera manufacturers, and important advances are announced with increasing frequency. The ability to accurately reproduce a scene with a high contrast range distinguishes high-quality industrial-grade and professional cameras from their less ex-pensive counterparts. Although most portable color cameras can produce a bright, clear, and attractive picture, sometimes more expensive cameras can do it in a greater range of circumstances and with less time-consuming attention to manipulation of the environment.

 # Color

Baselight and contrast range deal with the *amount* of light and its effect on a scene in terms of its overall brightness. The *quality,* or color, of that light constitutes the other half of the problem the videographer must solve in each shooting.

Additive and Subtractive Color

Two complementary theories of color must be understood before proceed-ing further. One, termed *additive,* concerns the mixing of colored light; the other, called *subtractive,* concerns the mixing of pigments.

Additive Color.   Physicists have demonstrated that visible light is re-ally electromagnetic radiation that can be manipulated (see Figure 6.4). A beam of light can be bent with a magnet, and different colors are formed through adjustment of the electromagnetic frequencies. Each color is formed by a different frequency. When all of the frequencies in the visible spectrum are added together, white light is formed. Along the way, some surprises occur. For example, mixing red and green light (adding the fre-quencies) produces yellow light.

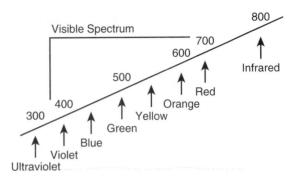

Figure 6.4 Frequencies of Visible Light

The **additive primary colors** of light—red, green, and blue—are the minimum colors necessary to mix all other colors (see Figures 6.5 and CP-3). Inspection of a color television picture reveals that the illusion of a picture is created through the presentation of many thousands of colored dots in sets of three. Each set contains a red, a green, and a blue dot. Varying the intensity of each dot in the set "mixes" a general impression of the desired color.

Subtractive Color.   The other theory of color important to the video producer is that of **subtractive color.** It concerns the mixing of pigments, paints, inks, dyes, and so on. The subtractive primary colors are magenta, cyan, and yellow. In your grade-school watercolor set, you probably knew these subtractive primaries as red, blue, and yellow (red and blue approximate magenta and cyan closely).

Figure 6.5 Additive Primary Colors of Light

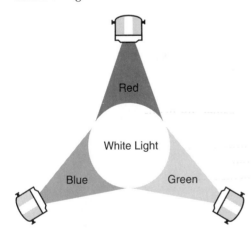

In theory, mixing all the colors in your paint set together would have resulted in black. Why? Because each color really absorbs all of the frequencies of light *except* that which it reflects and therefore appears to be. An orange appears to be orange because it absorbs (and changes into heat) all frequencies except orange. Black absorbs the most frequencies (and generates more heat) than does white (which reflects most frequencies and remains cooler). You have tested the truth of this theory if you have ever walked barefoot on pavement in the summer—the white lines on an asphalt road are always significantly cooler than the black asphalt next to them.

When does an orange not appear orange in color? When it is illuminated by a light containing no orange frequencies to be reflected; green light will do the trick. Under a green light, the orange fruit appears black and no amount of adjusting the intensity of the green light will change the orange from black.

This is extreme, but the principle applies to the illumination of the human face just as clearly. In field production, that illumination can come from the sun and household incandescent lights simultaneously; one side of the subject's face will be in blue light, the other in yellow orange. Skin pigmentation will not be reproduced accurately in video. The nature of the light distorts the reality of the subject. Sometimes this acts in a positive way; most of the time it creates a problem.

Videographers must remember that the subject (a clothed person, in most cases) is a collection of many pigments and that available illumination also is a collection of direct light and light reflected from nearby surfaces, each of which can change the quality of light in the scene. Remember, the *quality* of light (its constituent frequencies) and the *intensity* of light (its overall brightness) are different, and different means of control are necessary. Remember also that light meters measure light intensity, not the quality of light.

Color Temperature

In addition to the relative brightness of objects in a scene and the consequent attention that must be given to the contrast range capabilities of the camera, the videographer must also control or accommodate the quality of light in a scene. Unlike studio production, where this element is under complete control, field production is characterized by a lack of unity in the quality of light, especially when multiple locations are integrated into a single program.

These changing circumstances result in pictures that do not match in important respects, the most obvious being the colors of skin, clothes, grass, bricks, sky, and anything already known to the audience. The reason for this is that the light available in different locations does not consist of the same mix of electromagnetic frequencies. Therefore, a different mix is reflected from the subject to the camera. Remember not to confuse this with brightness or contrast range; it concerns the inherent quality of the light itself, not how much of it there is.

Automatic white balance circuitry in camcorders is designed to adjust the signal as conditions change; thus, video color values are maintained even when different color temperatures dominate the beginning and ending of a single shot. Automatic aperture controls respond to changes in the intensity of light, not to differences in color.

The appearance of color is determined by the pigments present in the object being photographed and the quality of the light illuminating them. What appears to be white light to the human eye does not always appear white to the video camera. For example, consider the qualities of light emitted by a fluorescent light and a standard household light. The household light has a tendency to be redder or warmer than the fluorescent light, which has a cool, blue-green quality. These variations in the quality of what appears to be white light are called differences in **color temperature**, and they are measured in a system of degrees Kelvin (°K). Video cameras are particularly sensitive to changes or differences in the color temperature of light. Some further explanation of this phenomenon is necessary.

Laboratory experimentation has shown that the extent to which a filament is heated (by passing an electric current through it) is related directly to the color it turns and the color of the light it radiates. At low temperatures, the filament glows red and casts a reddish light. Increasing the current increases the heat, and the filament glows yellow. Still more heat causes the filament to become white-hot and to cast a white or seemingly colorless light—a light that contains all frequencies and therefore does not change the appearance of the pigments it illuminates.

To further complicate matters, not only do different types of lighting instruments differ in color temperature (fluorescent versus incandescent versus tungsten-halogen lights, for example) but also they all differ from natural sunlight. In addition, not even sunlight has a constant color temperature—it changes depending on the time of day and the amount of atmosphere, clouds, and smoke it must penetrate to reach us.

Video studio lighting systems solved the problem of color temperature in a simple way. All lighting instruments are matched at 3,200°K so that colors remain constant regardless of camera position or time of day. Because offices, factories, stores, and exteriors are illuminated by a complex range and mix of light sources, this stands as a major difference between studio and remote production. The field videographer must learn to recognize the sources and qualities of illumination available on location and make the necessary adjustments in order to produce pictures with accurate color.

Because handheld color temperature meters, or **kelvinometers,** are not widely used in remote video production, attention continues to be focused on the source of the illumination in question. Rough guides disseminated by equipment manufacturers translate the numerical degrees Kelvin of various light sources into descriptive adjectives that nonphysicists are likely to recognize. Table 6.1 presents a list of common light sources and the color temperature of the light they emit.

White Balance

Adjustment of the video camera for the color temperature of the dominant light source is accomplished either through built-in automatic circuitry or by using the appropriate filter for the lens, and then by *white-balancing* the camera. Built-in **filter wheels** allow the camera operator to accommodate

Table 6.1 Color Temperature of Various Light Sources

Color Temperature[a]	Light Source	General Description
1,800°K	Open flame	Warm (red evident)
2,000°K	Warm-shaded household lamp	
2,800°K	Unshaded frosted white household lamp	
3,200°K	Television studio standard (tungsten-halogen) lamp	
3,500°K	Home-type photo floodlight	
4,800°K	Fluorescent lamp	
5,600°K	Direct sunlight (noon)	
6,500°K	Overcast daylight	
8,000°K	Blue sky	Cool (blue evident)

[a]Color temperature given in degrees Kelvin.

the existing lighting conditions somewhat. Inexpensive cameras may have a simple indoor-outdoor, two-position filter. More expensive cameras typically have filters to accommodate a variety of lighting situations: television-standard tungsten-halogen lights (3,200°K), fluorescent lights (4,800 °K), or a sunny day (5,600°K). In addition, one or more **neutral-density filters** may be built into the filter wheel. These do not change the color temperature of the light but simply reduce the quantity of light hitting the image sensor. They are most frequently used when existing light is simply too bright for the camera to handle (see Figure 6.6).

To adjust the camera for the color temperature of the existing light, a white card is held in front of the camera in the actual light that will be used in the scene or shot. If the camera has automatic white balance circuitry, it is engaged. If not, the correct filter must be selected for the existing conditions. Then, the camera operator zooms in to fill the frame with the white card and sets the **white balance.** On most cameras this is a simple process: the button used to set the white balance is depressed until the appropriate viewfinder display indicates that the camera has adjusted itself to the light. The electronic adjustments automatically made inside the camera guarantee that the white card will have the proper ratio of red, blue, and green in the video signal. Because the camera now knows what white looks like, it will also accurately reproduce any other colors in the scene. This process of white balance adjustment is made with each change of lighting, scene, or location (see Figure CP-4).

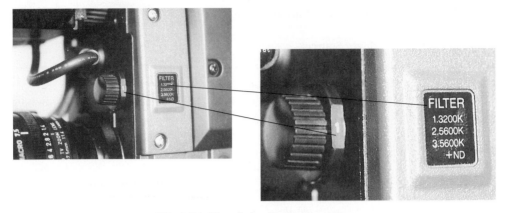

Three-Position Color Correction Filter

1. 3200K = Tungsten-Halogen Light
2. 5600K = Daylight
3. 5600K + ND = Daylight with a Neutral Density Filter

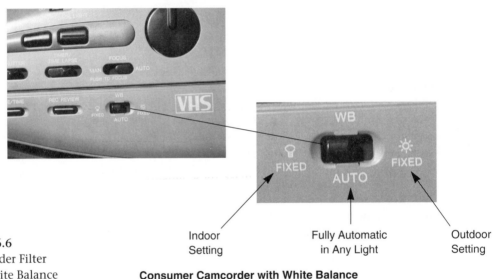

Indoor
Setting

Fully Automatic
in Any Light

Outdoor
Setting

**Consumer Camcorder with White Balance
(WB) Controls**

Figure 6.6
Camcorder Filter
and White Balance
Controls

Gels

In some situations, you can adjust the quality of light found in the field by using filters of one sort or another. The most common types of filters are called **gels**, from the word *gelatin*, which is the substance from which they were made in the past. Today's products are made of plastic or polyester and will not dissolve in the rain. They can be used to cover a window or they can be placed in front of a lighting instrument to change the color temperature of the light passing through it.

Blue gels, or **dichroic filters** (filters that allow only certain frequencies of light to pass), can be applied to lamps emitting light in the range of 2,000 to 4,800°K to convert them to the color temperature of average daylight. This is necessary if you need to augment natural daylight on a scene with additional illumination from tungsten-halogen lamps. Remember, much light intensity is lost with the use of such filters, and more lamps may be necessary to complete the effect.

Similarly, amber gels can be placed on windows to convert the color temperature of the light coming through them on a sunny day to the color temperature of interior lights—but this is not an easy process. The gel must be large enough to cover as much of the window as is visible in the shot, and it must be applied smoothly with no distracting air bubbles or creases that might be visible to the camera.

Neutral-density gels (similar in function to neutral-density lens filters) are available if windows causing brightness problems must appear in the shot. These gels appear to be transparent, but they reduce the amount of light passing through the window into the room without affecting the color temperature.

There are several things to keep in mind if you use gels on a light source: the greater the correction attempted, the less light actually reaches the subject; the less light produced by an instrument, the more instruments needed; the more instruments used, the more power cables, adapters, stands, and electrical circuits needed; the more equipment used, the larger the crew to be hired and the longer the hours they will work; ad infinitum. Clearly, accurate assessment of the problem is needed in the first place, as well as selection of the proper equipment for the job. Those who, through study and experience, can make these judgments correctly are an invaluable production resource.

Lighting Equipment

Obviously the capabilities of the equipment are important in determining the lighting problem. Light can be manipulated to make up for camera shortcomings where base illumination, contrast range, and color temperature are concerned. Of course, each manipulation requires time, and the results may not be known until the finished videotape is later examined on a waveform monitor and vectorscope in the editing facility. These technical devices display data relative to the strength and purity of the signal recorded. Given the small size of the typical field production crew and the

Figure 6.7
Portable Waveform/Picture
Monitor and Vectorscope

premium placed on speed—for example, one ENG crew may cover three stories in a single morning—such technical inspections are not the order of the day.

Portable units containing a color TV and a waveform monitor are widely available. Their use promises to reduce further the quality gap between field and studio production. (See Figure 6.7.)

Basic Lighting Instruments

The videographer must recognize the nature of the light on location as well as the capacity of the portable instruments available. With improvements in light-gathering capacity and contrast range of cameras, changes have been made in basic lighting needs. Increasingly, cloth reflectors have replaced floodlights as the major illuminator. Light reflected from aluminized cloth is used to provide bright yet diffused light that models the subject or reduces the contrast created by deep shadow areas.

The basic lighting instruments used in the field include **spotlights**, which produce a narrow beam of hard-edged light; **floodlights**, which produce a wider beam of soft-edged light; a variety of aluminized fabric reflectors coupled with high-intensity lamps (increasingly lumped together under the category **"soft light"**); and the newly developed portable full-spectrum fluorescent units. Depending on the complexity of the production, the lighting instruments used in the production will vary widely. An ENG cameraperson may well use only one small camera-mounted spotlight to illuminate a single individual who is the subject of an interview. A small-scale EFP crew working on a magazine-style program might use a combination of spotlights and floodlights to illuminate the subject and background areas. On a very large-scale production, a full array of open-face spotlights, reflectors, and diffusers, as well as an electrical power generator, might be employed.

Portable Lighting Instruments

Lamps. Three types of lamps (or bulbs) are commonly found in video lighting instruments. **Incandescent lamps** are similar in construction to common household bulbs. They have a tungsten filament within an evacuated glass bulb and are relatively inexpensive.

Tungsten-halogen lamps, sometimes called *quartz-halogen* or *quartz lights,* are the industry standard and are found in most professional video lighting equipment. The filament in these lamps is tungsten, and the quartz glass bulb is filled with halogen. The halogen prevents the tungsten filament from evaporating and coating the inside of the bulb with particles of tungsten that would affect the color temperature of the light. Unlike conventional incandescent lamps, whose color temperature decreases with age as the glass bulb becomes coated with particles of the filament, the tungsten-halogen lamp maintains a constant color temperature throughout its life (see Figure 6.8).

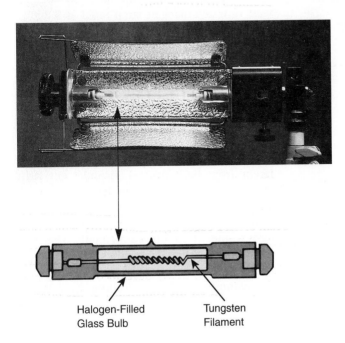

Figure 6.8
Tungsten-Halogen
Lamp

Halogen-Filled
Glass Bulb

Tungsten
Filament

Figure 6.9 Portable Lighting Instruments

Variable-Beam Spotlight with Barn Doors
(Lowell Omni-Light)

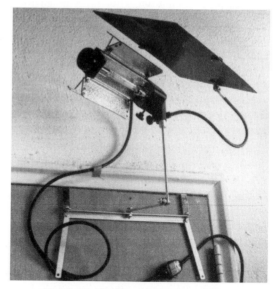

Floodlight with Flag Mounted on a Door
(Lowell Tota-Light)

Floodlight with Gel Mounted on a Floor Stand
(Lowell Tota-Light)

Many instruments in use in the field are open face (have no lens), contain a 500- or 750-watt tungsten-halogen lamp rated at 3,200°K, and operate on common 110-volt, 60-cycle power. The tungsten-halogen lamp must never be touched by bare fingers—if oil from the skin is deposited on the glass, it may cause the bulb to explode when it gets hot.

Fluorescent lamps provide the standard illumination in the American workplace. They have been a problem in video production because their color temperature was so different from both normal incandescent light and daylight. This problem has been solved, and portable equipment now includes fluorescent tubes that produce either 3,200 or 5,600°K light to meet location requirements. The term *luminescent* distinguishes these professional-quality video production instruments from the common fluorescent ceiling fixtures (see Figure 6.9).

Figure 6.9 Continued

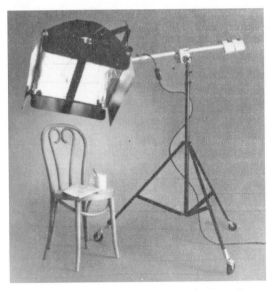

Softlight with Barn Doors (Lowell Softlight 2)

Videssense Portable Luminescent Lights

Fixed- and Variable-Beam Spotlights.

Two types of spotlights are commonly used in remote production: variable-beam and fixed-beam. On *variable-beam spotlights,* the width of the beam of light produced by the instrument can be adjusted by moving a control on the back of the light. This moves the lamp toward or away from the reflective surface inside the instrument, causing the width of the beam to increase or decrease (see Figure 6.10). A narrow beam concentrates all of the light produced by the lamp into a small area and, because it seems to radiate from a single point, the beam has a hard edge. The wider beam spreads that same light energy over a larger area, thus lowering the intensity at any point within the area illuminated. Because the light is reflected from many points on the reflector, it is more diffused and has a softer edge. *Fixed-beam spotlights* do not allow adjustment of the beam width and beam intensity.

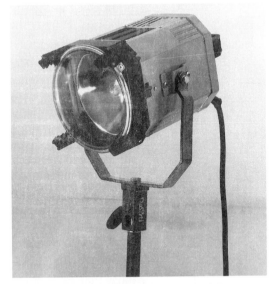

DeSisti 200-Watt Portable HMI Light

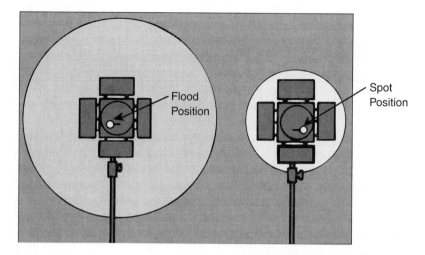

Figure 6.10 Changing Light Intensity with an Adjustable-Beam Instrument

Most spotlights are equipped with **barn doors**. These metal flaps can be attached to the instrument to control the shape of the beam of light. They are useful in restricting light from selected parts of a scene.

Light Quality—Hard and Soft Light.

Variable- and fixed-beam spotlights are designed to cast a hard light, one that creates sharp-edged shadows. The light created is highly directional, which is good for modeling—delineating the three-dimensional nature of people and objects. This was important given the relative insensitivity of early television cameras.

The more sensitive cameras in use today have allowed video lighting directors to develop lighting techniques that take much greater advantage of soft light. Soft light is less directional and produces fewer shadows than hard light. The shadow areas that are produced tend to be lighter and more transparent than the harsh, dark shadows that characterize hard light.

Soft Lights.

A variety of folding-reflector floodlights are available today that are extremely useful to the field producer. The cloth reflector is aluminized or coated with other highly reflective substances and stretched over a tent-like frame. Known as **soft lights**, they provide a bright light that is even more shadow-free than that produced by open-face floodlights. When erected, they occupy more workspace than do open-face floodlights but produce superior illumination.

Lighting Umbrellas.   Lighting umbrellas are widely used in conjunction with open-face spotlights to soften and diffuse the quality of light produced by those instruments. The small umbrella is opened and attached to the lighting instrument. As is the case with a soft light, the lamp faces into the umbrella, which then reflects the light out to the subject. The quality of the light that results from this technique is much softer and less harsh than the quality of light produced by the same instrument aimed directly at the subject (see Figure 6.11).

Fluorescent Lights.   Fluorescent light has been improved to the point that several companies are competing to provide such equipment to the field production market. Used to augment existing conditions, units are available to match either tungsten, at 3,200°K, or daylight, at 5,600°K. (See Figure 6.12.) Additionally, these new units require little electrical power, generate little heat, are marketed in a variety of sizes (down to 4" tubes), and have remote ballasts, all of which make them ideal in the smallest of locations (see Figure 6.13).

Figure 6.11   Spotlight and Umbrella Combination

Figure 6.12   Fluorescent Instruments at Work in the Field

In order to provide a more focused quality of light capable of producing slightly harder shadows and modeling effects, some fluorescent instruments can be equipped with a clear plastic focusing lens. Aluminum or
plastic grids or louvers that resemble a honeycomb can be attached to the
front of the fixture to reduce the amount of spill light by providing more
control over where the light falls. (See Figure 6.14.)

One drawback to the use of fluorescent lights is that the intensity of
the light they produce is rather weak. Therefore, they are most effective
when positioned relatively close to the subject being photographed.

Halogen-Metal-Iodide Lights.   A problem is created when natural
light in an exterior scene proves to be insufficient and needs to be boosted.
The AC-powered tungsten-halogen spotlights and floodlights provide the
wrong color temperature (3,200°K), and the mix with natural daylight

Figure 6.13 Small
Fluorescent Instrument

(5,600°K) may prove troublesome. Dichroic filters are available to convert the 3,200°K to 5,600°K—close enough to the color temperature of daylight for video purposes—but then additional instruments may be necessary.

The industry responded to this problem with a filterable light to serve such field production purposes, the halogen-metal-iodide (HMI) light. It is twice as efficient in terms of foot-candles per watt as tungsten as a basic source of illumination and four times as efficient when tungsten is filtered from 3,200°K to the equivalent of daylight. The special needs of the small-crew videographer led to the development of lighter-weight power transformers and of an adjustable-beam PAR unit (a parabolic reflector molded around a filament into a single lamp), which combines the focus advantages of an external lens with a lamp powerful enough to be effective in scenes dominated by direct sunlight. (See Figure 6.9.)

Figure 6.14 Reflectors and Louvers Help Focus Fluorescent Light

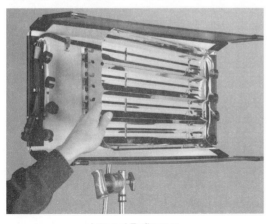

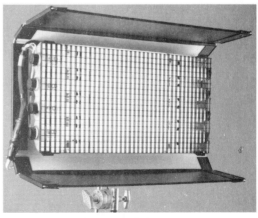

Internal Reflectors   Honeycomb Louver

167

Reflectors. A variety of reflectors are available to the field videographer. The principles upon which they operate are simple (see Figure 6.15), and they can be constructed at home with excellent results. Commercial products are often sturdier than homemade reflectors, but to make your own, you need only find a piece of cardboard or styrofoam at least three feet by three feet. (Cardboard curls and styrofoam breaks, so commercial products do have an advantage.) Glue aluminum foil to one side of a sheet of cardboard, avoid wrinkles, and make it as flat and shiny as possible. This will reflect a hard light. To the other side, glue a pebble-grained or finely wrinkled foil, which will diffuse the light it reflects and soften the edges of the shadows. Because aluminum foil is silver in color, it will not affect color temperature much.

Figure 6.15
Using a Hand-Held
Reflector

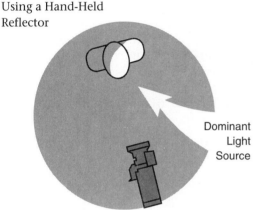

A Dominant Light Source Produces a Harsh Shadow.

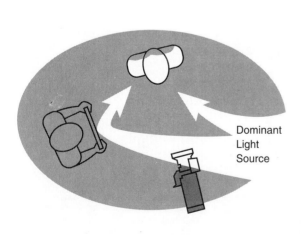

A Reflector Can Be Used to Reduce the Shadow Area.

Circular automobile windshield sunlight reflectors also work well and are available at a fraction of the cost of commercial reflectors purchased through photographic supply houses. White styrofoam by itself is an effective reflector; the light reflected is soft and lightens the shadows on the subject's face. However, it is easily damaged by clamps and it soils from everyday use. A white bedsheet can be used to reflect or diffuse sunlight, and a lightweight frame can be constructed to hold it.

Colored reflectors, usually gold, are available commercially or can be constructed for specific purposes. The light they reflect is warm and can match the color temperatures associated with open flame, sunsets, and incandescent lights.

Diffusers.   Light diffusers, also called **scrims**, are often used in field production to change the amount and quality of light in a scene. Professional lighting instruments are fitted with frames or slots to hold these diffusers, although a wooden clothespin can safely be used to hold a diffuser in front of a lamp that lacks such a feature.

Common aluminum window screening can be placed in front of a lamp to reduce its effective intensity and soften the edges of shadows slightly without changing the color temperature of the light appreciably. Several layers of screen can be used if the problem is extreme. The commercial diffusers on the market provide a more subtle range of control.

Silks are giant diffusers used to control light intensity and color temperature in outdoor productions. They are used like an awning or tent—above the picture and situated to filter all the light from the sky. Because they are difficult to rig and keep in adjustment (especially in the wind), they are associated only with the most expensive productions. At best, they facilitate production in bright sunlight by creating the even effect of a hazy day. A simple-to-make alternative can be constructed by taping the diffusion material to PVC pipe and assigning it to one or two crew members to keep between the sun and the subject—a challenge during a windy day at the beach!

Flags.   The well-equipped field producer may also have a variety of flags. **Flags** are opaque cards of assorted sizes that have handles which can be clamped to floor stands and other equipment to create a shadow by interrupting a beam of light. They are often used to keep the light of one instrument from illuminating the wrong part of a set or to keep sunlight off a subject.

Light Supports

When external lights such as those previously described are used in remote productions, some means of supporting the lights must be provided. Typically, one of the three following methods is chosen.

Floor Stands.   Most portable lights can be attached to telescoping **floor stands.** These stands are usually made of lightweight aluminum, and they provide a reasonable amount of stability for the lighting instrument. Because they telescope upward, the height of the lighting instrument can be adjusted to control the angle of light as it falls on the subject. Counter-weighted booms are increasingly used to place instruments exactly where they are needed. One word of caution: The higher the stands are extended, the more unstable they tend to become. Be careful not to bump into the stand or tug on the power cord, as even a slight force may cause the light and stand to fall.

Camera Mounts.   Camera-mounted lights attach directly to the camera and operate from battery power (see Figure 6.16). They are widely used in electronic news gathering (ENG) production activities to provide quick illumination of the reporter or interview subject in those situations when an additional crew member is not available to assist with lighting, or when necessary movement of the camera or the on-camera reporter/interviewee makes it impossible to set up fixed-position lighting instruments. Camera-mounted lights can produce harsh shadows on backgrounds and over-bright faces that lack recognizable features, unless they are controlled properly. Increasingly, camera-mounted lights are equipped with diffusion filters to produce a softer quality of light.

Handheld Supports.   Handheld lights are often used in remote pro-ductions. The lighting instrument or reflector can be positioned to fit the needs of the scene and to enhance the modeling of the subject.

Figure 6.16
Camera-Mounted Light

Sony 9WS Betacam SX™ Camcorder

Power Requirements

Electrical power for lights and camcorders is not available at every remote location. Although offices, hospitals, and factories have sufficient power available for video production, the outlets may not be in the most convenient locations, and several power cables and adapters may be needed. Permission to lay such cable in hallways may be required and may be granted only if rubber mats are taped in place over the cables as a pedestrian safety measure. Other locations, such as exteriors and some interiors in old buildings or warehouses, may not have any electrical power available. In these cases, the videographer must augment natural light with mechanical means, such as reflectors, or rely on battery-powered instruments.

Each solution has its limitations. There may be insufficient light to reflect, especially in late afternoon or at night, and batteries are reliable for only minutes, not hours. Lighting instruments lose intensity and the color temperature drops as batteries weaken. The time constraints of ENG make battery-powered lighting instruments useful on an individual production basis, but they may become a source of concern if a number of stories are to be covered in a single morning. ENG crews carry replacement batteries because of their short service life, and as soon as the crews return to the station, they immediately begin recharging the batteries. Many ENG vans are equipped with a rack of batteries and a battery-charging system so that a ready source of battery power is always on hand.

Formula for Alternating-Current Power

The videographer must also consider the capacity of the alternating current (AC) electrical circuits available. Depending on the wattage of the lamps being used, two or three instruments may be powered by one household circuit. If at all possible, cameras and audio equipment should be powered on circuits separate from lighting instruments (and refrigerators, microwaves, computers, space heaters, etc.) so that the act of turning the camera on will not overload a circuit already operating at capacity.

You can calculate how much power is available to you by using a simple formula:

watts = amps × volts

To use this formula, first determine the number of amps that the electrical circuit is rated for. In most homes and offices, standard 15-amp circuits are in place. (The amp rating is listed on the fuse box or circuit breaker.) The

171

line voltage of most household electrical power in the United States is 110 volts. Therefore, you can determine the wattage of the circuit by plugging the numbers into the equation. Because watts = amps × volts, using the figures above, your circuit would deliver 1,650 watts (15 amps × 110 volts).

Next, examine your lighting instruments. If you have 650-watt lamps, you will be able to run only two of them safely on any one circuit (2 × 650 watts = 1,300 watts). Three lamps will blow the fuse or trip the circuit breaker because they will exceed the capacity of the line (3 × 650 watts = 1,950 watts).

Outlets and Circuits

Most rooms have a number of electrical outlets but seldom more than two circuits or electrical lines. A room with four outlets is typically arranged so that there are two outlets each on two different circuits (see Figure 6.17). An easy way to determine whether different outlets are on the same or different circuits involves the use of a simple light. Plug a light into an outlet and then turn off the circuit breakers one at a time at the main power source. When the light goes out, you will know which circuit it is on and which circuit breaker controls it. Repeat the procedure for all the outlets in the room. If there are multiple electrical lines (circuits) in the room, you will be able to identify each, the outlets on each circuit, and the circuit breakers that control them.

In calculating the amount of power you need, don't forget to compute the power drawn by the camcorder—it can be found among the list of technical specifications in the operating instructions manual.

Figure 6.17   Electrical Circuits and Outlets

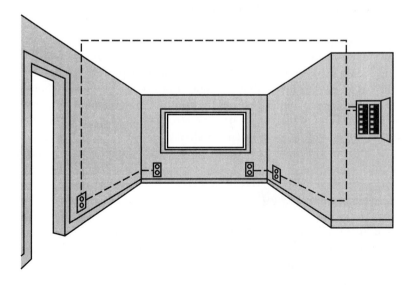

Controlling the Intensity of Light

Light intensity can be adjusted through the use of dimmers, by varying the beam width on those instruments with focus controls, by changing the lamp-to-subject distance, and through the use of diffusers.

Dimmers

Dimmers work by varying the wattage supplied to the lighting instrument. In this way, the intensity of the light can easily be changed. If a light is too bright, the wattage can be reduced until the light is at the proper intensity. Dimmers are extensively used in television studio production; however, they are seldom used in field production because of their weight and size.

It is just as well that dimmers are not carried in the field because they can affect the color temperature of the lamps being dimmed. As a lamp is dimmed, the color temperature decreases and the light it produces becomes progressively redder. The effect is more noticeable on incandescent lamps than on tungsten-halogen lamps, but it is nonetheless present for both. Videographers should not attempt to dim a lamp more than 10 percent of its brightness—beyond this, the color shift will affect picture quality.

Varied Beam Width

The variable beam found on many portable spotlights is extremely valuable for field production. Without changing the position of the instrument, the intensity of the light can be increased or decreased by adjusting the beam width. No dimmers are involved, and the light generated by a constant flow of electrical power (no color shift) can be spread widely or focused on a narrow area. The intensity of the light at any point within the beam depends on how concentrated the beam is.

Lamp-to-Subject Distance

Another easy way of altering the intensity of a specific light source involves simply moving the light. A change in the distance from the lamp to the subject affects the intensity of the light falling on the subject. Doubling the distance reduces the intensity of the light reaching the subject to one-fourth of its original strength (see Figure 6.18). This is the **inverse square rule**, and it is an important tool in remote video production (see Appendix 3).

Figure 6.18
Inverse Square Rule

|←X→|

Distance X
Intensity Y

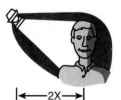

|←—2X—→|

Distance 2X
Intensity $\frac{Y}{4}$

173

Adjusting the lamp-to-subject distance is often the most effective way of changing the intensity of a light that does not have the variable-beam feature. However, adjusting the lamp-to-subject distance often has a negative side effect: the angle of the light relative to the subject also changes, and with it, aesthetic properties are changed. This will be discussed in greater detail later in this chapter.

Diffusers

As was discussed earlier, the intensity of light can be reduced by placing a fiberglass or screen diffuser between the source and the subject. Screens can be built up by adding layers at precise points to control different areas of the scene illuminated by a single instrument. Videographers are well advised to examine the entire array of products available from commercial photographic supply houses.

Other Equipment

Every list of the remote video producer's equipment includes two essential items: duct tape and aluminum foil. The uses for the tape are many and constant; subjects who cannot remain in position or in the light can even have their shoes taped to the floor! Aluminum foil can be used to extend barn doors on lighting instruments, to act as a hard or semisoft reflector, or to flag an errant light source.

Even the most exotic locations may benefit from some special applications of light. Geometric or nature-like shadows can be projected onto both on-camera talent and backgrounds to add to an effect. The egg-crate-type spill reducers mounted on some fluorescent units can be used with other instruments to generate an interesting pattern of light and shadow on an otherwise featureless wall.

Figure 6.19 Three-to-Two-Prong AC Adapter

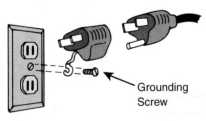

Grounding Screw

Caution: Always Connect the Ground Wire to the Screw in the Center of the Outlet Faceplate.

Finally, three-to-two-prong adapters are of paramount importance when using locations in older parts of town (see Figure 6.19). All professional lighting equipment comes equipped with the familiar three-pronged plug. However, many older homes and offices are still outfitted with two-pronged outlets. Safe operation of electronic equipment requires that all equipment be grounded properly. This is the function of the round third prong on three-prong plugs. Failure to properly ground electronic equipment may result in damage to the equipment and severe electrical shock to anyone who comes into contact with the equipment. *Under no circumstances should the ground pin be removed from a power cable to enable a three-pronged plug to be connected to a two-pronged outlet.*

The astute field producer always carries a number of these three-to-two-prong adapters to ensure a fast and safe AC hookup. After connecting the adapter to the three-pronged plug on the power cable to your equipment, be sure to connect the small wire or clip on the adapter to the small center screw on the faceplate of the electrical outlet. If the outlet has been installed properly, connection of this ground wire or clip will effectively ground your equipment.

Lighting Safety

A few practical warnings are in order with respect to lighting safety. Caution is imperative when lighting on location. For this reason, it is usually best to delegate responsibility for lighting supervision to one member of the crew who will see to it that safety requirements are met. Consider the following points when lighting on location:

1. *Do not overload electrical circuits.* Always calculate the amount of power your lighting instruments draw, and compare that with the amount of power the electrical circuits deliver. At best, an overloaded circuit can result in a blown fuse or circuit breaker; at worst, the outcome is a fire.

2. *Make sure all electrical cables are properly grounded.* Always connect three-pronged plugs to grounded outlets. If you must use a three-to-two-prong adapter, always connect the ground wire or clip on the adapter to the center screw on the faceplate of the electrical outlet.

3. *Keep fingers off tungsten-halogen lamps.* Finger oil on the quartz bulb may cause the lamp to explode. Always use a soft cloth or the piece of foam rubber supplied with the lamp to shield it from your skin if you have to touch the lamp (for example, when replacing a burned-out lamp).

4. *Make sure lights are securely mounted.* If you are using floor stands, make sure that the telescoping rods are securely fastened. If possible, tape the floor stand down. Tape the electrical cord to the floor at the base of the floor stand; if someone accidentally pulls on the cord, the shock will be absorbed by the tape and the light might remain standing.

5. *Keep the face of the lighting instrument a safe distance away from any flammable surface.* Lights get extremely hot. Be careful when operating them near draperies or any other flammable material. Keep lights a good distance away from people, and after your shoot, make sure you do not touch an instrument until it has cooled down.

fire

6. *Carry insulated electrician's gloves.* If you have to move a hot light in an emergency, insulated gloves will protect you from the instrument's heat.

burn

Always observe the standard rules of electrical safety. Avoid water, tape exposed wires, tape all cable securely to floor or walls, and try to keep children and animals well away from electrical equipment.

PART TWO
Aesthetic Factors

Modeling

Once the videographer recognizes the principles of illumination, the camera requirements, and the capacities of the lighting equipment, attention can be focused on the aesthetic factors of lighting. These make the picture effective in the context of the news being reported, the report being submitted, or the story being told. Chief among these aesthetic factors is creating an illusion of space and of three-dimensional subjects and objects on the two-dimensional piece of glass that is the television screen. The process of creating this illusion through lighting is called **modeling**.

Scenic painters and grade-school artists approach the problem of illustrating space in the same way: they simply invent objects and relationships that illustrate the idea. The field videographer, however, must use real elements of the existing location to capture the illusion of depth and bring it to the viewer's attention. Many techniques are available: the use of diminishing size, overlapping planes, changing focus, darkening colors, diminishing brightness, and differences in apparent movement linked with distance from the viewer. In addition, the video artist can enhance the separation of objects by contrasting their apparent textures.

Remember, the viewer is not a static, unfeeling being; the viewer wants to experience the dynamic qualities of the special location you are using. The successful videographer, through manipulation of the elements in the picture, provides an unusual experience for the viewer. This is as true in the presentation of the workings of an automobile assembly plant as it is in the presentation of eggs in a bird's nest.

Illumination

Much of the special feeling we can generate for familiar objects is related to the manner in which they are presented. For example, the pinecone is a common, undistinguished brown object found throughout the forest. Some may even believe it litters paths and, along with dead leaves and decomposing matter, contributes to the generally unkempt appearance of things. But remove this pinecone from the forest, place it in a gallery on a polished black marble pedestal in front of a soft ivory wall, illuminate it with a single shaft of light from above, and you will have produced art. By its presentation, the viewer can savor its eternal qualities and the genius of its design. So it can be with the presentation of people and objects via the video medium. Light can dominate our attention, describe form, and express mood.

Attention to the base illumination requirements of cameras has led to the observation (often true) that the picture appears flat and lifeless. Base illumination is half of the lighting problem; modeling is the other. **Base illumination** is light that is everywhere but that comes from no particular direction. Away from direct sunlight, nature creates this effect; with a collection of floodlights and reflectors, we can achieve the same effect. Instruments are placed so that the same intensity of light reaches every object in the scene and so that shadows caused by one instrument are neutralized by light from another. The even brightness provides no clues to the relative placement, dimension, shapes, or surface textures of the objects.

By varying the illumination, the videographer can invite attention to one object among many. Generally, the eye is attracted to the brightest object in the scene unless that impulse is countered through manipulation of focus or framing. The human face is most often the brightest object in a scene, and it is usually photographed in a way that reinforces its importance: from a medium close-up or close-up camera angle, with the face in sharp focus and the background slightly out of focus.

Directional Light

Careful control of relative brightness can enhance the visibility of objects, but it is not the whole solution to the problem. In nature, the directional quality of sunlight creates the pattern of highlights and shadows that describes solid objects. This same sunlight is reflected throughout the scene (from haze, clouds, foliage, walls, etc.) to provide the base illumination as well. The videographer selects camera angles that allow the sun (or other dominant directional light source) to cast the most recognizable pattern of highlights and shadows—to define the structure of objects in the scene (see Figure 6.20).

The pattern of shadows created by the directional light depends on the hardness of the light (the extent to which it represents illumination ra-

Figure 6.20
Shadows Created by Directional
Sunlight Reveal the Structure of
an Object

diating from a single point) and the relative positions of the subject, the light, and the camera. The illusion of depth is a function of the contours of the object, the camera positions, and this dominant light. Because of its importance, it is termed the **key light.** Remember, there is no standard position for this source: its effectiveness is relative to the position of the camera and the desired effect. Audiences are familiar with this function of sunlight and expect it to dominate scenes. Videographers creating a second set of shadows in conflict with sunlight, whether in outdoor scenes or sunbathed office settings, will be distracting these audiences.

Camera Position

Video production is complicated by the use of several camera angles in a given scene or interview. To light the scene effectively from one camera angle is to weaken the effect from another angle. If time is not a factor and coverage is of continuing action—live action that can be restaged—video producers can use **film-style lighting**, also called *single-camera lighting*. That means each scene is lit for each camera angle. In film-style lighting, the lighting setup is changed each time the camera position is changed, and lighting is done shot by shot. Film-style lighting gives the video producer a great deal of control over the lighting within a production. However, such attention to lighting detail has a price: time. Film-style lighting is a slow and meticulous process.

To get the most out of a given situation or location, the field videographer determines where the camera is going to be placed before attempting to light the scene. If multiple angles are to be used, all camera positions must be determined before the lighting is set. In this process, the greatest attention should be given to the close-up shots that will be of prime importance to the interview or story.

What factors determine camera position? First, the producer considers the reason for the choice of location. If that reason encompasses more than the location of a certain person and includes interest in a specific activity or facility, the camera must be placed where that action or facility can be seen and understood by viewers. The atmosphere of the actual location should be communicated to the viewer. The videographer's task is to provide more than what is already common knowledge to the viewers and more than what is possible in the studio.

Once the optimum angle or angles are chosen, an inventory of possible distractions should be made. Are there brightly illuminated windows in the background that could cause contrast range problems in the picture? Are there highly reflective glass or metallic surfaces that could ruin the picture? Next, are sufficient circuits available to power the instruments necessary to the videotaping? Is there enough room for the necessary lighting instruments? Will the instruments be too close to the subjects to maintain control of brightness? When these questions are answered satisfactorily, the production can proceed. The ENG producer has as little as five minutes to make these decisions; the EFP producer will visit the site prior to the production date to survey the location so these questions can be answered.

Three-Point Lighting

In theory, lighting to create the illusion of the third dimension involves three tasks: establishing the form (the key light), reducing the intensity of the shadows created by the key light (the fill light or lights), and separating the object from its background (the backlight). This technique is known as **three-point lighting** (see Figure 6.21).

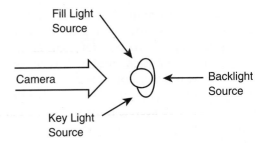

Figure 6.21 Three-Point Lighting Diagram

It is important to understand that these "three points" identify the functions of light that you will need to manipulate to produce the desired effect. Field production differs from studio production in that some light or combinations of sources of illumination already exist and are identifiable as part of that remote location. The challenge is to gain control of the lighting conditions by augmenting the existing illumination to produce the desired lighting effect. In studio production, illumination must be created in its entirety through the use of the appropriate lighting instruments, each of which may fulfill one of these principal lighting functions.

The augmentation of existing, or "location," light may address concerns with base illumination, modeling of subjects, apparent forms or textures of objects in the scene, the range of light-dark contrast in the scene, or a need to separate a subject from the background. Control of these functions of light can require the use of extra lighting instruments, reflectors, and diffusers. Such control may also involve staging action in a different direction relative to location light sources, such as waiting for clouds to move or the sun to progress a few degrees. Does all this seem complicated? It can be unless you scout the location well ahead of the scheduled shoot.

Key Light

The **key light** is the brightest, and therefore often the most important, light on a scene. The key light has the primary responsibility for establishing the form of the object being videotaped. It does this by providing bright illumination for the subject and by producing the shadows on the object. In many situations, it is the distribution of shadows on an object or in a texture, rather than general illumination itself, that provides the most significant information about the object's form.

As a consequence of viewing television for some 50 years or so, the public has come to expect certain types of presentations. News or formal announcements are commonly delivered by a person facing the camera in a studio setting—in nowhere, so to speak. A medium shot or medium close-up is used. There is nothing of note concerning time or place. One announcement looks like any other, regardless of the television channel or time of day. The key light conveys no expositional information and the subject is meant to appear absolutely normal, as if it were about 2:30 in the afternoon on a hazy day. To accomplish this, the key light is placed on a line from 30 to 45 degrees above the camera-subject axis and from 30 to 45 degrees to the right or left of that axis (see Figure 6.22). A pattern of highlights and shadows created by the key light on the face of the subject that makes the subject appear normal is found somewhere within these angles (see Figure 6.23).

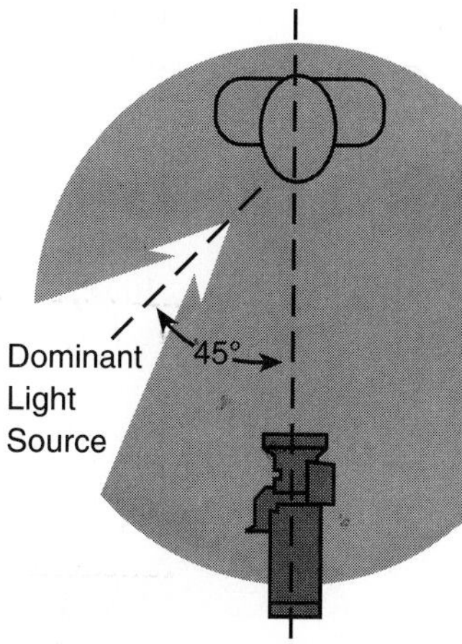

For many field production situations, this type of lighting may be all that is needed. If there is sufficient existing light for proper camera operation, and if the production features only one camera angle and one reporter in a city hall lobby, a single key light source might provide enough modeling, brightness contrast, and sparkle to do the job.

Figure 6.22 Typical Angle of Key Light

If the scene is to be shot outside on the steps, the reporter should be placed so that the sun acts as the key light. If the steps are out of the direct sunshine, the key light might be in the form of a reflection from a nearby white wall or a portable reflector (aluminum or white) held outside the field of view of the camera. Remember to adjust the camera filter for daylight. If a lighting instrument is used in this situation, a gel may be necessary to maintain a constant color temperature by converting the color temperature of the instrument to the color temperature of daylight.

Fill Light

Many scenes are more complex than this and involve the use of several lighting instruments. In a location that is too dark for video production, using only a key light might aggravate the situation by creating extreme contrasts between highlights and shadows. You may be tempted to use two bright lights, one on each side of the camera axis. This will illuminate the subject, but if the lights are of equal intensity, the effect of modeling will be neutralized completely.

The solution to the problem lies in the use of a fill light to control the degree of light-to-dark contrast within the scene while allowing the key light to describe the structure or texture of the subject or object. **Fill lights** increase the overall light level on a scene and fill in somewhat, but not completely, the shadows created on the subject by the key light (see Figure 6.23). Fill lights should be adjusted to produce from one-half to three-fourths of the intensity of the key light. Set the intensity of the fill light no lower than the base illumination level required for the camera. It may be higher if it is used in a portion of the scene that should be brighter than the rest for purposes of attracting attention.

Color television production of the past was notorious for its use—and in many cases, overuse—of fill light. This situation evolved because of the problems many older-generation color cameras had in accurately reproducing colors in shadow areas. Rather than reproducing a shadow area simply as a darker shade of the same color in a lit area, quite often a color

Figure 6.23   Effects of Three-Point Lighting

Effect of Key Light

Effect of Fill Light

Effect of Backlight

Effect of Key, Fill, and Backlights

shift or video noise occurred in the shadow area. To prevent such unsightly distractions, enormous amounts of fill light were added to eliminate shadows altogether. The practice also acted to reduce the time it took to set up a scene and, for that reason, still characterizes some network-level production (e.g., situation comedies).

Fortunately, the rapid improvement in light-gathering capacity of field cameras (represented by the CCD technology) reduced the need for so many picture-flattening fill lights. The subtle blending of skin tones from highlight to shadow is captured effectively by most cameras using only one soft light to augment natural illumination of the scene.

Whether the key light is provided by the sun or a lighting instrument, look closely at the shadow area to determine whether fill light needs to be added by an additional instrument or through the use of a reflector.

Backlight

The **backlight** has two functions: it separates the subject from the background by outlining the subject's head and shoulders with a thin line of bright light; and it supports the modeling effect by describing facets of the form untouched by the key light, which reveals the dominant structure (see Figure 6.23). The backlight is extremely valuable in giving form to hair or clothing that would otherwise blend into the background. Because so little of it is reflected to the lens, the backlight is maintained at an intensity level at least equal to that of the key light, and often brighter. It is placed behind and well above the subject. If it is placed too high, it will illuminate the subject's hair and nose out of proportion to the rest of the picture. If it is too low, its light on the subject will be lost to the camera. If it is even lower, it will radiate light directly into the lens and produce distracting lens flare.

The position of the backlight (or separation light) presents a real challenge to the field videographer. Because most portable lights are mounted on floor stands, a backlight set up directly behind the subject may appear in the shot. Two other solutions to the problem are commonly used. The backlight can be suspended above and behind the subject rather than mounted on a stand. This should put it out of the camera's field of view. (Make sure the light is fastened securely.) Another solution is to use **bounce light** as backlight. Aim a lighting instrument at the ceiling or the wall behind the subject so that the light bounces off that surface onto the back of the subject. If the rear wall is used as the reflecting surface, make certain that it does not appear in the shot, as it will undoubtedly be too bright and will create a distraction. If a backlight cannot be positioned satisfactorily, the use of a background light to illuminate the background behind the subject and to provide separation via brightness contrast can be an effective solution to the problem.

183

Three-Point Lighting: Ideal versus Real

The ideal concept of three-point lighting is easily illustrated, but in reality, the lighting setup may differ considerably from the ideal. Ultimately, the final decision about whether the lighting has been set correctly is a subjective one that should be made on the basis of how the scene looks on camera (or on a monitor), not by whether the position and intensity of the various lights correspond to the ideal formula for three-point lighting (see Figure 6.23). The lighting relationships previously discussed, then, provide a point at which to begin lighting a scene rather than the point at which one must always end.

Motivated and Unmotivated Lights

Key lights, backlights, or both can be motivated or unmotivated. *Motivated lights* are related to a light source identified with the specific location, such as a window to the sunlit world, a streetlight, or the flashing lights on an emergency vehicle. The audience is conscious of its presence (assuming the videographer lets the audience see the remote location in an establishing shot). *Unmotivated lights,* like those in a flatly lit news set, are simply present to provide illumination for the scene. They are not defined by a motivating source, e.g., the sun.

Light passing through windows is often important to shots on location, and it often generates production opportunities as well as problems. If the sunlight coming through a window dominates the scene, all other light sources and the camera itself must be adjusted to the color temperature of the sun at that moment. This can be a costly process in terms of both time and equipment because the color temperature of sunlight varies with time of day and atmospheric conditions. If the sunlight cannot be allowed to dominate the scene, windows must be covered by color-correcting gel or curtains, and furniture must be moved to keep the sunlight out of the picture. Repositioning the camera is also often necessary.

Table or desk lights solve the problem of identifying a motivating light. If the lamp has a translucent shade, or if the light from it strikes an object close by, it will violate the contrast range limits of the shot and create a major visual distraction. If the light is necessary to the scene, it is customary to place a low-intensity bulb in it for effect (and to reduce color temperature complications) and to apply directional lights from outside the scene. Be careful to avoid casting on the wall a full shadow of the lamp that is supposed to appear to be illuminating the scene. (In reality, table lamps seldom cast full shadows of themselves on nearby walls.)

Lighting for Texture

In addition to controlling the brightness of the background relative to the subject, care must be taken to bring out any textures or architectural features that contrast with the subject. This makes the whole scene more interesting and adds to the visibility of the subject. Base illumination alone usually does not make the actual textures apparent to the viewer.

Just as a directional light is needed to model a human face, a directional light is also needed to create a pattern of highlights and shadows that form a recognizable texture. The closer this directional light comes to paralleling the plane of the background (skimming the surface of the background), the more visible the shadows become (see Figure 6.24). Draperies, tile, brick, paneling, cork, and plaster all have recognizable textures that contrast effectively with the human face. This background element is important for identifying the spatial quality of the location and should be featured.

The directional light used to reveal natural texture is most effective if it seems to come from an existing motivating element—commonly a lamp or window. A wall next to a window is often chosen to serve as a background for two reasons. First, the window is a troublesome background (it often creates brightness and color temperature problems), and second, it can act as a mirror and reflect the production crew back to the camera. Light coming from a window and falling on an adjacent wall skims the surface of that wall and provides the desired texture effect. Such background light seldom creates a color temperature problem because the audience will not know what color the wall was supposed to be. Care must be taken to keep the subject away from such a background so that the shadows indicating texture are not washed out by illumination of the subject.

Figure 6.24   Lighting for Texture

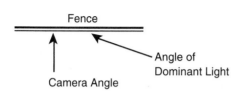

Directional Light Reveals the Texture
of this Fence.

Background Shadows

When selecting the camera position, which influences the location of any instruments necessary to augment local illumination, the videographer must be careful to put as much space as possible between the subject and the background. The greater the space, the less likely the shadow of the subject will appear on the wall. In the minds and experience of the audience, such a shadow is unusual and calls attention to the facts of the production rather than to its purpose. Note also that the smaller the office or other location, the more difficult it is to control all the elements that may affect the picture quality. When each pictorial improvement brings distractions with it, it may be best to concentrate on the subject's face and to keep everything else gently out of focus. Lower-than-normal light levels facilitate this. In such a situation, the f-stop on the lens will have to be opened and, as a consequence, the depth of field will become shallower.

Using Background Light to Indicate Time and Mood

Background light is probably the most important lighting variable that can be manipulated to influence the viewer's perception of the time of day or mood of a scene. **Background light** is different from backlight; background light falls on the background of a scene, not on the subject.

Our everyday experience tells us that there is a big difference between day and night in terms of light. If video cameras processed light as efficiently as the human eye, creating the illusion of night would be relatively simple—we could simply turn off all the lights. Unfortunately, when this is done, the camera no longer produces a usable picture.

The key to creating the illusion of night lies in control of the background light. A scene set at night should have a fairly dark background, even if it takes place indoors. A scene taking place during the day should have a bright background. In either scene, night or day, the foreground illumination should provide enough light to satisfy the minimum baselight requirements of the camera. Foreground shadows and automobile lights in the distance help to complete the illusion of night outdoors.

Similarly, background light can be an effective determinant of mood. Bright backgrounds, typical of daytime, tend to be bright also in mood. Dark backgrounds, on the other hand, introduce significantly more contrast into a shot or scene and are somewhat more ominous and mysterious. Again, in both scenes, the foreground lighting may remain constant from one situation to the next. It is the background light that determines whether the scene is a bright, happy comedy or a deep, dark mystery or drama.

The visual impact of interviews conducted in rooms with drab-looking walls or drapes can be markedly improved by adding some color to the shot. Attach a colored gel to a spotlight and position it to illuminate the background behind the subject. Used in conjunction with a pattern, or focused to bring out the texture in the background, this can produce a very dynamic and visually interesting effect.

Lighting Problems

Multiple Subjects

Thus far, we have focused on the problem of lighting a single subject in a remote location. Illuminating a conversation between two subjects poses several problems. First, at least two camera angles may be used. Second, there may not be enough lights, circuits, or time to light each subject separately.

The videographer will probably not place the camera perpendicular to the subject-to-subject axis because this results in all close-ups being profiles of each subject (the great American ear shot). Also, from this camera position, wider shots place the subjects at opposite ends of the screen, like bookends. This camera position lacks any dynamic quality and is useful only in expressing a static situation between two antagonists. The practice of placing the lighting instruments next to the camera or of keeping the bright sun behind the camera makes the resulting picture even more bland. The faces will appear flat and featureless. Avoid this setup (see Figure 6.25).

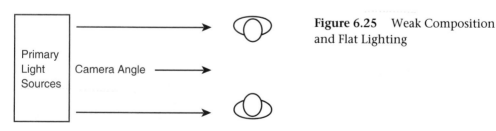

Figure 6.25   Weak Composition and Flat Lighting

When the Light Source Is Parallel to the Camera Angle, Minimal Shadows are Created, "Flattening" the Contours of Faces.

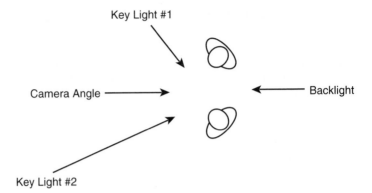

Figure 6.26 Lighting for Standard Composition: Cross-Keying

A second method the videographer might follow is the common studio practice of facing the subjects at a 90-degree angle to each other. This allows close-ups of each face and provides a pleasing two-shot. It also requires the use of three or four lights in addition to background considerations and is not particularly flexible in special locations. With this subject and camera blocking, two key lights are used—one for each subject—and each subject's face is illuminated toward the other. Neither person is hiding in the shadows during the conversation (see Figure 6.26).

Given the difficulty of controlling the spill of light in the constricted space characteristic of many remote production sites, the use of spotlights with this *cross-keying* method does not produce the most attractive modeling. The illumination levels become too high to exercise the subtle shadings that produce a rich picture. Multiple softlights or reflectors reduce this problem, but there is often a better solution.

A third method has evolved that uses as few as two lights beyond the fill and background requirements, produces attractive modeling, and lends itself to the comparatively dynamic z-axis camera and subject blocking treatment. The **z-axis** is an imaginary line extending from the camera into the scene. The arrangement of people or objects in the scene at different points on the z-axis increases the sense of depth in a scene. In this method, the subjects face each other, and the key light and backlight are combined, as each instrument serves two purposes. One source serves as a key for subject A and as a backlight for subject B. The other light keys subject B and backs subject A. The camera can be placed for an **over-the-shoulder shot** in either direction (see Figure 6.27).

This method generates a theatrical touch that fits the purpose of shooting on location. The directional highlights seen on the subjects suggest motivated light of some sort and, in so doing, make the location seem more interesting. The subjects do not seem to be illuminated by the same hazy sky that illuminates so much of television.

A soft light or large reflector can be substituted for one of the instruments with good results. The sun or other location light source can be used from one direction while the reflector reverses that illumination from the other.

The action in the scene is arranged along the camera axis with this method. The foreground subject appears larger and overlaps the background subject, whose face is toward the camera in position for an easy zoom to a close-up. Subjects can be seated on opposite sides of a desk, pieces of construction equipment, or whatever. It is easy to include elements of the location with this camera blocking and lighting method.

Image Compositing

Often termed *chroma keying,* the blue-screen technique (sometimes green is used instead of blue) has been used in video production since the advent of color. Video switchers were designed to combine one image (often the meteorologist) with another image (an animated map used as a background). Today's equipment allows foreground and background signals to be combined through a selective processing of the RGB levels (see Figure CP-5). Fine detail in foreground images (the meteorologist's hair, for example) can be processed accurately and foregrounds can be made to seem transparent if desired.

Today these compositing effects can be performed in a computer workstation equipped with software designed to produce video graphics and special effects. With the increasing use of **virtual sets** in video production (computer-generated images that take the place of actual sets and props), there is an even greater emphasis on the use of this production technique.

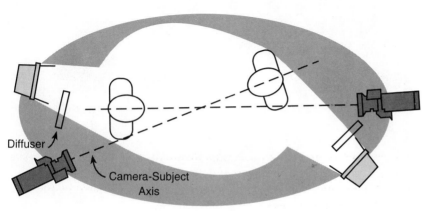

Diffuser

Camera-Subject
Axis

Figure 6.27
Lighting for
Dynamic
Composition

In a chroma-key-composited image, the foreground subject is typically recorded in a studio against a blue or green background. The chroma-key background may be either a seamless hard wall or a blue or green **cyclorama** (curtain) pulled taut to eliminate the wrinkles and folds in the fabric. A different background image is recorded separately or generated via computer. When the two images are combined, the blue or green chroma-key background is subtracted from the foreground picture, which is then combined with the new background image. (See Figure CP-5.)

In order for the effect to work properly, the blue or green chroma-key background must be evenly illuminated and free from shadows. Fluorescent instruments are particularly well suited to this lighting task, because they emit an even, soft light, at a precisely controlled color temperature, that can provide relatively shadowless illumination across large background areas. Although fluorescent instruments cannot throw light a great distance, they can be positioned close enough to the blue/green chroma-key background for maximum lighting efficiency. (See Figures 6.28 and CP-6.)

Planning

Competence and speed in lighting for remote production develop through systematic practice in determining the dimensions of the problem, the application of basic principles, the capacities of the equipment and materials

Figure 6.28
Fluorescent Lights
Provide Even
Illumination
for Blue-Screen
Backgrounds

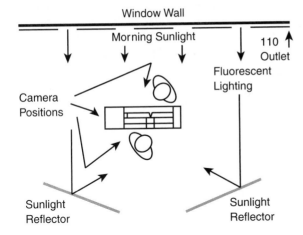

Window Wall

Morning Sunlight

110 ↑ Outlet

Fluorescent Lighting

Camera Positions

Sunlight Reflector

Sunlight Reflector

Figure 6.29 Sample Light Plot and Blocking Diagram

available, and the conscientious observation of the nature and quality of light produced in each setup. Classrooms, offices, cafeterias, and service stations each provide opportunities to plan for remote video production. A purpose is established for each of these potential remote locations, and the videographer identifies the opportunities and problems associated with each. Camera and subject **blocking diagrams** and tentative **lighting plots** should be prepared along with detailed equipment and materials lists (see Figure 6.29). This planning should precede the actual use of the equipment and will help you to use it more efficiently.

Once the equipment is on hand, the accuracy of the plan is tested. Detailed records of changes needed provide a base for discovering new techniques. Through a rigorous approach such as this, the videographer learns that some effects can be achieved without the optimum equipment. Through comparison of the amended plan with the actual picture as it appears in the video monitor, the videographer learns to identify and solve production problems—and to turn production problems into eye-catching production opportunities.

Common Lighting Problems

Location lighting, perhaps more than any other part of video field production, gives the videographer the opportunity to become a creative problem solver as he or she attempts to establish control over the natural lighting conditions present at the remote location. The number of problems en-

191

countered while shooting on location are as varied as the locations themselves. However, a number of common lighting problems are often encountered by beginning videographers. Table 6.2 lists 10 of these common problems, along with their probable causes and possible solutions.

Table 6.2   Common Lighting Problems

Problem	Probable Cause	Solution
Dull colors; everything looks grayish, grainy, or noisy.	Not enough light; aperture not open wide enough.	Add light; open aperture.
Colors too bright; pictures have hot spots that are white and glowing.	Too much light; aperture open too wide.	Reduce light; use a scrim; flood out the light; close aperture.
Weird skin tones; people look blue, green, or other unusual colors.	Filter wheel incorrectly set; improper white balance.	Check filter wheel; reset white balance.
People and faces appear in silhouette and are darker than the background.	Too much light on the background. Is subject in front of window, sky, or a white wall?	Change the background; cover it up so it appears to be darker, or move.
Inaccurate colors appear in shadow areas.	Too much shadow.	Use fill light to reduce the density of the shadows.
A strange green line outlines brightly lit objects.	Too much contrast between lit and unlit areas.	Try to even out the lighting and reduce overall contrast.
Flare appears in viewfinder.	A light or the sun is shooting directly into the camera lens, creating lens flare.	Use a lens hood; change the position of the offending light, control its spill with barn doors or a flag, or move the camera.
All the power goes out when you turn on lights.	Circuit is overloaded; circuit breaker has tripped.	Unplug something from the circuit and try again.
Glare from lights is being reflected directly into the camera by glass on pictures on the wall.	Angle of lights and reflective surface.	Change either the angle of the picture or the light, so that light is reflected away from camera.
Distracting shadows are being cast on rear wall by actors or set pieces.	Angle of light; action too close to the wall.	Move actors and set pieces away from the wall; raise lights so shadows are thrown onto the floor, not walls.

192

7

Sound

PART ONE
Technical Factors

There is a tendency to concentrate almost exclusively on the picture portion of the message when talking about video production. Indeed, the word *video* is derived from the Latin word *videre* (to see). Yet video is an audiovisual medium—one in which both picture and sound are important.

The importance of sound in video production has been given significant impetus by improvements in sound distribution and reproduction technology. Stereophonic sound was introduced to television broadcasting in the United States in 1984, and the development of HDTV carries with it the promise not only of improved picture resolution but also of the delivery of five channels of CD (compact disc)-quality sound. Today, most television receivers are capable of reproducing stereo sound on their own high-quality speakers, and "home theater" display systems rely as much on high-quality sound amplifiers and speakers as they do on large-screen video display. Beyond these technical factors, sound is an important aesthetic element that makes a significant contribution to the overall impact of program material.

Video field production offers a particular set of challenges and opportunities with respect to sound recording. While location sound can provide a dimension of realism frequently not found in studio productions, it can also be unpredictable and difficult to record. The controlled recording of sound on location is one of the great challenges facing video field producers.

Sound in Video Field Production

In general, video field producers are concerned with sound in three different situations: location recording, adding sound to prerecorded videotape (audio dubbing), and sound manipulation during postproduction editing. In all three applications of sound production, the video producer must have a clear understanding of the nature of sound, the capabilities and limitations of the equipment used to record it, and the impact of the manipulation of sound on the audience's perceptions.

Because the sound portion of a program carries a significant amount of information, at a very simple level of operation there is a necessity for all programs to have good, clear, clean sound. We can define **sound** as any aural component of a program that is intentionally present. **Noise**, on the other hand, interferes with sound—it obscures sound and makes it more difficult to understand. In many cases, noise is an unintentional element that has been introduced into the program.

In many ways, recording sound for video is similar to lighting. Just as it is fairly easy to make an image visible to the camera, so it is easy to record sound. However, there is quite a difference between simply recording *any* sound and recording *effective* sound. Indeed, the art of recording and manipulating sound may be compared to playing the guitar. It is one of the easiest things to do poorly and one of the hardest things to do well.

Sound: Technical Bases

Sound can be thought of simply as a pattern in the vibration or movement of molecules of air. When a sound is made, air is moved in waves (thus the term *sound waves*). Although the movement of sound waves is a complicated phenomenon, we will discuss only two characteristics of sound waves: amplitude (intensity) and frequency (pitch). For our purposes, these two characteristics of sound are the most important.

Sound Amplitude, or Intensity

Differences in the loudness, or intensity, of a sound can be seen as differences in the **amplitude,** or height, of the sound wave (see Figure 7.1). Loudness is measured in **decibels (dB).** Decibels are the standard unit, or ratio, of measure used in all audio equipment to gauge the relative **intensity,** or **volume,** of sound.

Amplitude

Wave A and Wave B have the same frequency—one cycle per second. The amplitude and intensity of B are greater than those of A.

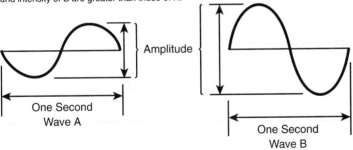

Frequency

Wave A and Wave B have the same amplitude, but different frequencies.

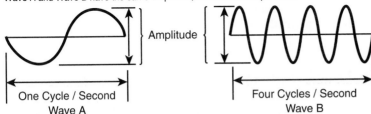

Figure 7.1
Differences in
Amplitude and
Frequency of
Two Sound Waves

The decibel scale is a logarithmic scale. This means that a sound that is 3 dB greater than another is twice the intensity of the first sound. In reality, a 3 dB change in intensity is very difficult to perceive, and a sound may have to increase in intensity as much as 6 dB before a listener perceives it to be twice as loud as the previous sound.

The human ear responds to a great range of sound intensities, from 0 dB (the threshold of hearing) to 120 dB (the threshold of pain). Sounds louder than 120 dB can be heard, but they may cause pain and/or deafness.

Sound Frequency, or Pitch

The other important characteristic of a sound is its pitch. **Pitch** refers to the way in which some sounds are higher or lower than others. For example, women's voices are usually higher in pitch than men's voices. (Remember, this is not a difference in loudness, although such a difference might also exist. Rather, it is a difference in the tonal quality of the sound.)

Differences in pitch are visible in sound waves as differences in the frequency of the waves. **Frequency** refers to how often the wave repeats itself in one second (see Figure 7.1). Each complete pattern of the wave—from one peak to the next—is called a cycle. When we talk about the frequency of different sounds, we use a standard unit of measure: **cycles per** second (CPS). These are called **hertz (Hz)** in honor of the German scientist Heinrich Hertz, whose influential work on electromagnetic wave theory in the late 1800s led to the invention of radio.

Humans can hear a range of frequencies that extends from a low of about 20 Hz up to a high of about 16,000 Hz. A 20 Hz sound is extremely deep and bassy; a 16,000 Hz sound is extremely high in pitch.

Not only are the concepts of sound intensity and frequency important in the theoretical sense but also they are important because they have practical applications in almost all areas of sound production. **Volume unit (VU) meters**, for example, are calibrated in decibels and are used in audio production to determine the relative strength of the audio signal. Microphones vary from one another with respect to their frequency response. Some microphones are more sensitive to certain frequencies of sound than others. The frequency response of a microphone, then, becomes an important variable to consider when deciding which microphone to use in a particular recording situation.

Audio-Level Meters

A VU meter contains a scale that is a standard calibration of signal strength used in all broadcast and nonbroadcast media facilities. The scale is calibrated in decibels, and ranges from a low of –20 dB to a maximum of +3 dB. Ordinarily, the –20 dB to 0 dB range of the scale is represented in black, and the 0 dB to +3 dB range is presented in red. Sometimes the scale also contains a percent scale, with –20 dB representing 0 percent and 0 dB representing 100 percent. A small needle indicates how high or low the signal is.

Two types of VU meters are used: one type uses a needle to indicate the volume of each sound channel (see Figure 7.2). In the other type, the needles are replaced by light-emitting diodes (LED) or bar graph displays (see Figure 7.3) that correspond to the various points on the VU scale. No matter which metering system is used, loud, dominant sounds should be kept in the range of –3 dB to 0 dB. Sounds recorded above 0 dB ("in the

Figure 7.2
VU Meters

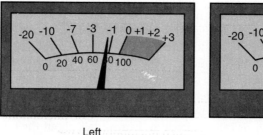

Left

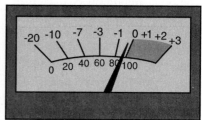

Right

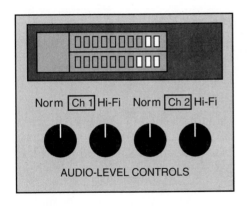

Norm Ch 1 Hi-Fi   Norm Ch 2 Hi-Fi

AUDIO-LEVEL CONTROLS

Figure 7.3 Camcorder
Audio-Level Controls

red") may be distorted; sounds record too low ("in the mud") will lack clarity and may need to be amplified, which will add noise to the signal.

Another type of meter sometimes found on audio equipment is the **peak program meter (PPM).** Peak program meters are somewhat more accurate than VU meters in terms of responding to rapid changes in the peak level of an audio signal, but they tend to be used more widely on studio equipment rather than on equipment designed for portable use in the field.

 ## Microphone Characteristics

Location sound is picked up and channeled into the video recording system with a microphone. A **microphone** is a transducer, just as a CCD is a transducer. However, the function of the CCD is to change light into electrical energy, whereas the function of the microphone is to change sound into electrical energy.

Sound is often difficult to control in the field because the field environment is unpredictable. Jet planes fly overhead, train whistles blow in the distance, wind and clothing rub against microphones, and so on. The world is not silent, and the microphone does not discriminate between wanted sound and unwanted noise as it picks up sound on a location shoot. Therefore, one of the most important elements that can be controlled to ensure a good recording of field sound is the microphone. The choice of a particular microphone and its placement depend on the particulars of the recording situation. Several characteristics of microphones should be considered before deciding which microphone to use.

Microphone Pickup Patterns

The **pickup pattern** of a microphone refers to the directions in which it is sensitive to incoming sound (see Figure 7.4). Microphone pickup patterns are important to understand and use in production because microphones, unlike the human ear, are not selective about what they hear. They respond to all incoming sound; they cannot distinguish between important sound and unimportant sound. If you are standing in the middle of a large group of people who are all talking, and you are particularly interested in hearing the conversation of only a few people, you can listen selectively to them and mentally block out all the other conversations. We practice this type of selective perception all the time. Place a microphone in the middle of a crowd, however, and no such selective perception is possible, unless the pattern of sound picked up by the microphone is controlled. If the microphone is sensitive to sound coming in from certain directions and insensitive to sound coming in from other directions, then a kind of selective pickup can be achieved.

Figure 7.4
Microphone Pickup Patterns

Omnidirectional

Cardioid

Supercardioid

Microphones that are sensitive in all directions are called **omnidirectional** microphones. Some microphones are sensitive in the front and back but not on the sides. These are **bidirectional** microphones. Other microphones have a heart-shaped pickup pattern. They are extremely sensitive out front but somewhat less sensitive to the sides and rear. These are **cardioid** pickup patterns. **Supercardioid** microphones exaggerate the sensitivity in front. They are very directional and generally are most sensitive to sounds in a very narrow angle in front of the microphone. Because these microphones are often extremely long and narrow, they are referred to as **shotgun microphones.**

Omnidirectional, cardioid, and supercardioid microphones are the kinds most often used in video field production. Omnidirectional microphones are useful if sound needs to be picked up from a wide area or if one microphone is needed to pick up sound from several people. Cardioid and supercardioid microphones are useful if more selectivity in the pattern of sound pickup is desired. For example, if you want to isolate sound pickup to a narrow area—one person in a group, for instance—a microphone with a narrow pickup pattern should be used.

Microphone Types

In addition to differences in pickup patterns, microphones also differ with respect to the way they are constructed. Microphones work by sensing changes in the sound waves created by the sound source. Within each microphone is a diaphragm that is sensitive to these changes in sound intensity and quality. The diaphragm converts the sound waves into an electrical audio signal. Not all microphones use the same type of mechanism to change sound into electrical energy. These differences in microphone mechanisms provide one of the principal ways to distinguish microphone types.

The two most popular microphone types found in video field production are dynamic microphones and condenser microphones (see Figure 7.5). The **dynamic microphone** contains a diaphragm that is attached to a coil of wire wrapped around a magnet. When the diaphragm moves, so does the coil; this causes a change in the magnetic field within the microphone and generates a corresponding amount of electrical voltage. This is the audio signal. The variations in the amount of voltage produced correspond to the variations in the frequency and loudness of the sound waves hitting the microphone's diaphragm.

Dynamic microphones are extremely rugged and may be the most widely used microphones in television production. They are relatively inexpensive (for professional-quality microphones) and usually have good frequency response. However, they tend to be somewhat less sensitive to high-frequency sounds than are condenser microphones.

Condenser microphones use an electric capacitor, or condenser, to generate the signal. This consists of a moving faceplate at the front of the microphone and a backplate in a fixed position behind it. Both plates are electrically charged, and sound hitting the faceplate causes a change in voltage. Because the voltage produced is very weak (much weaker than the signal produced by a dynamic microphone), condenser microphones need a source of power to amplify the signal. Condenser microphones designed

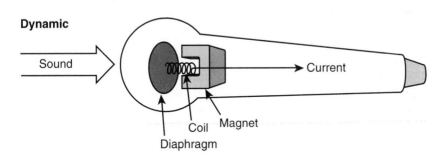

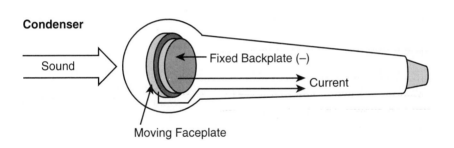

Figure 7.5
Microphone
Construction

for field production are typically powered by a small battery; others use "phantom power" in which power is supplied to the microphone via the microphone cable from an audio mixer or other power supply unit. This eliminates the need to check and replace microphone batteries because no microphone batteries are used in these systems.

Electret condensers are a popular type of condenser microphone. They differ in construction from conventional condenser microphones. Electrets are manufactured with a permanent electric charge in the capacitor and therefore require the use of only a very small battery as a power source to boost the output signal of the microphone to a usable level. As a result, electret condensers tend to be significantly smaller than other condenser microphones. They are frequently used as built-in microphones on portable cameras and in other situations requiring a small, inconspicuous microphone.

Professional-quality condensers and electret condensers are widely used in broadcast television production. Many dramatic productions use high-quality shotgun condenser microphones for sound pickup. Electret condensers are often used as clip-on microphones. Because of their small size, they are very unobtrusive.

Condenser microphones have several advantages over dynamic microphones. They are highly sensitive, particularly to high-frequency sounds. In addition, they can be made extremely small. On the negative side, they are often very expensive, fragile, and need a power source. Because the typical power source is batteries, they can be expected to fail when it is least convenient. Always begin recording with fresh batteries in the microphone, and carry a supply of replacement batteries in case of failure.

Another type of professional microphone is the **ribbon microphone** (sometimes called *velocity microphone*). Ribbon microphones contain a thin ribbon of metal foil mounted between the two sides of a magnet. Early ribbon mikes, designed for use in radio and noted for their excellent voice pickup, were generally large and bulky and not suited for field video production. Modern ribbon mikes are much smaller, but, like their radio counterparts, they are very fragile. Although voice pickup remains excellent, they are not a good choice for field production, because they can be easily damaged by loud sounds or by blowing wind.

Frequency Response

The way in which the microphone is constructed is important to the field producer because it determines how the microphone will perform. The **frequency response** of the microphone refers to its ability to accurately reproduce a wide range of frequencies. No microphone is capable of capturing the full spectrum of frequencies from 16 Hz to 16,000 Hz. However, professional-quality microphones are generally able to pick up a wider range of frequencies than are inexpensive microphones. This wider frequency response extends both down to lower frequencies and up to higher frequencies. An inexpensive microphone may well pick up middle-range frequencies but exclude the highs and the lows. In addition, many microphones are designed with specific uses in mind. A microphone designed for voice pickup will not have the high-frequency response that characterizes microphones designed for music pickup.

Specifications for microphone frequency response are provided by the manufacturer. Correct microphone usage and selection depend on matching the proper microphone—in terms of its frequency response—to your particular recording situation.

It is important to note that the frequency response of a microphone also depends on correct placement of the microphone. Reflected sound— sound that bounces off one or more room surfaces—sounds different to the microphone than sound picked up directly from the sound source. The distance of the microphone from the sound source also affects frequency response: the farther away it is placed, the poorer the sound pickup quality. In addition, the direction from which the incoming sound is coming must match the microphone's pickup pattern to maximize frequency response. That is, a microphone's pickup is better for on-axis sounds than for off-axis sounds. For example, a microphone with a very directional supercardioid pickup pattern responds better to high-frequency sounds hitting the sensitive front of the pickup pattern (on-axis) than to similar sounds coming from the side or rear of the microphone (off-axis).

Microphone Impedance

Finally, the field producer must consider the impedance level of the microphone. **Impedance (Z)** is a measure of the amount of resistance to electrical energy in a circuit. Impedance is measured in **ohms** (Ω), and two impedance categories are commonly found in audio equipment. **Low-impedance**, also called **low-Z**, refers to equipment rated at an impedance of 600 ohms or below. **High-impedance**, or **high-Z**, equipment is rated above 600 ohms.

All professional-quality microphones are low-impedance and are usually rated at 150 ohms. Similarly, VCR and camcorder audio inputs are low-impedance inputs. The rule of thumb is simply to match the impedance levels of the audio sources that you are connecting. Low-impedance sources connect to low-impedance inputs, and high-impedance sources connect to high-impedance inputs.

The principal advantage to using low-impedance microphones and other sources is that the audio signal can be sent over several hundred feet of cable with very little loss in signal quality. High-impedance lines, on the other hand, tend to noticeably affect signal quality if cable lengths exceed 25 feet or so.

Camera-Mounted Microphones

The **camera microphone** is a standard feature of many portable video cameras and camcorders. In inexpensive consumer camcorders, the microphone is commonly built into the camcorder. In industrial and professional-quality equipment, the microphone generally is attached to the camera but can be removed. In all these systems, the camera microphone can be used to record the audio simultaneously with the recording of the picture. Indeed, this is one of the great advantages of videotape over film—not only are picture and sound recorded simultaneously but also they can be played back as soon as the recording has been completed.

Built-in Microphones

Built-in camera microphones are most often electret condensers by construction. They are often located on the front of the camera body above the lens. On consumer-quality camcorders, they are sometimes located at the front of the camcorder's pistol grip.

Attachable Microphones

Professional-quality cameras frequently contain a mount into which a microphone may be inserted. If no mount exists, gaffer's tape may be used to attach a microphone to the camera. Typically, the rear of the camera is equipped with an XLR (Cannon) input, thus making it possible to connect any professional-quality microphone to the system's audio input through the camera (see Figure 7.6).

Obviously, cameras that can accommodate a professional-quality attachable microphone allow for better sound recording than those equipped with a fixed-position, built-in microphone. Good sound pickup depends on the use of the correct type of microphone. Because microphones vary with respect to sensitivity and pickup pattern, a microphone suitable for use in one situation may be the wrong one to use in another situation. The use of attachable microphones gives the videographer flexibility that does not exist in cameras with built-in microphones.

Advantages and Disadvantages of Camera Microphones

The most significant advantage to the use of camera-mounted microphones is the convenience they provide. They are particularly useful if one person is operating the camcorder with no additional production crew. No special provisions need be made for recording audio. You simply point the camcorder and shoot, and the camera microphone picks up the sound from the direction in which it is pointed, subject to its sensitivity, frequency response, and pickup pattern.

Figure 7.6
Attachable
Microphones

Audio Inputs on a Professional Camcorder

Four XLR connectors are used to connect audio inputs and outputs to this professional-quality M-II camcorder.

Camcorder with Shotgun Microphone Attached

A camera-mounted microphone is very convenient to use but presents some significant disadvantages. The most important disadvantage lies in the distance of the microphone from the principal sound source. Unless the camera is precisely at the sound source, the microphone will be a considerable distance away from the sound. Because the quality of a recording usually demands that the microphone be close to the principal sound source, this is a significant problem.

The second principal disadvantage to using a camera-mounted microphone lies in the fact that sound sources close to the microphone tend to be the prominent ones in the recording. Unfortunately, the sound sources closest to the camera are seldom what one wants to record: the sounds of the electrical motors that drive the zoom lens and lens focus mechanisms, breathing or talking by the camera operator, and other ambient noise close to the camera microphone will all achieve prominence in the recording. Unfortunately, close sounds tend to be louder than sounds farther away. Because the microphone has no way of knowing what is intentional sound and what is noise, all sound is recorded as it is received. Although the problem of intrusive proximate noise can be reduced somewhat by using a shotgun microphone on the camera instead of an omnidirectional one, it cannot be eliminated. Camera-mounted microphones usually provide recordings with inferior sound quality and levels compared to those produced with properly placed and selected external microphones.

Camera-mounted microphones can be used advantageously if all you want to pick up is general, rather than selective, sound from a location. A camera-mounted microphone will effectively pick up the on-axis sounds of a cheering crowd as the camera pans the grandstands, or the noise of traffic on the freeway as cars and trucks whiz by the camera. If, however, you want to isolate sound pickup to a particular person in the crowd or if you want to clearly pick up sounds that are off-axis to the camera microphone, then microphone choice and placement must be more selectively controlled.

External Microphones

External microphones are any microphones that are not built into or mounted onto the field camera. Once the field producer decides which type of microphone is best suited to the field recording situation at hand, a decision needs to be made about where to position the microphone and how to place it in that position. Microphones can be handheld, pinned onto the performer's clothes, hidden on the set, hung from the ceiling, supported on booms off camera, or attached directly to the object making the sound. Field producers use all these techniques and others.

Handheld Microphones

Handheld microphones are commonly used in ENG-type productions, particularly when an on-camera newscaster conducts an interview and only one microphone is available. Handheld microphones are usually dynamic microphones with a barrel that is relatively insensitive to sound. This does not mean that it is totally immune to picking up barrel noise—no microphone is. (If you tap your fingers along the barrel, it most certainly will pick up this sound.) However, in comparison with other microphone types, the handheld microphone is relatively insensitive along the barrel and therefore is widely used (see Figure 7.7).

When using a handheld microphone, it is important to remember that the person who holds the microphone controls the quality of the sound pickup. The on-camera interviewer must remember to speak into the microphone when asking a question and to move it when the respondent answers. Failure to position the microphone correctly to keep the principal sound source on axis reduces the quality of the sound pickup. In addition, many directional microphones contain small openings, or

Figure 7.7
Handheld
Microphone

ports, that cancel sound coming from unwanted directions. Be careful not to cover the ports on the barrel of the microphone with your hand as you hold it, as this will interfere with the directional pickup of the microphone.

The cardinal rule to follow when using a handheld microphone is to never relinquish control of the microphone to the person you are interviewing. Some interviewees instinctively grab the microphone when it is their turn to talk. Control of the interview, and of the microphone, should be maintained by the on-camera interviewer.

Figure 7.8   Lavaliere Microphone

Lavaliere Microphones

Lavaliere microphones are very small microphones that are pinned onto the clothing of the person who is speaking. The literal definition of *lavaliere* is a pendant worn on a chain around the neck, and some lavaliere microphones are actually hung around the subject's neck with a string. However, most current models have a small clip that pins the microphone onto the subject's clothing (see Figure 7.8).

Most lavalieres are either electret condensers or dynamic microphones. The electret condensers are the smaller of the two varieties and are widely used in field (and studio) production. The dynamic microphones are slightly larger but considerably more durable.

When using a lavaliere, try to position the microphone close to the subject's mouth. Quite often, it is pinned onto a jacket lapel or shirt collar. However, be careful when positioning the microphone to avoid placing it where the subject's clothing or jewelry may rub against it and create distracting noises.

When using a condenser lavaliere, be careful not to place it too close to the subject's mouth. Condensers are extremely sensitive and if the sound source is too loud (which often happens if it is too close to the microphone), it may distort the audio signal. This is known as **input overload distortion.**

If you are using a battery-powered electret condenser, remember also to check the battery before you begin recording. Make sure that it is correctly placed inside the microphone's battery compartment. If the positive and negative poles of the battery are not correctly seated in the compartment, the microphone will not work. Always carry a spare battery or two in case one of the microphone batteries gives up the ghost during your production.

Surface-Mounted Microphones

Although several manufacturers have developed boundary effect microphones of one design or another during the past two decades, the success of one is such that the trade name now identifies the microphone type. That name is Crown International's **PZM (pressure zone microphone)**.

These microphones are designed to be placed on the hard surface of a wall, desktop, or floor, where, in theory, the sound waves are not disturbed by reflections from other nearby surfaces. Multiple reflections of sound waves can act to change the volume and frequency of those waves. Reduction of this source of audio distortion results in comparatively clean processing of the human voice.

The pickup pattern of this microphone type is hemispherical. When mounted on the floor, it is often placed at a distance from a speaker equal to his or her height. For musical or theater groups, the microphone can be used effectively at a distance equal to the width of the group.

PZM-type microphones are used in confined spaces with excellent results. If such a space does not have a hard surface onto which to mount the microphone, it can be mounted on a flat piece of rigid plastic that is placed in the scene outside camera range. Scenes in automobiles, aircraft cabins, canopied beds, or the like can be recorded in this manner. Typical uses include mounting the microphone inside the cover of a piano, or on a conference table to pick up voices when there are a number of participants seated around the table.

The PZM microphone also delivers better sound in city exteriors than can be obtained with the traditional omni-on-a-pole method. If the program type or camera usage is such that the PZM will not be in the scene or will not matter if it is, it is the best choice. If camera work or dramatic illusion cannot be compromised in order to use a PZM, wireless microphones or fishpoles provide the best alternatives.

Shotgun Microphones

Shotgun microphones are widely used in remote production (see Figure 7.9). Because they have a very directional pickup pattern, they are often held off camera and aimed at the principal sound source. Thus, they do not intrude into the picture, but they provide sound pickup on a precise spot. They can be used to isolate sound pickup to one or two people in a crowd or to a particular location where activity is taking place.

207

Figure 7.9
Shotgun
Microphone with
Windscreen

Most shotgun microphones are extremely sensitive to barrel noise. For this reason, some have **pistol grips** attached to the microphone, which are used when it is handheld. When shotguns are attached to microphone booms, **shock mounts** are often used to insulate the microphone from the noise of the boom, and a **windscreen** is almost always needed when shooting outdoors.

Contact Microphones

Contact microphones are microphones that attach directly to an object. For example, say you want to clearly pick up the sound of roller skates or snow skis during an action sequence that is out of the range of a shotgun microphone. You can attach a microphone (perhaps a small condenser lavaliere) directly to the skate or ski. This will give very good pickup of the sound, even when the action takes place at a considerable distance from the camera.

Hanging Microphones

Hanging microphones are sometimes used indoors in remote production. These microphones are hung directly over the area where the action will take place or hung slightly in front of the action area and then aimed at it.

In either case, by hanging the microphone, you can usually get it out of the field of view of the camera. However, sound pickup usually suffers because the microphones tend to pick up a lot of the ambient background noise on the location.

Microphone Stands and Mounting Devices

Various types of stands and mounting devices are used to support microphones (see Figure 7.10). Stands have the advantage of holding a microphone securely in a fixed position. They also insulate the microphone from noise on the surface where it is positioned. **Desk stands**, for example, are small stands used to hold microphones on a desk or table in front of the person or persons who will speak. One microphone on a desk stand can be positioned to pick up the sound from two or more people. **Floor stands** are taller stands that telescope upward. They consist of a base, which supports the stand, and a telescoping rod, which allows the microphone height to be adjusted for correct sound pickup. Microphones on floor stands are frequently used to pick up sound from musical instruments and from people standing up to speak.

Fishpoles are extremely popular in field production. A fishpole is a metal rod that extends to allow placement of the microphone close to the sound source. It has many of the advantages of a handheld microphone, but it is insulated from barrel noise and allows the person holding it to remain off camera and move with the person who is talking.

A **boom**, a three-legged contraption that sometimes comes equipped with wheels and a telescoping boom rod, allows the microphone to be

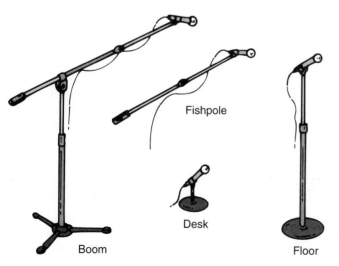

Figure 7.10
Microphone Stands

Fishpole

Desk

Boom

Floor

209

aimed, extended, and retracted. Booms are primarily used in dramatic production, where the movement of the actors is tightly controlled and limited to a relatively small action area.

Most field production situations use a variety of microphones and microphone supports. At a recent televised university gymnastics meet, the following kinds of microphones were being used by the remote television production crew: sportscasters used handheld omnidirectional microphones to conduct interviews with gymnasts; shotgun microphones were taped onto each portable field camera to provide background sound pickup for each camera shot; contact microphones were taped to the floor at intervals along the runway the contestants used when they sprinted toward the vault; a shotgun microphone on a floor stand was aimed at the vault to pick up the sound of contestants hitting it; and shotgun microphones on floor stands were aimed at the parallel bars and balance beam to provide precise sound pickup in each of these action areas.

Wired and Wireless Microphones

Once the appropriate microphone has been selected for the recording situation at hand, the audio signal needs to be transmitted to the appropriate input on the camcorder. Two types of microphone systems are commonly used in video field production: wired and wireless.

Wired Microphones

Wired microphones are widely used in field recording because of their ease of operation and reliability. After connecting a cable to the microphone and the appropriate audio input on the camcorder, you can begin recording.

Although this type of recording arrangement works well in most situations, the presence of the microphone cable sometimes causes problems. If the subject moves around a lot or is at a great distance from the camcorder, or if the presence of microphone cables will spoil the appearance of the event, you should use another method of transmitting the signal from the microphone to the camcorder.

Wireless Microphones

Wireless microphones—also called radio microphones—eliminate many of the problems associated with the use of microphone cables; therefore, they are extremely popular in field production. A wireless microphone sends its signal to a receiver via RF (radio frequency) transmission rather than through a cable. That is, it actually broadcasts the audio signal to the receiving station and thereby eliminates the need to use long cables to connect these two points. Wireless microphones contain three components: the microphone itself, a small transmitter attached to the microphone that transmits the signal, and a small receiver that receives the transmitted signal. The output of the receiver is then connected by cable to the appropriate audio input on the camcorder (see Figure 7.11).

In some wireless systems, the transmitter is built into the microphone itself—these are typically handheld microphones. Wireless systems in which the transmitter is a separate unit to which the microphone must be connected are called **body packs**, in reference to the fact that the transmitting unit is typically attached to the body of the person who is the source of the sound. Body-pack transmitters are usually used with lavaliere microphones because the lavaliere is too small to contain its own built-in transmitter.

Many types of microphones—handheld, lavaliere, and shotgun—can be obtained in a wireless configuration. For maximum flexibility and mo-

Figure 7.11 Wireless Microphone System

The LX Wireless Microphone System from Shure

bility, wireless systems designed for field use are battery powered, with both the transmitter and receiver operating off battery power.

Wireless microphones have several great advantages over wired microphones. They do not restrict the movement of the sound source, the microphone remains in the same relationship to the sound source even if the sound source moves, and there are no obtrusive cables to be seen. A wireless lavaliere microphone attached to a referee in a football game is always less than 12 inches from the referee's mouth, no matter where the referee is on the field. This ensures better sound pickup than a shotgun microphone on the sidelines aimed at the same official would get. No matter how the official moves or turns, the wireless lavaliere is always there to pick up the sound. In addition, because no cable is used, there is no chance of interfering with the movement of the players during the game.

Wireless microphones do present some problems, however. Because they demand power, either adequate AC or battery power must be available. More than one production has been ruined by failing batteries late in the day.

Although the transmitting part of the wireless body-pack unit is small, it nonetheless must be carried by and concealed on the sound source. Depending on how the subject is dressed, this may present problems. If you plan to use wireless microphones for sound pickup as you videotape a wedding, you may find that the transmitter and microphone can be easily concealed on the groom, whose jacket offers a good hiding place, but the bride's dress may not offer a suitable place to hide the equipment.

Because wireless microphones are actually small radio transmitters and receivers, they are susceptible to interference from other radio sources, such as police radios, CB radios, and so on. It is very distracting, to say the least, if the transmission of the wedding vows is interrupted by a radio message from the local police dispatcher announcing a burglary in the neighborhood.

The final and perhaps greatest disadvantage of wireless microphones for most producers is that they can be expensive. A professional-quality wireless system (microphone, transmitter, and receiver) can easily cost 5 to 10 times as much as an equivalent wired microphone.

Balanced and Unbalanced Lines

Whether your microphone system is wired or wireless, at some point it will be connected to the camcorder with a cable. Two types of cables, or lines, are commonly used to carry the audio signal to the recorder. Professional, high-quality systems utilize cables that are called balanced lines. A **balanced line** is a cable that contains three wires. Two wires carry the signal, and the third acts as a shield to protect the other two from outside interference. **Unbalanced lines** contain two wires. The wire in the center of the cable carries the signal, and the other wire acts both as a grounded shield and as a signal lead. Unbalanced lines are cheaper to manufacture, but they are also significantly more susceptible than balanced lines to interference from electrical lines, radio and television transmitters, and so on.

You can easily tell whether your audio cables or audio inputs and outputs are balanced or unbalanced by looking at the audio connectors. Three-pronged XLR (Cannon) connectors indicate that the line is balanced; mini-plugs, RCA/phono connectors, and phone connectors indicate that it is unbalanced. Incidentally, connecting a balanced line to an unbalanced input causes the line to become unbalanced, and the effect of the shield will be lost. This does not affect the signal quality, but it may make the signal more susceptible to interference. Unbalanced lines, however, do *not* become balanced by connecting them to a balanced input.

Recording Sound on a Portable Camcorder

Inputs

Sound that is picked up in the field with a microphone is routed into the portable camcorder through the appropriate input. All portable systems have at least one audio input, and most have two. If your camcorder has two inputs, each one corresponds to its own audio track, or channel. These will be labeled channel 1 and channel 2 or left and right.

Depending on the videotape format that you are working with, several different kinds of audio tracks may be available. Sound is recorded into linear, or longitudinal, tracks with one or more stationary audio heads. Most video formats have two linear sound tracks. There are no differences between these audio channels other than the fact that they occupy space on different places on the tape. They are equivalent in terms of size and the quality of the audio signal they are capable of recording.

Systems with high-fidelity sound record sound information along with the video information in the slanted video tracks on the tape. In these systems, the rotary video heads may also serve as the audio heads, or a separate rotary audio head may be used. Sound quality is significantly better than in linear-track recording because the tape-to-head speed achieved by the rotating sound head is significantly better than what can be achieved with the stationary head(s) used to record sound in the linear track(s). In addition, some systems (most notably 8mm/Hi8 and DV) are capable of recording high-fidelity sound digitally through a process known as *pulse code modulation* (PCM).

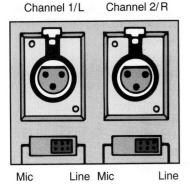

Channel 1/L   Channel 2/R

Mic   Line Mic   Line

Figure 7.12   Switchable Microphone/Line VCR Input

Input Level

It is important to know the kind of signal the input is capable of accepting. There are two different types of signals: microphone-level signals and line-level signals. A **microphone-level signal** is very weak because the electrical signal that the microphone produces is not amplified. **Line-level audio signals,** on the other hand, are amplified. They are considerably stronger than microphone-level signals. Line-level audio signals include the output from audiotape recorders, turntables, preamplifiers, and so on.

It is important that the level of the output signal be matched to the level of the input on the camcorder. Microphones should be connected to microphone-level inputs, and line-level outputs to line-level inputs.

On professional-quality equipment, audio input levels can often be switched from microphone level to line level. A small two-position switch near the input allows you to select the appropriate input level for your audio (see Figure 7.12).

Most consumer-quality camcorders are equipped only with microphone-level inputs. If you want to record a line-level signal, a pad must be used to connect the line-level source to the microphone-level input. A *pad* is a device that reduces the level of the signal from line level to microphone level. It is connected to the audio cable between the line-level source and the microphone-level input connector on the camcorder.

If you want to feed a microphone-level source into a line-level input, small amplifiers to boost the microphone-level signal to line level are available. These are relatively inexpensive and they simply connect to the cable between the microphone and the line-level input connector.

Input from the Camera Microphone

The audio signal generated by a built-in camera microphone is automatically routed to the camcorder's VCR and recorded onto one or both of the audio channels available on the videotape. In systems with a separate camera and VCR, the camera microphone audio signal is carried from the camera to the VCR through the camera cable.

In most systems, if an input from an external source is connected to the VCR in the same channel that has been allocated to the camera microphone, the external source will override the camera microphone, and the camera microphone input will not be recorded. This can cause disastrous results if you connect an audio cable to the microphone input on your camcorder but forget to connect the external microphone to the cable. In this situation no audio will be recorded: the connected audio cable will override the camera microphone, but with no microphone attached to the cable no sound signal will be generated.

Automatic and Manual Gain Control

The camcorder's audio gain control circuits have already been discussed in some detail in Chapter 5. However, it is worth mentioning again here that the gain control—the control over the amplification of the signal—may be either automatic or manual. Most consumer-grade camcorders contain an automatic gain control mechanism built into the audio circuitry of the VCR. Manual adjustment of audio source levels that are patched (connected) directly into the camcorder is not possible on such machines.

Professional-quality camcorders and many full-size VCRs contain manual gain control circuitry. Typically, there is a switch that allows you to choose either automatic or manual gain control. If manual gain control is chosen, a small potentiometer must be adjusted to bring the level up to the appropriate peak without overamplifying, and consequently distorting, the signal (see Figure 7.3).

Limiters

Many VCRs contain audio peak limiters. A **peak limiter** is an electronic device that prevents the audio level from exceeding 100 percent (0 dB) on the volume unit (VU) meter scale. Usually, the limiter is controlled with a simple on/off switch. Limiters are useful if the sound in your recording situation is very unpredictable. If loud noises appear at random intervals, the limiter ensures that the recorded signal is kept within acceptable parameters. If the sound in the remote location contains predictable peaks, the recording level can be manually set with the limiter off, and the recorded signal should meet acceptable technical standards.

Connectors

As equipment becomes standardized, so do the connectors that carry the audio signals in and out. Presently, however, a wide variety of connectors perform essentially similar functions (see Figure 7.13). Professional-quality

215

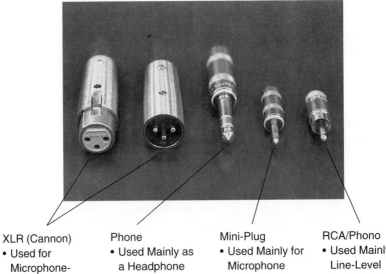

XLR (Cannon)	Phone	Mini-Plug	RCA/Phono
• Used for Microphone- and Line-Level Signals • Professional Quality • Balanced Line	• Used Mainly as a Headphone Connector or for Microphone or Line-Level Audio Signals • Unbalanced Line	• Used Mainly for Microphone Inputs and Earphones • Unbalanced Line	• Used Mainly for Line-Level Inputs and Outputs • Unbalanced Line

Figure 7.13   Typical Audio Connectors

machines utilize three-pronged XLR (Cannon) connectors for all audio inputs and outputs. These balanced connectors carry either line-level or microphone-level signals.

Microphone inputs on many consumer-level camcorders often accept mini-plug connectors. These are unbalanced. Line-level inputs and outputs on consumer- and industrial-grade equipment frequently utilize RCA/phono connectors, which are also unbalanced lines. Finally, some machines use phone connectors for microphone- or line-level signals. Again, these are usually unbalanced lines.

If you are not working with professional-quality video equipment with standardized audio connectors, it is to your advantage to acquire a set of audio adapters that will enable you to adapt any type of microphone or cable to any type of input connector. Adapter kits are available from most audio-video supply houses, or you can simply go to a local electronics store and buy the ones you will need. The importance of making connections properly cannot be overemphasized. If you cannot get the audio signal into the camcorder, you cannot record it. Well-prepared field producers are certain to have the connectors or adapters they will need to route the signal into the recorder being used.

Mixers

Most camcorders have two channels available for audio information. However, if you have more than two audio sources, or if you want to record a number of sources together onto one audio channel on the videotape, you will need to use an audio mixer.

An **audio mixer** is a device that combines a number of independent audio inputs by mixing them into one signal. For example, say you are recording an interview in which three or more people—each equipped with a microphone—are speaking. Each microphone could be fed into a mixer where the signals would be combined. The output of the mixer—a single channel—could then be recorded onto one audio channel of the videotape.

Passive and Active Mixers

There are two different kinds of audio mixers: passive mixers and active mixers. *Passive mixers* simply combine a number of individual inputs into one output without amplifying the signal. Passive microphone mixers with two inputs and one output are extremely popular in video field production because the most typical field production situation involves the use of two microphone sources—usually an interviewer and a subject.

Active mixers give you control over the amplification of each of the audio sources. Each channel on the mixer has its own potentiometer as well as a potentiometer to control the *master gain*—the overall amplification of all the individual channels. Professional mixers are equipped with a VU meter so that levels can be set for the individual inputs as well as for the master gain (see Figure 7.14). The input signals may be microphone level (unamplified) or line level (amplified), with the inputs being switchable to either. In addition, the output level is also commonly switchable. It may be sent to the camcorder as a microphone-level signal or a line-level signal.

Make sure the mixer output and camcorder input are set to the same level. More than one production has been ruined by mismatched audio output/input levels.

Setting the Mixer Gain Levels

To use a portable mixer effectively, the gain levels for each of the input channels, as well as the master gain—the amplification for the combined signal of each of the individual channels—must be correctly set. Because

Mic/Line Inputs

VU Meter

Master Gain Control

Rotary Pots (Volume Control)

Shure FP32A Three-Channel Mixer

Figure 7.14   Portable Audio Mixer

overamplification of any signal increases the electronic noise inherent in the system, care should be taken to keep amplification levels within tolerable limits. A general rule of thumb to follow in setting levels is to keep the master gain control lower than the individual channel gain controls.

Using a Built-In Tone Generator.   If your portable mixer has a built-in tone oscillator, the channel and master gain levels can be easily and precisely set. Most portable mixers contain rotary pots marked in increments from 0 to 10. First, make sure that all individual potentiometers and the master gain potentiometer are turned down to zero. This prevents them from creating unwanted electronic noise. Then, turn on the tone generator and turn up the potentiometer on the channel to which the generator is assigned approximately halfway. Finally, turn up the master gain control until the needle on the VU meter reaches 100 percent. The mixer master gain level is now set.

Levels can now be set for each of the audio inputs. Turn off the tone generator and turn the channel potentiometer back to zero. Connect the appropriate input sources to the mixer, and set the level of each in turn by turning up the appropriate potentiometer until the VU meter shows an acceptable signal, usually between –3 dB and 0 dB on the VU meter for dominant, loud sounds and voice recording. Make a note of the setting for each channel. If an acceptable signal level cannot be obtained, you may need to increase the master gain. However, if all the sources are peaking in the red with their individual potentiometers at very low settings—1 or 2, for example—it may be necessary to turn down the level of the master gain.

Experimenting with Level Settings.   If no tone generator is available, you can experiment with level settings. Try a setting of 3 or 4 on the master gain, and then turn up one of the channel gain controls. If the VU meter peaks with the channel gain at a very low setting, then *decrease* the master gain level. If the VU meter peaks with the channel gain at an extremely high setting, then *increase* the master gain slightly. With a little experimentation, you will soon find the master gain setting that gives you the most control over the signal through the channel gain selector without overamplifying the signal or introducing spurious noise.

Standardized Recording Procedures

Very few standardized recording procedures can be found for any aspect of field production. Most producers simply adopt systems that they are familiar with or that have worked for them in the past. Audio recording procedures are no different. However, a few suggestions for a standardized approach to sound recording are in order.

Identify Channels for Recording

Perhaps the most important decision that needs to be made in the field with respect to sound is the decision about where (on which channel) to record the principal audio. If your system has only one available audio channel, the choice is simple, but if you have two available audio channels and are using one or more external microphones or other external sound sources, it is more complex. Two factors should be considered:

1. Which channel is safe in terms of the track layout?
2. If time code is added to the tape later, onto which channel will it be added?

Safe Track.   The safe track is the track that is located in the interior of the videotape. The unsafe track is the one closer to the edge. If you have a two-channel system, you will probably want to record the principal audio, usually the most important voice part of the program, on this safe track, and use the other track for additional audio—music, sound effects, other voice, and so on.

Time Code.   Although SMPTE time code is described in considerable detail in Chapter 10, the importance of time code and its relation to the audio tracks need to be mentioned here. Time code is an electronic signal that is recorded onto the videotape to aid in editing. If you plan to edit

219

using time code, you must know how your editing system will read the time code. Some systems are preset to read time code from only one of the two audio channels. It may be either channel 1 or channel 2, but in either case, it is probably not switchable. Therefore, you must record time code onto the channel that the editing equipment is set to read. If the time code editor reads time code from audio channel 1, then audio channel 1 should be left free for time code and all program audio must go onto channel 2. Similarly, if your system reads time code from channel 2, then channel 1 should be used for program audio. Familiarize yourself with the time code requirements of your editing system before you shoot any field tape to avoid the costly and time-consuming problem of switching audio and time code to opposite channels after they have been recorded onto the tape.

Count Down Stand-Ups and Voice-Overs

If you are recording a stand-up or a voice-over (VO) segment, you should identify it and count down to it. A **stand-up** is simply a shot in which the program talent, usually a reporter or the host of the show, talks directly into the camera at the remote location. Some identifying detail of the location is usually visible in the background. (Think, for example, of the traditional shot of a newscaster on the White House lawn.) A **voice-over,** by contrast, is narration that is delivered by an off-camera announcer. The voice of the narrator is heard over the visuals, but the narrator is not seen on camera.

If you are recording a stand-up to be used at the beginning of a news or documentary piece, you might simply face the camera and record the following: "Documentary introduction, take 1. Five, four, three . . . [Silently count: two, one, zero] Today at the state capitol, legislators passed two bills that would dramatically increase school funding. . . ." The countdown is useful to both the person on camera and the editor. If you will be speaking on tape, you can use it to pace your presentation. Always count off the first three seconds—"five, four, three." Remain silent for the rest of the countdown (two, one, zero) and then begin. This allows you to catch your breath and deliver the introduction without surprising the audio person, who has to set the levels. Count down at the same voice level that you plan to use to deliver the on-camera statement.

The countdown is also useful to the editor because it serves as a timing reference and cue for the beginning of your statement. In addition, should you happen to boom out the first few syllables, causing an audio-level problem that will need to be corrected during editing, the editor will know exactly where that point is on the tape. The editor can then decrease the level slightly for the first few syllables and increase it to the proper level for the rest of the segment.

Use a Slate

Identification **slates**—audio and video—should be used at the start of each tape. These should clearly indicate what follows on the tape. If you are shooting a fully scripted production, one in which each shot will be recorded individually, then each shot and each take of each shot should be slated. A production slate is a small board (often a chalkboard) that contains essential information about the production, such as the production title, date, shot number, take number, and so on. Sometimes, when a visual slate is not available, the slate information may simply be read into a microphone and recorded at the beginning of a shot. Such an audio-only slate is often used when recording stand-ups and voice-overs, as the essential slate information can be read by the talent immediately before the take.

By giving the take number on the slate, you will be able to easily identify the good take when you edit your raw tape. If four takes of the same introduction are recorded and the first three were all disasters, you will know to fast forward to take number 4 when you edit. Without the slate, you will waste valuable editing time by listening to each of the four takes to find the correct one.

 ## Monitoring Sound

Volume Unit Meters

Field sound should be monitored for quality as it is being recorded. There are two ways to check the sound during the recording process. First, the audio levels should be monitored by watching the volume unit (VU) meters. They give you an accurate indication of the level, or strength, of the audio signal going into the recording deck. Care should be taken to record sound with good, consistent levels in the field. If the levels vary a lot from tape to tape, source to source, or location to location, the editor will later have to continually adjust the audio record level during the postproduction process to achieve a consistent level in the final edited program. If audio levels on the field tapes are correctly and consistently recorded, the editor will not have to balance the levels in postproduction, and the overall sound quality and impact will be better.

Headphones

In addition to visually monitoring the levels on the VU meters, use **headphones,** an **earphone,** or the camcorder **earspeaker** to listen to the quality of the sound as it is recorded. Although headphones provide some information about the strength of the audio signal as it is being recorded, they are actually more important for other reasons.

Headphones tell you what the audio sounds like. Are you getting a clear recording? Is there any distortion in the recording? Are there any extraneous noises interfering with your audio? Are background noises overwhelming the important foreground sound? If you are using a mixer and mixing several inputs down to one channel, how does the mix sound? In an interview, can all the people on microphone be heard clearly? If you are recording a musical group with several instruments, how does the musical mix sound? Are the levels of each of the instruments correctly set in relation to each other? These questions cannot be answered by looking at a VU meter. They can be answered only by listening to the sound itself and by making a judgment based on what you hear.

Test Recordings and Field Checks

All field recording should include a test recording and field check of the recorded sound. If time permits, a test recording should be made before you travel to the field location. Record video and audio onto the VCR, and then play it back. Problems that are apparent in this test recording are unlikely to disappear by the time the equipment reaches the field. It is better to delay or postpone a shoot while correcting an important audio problem than to labor all day in the field only to find out that your audio has a problem, or worse, is altogether missing from the field tapes.

In addition to making a test recording prior to the shoot and monitoring the sound with VU meters and headphones while the shoot is in progress, be sure to conduct periodic field checks of the audio and video quality of the tapes. A good time to check is when you are switching tapes (if time permits) or during breaks in the action. Rewind the recorded tape in the VCR slightly and play it back. Monitor sound quality through headphones and picture quality in the camera viewfinder or an external color monitor. Loss of picture or sound may be caused by a poor connection, clogged head, or something more serious. Again, it is better to identify the problem early than to spend the day recording only to find that your tapes are blank or that you have a serious technical problem that will keep you from using them.

Hints for Recording Good Sound

Good field sound recording depends on several important variables, including correct microphone selection, correct microphone placement, and correct signal recording.

Microphone Selection

There is no such thing as the perfect, all-purpose microphone. All microphones are different, and selecting the proper microphone for field use depends on matching the microphone's characteristics with those of the recording situation.

Obviously, in choosing a microphone, you should consider how it will be used. First, consider what you are going to record—voice, music, and so on—and then identify the microphone that provides the frequency response best matching the characteristics of the sound source to be recorded. Next, consider the unique characteristics of field recording. Will you be able to use multiple microphones to selectively record each part of the audio? Or will one microphone be used to record everything? How will the microphone be mounted? Will it be handheld? Frequency response, pickup pattern, size, durability, and ease of operation are all factors to consider when choosing a microphone for field recording.

Microphone Placement

Because of the great possibility of interference from ambient noise when microphones are placed at a distance, the most important principle of microphone placement in field production is to get the microphone as close as possible to the sound source, but not so close, of course, as to create distortion. Remember also that some microphones tend to emphasize low-frequency sounds when placed too close to the sound source. This close-up sound distortion is called **microphone proximity effect.**

When only one microphone is to be used for an on-camera interview, a handheld shotgun may serve best. However, if you are able to attach a high-quality condenser lavaliere to each of the participants, you may be able to achieve excellent sound reproduction without the visual distraction of the handheld microphone.

In some situations, such as a sporting event, it is not possible to get close to the sound source. It is common practice to attach wireless lavalieres to the referees, but the players themselves present an audio pickup problem. Because microphones are fragile, they cannot be attached to the players. Pickup must be from a distance, and shotgun or *parabolic microphones* that reflect the incoming sound to the focal point of the parabola are most frequently used.

Close microphone placement may also be a problem if the nature of the production demands that the microphones not be seen on camera. If they cannot be hidden on the performers or the set, off-camera shotgun microphones will probably be used.

A general rule of thumb for microphone placement when two or more microphones are used simultaneously in close proximity is to ob-

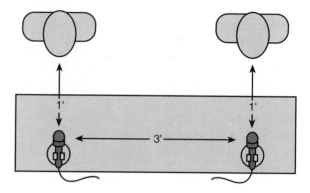

Figure 7.15   3:1 Microphone
Placement Ratio

serve a 3:1 ratio in which the distance between microphones is at least three times greater than the distance between either microphone and the person who is using it. For example, if two or more people are seated at a table and each one is miked with an omnidirectional microphone on a desk stand, and the distance between each person and his or her microphone is one foot, the distance between the two microphones on the table should be at least three feet. This type of positioning reduces the tendency of the microphones to cancel each other out when both are being used at the same time (see Figure 7.15).

Signal Recording

No matter how close the microphone is to the sound source or how well the microphone's response patterns match the characteristics of the sound source, the final recording will be only as good as you make it when you connect the inputs and adjust the recording level. Automatic gain control tends to overamplify the signal during periods of silence and then boom out the next loud sound. Manual gain control eliminates this problem, but care must be taken to correctly adjust the level. Adjust it too high ("in the red") and the signal will be noisy or distorted; adjust it too low ("in the mud") and the signal will be weak and the quality poor.

Analog versus Digital Audio

In the past, most camcorders recorded an analog audio signal—one in which the voltage of the electrical signal produced by the microphone varied continuously in relation to the sound that produced it. Increasingly,

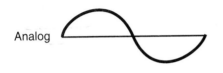

Analog

Sound Wave Is Continuous

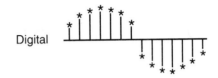

Digital

Sound Wave Is Sampled and Quantized

Figure 7.16 Analog vs. Digital Audio

however, analog signals are converted into digital signals for recording and processing. Both the DV and Hi8 recording formats, for example, record sound digitally.

The process of recording digital sound is similar to the digital video recording process described in Chapter 4. The analog sound wave is sampled at different points in time (sampling rate), and each of the points sampled is assigned a numerical value in a digital binary code consisting of "bits" made up of a pair of off/on (0/1) pulses. This is called **quantizing** (see Figure 7.16).

As you can imagine, the more frequently the sound is sampled, and the more bits assigned to each sampling point, the more accurate the digital code will be. A number of different sampling rates are used in digital audio recording. While the standard sampling rate for compact discs (CDs) is 44.1 kHz, the standard for VCRs recording broadcast quality digital audio is 48 kHz, meaning that the sound is sampled 48,000 times per second. Bit sampling rates vary as well. The accepted broadcast standard is based on 16-bit sampling. Lower quality recordings are made with systems using 8-bit and 12-bit sampling.

Special Problems

Location Acoustics

Unlike the studio producer, who operates in a tightly controlled acoustical environment, the remote producer is afforded very little control. Therefore, much attention should be paid to the acoustics of the remote location when the initial survey of the location is conducted (see Chapter 13).

Sometimes, problems caused by the acoustical properties of the location can be solved simply by the use of filters or by changing the position of the person who is speaking and/or the type and location of the microphone. Some microphones, and many portable mixers, contain **low-cut filters** that eliminate low-frequency sounds, thereby eliminating the booming that occurs in large rooms. If the remote location has an extremely hollow, boom-like quality, a low-cut filter can improve the quality of the sound.

We all know that hard, polished surfaces such as glass reflect sound, whereas soft, textured surfaces such as cloth tend to absorb sound. The proximity of highly reflective surfaces can cause sound problems that are easily corrected. Consider an interview being conducted in front of the glass window of a local coffee shop. The coffee shop is located on a very busy street with an almost constant flow of car and truck traffic. If the shop proprietor stands in front of the window and the sound is picked up with a shotgun mounted on the camera (or held off camera), the traffic sounds reflected off the glass will probably overwhelm the sound of the proprietor's voice. Use of a lavaliere microphone will improve the sound pickup, but the traffic sounds (which now enter the microphone as direct, rather than reflected, sound) will probably still be too loud. If, however, a lavaliere is used and you change the positioning so that the proprietor's back is to the traffic, the proprietor's body will physically shield the lavaliere from the traffic sounds. Thus, the voice pickup will be considerably improved.

Wind Noise

Figure 7.17
Microphone
Wind Screens

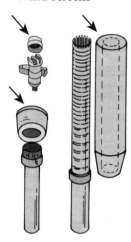

Wind noise is the most common problem encountered when recording outside. Even a light wind can sound like a hurricane when it passes over a microphone. For this reason, always use a windscreen on microphones when recording outside (see Figure 7.17). A **windscreen** is a foam cover placed over the microphone to screen out wind noise. Windscreens for most types of microphones are commercially available. If you cannot buy one, you can easily make one by cutting a piece of porous polyurethane foam to the dimensions of the microphone.

Foam windscreens work best in situations where the amount of air moving against the microphone is minimal. For more severe wind conditions in locations outside, a *blimp-type* windscreen will be necessary (see Figure 7.9). These large, fuzzy microphone covers may look strange, but they are quite effective. More specialized filter material is used in commercially available *rain diffusers,* which reduce the noise of rain hitting the microphone.

Some microphones have built-in **pop** or **blast filters.** These filters protect against sound distortion caused by particularly strong blasts of breath when a microphone is placed very close to the subject's mouth. Pop filters also provide some protection against wind noise.

Ambient Noise

Ambient noise—unwanted background noise—is the scourge of field production. A shot of a tranquil suburban street with birds chirping in the background can easily be destroyed if the local public works department selects your shooting day to bring out a jackhammer crew to remove part of the pavement on a nearby street. Freeway and airport noises often seem much louder when you watch your field tapes back in the editing facility than they did when you recorded a stand-up on a freeway overpass or near the airport passenger terminal.

The problem with ambient noise is that it is often unpredictable and uncontrollable. You might be able to persuade the jackhammer crew to take a short work break while you get your shot, but you probably will not have much luck in controlling the freeway traffic or air traffic.

The most severe problems can be avoided by thoroughly surveying the location before the shoot and paying close attention to the sounds of the location. Correct selection and placement of microphones can also help to reduce the pickup of unwanted ambient noise.

Camcorder Noise

Sometimes the noise created by the camcorder itself—noise made by the zoom lens motor or by the tape transport and rotating video heads—will be picked up by the sensitive microphones used to record sound on location. Wrap the camcorder in a blanket to muffle the sound, or shield it with your body to reduce this unwanted noise.

Radio Frequency and Electrical Interference

Interference from electrical or radio frequency (RF) sources causes a consistent problem in location sound recording. Unbalanced lines may pick up outside electrical or **RF interference** that will be extremely difficult to remove from the final audio track. Balanced lines provide protection against this, but only if all the connections are solid. If the shield solder comes loose or if the cable has a break in it, signal quality may be adversely affected.

No cable, balanced or unbalanced, can withstand radio waves if it is placed too close to a transmitter. In effect, cables act like antennae. If you are in the line of sight of a radio or television transmitting tower or if you are extremely close to a microwave transmitter, your audio cable may pick up the sound of the radio station or the microwave transmission. Depending on the circumstances, the interference may be louder than the wanted audio signal. The problem can sometimes be corrected by changing the position of the cables, but occasionally the problem is so severe that the only solution is to move to a new location that is farther away or out of the line of sight of the offending RF source.

High-voltage electrical lines, electrical transformers, and motors may also interfere with the audio signal. Always try to keep audio cables away from such sources. Sometimes, cables can be wrapped in black electrician's tape to provide insulation against electrical interference. Noise from motors, particularly if they run intermittently, is often more difficult to identify and control.

 ## Equalizing and Filtering to Improve Sound Quality

In extreme cases of interference, the audio on prerecorded field tapes can be manipulated to improve sound quality. Two common types of sound manipulation involve the use of filters or equalizers. Audio **filters** allow you to cut out certain parts of the high or low end of the audio signal. The filter works by blocking out the parts of the signal above or below a specified cut-off frequency. For example, you could eliminate the high frequencies in a signal to create a bassy effect, or you could eliminate the low frequencies to give it a higher effect. **Notch filters** can be used to eliminate a particular range of frequencies in the signal. An obtrusive electrical hum, for example, might be isolated at 60 Hz. With the notch filter, you could eliminate this part of the signal and let the rest pass by.

Equalizers are similar to filters but are somewhat more complex. Equalizers break down the audio signal into a series of equally wide ranges of frequencies. The level (gain) of the signal can then be increased, decreased, or left unchanged in each of the intervals. By increasing the level of some of the intervals and decreasing the level of others, the overall quality of the sound can be changed.

Filters and equalizers can also be used to achieve a particular kind of production effect. For example, the tinny sound of an inexpensive portable radio can be achieved by using a low-frequency filter to cut out the rich, low-frequency part of the signal, allowing only the thin, high frequencies to pass. A normal audio signal can thus be manipulated to make it sound like a radio, telephone, loudspeaker, and so on.

Adding Sound to Prerecorded Videotape

So far, we have concentrated on discussing general aspects of sound and sound recording, particularly with respect to recording live sound on location. Indeed, this is probably the most common type of sound recording in video field production. However, another extremely important aspect of sound recording concerns adding sound to a prerecorded videotape. Perhaps you have recorded video onto a videotape and want to add background music. Or perhaps you want to add a voice-over (VO) narration to connect the visual sequences on the tape. Almost all video recording systems let you add new sound to the videotape in a number of ways.

Audio Dub

Many camcorders and most VCRs contain an *audio dub feature*. The audio dub control allows new sound to be added to one of the available audio channels. When the audio dub control is engaged, the audio circuitry for one of the audio channels goes into the record mode. An audio erase head erases the old audio signal from the designated channel, and the audio record head lays down the new audio signal. The new audio input signal can usually be either microphone level or line level, as long as it is connected to the proper audio input connector.

There are two complications with the audio dub feature. First, audio dubs can be made only onto longitudinal (linear) audio tracks. If your VCR or camcorder has high-fidelity sound that was recorded with the rotary video heads (or a special rotary audio head) along with the video information in the slanted tracks of video information on the videotape, you will not be able to make an audio dub into these tracks. Second, on VCRs or camcorders that record audio information in two separate linear sound tracks, the audio dub feature may be designed to work in only one of the two channels.

It is extremely important to monitor the sound level and quality when performing an audio dub. If background music is to be dubbed in, the music should not be so loud that it interferes with the quality of the voice on the other channel. The proper level can be set by watching the VU meters and by monitoring the sound with headphones. The quality of the mix can be monitored by listening to the mixed output of both audio channels. Simply set the audio monitor selector switch to "mix" (rather than to either channel 1 or 2), plug in the headphones, and listen. Adjust the level of the music so that it takes its proper place in the background, behind the voice.

229

Audio-Only Insert Edit

New audio information can also be added to either one of the two linear audio channels available in most tape formats by performing an audio-only insert edit. This is a form of electronic editing, and in order to accomplish this, you will need to use a special editing VCR. This is discussed in greater detail in Chapters 9 and 10.

 # Additional Sound Recording and Playback Devices

Not all sound used in video production is picked up by a microphone and recorded onto videotape in the field. Analog audiocassette recorders, digital audiotape recorders, compact disc players, and digital audio workstations are frequently integrated into the process of video field production and postproduction.

Audiocassette Recorders

Audiocassette recorders are an invaluable tool of the video field producer. Because the cassettes are so small—the $1/4''$ tape is contained in a plastic housing only 4″ long by 2″ wide—audiocassette recorders can be made quite small and extremely portable. Producers use audiocassettes to record preinterview discussions with potential production subjects as part of the program's preproduction planning process, as well as to make voice and sound recordings to be incorporated into the program during production and postproduction.

While the portability and relatively low cost of audiocassette recorders are advantages, the slow tape recording and playback speed ($1^7/_8$ inches per second) provides less-than-optimal recording quality, particularly in consumer-quality machines. Professional-quality audiocassette recorders equipped with Dolby® noise-reduction circuitry, which eliminates the characteristic tape hiss, provide the best-quality recordings.

Digital Audiotape (DAT) Recorders

Digital audiotape (DAT) recorders are capable of recording significantly better sound quality than are their analog relatives. DAT tapes are smaller than traditional audiocassettes and are not subject to the tape hiss problems of the analog format (see Figure 7.18). Frequency response and dynamic range (the range from softest to loudest sound) are much better than in analog cassettes. As a result, voice and music recordings made with DAT recorders can provide high-quality sound during field production and postproduction.

Figure 7.18 Portable Digital Audio Tape Recorders

Sony TCD-D10 Pro II Professional
DAT Recorder

Consumer-Quality Sony Walkman Portable
DAT Recorder

Compact Disc (CD) Players

Compact discs (CDs) have become the standard for the distribution of recorded music. The audio information on CDs is digitally encoded and read back by a laser. CD players allow random access to any track on the disc, making it easy to cue and play them.

Digital Audio Workstations

A **digital audio workstation (DAW)** consists of a personal computer equipped with appropriate hardware and software for the manipulation and editing of sound. DAWs are increasingly used to manipulate field-recorded audio in postproduction and to add music and audio special effects to the sound track of a program. With the use of SMPTE time code, audio tracks that have been processed in a DAW can be resynchronized with the original video footage. (See Figure 7.19.)

Figure 7.19   Digital Audio Workstation

Digidesign® AudioVision 4 System

PART TWO
Sound Aesthetics

Effective control of the sound portion of a program involves control of the aesthetics of sound as well as control of sound from a technical standpoint. Just as changes in lighting, camera position, and shot composition can affect the audience's perception of a scene, so can manipulation of the audio.

Types of Sound

Silent video productions are extremely rare. We have become so accustomed to the presence of sound within video productions that even a few seconds of silence seems out of the ordinary.

Sound, as we mentioned at the beginning of this chapter, is any audio element whose presence in the program is intended. Noise, by contrast, is unwanted or unintended sound. Sound is used to enhance communication; noise interferes with communication. Four types of sound commonly found in most video productions are voice, natural sound, music, and sound effects.

Voice

Voice is probably the most common type of sound found in video field productions because many remote productions are interviews. The two most common uses of voice are dialogue and narration. **Dialogue**, conversation between two or more people, may be scripted or unscripted. Scripted dialogue is found most often in a drama or simulation; unscripted dialogue is found most often in interviews.

Narration is another extremely common use of voice. Narration may be on camera or off camera. In either case, the narrator describes the situation at hand and generally serves to link together portions of the program for the viewer. When narration is given off camera, we usually see visuals on the screen that correspond to someone or something other than the narrator (B-roll footage). Off-camera narration is referred to as **voice-over (VO)**. When the narrator (or any other person on camera) is shown while speaking, this is called **sound on tape (SOT)**.

Natural Sound

Natural sound is an extremely important component of video field production. One might argue that it is natural sound that distinguishes field production from studio production, because, strictly speaking, there is no natural sound (other than noise from the video equipment, studio personnel, and air conditioning!) in the studio. Natural sound is sometimes called *location sound* or *ambient sound*—it is the sound present in the location in which the action is taking place. For example, in an interview with a shipyard welder, the natural or location sound would be the sound produced by the workers and machinery in the shipyard, or the sound produced by the welding equipment itself. In a sequence on waterskiing, the natural sound would be the sound of the boat engines and the sound of the water against the boat's hull and the waterskis.

Natural sound adds an important dimension of detail to remote productions. Tape shot in the field that does not include natural sound seems flat and lifeless. You have all seen those weekend television sports programs, usually of fishing or hunting, in which a voice-over is used with silent footage of the sporting activity. Such a technique gives the program a distance and sense of unreality that is immediately noticeable. The viewer, consciously or unconsciously, is aware that something is missing. Something is indeed missing—the sounds one would hear if one were alongside the hunter. We expect to hear natural sound any time we see a picture because this is how we experience things visually and aurally in the real world. The importance of recording natural sound, particularly when shooting B-roll video footage that will be edited to match the voice-overs, cannot be overemphasized.

Music

In contrast to the naturalness and reality of natural sound, music is one of the most unrealistic sound elements within a program. How many times in real life has music been present as a background to your activities? Yet, ironically, a program without music often seems as flat, lifeless, and unnatural as one constructed without natural sound! The reason that music seems so natural is that we have become conditioned to its presence within visual presentations. The use of music is an easily understood convention that viewers have come to expect. A car chase without music to heighten the drama would be unusual indeed!

The principal use of music is often to reinforce or create a mood, as in the heightened drama that results from the music in the car chase. Music can also be used to present important information about locale (place) or time. A desert without music is simply a desert. However, with the appropriate background music it can become the desert of the American West, the desert of ancient Asian nomads, or a lunar desert in a futuristic space adventure.

Music, like natural sound, is important because it adds another layer to the audiovisual mosaic. As more layers are added, the mosaic becomes more complex and consequently more interesting to the viewer. Music, then, can be used to add energy to a scene that might otherwise seem to be slow or lifeless.

Another common use of music is in program themes. It is particularly noticeable and useful when used to introduce a program. While we would probably object to the use of background music during an interview with a leading head of state, we nonetheless readily accept it at the beginning of the news program that contains the interview. The reason for this is that music serves an important cuing function. It tells us when something new is about to happen. For this reason, it functions effectively to introduce a program, where it is used to catch the viewers' attention.

Music is used similarly as a punctuator within a program. Music introduced into a previously silent scene may tell us that something is about to happen or it may simply reinforce the situation as it has been presented.

Sound Effects

In studio video production, **sound effects** are often used to present the natural sounds of the location being depicted. The sounds of birds gently singing in the background during a scene supposedly taking place on a porch swing on a warm summer day will most certainly need to be added as a sound effect if the scene is staged in a studio. On the other hand, if the scene is shot on location, these background sounds may actually be present on the location as natural background sound.

Sound effects are widely used in both studio and remote production to suggest something that is happening off camera. Explosions, car wrecks, rocket launches, and other events of proportions that are difficult to stage can effectively be represented through the use of off-camera sound effects.

For a sound effect to be effective, it must be believable to the audience. Believability is achieved if the sound effect accurately represents the sound of the phenomenon in question. To do this, the sound effect must be characteristic of the phenomenon, and it must be presented at the proper volume and have the proper duration. A car crashing sounds different from a bottle breaking, and the sound of the engine of a passenger car is different from the sound of the engine of a high-performance racer. To be effective, these and any other sound effects must accurately match the sound of the event depicted, or the effect will be comedic. Show a man talking and dub in the voice of a woman, or show a rabbit with its mouth moving and dub in the sound of a chicken, and the audience will almost certainly laugh.

Sound Perspective and Sound Presence

Sound Perspective

Two important aesthetic variables commonly associated with sound are perspective and presence. **Sound perspective** refers to the way in which the perspective of the sound matches the perspective of the visuals related to that sound. A train in the distance appears to be small on screen, and the sound created by the train is faint. As the train gets closer, its image becomes larger and the sound becomes louder. This is the phenomenon of sound perspective.

Although this may seem straightforward and simple to achieve, in fact we often violate rules of absolute perspective in video production. In an interview, for example, when cutting from a long shot to a close-up, we seldom vary the perspective of the sound, although an absolute faithfulness to the principle would demand that we do so.

Problems with sound perspective frequently occur when shooting in the field. They usually result from the camera changing its perspective of a scene (by zooming in or out, for example) without a change in perspective of the sound picked up by the microphone. This occurs particularly if the microphone is attached to the camera or mounted in a fixed position. Tight shots look very different from wide shots, and we would expect the sound to be different if we strictly adhered to the rules of sound perspective. However, the microphone picks up sound in a consistent manner, whether it is attached to the subject or the camera.

Another problem with sound- and visual-perspective mismatch occurs when the sound source moves. The following example illustrates the problem. Visualize a shot in which the movement of a car is recorded as it proceeds down a narrow country road toward the camera. At the beginning of the shot, the car is far off in the distance and the sound of its engine is almost inaudible. The lens then zooms in all the way, so that the car fills the screen. Yet, in reality, the car is still quite a distance from the camera, where the microphone is mounted. Consequently, the sound of the engine is still rather weak. The camera holds the shot of the now empty road, while the car, now off camera, continues to approach the camera position. Several seconds later the car actually passes the camera and the engine sound swells to the full volume that was expected when the car's image filled the screen. What has happened is that the sound has become detached from the visual and does not match the perspective change of the visual. The sound seems to follow the car rather than to have been created by it.

Sound Presence

Nearby sounds are different from sounds far away. One obvious difference between the two is volume, as we have seen in the discussion of sound perspective. However, not only are nearby sounds louder than faraway sounds but also they have a different sound quality. This difference in sound quality is called **sound presence.** Nearby sounds not only sound loud but also sound close. This difference in quality results from the fact that microphones respond differently to sounds that are close than to ones that are farther away. At close distances, microphones pick up subtle tonal qualities of the sound that are inaudible at greater distances.

The effect of sound presence, then, can be created by closely recording the sound source. A handheld microphone held inches away from the speaker's mouth has a greater presence than a lavaliere held 15 inches away. And the lavaliere has a greater presence than a shotgun microphone located 15 feet away from the subject. Many video programs feature relatively close shots of speaking subjects, and it is important to capture as much of the sound presence of their speech as possible to facilitate the audience's perception of closeness.

Constructing the Audio
Portion of a Program

Just as a series of technical decisions must be made about the type and placement of microphones to ensure high-quality sound pickup, so must a series of strategic decisions be made about the design of the audio portion of a program.

Narrator versus
No Narrator

In any kind of documentary or informational program, basic decisions about the structure of the audio portion of the program center on the presence or absence of a narrator or host. Some documentarists prefer to let the story tell itself and are therefore resistant to the use of a narrator. Whether or not to use a narrator is a matter of both your personal preference and the goals of the program. A narrator might be an unnecessary intrusion into a program designed as an ethnographic study of people in a particular community. On the other hand, a program on the local pasta factory might be difficult to complete without a narrator to explain the technical elements of the factory's operation and to link together the program's various segments.

Narration serves many useful functions. It can quickly provide expositional details that might take considerable time to develop if left to emerge from the comments made by the participants in the program. Also, narration can effectively present technical information in nontechnical terms. Often, experts on a particular subject present information that is too detailed or complex. Narration is an effective way of providing transitions or bridges from one segment of the program to another. In addition, narration is often used to introduce speakers as they appear within a program. This is an effective and economical technique that eliminates the need for intrusive name superimpositions.

On-Camera and Off-Camera Questions

One of the first decisions that must be made when designing an interview-based program is whether the interviewer's questions will be incorporated into the final program. If the questions will be used, the interviewer must be miked. Furthermore, if you plan to include the questions, you must decide whether the interviewer will appear on camera or whether the questions will be asked from off camera.

In a single-camera shoot, on-camera questions are typically recorded after the interview is completed. This technique is called shooting **question re-asks.** Two important factors must be considered when shooting question re-asks:

1. The questions must be re-asked accurately; they should be the same questions as originally asked.
2. The camera must be correctly positioned so that the question re-asks can be edited together properly with the rest of the original interview material.

If the interview questions are scripted, then the same script of questions can be used to shoot the question re-asks. If the interview questions are asked spontaneously (ad-libbed) rather than from a script, the production assistant (PA) should write down the questions as they are asked. If this is not possible, or if the PA is not sure of having accurately written down the questions, then the audio portion of the videotape should be reviewed to produce an accurate transcript of the questions. The question re-asks can then be shot using this transcript as a guide.

Question re-asks should be shot immediately after the interview is completed and in the same location in which the interview was recorded. Move the camera and shoot the interviewer from an angle complementary to the angle at which the interview was shot. Care should be taken to ensure that the questions will cut together with the answers in terms of the screen directions of interviewer and interviewee. Care should also be taken to guarantee that the backgrounds for the interviewer and interviewee are consistent. They need not be exactly the same, but enough background information should be given for the viewer to know that the questions were asked and answered in the same locale.

Another important reason for shooting question re-asks in the same location as the interview is to guarantee that the sound quality of the questions matches the sound quality of the answers. The presence of consistent ambient room noise is particularly important in determining that the sound quality matches.

In addition to shooting the question re-asks in the same location, many videographers make it a practice to record some additional **room tone**—wild sound of the ambient sound present in the room. If a question needs to be reconstructed, recorded, and inserted into the program later on, room tone can be dubbed in under the question so that it will not sound like the question was asked at a different time or in a different place. Room tone can be recorded directly onto videotape by letting the camcorder run for several minutes. If the camcorder has a good-quality microphone attached to it, this will usually provide an acceptable room tone recording. Remember to keep quiet on the site while recording room tone. It is good practice to record at least 60 seconds of room tone at each location to be used if needed in editing.

Natural Sound

Every attempt should be made to record as much natural sound as possible while shooting in the field. Natural sound should be recorded onto the videotape along with the visual material that corresponds to it. Even if the tape is merely being shot to be used as the background visuals (B-roll) for narration voice-over segments, the natural sound should still be recorded. A segment with natural sound under the voice-over is usually more effective than the same visual sequence with narration and no natural sound.

Music and Sound Effects

The need for music and/or sound effects should be assessed early in a program's production. Indeed, the selection of music or effects is just as important as the selection of individual **sound bites**, or voice segments, and visual sequences.

Aside from the legal questions regarding permission to use music (see Chapter 13), great care should be taken in the selection and use of previously recorded music. Probably the greatest problem with prerecorded music is the fact that it may be familiar to a large part of the audience and may have very unique associations for different audience members. The lilting instrumental signifying blissful romance to one person may have been popular at the time someone else was enduring a bitter divorce. It may therefore symbolize loss rather than fulfillment to that audience member. This is one of the principal arguments for the use of original music. Uniquely composed original music can exhibit the expressive characteristics called for by the production, and therefore will facilitate rather than inhibit communication.

When music plays a supportive or reinforcing function within a scene, care should be taken to match it to the visuals in terms of mood, location, and historical time. Just as ragtime piano music would most likely be inappropriate as background music for a solemn funeral scene, so would bagpipes be inappropriate as the background for an Italian wedding—unless one intends a comic effect. Electronically synthesized music would similarly fail to match the historical time of a scene supposedly taking place in medieval England.

One final caution about music concerns the use of music with lyrics. Instrumental music is usually more easily incorporated into a production than is a song with lyrics for the simple reason that the lyrics may provide unwanted, unnecessary information to the viewer. When music is used as background, lyrics often compete for the viewer's attention. Lyrics create an almost insurmountable distraction to narration or dialogue. Furthermore, lyrics become even more distracting if the music fades out before the lyrics reach their conclusion. Music with lyrics should be used only if there is a precise reason for the inclusion of the lyrics—for example, if a particular song is being used for historical accuracy or if the lyrics reinforce or describe the visual action of the scene.

Making a Track Chart

Most videotape recording formats provide at least two tracks for recording sound in the field, but the number of tracks available during postproduction may be significantly larger. In nonlinear video editing systems and digital audio workstations designed for postproduction there commonly will be 4, 8, 16, or more available tracks. Even in a fairly simple video production with VO, SOT, natural sound, and music, you may find that you need four audio tracks to accommodate all your sound sources during postproduction.

An **audio track chart**—simply a log of each of the sound sources arranged along a time line of where they occur in the program—is a useful

Figure 7.20 Audio Track Chart

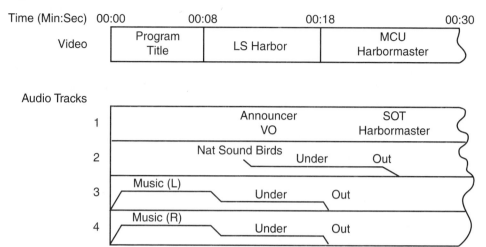

device to help plan and organize your production. First describe each of the video shots in sequence and then assign each of the sound sources to a different audio track in the time line. Be consistent about where you place similar sources. For example, in a four-track plan you may want to keep principal voice segments (VO and SOT) in track 1; natural sound and/or sound effects in track 2; and stereo music in tracks 3 and 4 (3 = left music channel, 4 = right music channel). (See Figure 7.20.) When the production is complete, the multitrack version of the program can be mixed down to two tracks on the program master.

The Visual Impact of Microphones

Obtrusive versus Unobtrusive

No discussion of the aesthetics of sound would be complete without mention of the visual impact of microphones. A microphone visible in a scene affects that scene. If characters in a drama all carried visible microphones, the illusion of the drama would be destroyed. For that reason, great care is taken to hide microphones in dramatic presentations. They are mounted on booms out of camera range, hidden in plants on the set, or cleverly concealed on the actors themselves—all to preserve the illusion of reality that the drama intends to convey.

In an interview-based presentation, microphones seem to be a necessary evil. We accept their presence unquestioningly. However, some care should be taken if you want to achieve a documentary effect in which the recording crew and its technology are unobtrusive. For example, in an ethnographic production, the story tells itself: no narrator is used, and the questions are not heard within the program. This illusion of objectivity should be supported through the relative invisibility of microphones.

Relatively unobtrusive lavaliere microphones can be used, or if the presence of any microphones will destroy the illusion, then a shotgun microphone held out of camera range may be most appropriate. The ENG-style intrusion of the microphone in someone's face is inappropriate in most circumstances other than on-the-street news interviews and should be avoided.

Consistent Use of Microphone Types

If microphones are to be visible in various shots, then an attempt should be made to be consistent with respect to the types of microphones used. If lavalieres are used, then the same type of lavaliere should be used on all interview subjects. Similarly, if a handheld microphone is used, the same type should be used consistently throughout the program. This is particularly important if an on-camera narrator does stand-ups throughout the piece. The same type of microphone should be used because it provides both visual and aural continuity. When different program segments are edited together into a complete program, consistent microphone use helps give the program unity, whereas inconsistent microphone use draws attention to differences in sound quality and will fragment the program.

8 Editing Aesthetics

Editing is an invisible art. When it is done well, it is hardly noticed—yet almost every visual message in television and film has been edited.

If we define *editing* as the process of selecting and ordering shots, we can identify two kinds of video editing: editing done during a program's production and editing done after the program has been videotaped. This latter type of editing is called *postproduction editing*.

Television directors have always had the ability to choose and order the shots within a program. Until the advent of postproduction editing, these decisions were made live, as the program was being taped or broadcast. The signals from several television cameras were simultaneously fed into a video switcher, and their pictures were displayed on monitors in a control room. The director would look at the monitors and call for the shots desired. This type of production is still widely done. Shot selections in most live news broadcasts, sports telecasts, and discussion programs are still made by a director in a control room who calls the shots as the program unfolds.

Video editing in postproduction eliminates the need for making editing decisions while a live program is in progress. Production personnel can concentrate on getting the information they need onto tape, without worrying about the arrangement of the shots until after they have finished taping the program. In addition, whereas video switching is often tied to events in one locale, postproduction editing allows gathering of material for a program from different locations over a longer time.

Postproduction editing, simply referred to as editing from here on, is extensively used in video production. Many programs that look live—such as interviews and variety shows—have been edited in postproduction, long after the initial material was taped.

Editing is the process of arranging individual shots or sequences into an appropriate order. The appropriate order is determined by the information the editor wants to communicate and the impact the editor wants to achieve with the material. The process of editing includes making a series of aesthetic judgments, through which the editor decides how the piece should look, and performing a series of technical operations to carry out the editing decisions. This chapter focuses on the aesthetic elements involved in editing.

Role of the Editor

The video editor is potentially one of the most creative members of the production team. No single-camera production shot with postproduction editing in mind would ever appear on a television screen without the services of a competent video editor. However, the importance of the editor to the production team depends on both the role and the amount of creative freedom given to that editor. In video production, two broad categories of editors are typically found: the autonomous creative editor, who makes the principal editing decisions, and the subordinate technical editor, who carries out editing decisions made by someone else.

The Creative Editor

The autonomous **creative editor** is an individual with significant responsibility for making and executing editing decisions. The creative editor must understand both the aesthetic principles of editing as well as how to operate the video editing equipment. Working in a variety of production situations, the creative editor may be given a brief story outline and a dozen cassettes of field tapes from which to edit a story segment that conforms to the general conventions of the program. Here, the editor has an incredible amount of creative freedom. Decisions about the use of music, sound effects, sound bites, shot sequences, and even the structure of the segment may be left to the editor's discretion. However, the segment or program producer or director usually retains veto power.

At the other end of the spectrum, the creative editor may edit material for a program that was shot from a full script. In this situation, the editor's role is to make the raw material conform to the script. Even within this process, the editor has considerable creative freedom. The editor works with multiple takes, from similar or different angles, of a number of individual shots. Although the basic structure and dialogue of the scene are given in the script, the editor can significantly influence the shape and impact of the scene by selecting the particular shots and takes that work best.

The Technical Editor

The subordinate **technical editor** is usually (but not always) primarily a technician or engineer who is thoroughly familiar with the operation of the editing system from a technical standpoint. The technical editor executes editing decisions made by someone else.

Many video production companies do not own production equipment of their own, choosing instead to rent or lease production equipment and facilities from companies that specialize in providing these services. This is often the case with video editing equipment. Because editing systems vary in complexity and flexibility from one facility to the next, when a suite of video editing equipment is rented at a postproduction facility, an editor is usually provided from the staff of the postproduction facility to operate the equipment in an efficient, cost-effective manner. Creative control of editing decisions is retained by the producer or director of the program, and the technical editor performs the edits as they have been determined by the individuals with creative control over the program.

It would be grossly unfair to say that technical editors understand only the technical process of editing and not the aesthetics of editing. In reality, most technical editors know what edits together well and what does not. The principal difference between creative and technical editors lies in the location of creative control over editing decisions. The autonomous creative editor has such control, whereas the subordinate technical editor usually does not. However, most good subordinate technical editors make suggestions about the aesthetics of the edit and, for that reason, they too are partners in the creative editing process.

In many production situations, one individual performs both of these editing functions. Indeed, in many small video production companies and in video production units located in educational institutions, corporations, cable television, and sometimes even broadcast television, one person may produce, direct, and shoot the entire production as well as edit it! Therefore, it is extremely important to understand both the aesthetic and the technical aspects of video editing, and how to plan and execute a production reflecting both of these areas of concern.

The Editor as Graphic Artist

In addition to the technical and aesthetic elements of editing, today's video editors are increasingly being called upon to integrate significant graphic design elements into the programs they edit. Modern digital non-linear editing systems not only allow audio and video to be edited quickly and efficiently but also allow for easier integration of graphics and special effects than the tape-based systems they are replacing. Increasingly, editing, graphics, and effects software are installed on the same computer system, and one person has the responsibility of performing editing, graphics, and effects tasks. The technical editors of old are being replaced quickly by more creative editing personnel who are as familiar with graphic design as they are with editing.

 ## Types of Editing

There are two general techniques, or styles, of editing. One is continuity editing; the other is dynamic, or complexity, editing. These two terms represent somewhat of an oversimplification of many ways that editing can be approached. Editing is seldom solely one technique or the other. In most cases, it is a combination of the two techniques. However, these two terms, *continuity editing* and *dynamic editing,* provide a useful place to begin talking about different kinds of editing.

 ## Continuity Editing

The goal of **continuity editing** is to move the action along smoothly without any discontinuous jumps in time or place. It is easier to perform continuity editing of visual sequences if the material has been shot with postproduction editing in mind. (You may want to review the guidelines for shooting to edit in Chapter 3.)

However, even if the field tape has not been shot according to the rules, there are a number of guidelines that the editor can follow to achieve continuity in editing. Four of the more important guidelines are discussed here.

Establish and Maintain Screen Position

Establishing Shots.   The use of the **establishing shot** is an important feature of continuity editing because it identifies the location and the position of the people in the shot in relation to their environment. Once a scene has been set up through an establishing shot, many of the other principles of continuity editing follow logically.

Cut In and Cut Out.   By their nature, establishing shots tend to be medium or long shots. These shots often do not have the dynamism or energy of the close-up shot. Once a scene has been established, it is standard editing technique to then **cut in** to a close-up of some detail of that scene. The interview that begins with an over-the-shoulder 2-shot of the interviewer and subject is frequently followed by a cut-in to the close-up of the subject. In a demonstration of a product or machine, the establishing shot may present a shot of the object and the person with the object. The cut-in presents important details not visible in the longer shot.

Conversely, once the cut-in establishes the important detail, it is frequently necessary to **cut out** again to the wider shot, particularly if action is about to take place. A shot sequence utilizing the techniques of the establishing shot, cut-in, and cut-out is shown in Figure 8.1.

When cutting in to a tighter shot from a wide shot, objects and people should maintain their same relative place in the frame. Someone who is on the right side of the frame in the wide shot should remain on that side of the frame, or in the neutral center of the frame, when you cut into a medium close-up. The cut in should not cause the person to flip to the other side of the frame (see Figure 8.2).

Establishing Shot

Close-Up

Close-Up

Wide Shot

Figure 8.1   Establishing Shot, Cut In, and Cut Out Sequence

Poor Edit

Woman's Screen Position Changes

Good Edit

Woman's Screen Position Is Maintained

Figure 8.2
Screen Position
Reversal

Jump Cuts and Matched Cuts.

Jump cuts and matched cuts violate the conventions of continuity editing because they destroy the invisible, or seamless, quality of the editing. A **jump cut** occurs when something is removed from the middle of a shot and the two remaining end pieces are joined together. If the size and position of the subject are not exactly the same, the cut from the beginning shot to the end shot will cause the subject to appear to jump in the frame. Look at the two sequences of images in Figure 8.3. In the first sequence a woman walks toward her friend, sits down at the table, and drinks from her cup of coffee. All of the essential action of the event is represented in the shot (approach, sit down, drink). If the middle part of the shot where the woman sits down at the table to join her friend is removed, and the first and last parts of the shot are joined together (approach, drink), the woman on the right-hand side of the frame will instantly jump from her standing position next to the table to a sitting position at the table with the coffee cup raised in her hand. This is an extreme example of a jump cut.

Matched cuts are similar to jump cuts. A **matched cut** is a cut from one shot to another that is similar in terms of angle of view and camera

Continuous Sequence

Woman Approaches

Woman Sits

Woman Drinks Coffee

Jump-Cut Sequence

Woman Approaches

Woman Is Seated,
Drinking Coffee

Figure 8.3
Jump-Cut Sequence

position. When the two shots are joined together, the effect is of a jump or change in the screen position of the people and objects in the shots (see Figure 8.4).

Avoid jump cuts and matched cuts because they are visible and obtrusive. They look like editing mistakes because they violate the spatial continuity of the subject in the frame. When the subject jumps or moves from one part of the frame to another without any motivation, continuity is lost.

Figure 8.4
Matched Cut

Shot 1   Shot 2

Subject jumps in frame when cutting from shot 1 to shot 2.

Use Eyelines to Establish the Direction of View and Position of the Target Object

An **eyeline** is simply a line created by your eyes when you look at a **target object**. If you look up into the sky at a bird, the bird is the target object and the eyeline is the imaginary line between your eyes and the bird. Look down at your feet and a similar eyeline is created between your eyes and their target.

Eyelines and the position of the target object are very important in creating continuity. A close-up of someone looking up, followed by a close-up of a bird, makes sense (see Figure 8.5). The same close-up of a person looking up, followed by a shot of the subject's feet, does not.

Eyelines are formed between people when they talk, and they can be used to create continuity when the conversation is edited. This type of continuity editing is facilitated if the original material has been shot utilizing complementary angles. A simple scene with two people illustrates the point, which can be applied to interviews as well. Assume that an establishing shot has been recorded. The first sequence in Figure 8.6 shows the establishing shot as the editor sees it on tape. Close-up details of each of the people in the shot have been recorded using complementary angles—one looks to the right side of the screen, the other looks to the left side of the screen. When the establishing shot and two close-ups are edited together, the shot sequence reveals the two people talking to each other.

Violating the rule of complementary angles produces a discontinuous, if not comedic, effect. In the second sequence of shots in Figure 8.6, the characters are facing the same angle on camera in their MCU shots. These two shots cannot be edited to make it look like the two people are talking to each other because the people in the shots are not in the target positions created by their eyelines.

Figure 8.5   Eyelines Establish Position of Target Object

Eyeline   Target Object

Establishing Shot

Two Medium Close-Ups Shot at Complementary Angles

Establishing Shot

Two Medium Close-Ups *Not* Shot at Complementary Angles

Figure 8.6   Complementary Angles

Maintain Continuity in the Direction of Action

Perhaps nothing is more important to maintaining the continuity of action than maintaining **directional continuity**. Characters or objects moving in one shot should continue to move in the same general direction in a subsequent shot. Directional continuity will be apparent in the raw footage if the videographer has paid attention to the 180-degree rule and the principal action axis when shooting the original field tapes (see Chapter 3).

Mismatches in directional continuity are most apparent when a strong horizontal movement in one direction is immediately followed by another movement in the opposite direction, as in the example in Figure 8.7. In the first shot, action moves from left to right in the frame. In the second shot, the screen position of the subject is reversed, and the woman now appears to be moving from the right side of the frame to the left. If the editor needs to use discontinuous shots, they should be bridged by a neutral shot in which the action moves directly toward or away from the camera. The second shot sequence in Figure 8.7 illustrates how a neutral shot can be used to bridge a discontinuous shot sequence.

Discontinuous Action Sequence

Action Moves to the Right   Action Moves to the Left

Bridging Discontinuous Action with a Neutral Shot

Action ⟶ Neutral ⟵ Action

Action Moves Toward Camera

Figure 8.7   Bridging Discontinuous Action with a Neutral Shot

Use Shot Content to Motivate Cuts

In continuity editing, each edit or cut is usually motivated. That is, there should be a reason for making an edit. The two principal motivators of cuts are dialogue and action.

Much editing is motivated by what is said. For example, a question demands an answer, and each line of dialogue in a dramatic scene must be met with another. In these situations, the editor's task is to cut the material together so that what is said makes sense and so that the visual and aural sequence flows smoothly. The rhythm of the editing should match the rhythm of what is being said in the scene. To do this, edits are usually made at the natural breaks in the dialogue.

The other great motivation for a cut is action. Indeed, one of the cardinal rules of cutting is to cut on action. Look at the sequence in Figure 8.8. This sequence contains two shots of a chef whipping ingredients in a bowl.

Shot 1—LS Chef and Bowl   Shot 2—CU Chef Whipping Bowl

Figure 8.8
Cutting on Action

Shot 1 is a long shot of the chef and bowl; shot 2 is a close-up of the bowl. The best time to cut to the close-up of the bowl is when the chef begins to whip the ingredients. The editor needs to match the edit point carefully on the two shots. Because the action is repeated in both shots, it must be edited in such a way that no duplication of action is visible. The sequence should look as if it is happening in real time.

As this example demonstrates, it is easier to cut on action if the editor has several shots repeating the action from different angles. A good field producer makes certain that this material has been shot.

Other Continuity Issues

Beyond the issues of continuity related to placement of the subjects in the frame, the editor should pay attention to several other continuity problems as well.

Lighting Continuity. Field video production is characterized by shooting at different locations on different days and at different times of day. Unlike studio video production, where tight control of lighting can be achieved, light values in field video production tend to vary from location to location and by time of day.

Sometimes changes in the quality of light from shot to shot will make sense in the context of the story being told; other times such changes will make the action seem discontinuous. For example, outdoor material shot on a foggy day with soft, diffuse light will not cut together well with material shot at the same location on a sunny day. If you have to make a continuous sequence of shots recorded under differing lighting conditions, care needs to be taken so that shots with widely varying light values are not juxtaposed.

Sound Continuity.   As is the case with light, sound conditions vary from location to location as well. Although this may be an advantage in differentiating one locale from another, it can also present a problem, particularly where the voice tracks are concerned. The sound quality of interview material should be consistent, and a good editor will use plenty of room tone or background sound to smooth cuts from one sound bite to another.

Physical Appearance of the Subjects.   Attention also needs to be paid to the general physical appearance of the principal subjects in order to ensure that their appearance does not change radically within the program or segment. Audiences readily accept that a subject's clothing may be different in interview shots and in B-roll footage shot on location. However, if some other aspect of the subject's appearance changes radically, it may confuse your viewers.

For example, consider a subject photographed with a full head of hair in an interview, who then appears with his head shaved bald in B-roll footage recorded some time after the interview. If the subject's appearance changes radically, it may have to be explained in the script, particularly if the change is so dramatic that viewers will not easily recognize the "before" and "after" subject as the same person!

Dynamic Editing

Dynamic editing differs from continuity editing in two important ways. It tends to be a bit more complex in structure, and it frequently utilizes visual material to create an impact rather than simply to convey literal meaning. Dynamic editing, then, is more *affective* than continuity editing. This is not to say that continuity editing must be listless or boring or that dynamic editing cannot be used to convey a literal message. The differences between the two are often differences of degree rather than of substance.

Editing to Maximize Impact

Dynamic editing attempts to maximize a scene's impact rather than simply to link together individual shots into an understandable sequence. The selection of shots for use in dynamic editing, therefore, is somewhat different than in continuity editing. Dynamic shot selection frequently includes shots that exaggerate or intensify the event rather than simply reproduce it. Extremely tight shots or shots from peculiar angles are frequently incorporated into dynamic shot sequences to intensify a scene's impact.

Manipulating the Time Line

Dynamic editing frequently is discontinuous in time. That is, rather than concentrating on one action as it moves forward in time (a technique typical of continuity editing), dynamic editing can use **parallel cutting**—cutting between two actions occurring at the same time in different locations or between events happening at different times. The dynamic editor might intercut frames of past or future events to create the effect of a **flashback** or a **flashforward.**

Editing Rhythm

Continuity editing is usually motivated by the rhythm of the event (either the action of the participants or the dialogue of the characters); dynamic editing is more likely to depend on an external factor for its motivation and consequent rhythm. Two common techniques include editing to music and timed cuts.

In its most common form, **editing to music** involves editing together a series of related or unrelated images to some rhythmic or melodic element in a piece of music. In the most clichéd type of editing to music, the editing matches a regular rhythmic beat and does not deviate from it. Editing that uses various musical components—the melody or a strong musical crescendo, for example—to motivate the edits is more energetic and interesting.

A **timed cut** is one in which shot length is determined by time rather than content. You can edit together a sequence of shots that are each two seconds in length, or you can use shot length like a music measure to compose a sequence with a rhythm based on the length of the shots.

The Rule of Six

Although this discussion of editing began with a description of how to achieve continuity of the subject in time and space, editing that is "correct" as far as continuity is concerned may not be good editing unless other factors are considered as well. Veteran film editor Walter Murch suggests that six elements should be considered to evaluate each edit made:

1. **Emotion.** Does the edit make the audience feel what you want them to feel at that moment?
2. **Story.** Does the edit advance the story in a meaningful way? Does the edit help your audience understand the story, or does it confuse them and/or complicate the story?

3. **Rhythm.** Does the edit occur at the point that is rhythmically correct in terms of the edited shot sequence? When you review the edit, does it feel right?

4. **Center of Interest.** Does the edit respect the visual center of interest of shots that precede and follow it? Is the viewer's eye readily led to the center of interest in successive shots, or is the viewer forced to search for the center of interest?

5 and 6. **Two- and Three-Dimensional Screen Space and Continuity.** Does the placement of subjects in the frame and in relation to other subjects and the environment in the shot respect the conventions of visual continuity? Are the spatial relationships between characters understandable in the shot sequence?[1]

 # Transitions
and Effects

Transitions

For most video producers with simple editing systems, the cut is the only visual transition possible from shot to shot. The most frequently used transition in video and film, the **cut** is an instantaneous change from one shot to another. It approximates the effect achieved by blinking, without leaving a blank or black space between shots.

For the producer with access to an A/B-roll editing system or a non-linear editing system, a number of other transitions are available.

A **fade** is a gradual transition from black to an image or from an image to black. Fades are usually used at the beginning and end of a program; thus, we have the terms *fade in* and *fade out*. However, fades are also used within a program. A fade signals a break in continuity of the visual message. Fades are used to insulate the program material from a commercial, to signal to the audience that an event or episode has ended, that time has passed, and so on.

The **dissolve** is similar to the fade except it involves two visual sources. One gradually fades out as the other fades in, and the two sources overlap during the transition. The effect is one image changing into another. Dissolves, once widely used to signal passage of time, now are more often used to show the relationship between images, particularly structurally related images. A dissolve from a photograph of a young man to another photograph of the same man in old age not only clearly shows the passage of time but also represents the metamorphosis of one image into another.

A **wipe** is a transition in which one screen image is replaced by another. The second image cuts a hard- or soft-edged pattern into the frame as the transition takes place. The wipe pattern is selected and preset by pressing the appropriate button on a video switcher. Most video switchers are equipped with a standard array of wipe patterns: circles, squares, diagonals, diamonds, and so on.

Digital Video Effects (DVE)

Once extremely popular in television commercials but seldom used in news or dramatic productions, wipes have now largely been replaced by **digital video effects**. Digital video effects are made possible by digital processing equipment, which digitizes and processes the video signal. Common digital effects include **page push** and **page pull** (the picture appears to be pushed or pulled off the screen by another), **page turn** (this looks like the page of a book or magazine turning), and a host of three-dimensional effects that transform the image into a sphere, the side of a cube, and so on.

Figure 8.9   Digital Video Effects

This sequence of shots was manipulated digitally. The image was flown into the frame and then compressed to create a photograph-like image.

257

Figure 8.10 Sample of Transitions Available in a Nonlinear Video Editing System

Other common digital video effects include **image compression** and **expansion,** which result from stretching or squeezing the horizontal and vertical dimensions of the picture. Through image compression, a full-frame image can be reduced to any size and positioned anywhere in the frame. Similarly, through expansion, a reduced image located in a section of the frame can increase in size until it fills the frame (see Figure 8.9).

Digital video effects are often used as transitions. Once, only state-of-the-art production houses and television studios had the sophisticated video switchers with the processing equipment necessary for these effects. But with the increasing convergence of computer and video technology, many of these special effects are now available in cost-effective desktop video systems. (See Figure 8.10.)

Camera-Generated Transition Elements

Despite the availability of this wide range of transition devices in many sophisticated editing systems, much video editing is accomplished on rather simple systems that allow only cuts for transitions. The creative challenge, then, becomes to plan for transitions during the shooting process so that effective and interesting transitions can be achieved even with the cuts-only limitation.

For example, the effect of a dissolve can be approximated by cutting on shots that are out of focus. As you are shooting what will be the first shot in your edited sequence, roll the image out of focus and record this. Begin shooting the second shot in the sequence with the image out of focus and then bring it in to focus. If the focus rolls are timed well and the edit is made at the point where shot 1 ends (out of focus) and shot 2 begins (out of focus), the edit will be relatively invisible and the edited sequence will provide an effect similar to a dissolve. Similarly, fades can be achieved by using the camera iris to fade shots in or out when they are originally recorded. Many consumer camcorders contain a fade-in/fade-out control that accomplishes this electronically.

Camera movement can also be preplanned to accentuate the editing process by controlling the speed and direction of pans, tilts, and zooms during the field production phase of the program. Shots can then be cut together in which camera movement continues in the same direction and at the same speed from one shot to the next, or sequences can be constructed in which the direction of camera movement reverses from one shot to the next.

Motion Effects

The speed at which shots are replayed can be manipulated during the editing process. Although all field video is recorded at normal speed, during editing the playback speed can be increased or decreased. In linear editing systems, this is accomplished by VCRs capable of slow- or fast-motion playback; in nonlinear editing systems, motion effects software is used to control the speed of the images. *Slow-motion* effects are the most common, with the action taking on a smooth, almost dream-like quality. *Accelerated-motion* effects can be created by increasing the playback speed of source materials.

Color and Brightness Effects

Color and brightness values of recorded images can also be manipulated during editing. Hue, saturation, and brightness can be adjusted to correct the color values of video recorded in the field and to make it consistent with the other shots in a program, or color and brightness values can be purposefully distorted to achieve a particular effect. Color images can be converted into black-and-white images by eliminating all of the color information in the video signal, or the range of color values present in normal video can be replaced with one particular value—for example, sepia, or blue, or any other color—to achieve the desired effect.

Sound in Editing

Sound is one of the most important components of video editing. From a technical standpoint, control over sound is essential to avoid distortion and make a clear recording. From an aesthetic standpoint, sound plays an important role in influencing the mood and pace of the edited piece and, subsequently, the audience's response to the program. Control of sound during the editing process involves a number of different steps, including sound selection, sequencing, layering, and processing.

Sound Selection

The most basic decision to be made about sound while editing is deciding which sound segments to include and which not to include. The editor must first choose from the material available on the unedited videotapes and then must decide what material needs to be added. Additional material may include narration, music, or sound effects.

If the unedited material is interview-based, the editor will need to identify those sections of the interview with the most impact and/or those that concisely present the speaker's point of view. These segments are called **sound bites** when they are edited into the program.

A narrator can link together these sound bites. **Narration** will then need to be written and recorded for these transition segments. When the narrator is heard but not seen on screen, this is called a **voice-over (VO).** If the narrator is seen on screen while speaking, this is referred to as **sound on tape (SOT).**

Music and sound effects can later be edited into the program as well. The process of recording these sound tracks is known as **laying down tracks.**

Sound Sequencing

Once the principal sound segments have been selected, the editor must put them into the proper sequence. No matter what the purpose of the segment is, some kind of order is needed. In an instructional or dramatic program, the presentation of the basic material may follow a rigid structure that is geared to maximize the learning or dramatic impact of the program. In an experimental production, sound sequence may be determined by other concerns. In both types of productions, however, basic decisions need to be made about the order of presentation.

In addition to determining the sequence of the sound segments, the editor must also determine the kind of transitions that will be used between them. When editing voice, the most common transition is a straight cut. When one audio segment ends, the next one begins, leaving a natural pause between segments. In other kinds of audio sequences, segues or crossfades may be used.

A **segue** (pronounced "SEG-way") from one sound to another is a transition in which the first sound gradually fades out. When the sound has faded out completely, the next sound is gradually faded in. There is a slight space between the two sounds but no overlap. In a **crossfade**, the first sound fades out but the second sound fades in before the first one fades out completely. This results in a slight overlap of the two sounds.

An edit that simultaneously affects both audio and video is known as a **both edit**—that is, both audio and video are edited at the same time. Most dialogue and interview editing is of this type. An on-camera SOT introduction from the field news reporter that is immediately followed by an SOT statement from a county official under arrest for corruption is an example of a both edit. One picture and its corresponding sound are immediately replaced by another picture and its corresponding sound.

Another sound-editing technique is the **split edit.** In the split edit, an edit is made first on sound (or picture) and then is followed by the edit to the corresponding picture (or sound). Two separate edits—one on audio, the other on picture—are made, and one follows the other in time.

Consider a sequence in which an on-camera news field reporter, standing outside the local federal building, announces that a noisy protest by tax resisters is going on inside. Instead of cutting from the reporter to the video and audio of the protesters inside, the editor can first cut in the sound of the protesters under the shot of the newscaster giving the introduction. Then the editor can follow with the video of the demonstrators after the introduction is complete. In an interior scene in which a distraught father is waiting for word from the police about the condition of his missing daughter, we see the father glancing nervously out the window. An audio-only edit can introduce the sound of the police car approaching at high speed, followed by a video edit to the patrol car itself, with the sound in sync as it grinds to a halt in front of the house.

Sound Layering

The sound portion of a program can include several sound sources heard simultaneously. When voice-over narration is used, the voice is usually heard over both a picture and some kind of background sound. A more complex example of sound layering might include hearing voice-over, natural sound, and music simultaneously in the same shot. The editor, therefore, not only must select the appropriate sound sources but also must layer or **mix** them together appropriately.

The relative strength of each of the sounds layered together is usually determined by its importance in the scene or sequence. The editor must correctly mix them so that their relative volume matches their importance. A voice-over should not be overwhelmed by the natural sound or music that is supposed to be in the background. However, in a highly dramatic scene, the music may well come to the foreground as it overwhelms the background and other sounds in the scene.

Sound layering, then, involves determining which sounds should be heard in the foreground, in the background, or in between. It also involves achieving the proper layering effect through volume manipulation when mixing the sound in the editing process.

Sound Processing

Sound quality is also frequently manipulated during the editing process. Audio filters and graphic equalizers are widely employed either to correct a problem in the field audio or to manipulate an audio source to achieve a particular effect. The editor must consider all the available sound sources and determine whether manipulation of the sound quality is needed. If there are inconsistencies in the quality of the voice recordings on various field tapes, an equalizer should be used to achieve maximum consistency.

NOTE

1. Murch, Walter, *In the Blink of an Eye: A Perspective on Film Editing,* Beverly Hills, CA: Silman-James Press, 1995.

9 Linear, Cuts-Only Videotape Editing

The technology of video editing has undergone significant change in the past several years. Two different technologies are now used for video editing: the traditional linear videotape-based editing systems and the more recently developed digital nonlinear editing systems. This chapter will concentrate on linear, cuts-only videotape editing. Chapter 10 focuses on multiple-source (A/B roll) linear videotape editing, and Chapter 11 focuses on digital nonlinear systems.

In **linear videotape editing** systems, videotape is the recording medium. Edits are made in a sequential fashion, one after the other, starting at the beginning of the program or segment and working to the end. The simplest systems are capable of making only one kind of editing transition—a cut.

Electronic Videotape Editing

Electronic editing with videotape is simply a process of rerecording information into a new sequence. Two videotape machines are used: the playback VCR, or source VCR, which contains the original videotape; and the record VCR, or editing VCR, which contains a blank videotape (see Figures 9.1 and 9.2). Material from the source VCR is recorded onto the editing

Source VCR

Editing VCR

Edit Control
Unit

Figure 9.1
JVC ½″ VHS/S-VHS
Edit Desk System

VCR in the desired sequence. After editing, the new edited version is on the videotape in the editing VCR, and your original tape remains in its original form on the source VCR. You have made a copy of certain portions of the original, rearranged in a new order.

Although this sounds simple, electronic editing is complicated by the fact that the video signal can be reproduced only when the videotapes are already moving through the machines. Therefore, you need a system that can make an edit at a precise point while both the source VCR and the editing VCR are rolling. In this respect, making an edit can be compared to passing a baton during a relay race. As the runner with the baton ap-

Figure 9.2 Cuts-Only Editing
System Schematic

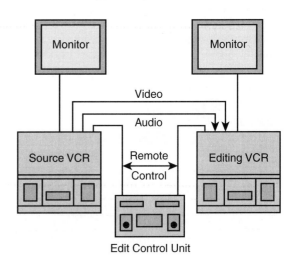

proaches the baton-pass area, the second runner, who will receive the baton, begins to run. When the baton actually passes hands, both runners are moving at full speed.

Editing System Components

A complete editing system (see Figure 9.2) generally includes the following components:

1. Playback (source) VCR, to play back the original, unedited videotape
2. Record (editing) VCR, capable of making a clean edit in the vertical interval between frames
3. Monitors for the source and editing VCRs, to allow you to see and hear the audio and video from each source
4. An edit control unit for controlling both VCRs, so that edit points can be found and edits precisely made by incorporating an adequate preroll time that allows the machines to stabilize and reach their edit points at the same time

Editing Videocassette Recorders

To edit electronically, a special type of videocassette recorder—the **editing VCR**—is used. An editing VCR accomplishes an edit by synchronizing the incoming signal from the source VCR with the signal on the editing master tape. The *editing master tape* is the tape in the editing VCR onto which the program material is being edited. For the edit to be accomplished cleanly, the editing VCR must begin recording a new field (track) of information at precisely the same instant that the source VCR plays back that field of information. In addition, the edit must be made in the vertical interval between frames of information on the videotape in the editing VCR (see Figure 9.3).

This synchronization is achieved in two ways. First, the editing VCR reads the incoming vertical sync pulses from the source VCR. This information is transmitted to the capstan servo, which adjusts the playback phase and speed of the editing VCR to correspond with the speed of the source VCR. This aligns the vertical interval of the video signal in the editing VCR with the vertical interval of the video signal on the source VCR (see Figure 9.3). When the video signals have been synchronized, the posi-

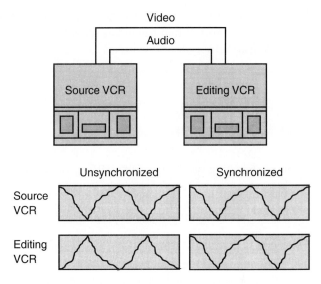

Figure 9.3 Synchronized Source and Editing VCR Signals

tion of the video record heads in the editing VCR is adjusted by the head servo so that they precisely scan the tracks of information on the tape.

If this sounds complicated, it is! Editing VCRs are marvels of modern electrical and mechanical engineering. They are complicated, sensitive, and sometimes temperamental pieces of equipment and deserve to be treated with respect.

Editing Control Units

The process of locating editing points and then **backspacing** the machines several seconds to allow adequate preroll time—also called backtiming, prerolling, or cuing—is done with **automatic editing control units** that read control track pulses or SMPTE time code.

Control Track Editing

The simplest type of edit cuing system relies on an *automatic edit control unit* to cue up the tape by counting the tape's control track pulses (see Figure 9.4). Commonly referred to as **control track editors**, these relatively inexpensive controllers are used in both broadcast and nonbroadcast production applications. Although they are sometimes criticized because they are not as accurate as SMPTE time code systems, they are considerably less expensive. In some applications, they also allow the editor to work faster. Simple control track edit controllers are widely used in many educational and institutional editing facilities.

Figure 9.4 Cuts-Only Control Track Edit Control Units

Sony RM 250

Panasonic AG A750

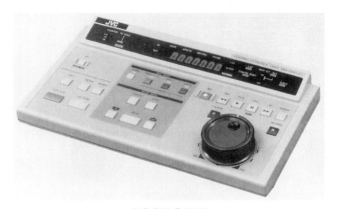

JVC RM-G800U

Standard Controls

All edit control units contain a set of standard controls. First, the controller contains a set of player (source VCR) and recorder (editing VCR) controls for both of the machines in any of their normal operating modes: play, fast forward, rewind, stop, and so on. Usually, the left side of the edit control unit contains a full set of controls for the source VCR, and the right side contains all the controls for the editing VCR. The edit control unit, then, is simply a remote control device that can be used to control the playback and record functions of the machine (see Figure 9.5).

Because editing demands that precise frames of information be found at the edit points, the control units also typically contain a **joystick** or **search dial** that allows the editor to look at the image on either machine in a number of different modes: frame by frame, slow motion, normal motion, and fast motion. Through the use of the joystick or search dial, the tapes can be jogged forward or reverse with the videotape against the VCR heads. The picture and sound are displayed in the monitor, allowing you to select the precise frame to be edited.

Most edit control units also contain a *digital time display* in hours, minutes, seconds, and frames for both the source and editing VCRs. This

Figure 9.5   Functional Diagram of a Cuts-Only Edit Control Unit

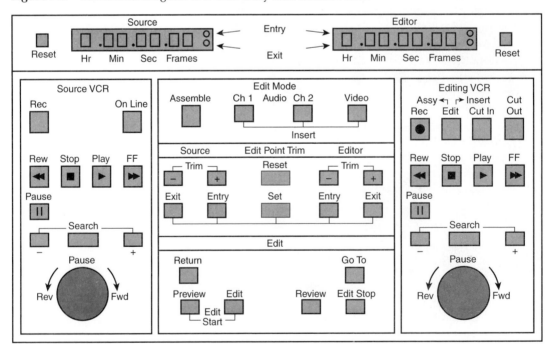

digital display works by reading the control track pulses on the tape. When you put a tape into a VCR and push the play button, a digital readout appears on the edit controller that displays the location on the tape. The edit controller is not displaying clock time. Rather, it is translating control track pulses into a time readout. This may seem minor, but it is really a very important point. The control track edit controller does not use a clock to tell time. It simply counts control track pulses and then translates the count of those pulses into a time readout: 30 pulses equals one second; 1,800 pulses equals one minute; 108,000 pulses equals one hour; and so on.

It is important to remember that the time readout on the edit control unit is accurate only if the counter is reset to zero at the beginning of the tape and if the tape has continuous control track on it. If the counter is reset to zero in the middle of a tape, the time readout will begin counting again from 0 hours, 0 minutes, 0 seconds, and 0 frames. The time readout, then, must be treated carefully. If it is *not* reset to zero at the beginning of a tape, or if it *is* reset to zero in the middle of a tape, the readout will not be accurate.

The center part of the edit control unit contains the editing controls. The *edit mode* buttons are used to select either the assemble- or insert-edit mode. (These modes are explained later in this chapter.) If the insert mode is selected, an additional group of buttons allows the operator to select video, audio 1, or audio 2 in any combination as the signals to be inserted. *Edit point* controls are used to enter the edit entry and exit points. **Trim** controls allow you to add or subtract frames from the edit points after they have been entered into the control unit.

Also included among the editing controls are those that set up the performance of the edit once the edit points have been selected. The *preroll* control (sometimes called the *cue* control) backspaces each machine five seconds before the edit entry points to allow enough time for the machines to get up to speed and stabilize before the edit takes place. The *preview,* or *rehearse,* control allows you to preview an edit without actually recording it. Both machines will roll forward and do a practice edit that you can view on the monitor of the editing VCR; however, the editing VCR will not ac-tually record the edit. If the edit meets with your approval, you can use the *perform edit* or *edit start* control to recue the machines and actually perform and record the edit.

Most edit control units also contain a *review* control. After the edit has been made, the control unit will stop both tapes and rewind the edit-ing VCR to the exit point of the edit just completed. When the review con-trol is depressed, the control unit rewinds the editing VCR to a point in front of the entry point of this edit. It then puts the machine into the play mode so the edit can be viewed at normal playing speed. You should al-ways review each edit at normal speed and in slow motion after it has been recorded. Make sure that the edit achieves the desired aesthetic effect, and

269

check it for technical accuracy and stability. The *go to* control moves the tape in either machine to a specified point—typically the entry or exit point of the previous edit, or in VCRs with SMPTE time code, to a particular time code location in the tape.

Setting the Edit Points

On control track edit control units, edit points are set by finding the precise frame on which the edit is to be made and then putting the machine into the pause mode at that point. The precise frame of the edit is found by using the joystick or search dial with the VCR operating in the search mode. Edit entry and exit points are then entered into the edit control unit by pressing the appropriate buttons to set the entry and exit points for the source and record VCRs.

On some systems, you can enter edit points *on the fly,* with the VCR in the play mode. When the editor sees the desired edit point (or hears it, if this is an audio edit), the editor pushes the edit entry control as the tape is playing. This enters the edit point into the system. The difficulty with entering the edit decisions on the fly is that accuracy depends on the speed of the editor's reaction. If the editor's reflexes are slow, the edit point may be off by a second or more. For this reason, the search mode is most often used to enter edit points by slow-speed searching for the precise frame and then putting the machine into the still-frame mode at the edit point.

Yet another option allows the editor to perform edits on the fly. Most editing VCRs and automatic edit control units contain a pair of buttons labeled *cut in* and *cut out.* If an input signal is being fed into the editing VCR (from a source VCR or other video source) and the cut-in button is depressed, an insert edit will be made. When the cut-out button is hit, the edit will end. You should exercise great caution when editing in this manner. As with setting edit points on the fly, correct edit points depend on quick reflexes. Furthermore, because the cut-in button actually executes the edit (and consequently erases and records over the original material on the edit master tape), you will not have a chance to correct a wrong edit.

Backspacing

Once the edit entry and exit points have been entered into the control unit, the VCRs need to be cued to a point before the edit entry points so that both VCRs can be backspaced. The control of this process—also called backtiming, cuing, or prerolling—is one of the most important functions of the edit control unit, and it is in the way the VCRs are backspaced that the meaning of the term *control track editor* emerges.

When you give the edit control unit the command to backspace the tapes, they typically back up to a point 5 seconds before the edit point. However, the control track editors do this *not* by measuring time but rather by counting control track pulses. Because there are (or should be) 30 control track pulses per second, the control unit counts off the control track pulses from the beginning of the edit point. When it reaches 150 pulses (30 pulses per second × 5 seconds = 150), it stops the VCR, which is now cued. Similarly, when the command is given to perform the edit, the control track editor does not know where the edit point is in terms of the video or audio content of the picture. It simply counts off the 150 control track pulses again and makes the edit when it reaches pulse 150.

Perhaps the most common problem encountered with the control track edit units occurs when you attempt to cue a tape that lacks enough control track in advance of the edit point to allow the control unit to backspace the tape. *Tapes must always have at least 5 seconds of continuous video information and control track before the edit point. Just to be safe, it is better to have more than 5 seconds (10 seconds is good).*

Let's suppose that you are trying to cue up a tape on the source VCR. You find a point that is 2 seconds into a shot and identify that as the beginning of the edit—the edit entry point. You then attempt to cue the shot by giving the control unit the command to backspace the tape. The edit control unit begins to count control track pulses and counts back to the beginning of the shot: 2 seconds = 60 control track pulses. However, it needs 90 more control track pulses to properly cue up the shot. Unfortunately, your video ends at the two-second mark. The VCR, oblivious to the fact that there is no video beyond this point, will simply continue to rewind the tape until it reaches the next control track pulse or until it reaches the beginning of the tape.

If your VCR refuses to park the videotape in the cue mode, and rewinds the tape to the beginning, chances are great that there is not enough control track in front of the edit point. The VCR is fruitlessly searching for the place at which to stop. Again, it is for this reason that *all tapes must have at least 5 to 10 seconds of usable video and control track before each edit point on both VCRs.* Without it, the edit control unit cannot cue the shot for the edit.

Problems with Control Track Editing

Control Track Pulses. The main weakness in control track editing systems lies in the fact that all control track pulses look the same to the edit control unit, which is capable of counting control track pulses only when it cues the VCR. An error in counting will affect the amount of time the VCR is backspaced, thereby affecting the accuracy of the edit.

For example, let's assume that one of your tapes is slightly wrinkled at the edge and that this wrinkle has destroyed one second of control track pulses (30 pulses). Let's assume further that these missing control track pulses come 2 seconds in front of the edit point. As the control unit counts back to 150, it will be at pulse 60 when it hits the spot where the pulses are missing. The tape will continue moving, but the control unit will not count pulse 61 until it gets to the next pulse. Because 1 second of pulses is missing, the control unit will count pulse 61 at the spot in the tape that should have produced pulse 91. When the control unit reaches pulse 150, it will stop the VCR. Instead of backspacing the tape 5 seconds, it will have backspaced it 6 seconds. But because its only time reference is control track pulses, it has no way of knowing this.

If this error is made as the tape on the source VCR is cued, when the command to perform the edit is given and both VCRs are rolled, the edit will be made at a point 1 second off the planned spot on the source VCR. This is a considerable difference, especially if you are trying to edit between words or in other places where a difference of a few frames may be critical.

Accuracy.   Control track editors are not **frame accurate.** That is, they seldom make the edit exactly on the planned frame. Most systems are accurate only within two to four frames on either side of the planned edit point. In many situations, this is good enough, but in some it is not. Two factors contribute to the inaccuracy of these editing systems: problems with counting and system mechanics. Pulse counting tends to be more accurate when edits are of short duration and less accurate when they are long. In a 1-*second* insert, only 30 control track pulses need to be counted to mark the edit entry and exit points. On the other hand, in a 1-*minute* insert, 1,800 pulses are counted and the chances of miscounting are magnified. If the pulses are not counted correctly, the edit points will be off the mark.

The other problem with the accuracy of control track editing systems lies in the mechanics of the machines. When the VCRs cue up a shot, they rewind 5 seconds and then pause the tape. However, the braking mechanism in the VCR is not always frame accurate. The VCR may overshoot the mark by two frames. However, because all control track pulses look the same, the control track editor will not know that the VCR is two frames off. When the perform edit command is given, it will simply count off 150 pulses—not 152—and will assume that it has reached the edit point correctly. For this reason, *the more times you preview or rehearse an edit, the greater the chance of the system making an error when it performs the edit.*

Some VCRs are more mechanically accurate than others. New VCRs are usually more accurate than old VCRs, and certainly well-maintained VCRs are better than abused ones. However, no matter how good the condition of your VCR and editing system, you will seldom be able to achieve frame-accurate editing with a control track editing system.

Varying the Preroll Time

Most control track editing systems use a 5-second preroll. On some systems, preroll time can be decreased. If your machines stabilize quickly, you may be able to reduce the time to 4.5 or sometimes 3.5 seconds. By reducing the preroll time, you can edit with less control track at the head of each shot, and you can save a second or so every time you make an edit.

Assemble and Insert Editing

There are two different modes of electronic videotape editing: assemble editing and insert editing. The differences between the two can be understood in strategic terms as well as technical terms. That is, we can talk about assemble and insert editing in terms of both how we approach editing and how the edits are physically accomplished within the electronic editing VCR. We'll examine the strategic differences first.

Editing Strategy: Assemble versus Insert Editing

Videotape editors commonly talk about *assembling* a program or program segment. A literal definition of **assemble editing** might therefore simply be to join the parts together. And, indeed, that is what an assemble-editing strategy is. When you assemble a program, new information is added to a tape shot by shot, or scene by scene, in proper sequence. At the beginning of the master editing tape, you lay down shot 1, then shot 2, then shot 3, and so on, until the program is complete. Or, perhaps you have already put together a number of different sequences or scenes, each of which contains a number of individual shots. You can assemble the final show out of these sequences by editing them together into the proper order. First one sequence is laid down, then another, and another, and so on, until all the sequences for the final program are assembled in a new order on the tape (see Figure 9.6).

Insert-editing strategy is significantly different from assemble-editing strategy because you insert a shot or sequence into a preexisting shot or sequence within the program. If you have already transferred shot 1 to the edit master and now want to put shot 2 into the middle of shot 1, leaving the beginning and end of shot 1 on the edit master, you are inserting shot 2 into shot 1 (see Figure 9.6).

Another use of the insert is to bridge a cut between two shots. Perhaps you have assembled shots 1 and 2 together, only to find that the transition point between the shots looks bad. Perhaps shot 1 shows the subject

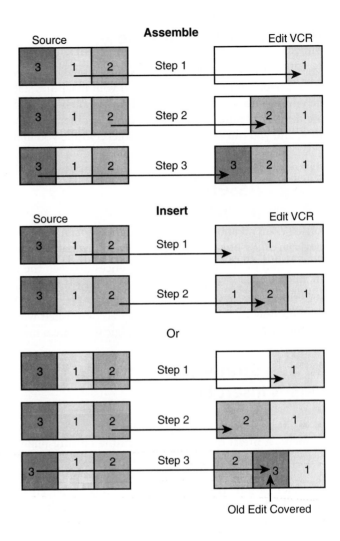

Figure 9.6 Assemble and
Insert Editing Strategies

looking to the left side of the screen and shot 2 shows him looking to the right. The transition between shots creates an obvious and irritating transition—a jump cut—that should be eliminated. So, take shot 3, a long shot of the subject seen over the shoulder of the interviewer, and insert it at the transition point. This insert of the cutaway acts as a bridge to eliminate the disturbing jump cut. Once again, you are inserting new material into a sequence that has already been recorded.

To summarize, laying down shots or scenes in a sequence one after the other is an assemble-editing strategy. Editing information into an already recorded shot or sequence, while leaving the head and tail (beginning and end) of the original shot or sequence intact, is an insert-editing strategy.

Technical Differences:
Assemble versus Insert Editing

Not only can we describe the differences between assemble and insert edits in terms of editing strategy but also there are some very large technical differences in the way assemble edits and insert edits are accomplished by the editing VCR. (The following discussion of the technical differences between assemble and insert editing describes those tape formats in which the control track signal has been recorded in a longitudinal track by a stationary head: e.g., VHS/S-VHS, $3/4''$, Betacam SP, M-II, and DVCPRO. The slightly different systems of 8mm/Hi8 and will be discussed separately later in this chapter.)

All high-quality editing recorders contain a control that designates the *editing mode* as assemble or insert. An assemble edit is the simplest type of edit, and in fact, when electronic editing was developed, many machines had only an assemble-editing mode. Assemble editing adds new information onto the end of prerecorded information on another tape. An assemble edit can be used for *editing in* only. The assemble mode allows you to get a clean edit where the edit begins, but the image breaks up where the edit ends. An insert edit, on the other hand, is really two edits: one at the beginning of the insert and the other at the end. The edit is executed cleanly at both points.

Assemble and insert editing differ technically in how the new information is recorded on the editing VCR. Of particular importance is what happens to the control track on the edit master tape and how the old information on the edit master tape is erased. In the assemble mode, *new control track and audio and video information are recorded onto the tape in the editing VCR*. In the insert mode, *the control track is left undisturbed, and only new audio and/or video information is laid down in place of the original information* (see Figure 9.7).

Whenever new information is added to a tape, the old information must be erased. The differences between assemble and insert editing result from the different ways in which the old information is erased. In the assemble mode, a stationary **erase head** erases the full width of information on the videotape before the new information is laid down by the spinning record heads. However, the use of the stationary erase head in the assemble mode creates a problem at the end of the edit, because the erase head completely erases the tape before it reaches the record heads. As a result, when the VCR stops at the end of an edit, there is a blank spot of tape between the erase head and record heads. This blank spot does not contain any audio, video, or control track information. For this reason, when you play back the tape, the beginning of the edit will be clean, but the picture will break up at the end of the shot. This occurs because both the control track and video information are missing.

275

Linear, Cuts-Only
Videotape Editing

Assemble Editing

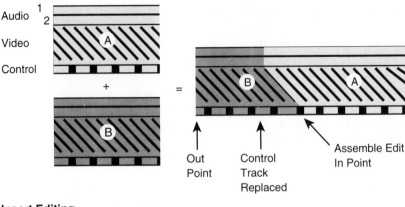

Audio 1 2
Video
Control

+ =

Out
Point

Control
Track
Replaced

Assemble Edit
In Point

Insert Editing

Original

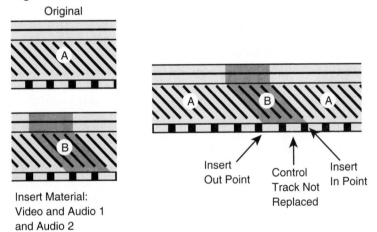

Insert Material:
Video and Audio 1
and Audio 2

Insert
Out Point

Control
Track Not
Replaced

Insert
In Point

Figure 9.7
Assemble and
Insert Editing—
Technical Differences

A = Shot #1
B = Shot #2

No such problem occurs in the insert mode. The control track is not erased because the stationary erase head is not used in the insert mode. When a video insert is made, only the video information (not the control track) is erased by a pair of **flying erase heads** located immediately in front of the record heads. This allows erasing of precise frames of information without leaving a gap in the recording as in the assemble mode. Audio inserts are accomplished by erasing only the tracks of linear audio information that are to be replaced by new information. In both the video and audio insert modes, the control track is not affected. The video flying erase head erases only those frames of information that are to be replaced by new information, but not the control track. Thus, continuous control track and video information is maintained, and the edit is clean at both the entry and exit points.

Please note: Audio-only inserts can be performed only when the audio information has been recorded into one or more longitudinal tracks of audio information. In videotape formats in which high-fidelity sound information has been recorded in the slanted tracks of video information with rotary record heads, an audio-only insert cannot be performed without affecting the video information.

Assemble-Editing Review

Let's briefly review what we know about assemble editing. An assemble edit involves the transfer of information from the source VCR to the editing VCR. Assemble-editing strategy means that shots or sequences are added onto the tape in the editing VCR in the desired sequence. From a technical standpoint, assemble editing means that each time an edit is made, the editing VCR records new video, audio (both channels if on a two-channel VCR), and control track. Furthermore, an assemble edit is used for editing in only—that is, it adds new information to the end of other video information already present on the tape in the editing VCR. The beginning of the edit is stable, but the end of the shot will break up where the edit ends because control track and video information will be missing from the tape in the small space between the location of the stationary full-track erase head and the place where the video record heads hit the tape.

Approaching Assemble Editing

To perform an assemble edit, two VCRs are needed: the source VCR containing the original unedited material, and the editing VCR containing the **edit master tape** (which is the tape onto which the edits will be made). Because assemble editing involves adding information to a tape in sequence, the tape in the editing VCR cannot be blank. It must have video information and control track on it for the edit to be made properly. If you already have some information recorded on the tape in the editing VCR, assemble editing is easily accomplished. You simply add new material to the end of the old material. But what do you do at the beginning of a program? How do you make the first edit of a program onto a blank tape?

To make the first edit in a program, it is customary to record some video black at the beginning of the edit master tape (see Figure 9.8). **Video black** is a black video signal. It can be produced by a video switcher and sync generator, equipment typically found in a video studio or editing facility. Video black can also be produced simply by capping the lens of a video camera and recording the black picture. This provides a video signal and all the synchronizing pulses that the editing VCR needs to make an edit, because control track pulses are recorded whenever a video signal is recorded on a VCR.

If a video signal and control track are not present on the edit master tape, the first edit will be unstable. The editing VCR needs control track to regulate its playback speed. Also, without video information on the tape, there is no way to synchronize the movement of the video heads so that they begin recording the new tracks of video information at the correct place on the tape.

Figure 9.8   Overlapping Edits

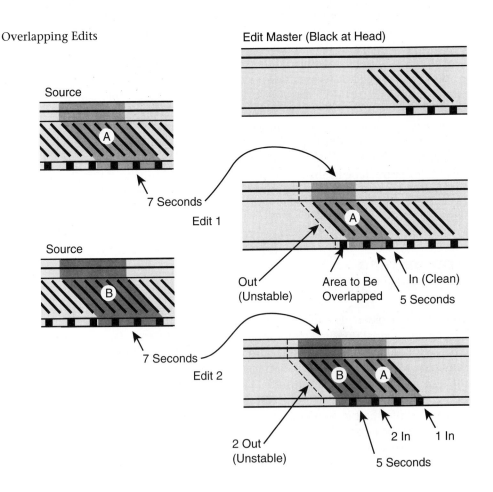

Overlapping Edits

When using assemble edits to construct a program, the technique of overlapping edits is employed. An **overlapping edit** is one in which the end of the last shot recorded on the editing VCR is erased and recorded over by the beginning of the next shot that is being transferred from the source VCR. This technique covers up the messy picture breakup that always comes at the end of an assemble edit.

Assume that you want to transfer seven seconds of shot 1 on the source VCR to the editing VCR. If you end the assemble edit precisely at the seven-second mark, the picture will break up, causing a problem in the program. The solution is to record more than the seven seconds you need. Then begin the next edit at the seven-second mark of shot 1 and erase the breakup after that point. Figure 9.8 illustrates this technique.

Whenever you are editing in the assemble mode, use this technique of overlapping edits. Always allow both the source and editing VCRs to roll several seconds beyond the planned end point of the edit, and then record the beginning of the next shot over this material (see Figure 9.8).

Problems with
Assemble Editing

Each time an edit is made in the assemble mode, a new segment of control track is recorded. If the edit is not made in precisely the correct place, or if there are any irregularities in the signal on the source VCR (which is now being recorded onto the editing VCR), this will cause a momentary loss of stability in the final edited program. For this reason, most professional editing is done in the insert mode, even if the editor is simply recording the shots in sequence. Using the insert mode guarantees a continuous, uninterrupted control track on the edited master tape because control track information is never affected in the insert editing mode.

Insert-Editing Review

Insert editing differs principally from assemble editing in that the edit master tape—the tape onto which you will edit—must already have a continuous control track. In the insert mode, the control track is not erased because the VCR's large stationary erase head is not activated. Rather, the insert mode uses the small flying erase heads, which are positioned immediately in front of the video record/playback heads. These flying erase heads erase only the tracks of video information that have previously been laid down on the tape. They do not affect the control track at all and may be used in conjunction with or independent of the stationary audio erase heads. The result is that in the insert mode you can insert new video, linear channel 1 audio, linear channel 2 audio, or any combination of the three. You can do video-only edits, in which new video information is laid down and the linear audio channels are left undisturbed. Or you can do audio-only edits, in which the old video information is left undisturbed. In addition, you can combine video and audio insert edits. For example, you can insert new video and linear channel 1 audio onto the master tape, leaving linear audio channel 2 undisturbed. Or you can insert new video and linear channel 2 audio, leaving channel 1. Insert editing gives the editor incredible flexibility during the editing process.

In those videotape formats in which video and high-fidelity audio are recorded together in the same slanted tracks of information on the tape, any video insert will affect the high-fidelity sound information as well. Similarly, any attempt to edit the high-fidelity sound will affect the video information. Audio inserts can be made independently of video inserts only if the tape format contains one or more longitudinal tracks of audio information or, as is the case with 8mm/Hi8 and DV systems, digitally recorded PCM audio tracks.

Approaching Insert Editing

To edit in the insert mode, the tape you are editing onto must have continuous prerecorded control track and video information for the entire length of the edited program. As explained, the control track is needed because new control track information is not recorded in the insert mode. Therefore, the master tape must have control track on it to regulate the tracking of the editing VCR. In addition, the control track must be continuous. If there are any breaks or interruptions in the control track, the edits will not be stable. The picture will break up wherever control track pulses are missing.

Therefore, before you can begin editing in the insert mode, you need to know the length of the finished program. You then need to record enough control track onto the edit master tape to safely cover the length of that program. For example, before you can begin editing a 10-minute program segment, you need to record at least 10 minutes of video black and control track onto the tape. It is always a good idea to lay down more control track and black than you think you will need. Then, if you slightly exceed the projected program length, you will still have some control track and video black to work with. To protect against running out of control track, most professional producers simply lay control track down along the entire length of the tape they are editing onto.

Video Black
and Crystal Black

Sometimes, you will hear videotape editors use the term *crystal black* instead of video black. **Crystal black** is simply a color-black video signal recorded onto a videotape—usually for the entire length of the tape—when the tape will be used as an edit master tape. This color-black video signal includes **color burst**, the pulse that controls the phasing of the color signal and activates the color circuitry in a television receiver, as well as the horizontal and vertical sync pulses associated with the video signal. When video black is recorded onto a tape, control track is automatically recorded as well, because the control track is triggered by the vertical sync pulses in the black video signal.

At this point, it is important to note that having video black is different from having no video signal. A videotape with video black recorded onto it is not a blank tape. A blank tape contains *no* video signal, whereas video black is indeed a video signal. If you look at video black on a monitor, you will see a stable black screen. If you look at the signal on a waveform monitor, you will see that it does indeed produce a video waveform, and you will be able to identify the sync pulses and color burst in the waveform.

Blank tape, on the other hand, has nothing recorded on it. There is no video signal, sync, or color burst. When you play back a blank tape and look at it on a monitor, you will see snow, or the screen will be black but the picture will jitter and roll. On some systems, the screen will be blue. If you look at a waveform monitor, you will not see the characteristic video waveform because no signals are recorded on the tape.

Video black is used in the editing VCR because it provides a stable reference signal into which your new video and audio information can be laid. Because control track pulses are recorded as the black video signal is laid down, the editing VCR will have the information it needs to maintain stability throughout the program.

Some videotape editors prefer to lay down **color bars** instead of video black for the entire length of the tape. The reason for this is that occasionally, when editing, you may accidentally leave a small bit of space between the end of one edit and the beginning of the next. In the insert mode, the end of the edit is as clean as the beginning of an edit, and these mistakes are sometimes hard to see. If you are editing onto a tape with video black recorded onto it, you may not see the space between the shots when you play back the tape. But, if you are editing onto a tape with color bars on it, the space between shots will reveal an unerased segment of color bars that will jump out at you like a red flag at a bull in a bullring. You can then correct this error by redoing the edit to eliminate the gap between the shots.

Assembling in
the Insert Mode

Although insert editing is most commonly thought of as the process of inserting new information into a prerecorded shot or sequence, it is also possible to assemble a program in the insert mode. You will recall from the discussion of assemble and insert editing the difference between the *strategy* used in editing and the *technical processes* used to execute the strategy. This distinction is important because one frequently wants to put a program together shot by shot in sequence (assemble strategy) while using the technical process of insert editing.

You may wonder why anyone would want to do this. The answer, of course, lies in what has already been said with respect to the control track.

Figure 9.9   Assembling in the Insert Mode

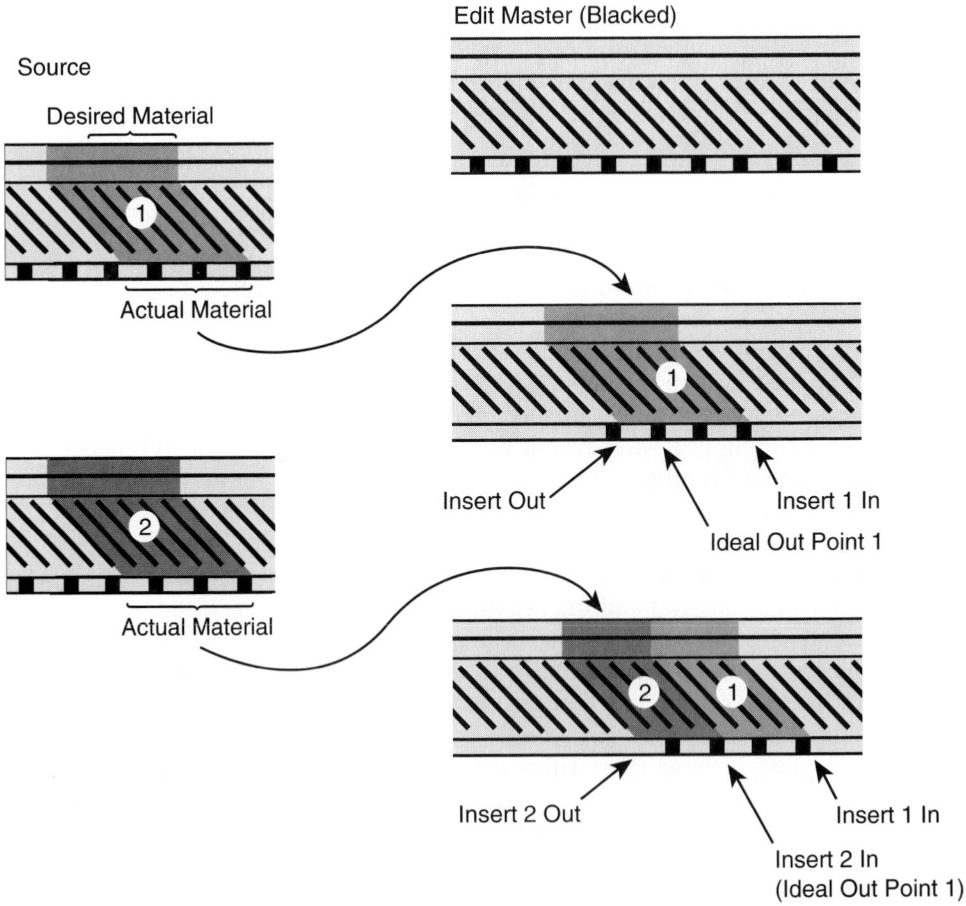

In the assemble mode (technical process), the old control track is erased and new control track recorded with each edit. The problem with this process is that you have a good chance of winding up with a slightly irregular control track. Even slightly inaccurate timing of any edits or inaccurate spacing of the edit master control track pulses results in an unstable edit that may cause the picture to break up or roll. In a program with several hundred edits, the chances are good that at least one control track segment will be bad.

In the insert mode, however, the control track is not affected during the editing process. Therefore, assembling the program in the insert mode usually produces a higher-quality finished product. As in assemble editing, the process of overlapping edits is usually followed. While this is not necessary from a technical standpoint, because the output of the edit will be clean and stable, overlapping edits are used because most editing systems are not frame accurate. Recording more information than you need as you lay down each shot on the edit master is a safety measure that prevents a black space from appearing in the tape between shots, even if the next edit is a frame or two late (see Figure 9.9).

8mm/Hi8 Editing

As you will recall from the discussion in Chapter 4, in the 8mm/Hi8 videotape formats, all the critical signal information (audio, video, control signal) is recorded in the slanted tracks of information by the rotating video/audio heads. There is no stationary erase head to erase the tape, no stationary head to record control track, and no stationary head to record audio because there are no linear audio tracks. Because all the recording and rerecording is accomplished with the rotary recording and flying erase heads, editing with 8mm/Hi8 more closely resembles insert editing in the other tape formats, but with some significant differences.

Because the audio, video, and control pulses are recorded in the same slanted tracks of information, whenever an assemble edit is made, all of the audio and control signals are replaced as well. Insert edits, on the other hand, can be performed independently on the video, time code, and PCM (digital) audio channels. 8mm/Hi8 systems also contain one or two AFM (high-fidelity) audio tracks. Because these high-fidelity audio tracks are recorded at the same place on the tape as the video information (the video and audio signals are actually recorded in the same track but at different depths in the magnetic-recording layer on the tape), audio inserts on the AFM audio tracks cannot be made independently of the video. Similarly, whenever a video insert is made, the AFM audio tracks are re-recorded as well. So, in order to achieve fully independent insert editing of video and audio, the PCM digital audio tracks, rather than the AFM high-fidelity tracks, should be used.

283

Wrong Field Edits

For an edit to be stable and clean, it must come at the appropriate point in the signal. The edit must be positioned correctly with respect to control track pulses and the tracks, or fields, of information on the videotape. However, in analog helical scan systems, each frame of video information is composed of two separate fields, and each one of those fields is recorded in its own track of information on the tape. Thus, there is only a 50 percent chance that an edit will be made correctly. A correct edit must come at the end of the second field of information of a video frame in the editing VCR and before the first field of information of the appropriate frame in the source VCR. A correct edit will look like this:

recorder field 1—recorder field 2—*edit point*—source field 1—source field 2

Edits that do not come between the end of the frame on the editing VCR and the beginning of the frame on the source VCR are called **wrong field edits.** Here are two examples of wrong field edits:

recorder field 1—*edit point*—source field 1—source field 2

and

recorder field 1—recorder field 2—*edit point*—source field 2

Editing VCRs contain a *frame servo* control. Setting this control to the on position in the editing VCR guarantees that all edits are made at the correct place, thus eliminating wrong field edits. Because wrong field edits can cause problems with stability and color reproduction, this control on the editing VCR is extremely helpful.

Interformat Editing

For years, it was standard practice to edit videotape onto the same tape format on which it was originally shot. However, given the proliferation of videotape formats and the advantages of some formats as field acquisition formats and others as editing formats, this is no longer always the case.

Because editing is an electronic process in which the signal from a source machine is rerecorded on the editing VCR, tapes that were recorded in the field in one format can be edited to master tapes in another format. This is known as **interformat editing.** For example, Hi8 and S-VHS have become popular field acquisition formats for many video field producers because the equipment is portable and relatively inexpensive. By using the appropriate format machine as the source deck in a compatible editing system, Hi8 or S-VHS field tapes can be edited to a master tape in a different format. Extremely high-quality video can be produced by shooting on S-VHS or Hi8 and editing onto Betacam SP. Producers aiming for even higher quality might shoot field tapes in Betacam SP, and edit to one of the digital tape formats for their program masters.

Tapes that have been shot in the field in one format can, of course, first be dubbed to another format for editing if the editing system format is different from the field-recording format. However, you lose a full tape generation in the process. Interformat editing eliminates the intermediate dubbing step and thereby saves one generation, as well as the time it would take to dub the tapes.

Editing systems can be extremely simple or complex. The level of complexity of an editing system is usually determined by two factors: your editing needs and/or the amount of money you want to spend on the system.

Let's turn our attention now to the fourth point in the list: systems or devices that can be used to cue up the source and editing VCRs.

Editing on a Cuts-Only System

Cuts-only editing systems are very basic, consisting of two VCRs (source and editing), two monitors (one for each VCR), and an edit control unit (see Figure 9.10). These simple systems are referred to as *cuts-only editing systems* because the only transition they allow the videotape editor to use is the cut. Dissolves, wipes, and other special effects require at least two source VCRs and a video switcher interface.

Videotapes

You will need at least two videotapes to edit. One or more tapes will contain the original unedited material. These tapes will go into the source VCR as they are needed. You will also need one blank tape, which will become the **edit master tape** and will go into the editing VCR. If you plan to edit in the *insert mode*, this tape should contain video black and control track for the expected length of the program. If you plan to edit in the *assemble mode*, you will need some video black and control track at the beginning of the tape so that the edit control unit can cue up for the first edit.

285

Source VCR Monitor

Editing VCR Monitor

Audio Patch Bay

Audio Headphones

Audio Mixer

Source VCR

Edit Control Unit

Editing VCR

Figure 9.10   Cuts-Only Editing System

Source VCR Setup

Once the basic editing system is in place and you are ready to begin editing, you need to prepare the source and editing VCRs. First, turn on the power to all elements of the system and insert your original tape into the source VCR. Before you can begin to edit, several switches and meters need to be set in the proper position on the VCR.

Remote Control.   To control the VCR from the edit control unit, place this switch in the *remote* position. When it is in the *local* position, the VCR is controlled by the tape transport controls on the front of the VCR.

Audio Monitor.   In the *mix* position, channels 1 and 2 will be heard on the playback monitor. For selective track monitoring, set to either channel 1 or channel 2. There may also be a set of switches to select either the normal or the high-fidelity audio track.

Input Signal Selector.   Set the input signal selector for the input going into the VCR. The *line* position is used to record audio and video signals from normal audio and video sources, and the *Y/C 358* position is used for S-Video inputs. If the source VCR is a play-only machine, it will not have an input signal selector, because it is not capable of recording an input signal.

Sync. The sync switch tells the VCR what the source of vertical sync is for this machine. In most situations, you should set the sync switch on the playback VCR to the *internal* position. This means the VCR will be synchronized to an internal crystal oscillator with a frequency of 60 cycles per second. In large editing facilities, the source VCR may be operated in conjunction with **house sync** (sync supplied by an external sync generator to all the video equipment in a given facility) or a **time base corrector (TBC)**, an electronic device that improves the stability of the playback signal. In both of these situations, set the sync selector switch to the *external* position.

Tracking. Once you have selected the correct sync position, put the VCR into the play mode. When the image appears on the monitor and stabilizes, adjust the tracking control so that the needle reaches the maximum position on the tracking meter. If all of your tape was shot on the same VCR, you will not have to adjust tracking again. However, if you are using tapes that were recorded on a number of different machines, or if you notice the tracking meter wavering from the maximum position, you will have to readjust the tracking control. Some source VCRs have a tracking control but no tracking meter. In that case, adjust the tracking control until the picture in the monitor is clear and stable.

Counter. With sync and tracking set and the VCR in the proper video mode, you can now rewind the tape and zero the counters on the edit control unit and the VCR. This will ensure that they both start counting from zero.

Editing VCR Setup

Once the source VCR is set, you can turn your attention to the editing VCR.

Remote Control. Set the switch to the *remote* position to control the VCR through the edit control unit.

Audio Monitor. Select *mix* (or channel 1 or 2) and either *normal* or *high fidelity*.

Input Signal Selector. This switch should be set either to the *line* position or the *Y/C 358* position, depending on the source recording.

Sync. Set the sync selector switch on the editing VCR to the *normal* position, unless you have an external sync input from a house sync generator or a time base corrector. The normal setting allows the editing VCR to reference to incoming sync from the source VCR, thus making editing possible.

Tracking.   The tracking level should be set with the tape in the play mode, just as tracking was set on the source VCR. If you are editing in the insert mode or the assemble mode and have video black recorded on the entire tape (insert mode) or just on the head of the tape (assemble mode), you will need to set your tracking level only once. No adjustment should be made after this initial adjustment.

Counter.   Once you have set the sync, tracking, and input controls, stop and rewind the tape. Then zero the counter, as you did on the source VCR.

Record Levels.   It is now time to set the record levels on the editing VCR. Video and audio levels can be set independently. Most machines allow you to set the levels on automatic gain control (AGC) or to adjust them manually. Most editors prefer to set the video level on AGC because video levels on field tapes tend not to vary greatly since much of the initial level control during recording is automated by the camera and the VCR. By contrast, because audio levels in field recording may vary greatly, it is typical to adjust the audio level manually.

Most audio and video meters on editing VCRs show audio and video levels when the machines are in the electronics-to-electronics, or *E-to-E mode*. Some machines go into this mode if the VCR is in the stop mode; others go into this mode if the record button is pressed while the machine is in the stop mode. In the E-to-E mode, the record circuits are engaged, and the output of the source VCR is looped through the editing VCR. This allows you to see the incoming audio and video levels on the editing VCR's meters and to see and hear picture and sound on both the playback and record monitors.

Once the levels are set, press the stop button on the editing VCR to break the E-to-E loop. Then press stop and rewind on the source VCR. Make sure that all tape counters on both machines are reset to zero. You are now *almost* ready to edit.

Editing Leader

One last thing requires attention before you begin editing. Every edited master tape should have a standard **leader sequence** at the head of the tape before the beginning of the program. This standard leader serves a number of purposes. First, it provides protection for the beginning of the program. Remember, the first part of the videotape is the part grabbed by the mechanical arm in the VCR and wrapped around the head drum. This part of the tape is therefore subjected to considerable stress, and is occasionally damaged. Try to avoid using the first minute or so of tape for critical information—such as the beginning of your program! By placing identifying leader at the head of the tape, the beginning of your program will be protected from the machine's mechanical maw.

The other reasons for using standard leader are to identify the program on the tape and to give your engineering staff a way of checking the audio and video signal levels before the program starts. Finally, the leader provides a way to cue up a tape so that the beginning of a program can easily be found. There is nothing more frustrating than watching someone try to find a 30-second program that was recorded somewhere on a 120-minute tape without any identifying leader before it.

Unfortunately, there is no standard videotape leader. Commercial producers, independent producers, broadcasters, and corporate producers all use somewhat different leaders. However, the following leader sequence is extremely useful:

Video black	10 seconds
Color bars with tone (0 dB)	60 seconds
Slate (program identification)	10 seconds
Countdown leader	8 seconds
Black	2 seconds
Program start	

This leader sequence provides all the necessary advantages. It provides a 90-second buffer between the beginning of the videotape and the beginning of the program; it gives the engineering staff video and audio reference levels; and its countdown allows the tape to be accurately cued up for playback. No edited tape should be produced without this or other similar leader.

You can assemble your own leader by editing together the material you need in the proper sequence. Use the camera to record video black if you do not have a switcher with a video black output available. Color bar and tone generators are common fixtures in all studios and postproduction facilities. If you do not have access to them, you can improvise. Many cameras now have a color bar output, and some audio mixers have a tone oscillator. You can combine the two to create color bars with tone. You can make your own slate and record it, and if you do not have a prerecorded countdown leader you can easily make one by editing together one-second segments of the numbers 10, 9, 8, 7, 6, 5, 4, and 3. Leave two seconds of black at the end of the countdown before the program begins.

Editing Strategy

Setting Edit Entry Points.
Try to set the edit entry points as accurately as possible. If you are editing to audio, try not to cut off the first part of the first word spoken by your subject. Sometimes, it is better to start with a brief pause than to risk cutting off someone in the middle of a word.

Setting Edit Exit Points. If you are editing in the assemble mode (or if you are assembling a program in the insert mode), use the technique of overlapping edits. Let the edit continue past your planned exit point, and then cut off this unwanted material when you set the entry point for the next edit. This gives you a little breathing room for the next edit. It is better to have a little room after the shot than to cut it so closely that you have to cut the tail off the shot on the edit master tape when you make the next edit.

Avoiding Overuse of the Pause Mode. It is a good idea *not* to leave either VCR in the cue/pause or preroll mode for any significant time while you are looking for the edit points on the tape in the other VCR. When a VCR is in the pause mode, the heads continue to hit the tape. This is what produces the still-frame image on the monitor. Excessive use of the pause mode may wear out the tape in that spot. The oxides may wear off the tape, causing the image to look bad or even causing the video heads to clog. Some machines automatically go into the stop mode if they are left in the pause mode for more than a few minutes.

An easy way to avoid leaving a tape in the pause mode for too long is to set the edit points on the source VCR before you set the edit points on the editing VCR. It usually takes longer to find the edit points on the source VCR because you may have a number of takes of each shot or perhaps a number of tapes from which to draw your material. On the editing VCR, however, the next edit is almost always made immediately after the last one on the tape, so it does not take very long to find the entry point.

Performing an Assemble Edit

Once the VCRs are set up, the tapes are tracked to a maximum, and your record levels are set on the editing VCR, you are ready to begin editing. To do this, you must follow these steps:

1. Select the *assemble-editing mode* on the edit control unit.
2. Find the edit entry and exit points on the source VCR, and enter them into the edit control unit.
3. Find the edit entry point on the editing VCR, and enter this into the edit control unit.
4. Cue the tapes, allowing the edit control unit to backspace them to the preroll point five seconds before the edit entry points.
5. Preview the edit. Watch the editing VCR's monitor to see if the edit takes place at the correct spot. Also, listen closely to the audio. Does it sound correct? Is the level correct? If the preview is satisfactory, continue to step 6. If the preview is not satisfactory, reset the edit point that is causing the problem.

6. Recue the tapes to the preroll point.
7. Perform the edit.
8. Stop the source VCR.
9. Stop the editing VCR and review the edit.
10. If the edit is satisfactory, continue on to the next edit. If it is not satisfactory, redo the edit.

Performing an Insert Edit

The following steps detail how to perform an insert edit:

1. Select the *insert-editing mode* on the edit control unit, and select the type of insert you want to make (video, audio 1, or audio 2).
2. Locate the critical out point of the edit. Is it on the tape in the source VCR? or is it on the tape on the editing VCR? Enter the edit entry and exit points for the critical tape. Enter the edit entry point on the other tape.
3. Cue both VCRs.
4. Preview the edit.
5. Recue the tapes.
6. Perform the edit.
7. Stop both VCRs and review the edit.

Getting More Complex: Manipulating Audio

If all you want to do is transfer material from the source VCR to the editing VCR, then the simple editing system and procedures described above will suffice. However, most editors want to do a little more with their material in the editing process. Most frequently, they also want to manipulate the audio.

Audio Patch Bay.   Every simple editing system should contain at least a simple *audio patch bay* or switch that allows the editor to manipulate the audio as it flows from the source VCR to the editing VCR. A simple device that allows you to send the source VCR's channel 1 to either channel 1 or 2 on the editing VCR and the source VCR's channel 2 to either channel 1 or 2 on the editing VCR is essential. Although it is possible to reach behind

291

the VCRs and simply repatch the audio inputs when you need to redirect the audio signals, an *outboard patch panel* can save a lot of wear and tear on the VCR's cables and connectors (see Figures 9.11 and 9.12).

Multiple Audio Sources. The next step up in complexity with respect to audio manipulation is having the ability to incorporate additional audio sources into your edited program. You will often need to add narration, music, and/or sound effects to the edited program. How can you do this? One way is to patch the additional audio sources directly into the editing VCR. Most machines have inputs for microphones or line-level inputs for audiotape recorders and turntables. However, with direct patching into the editing VCR, it is very difficult to lay down the information accurately at the edit point. If you do not manually activate the record circuits and cue the audio to roll at the right time, you are out of luck.

A much better way to deal with the problem is to record the audio information that needs to be dubbed into the program onto another videocassette. New or additional audio information can easily be integrated into

Figure 9.11   Schematic Diagram: Audio Mixer and Patch Bay

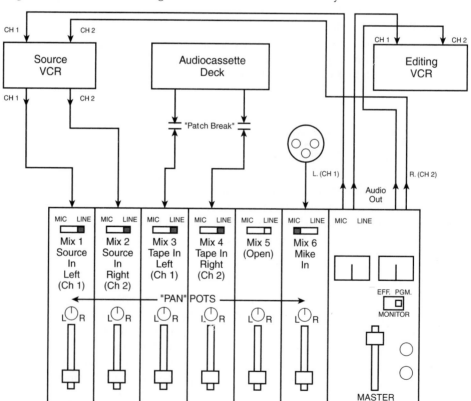

Equalization Controls

Pan Pots

Channel Gain Controls

LED Level Display

Main Mix (Gain) Control

Figure 9.12   12-Channel Audio Mixer (Mackie 1202-VLZ)

a program if it can be controlled and cued in the same way that videocassettes can be controlled and cued. For this reason, it is a good idea to keep several videocassettes on hand with video black and control track. If you need to add music to a program and you have it on audiotape, transfer it first to the appropriate audio channel of one of the videocassettes with the video black and control track. With the audio information recorded onto a videotape, it can now be cued by using the edit control unit.

New audio information can be added to the edit master tape by doing an audio-only insert into the appropriate linear audio channel on the editing VCR. Voice-overs can be added in the same way. Record the voice-over onto a videocassette that has been blacked, and then insert this cassette into the source VCR. All cuing can then be done with the edit control unit.

If multiple audio sources are going to be used during editing, an audio mixer should be incorporated into the editing system. The audio mixer can be placed into the audio line between the source and editing VCRs. Additional audio inputs can be patched into the system through the mixer. (See Figure 9.12.) The audio mixer allows for precise control of the level of each source sound. In addition, the mixer may incorporate equalization controls to adjust the tonal quality of the source sounds. And finally, many mixers contain *pan pots,* which can be used to send the source sounds either to channel 1 or channel 2 on the editing VCR, or to both channels simultaneously.

Monitoring Audio
While Editing

One aspect of audio that is frequently overlooked in the editing process is the quality of the audio speakers used to monitor the program audio. Many editing systems contain only the audio speakers in the video monitors for the source and record decks. These speakers are usually of very poor quality, and more often than not they mask the way the audio recording actually sounds.

For this reason, you should use a pair of good-quality audio speakers (one for each channel) to monitor the audio while editing. Bookshelf-sized loudspeakers do the job well, as do some of the high-quality minispeakers that have become available in the last few years. These should be used in conjunction with the normal television monitor audio speakers. The high-quality speakers let you hear things that may not be apparent on the television monitor speaker, whereas the television monitor speaker lets you hear the audio the way it will most likely be heard when the program is received at home and viewed on a conventional television.

If you are editing in a very noisy area, use headphones to monitor audio. This way you can hear the program audio without distraction from outside noise.

10 A/B-Roll Editing and SMPTE Time Code

Many productions that originate in the field reach their conclusion in an editing suite that is significantly more complex than a cuts-only editing system (see Figure 10.1). This chapter examines multiple-source (A/B-roll) editing, SMPTE time code and postproduction signal processing. The burgeoning area of desktop video production, emphasizing digital nonlinear video editing, is the subject of Chapter 11.

Figure 10.1
On-Line Editing Suite—Realtime Video, San Francisco, CA

A/B-Roll Editing

In contrast to single-source cuts-only editing systems, **A/B-roll editing** systems utilize two source VCRs and one editing VCR. A/B-roll systems are somewhat more complicated than single-source cuts-only systems and are used for three reasons:

1. To allow the videotape editor to perform multiple-source transition effects, such as dissolves and wipes
2. To allow precise control of additional audio sources
3. To key titles

Checkerboard Assembly

A/B-roll editing takes its name from the technique of A/B rolling in film production. To make splices between shots invisible or to dissolve from one shot to another, shots are arranged on rolls of film in checkerboard fashion. Shot 1 is put onto the A roll, and an equivalent length of black leader is placed on the B roll. Shot 2 is placed on the B roll, and a corresponding length of black leader is placed onto the A roll. Shot 3 goes onto the A roll, with black leader on the B roll. This alternating checkerboard pattern is completed for the length of the film. If only two rolls of film are used, it is called A/B rolling. If more rolls are used to build more complex effects, it may become A/B/C rolling, and so on (see Figure 10.2).

When the A and B rolls are sent to the laboratory for final assembly, the transitions are put into the film. To cut from shot 1 to shot 2, the last frame of film of the A roll (shot 1) must match the beginning of the first frame of shot 2 on the B roll. (The black leader is invisible and does not affect the quality of the picture.) Shot 2 and shot 3 are overlapped for the desired length of a dissolve. When the film is processed in the printer in the lab, the B roll is faded in as the A roll is faded out, creating the dissolve effect. The A/B-roll model has also been adapted for use in the time line of a number of popular digital nonlinear video editing systems.

Figure 10.2 Checkerboard Assembly (Film or Video)

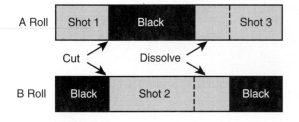

Automatic A/B-Roll Edit Control Units

Automatic A/B-roll edit control units are used in linear videotape editing systems to perform dissolves and wipes, and to key titles (see Figure 10.3). Automatic A/B-roll edit control units control two different source VCRs along with the editing VCR. After all the tapes have been cued, a dissolve (or wipe) is performed as follows.

First, the control unit rolls source A and the editing VCR. An edit is made at the first edit point, so that source A is now being recorded onto the editing VCR. At the appropriate cue point, source B is rolled. At the dissolve point, the edit control unit automatically brings up the video and/or audio level of source B as it simultaneously fades out the video from source A. During the transition, the two video sources appear superimposed. When the dissolve is complete, source A automatically stops. Source B continues to record onto the editing VCR until the edit out point of the shot is reached.

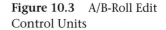

Figure 10.3   A/B-Roll Edit Control Units

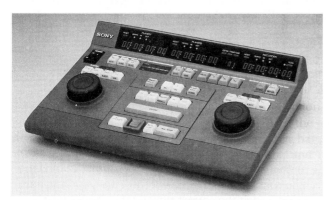

Sony PVE-500

Videonics Edit Suite

Matched Frame Editing

If the next desired transition is a straight cut, this can be performed as a normal edit between the appropriate source and editing VCRs. If, however, the next transition is a dissolve or wipe back to source A, then the technique of matched frame editing is used.

A **matched frame edit** is an invisible edit made in the last shot laid down on the editing VCR. In a matched frame edit, a single shot is broken into two individual shots. A part of the shot is laid down onto the editing VCR. The matched frame edit then joins the part of the shot on the editing VCR with the rest of the shot, which is supplied by the source VCR. The two parts of the shot are perfectly joined, so the edit is completely invisible. Indeed, the shot appears to be perfectly continuous.

The matched frame edit allows you to dissolve back to the other source machine. Once the matched frame edit has been made, the other source machine can be rolled, and the next dissolve can be executed (see Figure 10.4).

A/B-Roll Audio Editing

A/B-roll audio editing is often used to mix several audio sources. Consider this very simple example. Source A contains the principal video with sound on tape, to which you want to add background music. Source B contains a videocassette with music recorded onto the appropriate audio channel. Both sources can be controlled by the edit control unit, and the music on source B can be introduced at the correct time by the control unit.

Figure 10.4   Matched Frame Editing

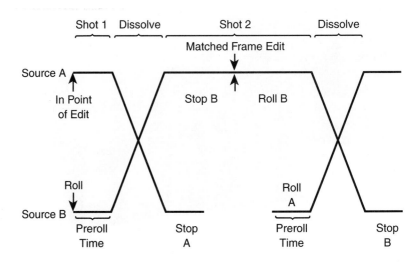

298

Of course, music can instead be added by playing it back directly from an audiotape recorder or CD. However, the A/B-roll audio editing system allows all sources to originate on videotape and thereby provides much more precise cuing and recording.

Keying

Some A/B-roll automatic edit control units contain a *keyer*, thus eliminating the need to use a video switcher for keys. The A/B-roll control unit can be used to easily control the points at which keyed letters are introduced and deleted. It also controls the way in which the letters are introduced: they can be cut in (abruptly appearing at full intensity on the screen); faded in; wiped in; or introduced as a *wipe-key*, a combination of a wipe and a key. The edit control unit usually lets the operator determine the speed at which keys are faded or wiped into the picture.

SMPTE Time Code

The most sophisticated editing systems utilize Society of Motion Picture and Television Engineers (SMPTE) time code. (The complete formal name for this code is SMPTE/EBU (European Broadcasting Union) time code, but in common practice it is simply referred to as SMPTE time code.) **SMPTE time code** is an identification system in which each frame of video information is given a unique code number that identifies it in terms of hours, minutes, seconds, and frames. The first frame of video information is coded 00:00:00:01 (0 hours, 0 minutes, 0 seconds, and 1 frame). A frame of information 10 minutes into the tape would be coded 00:10:00:00 (0 hours, 10 minutes, 0 seconds, and 0 frames), and so on.

SMPTE time code has a number of advantages over systems that lack time code, and it has become an important part of video production. Unlike other kinds of tape counters, which may vary from machine to machine and can be reset to zero by pressing the reset switch on the VCR, SMPTE time code becomes a permanent part of the tape. This provides an accurate and precise time reference for any frame of video information and allows you to find a particular point in a tape on any VCR that is capable of reading time code information.

Because of its accuracy, SMPTE time code is widely used in videotape recording and editing. Entry and exit points for each shot can be logged in terms of their time code numbers, and a complete list of all of the shots that will compose the program can be compiled. The edited master tape can then be assembled by referring to the time code numbers for each of the shots. If a mistake is made during the editing process, or if it is necessary to change the length of a shot or its order within the program, these modifications can be made much more quickly and with greater accuracy than with control track systems.

Types of Time Code and Where They Are Recorded

Time code information is recorded as digital electronic information on the videotape. It can be recorded during field production, or it can be added to videotapes that have already been recorded without it.

There are two basic types of time code: longitudinal time code (LTC) and vertical interval time code (VITC). **Longitudinal time code** is typically recorded by a stationary head in one of the longitudinal audio tracks on the videotape or in a special cue or *address track* that is found on some professional-quality VCRs. The VCR needs to be equipped with special heads and amplifiers in order to record and play back longitudinal time code accurately. On many VCRs, only one of the longitudinal audio tracks is capable of recording time code. By activating a special time code switch, the audio circuitry is converted to record and read the time code signal.

Because longitudinal time code is recorded in its own track, it can be recorded at the same time the video information is recorded or it can be added to a tape after the video has been recorded. This latter method of adding time code to a prerecorded tape is known as **poststriping.**

Vertical interval time code is recorded by the rotating video heads in one of the video tracks during the blanking interval between the fields of video information. Unlike longitudinal time code, which can be recorded at the same time the original video is recorded or added to a tape afterward, VITC is recorded in the vertical blanking area of the video signal on one of the video tracks, and it must be recorded at the same time the video information is recorded.

The advantage to recording the time code in the vertical interval or the address track is that it leaves both audio channels free for audio production. If the time code is added in one of the audio channels after the video has been recorded, only one audio channel is available for audio production because the other contains time code information.

As with many other elements of video field recording, there is no standard for where to record the time code information. Some editing systems demand that it be recorded in audio channel 1; others require audio channel 2. Most will work with the time code recorded in the vertical interval, and some will be able to handle a mixture of time code locations. For example, time code is often recorded on the edit master tape in the vertical interval when the video black is recorded. Field tapes, however, might include a mixture of time code recorded in the vertical interval and in one of the audio channels. Most sophisticated systems can read time code from any of these locations.

It is always a good idea to check your editing system's time code requirements before you decide where to record the time code on your tapes. There is nothing more frustrating than recording the time code in audio channel 2 and then finding out that your control unit or VCR only reads time code in channel 1. Planning is of the utmost importance here. If you record the time code in the wrong audio channel for your editing system, you should **ping-pong** the time code and audio information by making a dub of the tape and rerecording the time code and audio on the correct channels. Time code that had originally been recorded on channel 2, for example, would wind up on channel 1 in the dub, whereas the audio originally recorded on channel 1 would be rerecorded on channel 2. The problem with this procedure is that you lose a generation in your tape. Instead of editing from a first-generation original, your original now is a second-generation tape. This means that the edit master tape will be a third-generation tape instead of a second-generation tape, and some quality loss may be apparent.

Drop-Frame and Non-Drop-Frame Time Code

Normally, time code numbers are generated to match the 30-frames-per-second scanning rate of the video system. This is **non-drop-frame time code.** However, the frame rate for the American NTSC color standard is actually 29.97 frames per second. In order to correct for this discrepancy—which is equivalent to 3.6 seconds or 108 frames per hour—SMPTE time code generators are capable of generating **drop-frame time code.** Drop-frame time code generators drop (do not generate) two frames of time code information per minute each minute of the hour, with the exception of the 10th minute of each hour. To look at this another way, two frames are dropped during 54 of the minutes in each hour (2 × 54 = 108 frames/hour).

In many editing situations where time code is used, non-drop-frame time code provides sufficient accuracy. However, if absolute precision in the timing of a segment is necessary, particularly if it is a long program meant for broadcast distribution, drop-frame time code should be used.

You can tell if the time code on a tape is non-drop-frame or drop-frame by looking at the time code display. In non-drop-frame time code, the time code numbers are separated by colons (hr:min:sec:fr). Drop-frame time code is distinguished by the use of semicolons instead of colons (hr;min;sec;fr) or by dropping the top dot of the last colon in the sequence (hr:min:sec.fr).

Generating and Recording Time Code

The **time code generator** is the device that produces the time code information. Some time code generators are portable (they are built into some portable camcorders or can be attached to them; see Figure 10.5). Others are mounted in studio equipment racks and are not portable.

Figure 10.5
Time Code Generators

Portable Time Code Generator
(Future Video TCG-2000)

There are two different kinds of time codes: time-of-day time code and dedicated time code. **Time-of-day time code** is referenced to a 24-hour clock and runs continuously, day and night. At midnight, the time code reads 00:00:00:00; at noon, it reads 12:00:00:00; and so on. Time-of-day code is often found in large production houses where a central time code generator feeds the time code simultaneously to all the VCRs in each of the editing rooms, thus eliminating the need for each machine to have its own time code generator.

A more common type of time code used in video field production is called dedicated time code. **Dedicated time code** means that a particular VCR has its own time code generator. Dedicated time code is also called *zero-start time code*, because the time code generator can be set to start counting at 00:00:00:00 at the beginning of each tape. Typically, dedicated time code generators can be used in one of two modes: free run or record run.

In the **free-run** mode, the time code generator begins producing time code when the power to the VCR is turned on and continues until the power is turned off. Time code is produced as long as the VCR power remains on, although

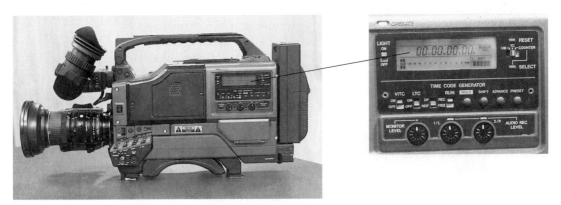

Camcorder Time Code Generator

the VCR must be in the record mode for it to record the time code. When the time code generator is in the **record-run** mode, time code is produced only when the VCR is in the record mode. The following example illustrates the difference between these two modes.

Suppose that after recording an opening shot, the camcorder's VCR is placed in the pause mode while the next shot is being set up. The time code at the end of the opening shot is 00:02:00:00, indicating that the first shot was two minutes long. In the record-run mode, the time code generator will stop producing time code until the next shot is recorded. The time code for that shot will begin with the next frame: 00:02:00:01. In the free-run mode, the next time code number recorded will reflect the amount of time that has elapsed between shots. If the crew took a 10-minute coffee break between shots 1 and 2, the time code at the beginning of shot 2 will be 00:12:00:01.

The most common mode used on portable VCRs is record run. This produces time code with no gaps in it. Time code on a 30-minute mini-cassette begins at 00:00:00:00 and ends at 00:30:00:00 if exactly 30 minutes of tape are used.

One nice feature on many portable time code generators is that the hour digit can be manually preset. This allows field producers to identify their field tapes by presetting the time code hour to correspond with the number of the tape. Field tape 1 begins with 01:00:00:00, tape 2 begins with 02:00:00:00, and so on. This technique can only be used if you are working with a videotape format with field recording capacity of less than one hour because recording time in excess of one hour will cause the preset hour digit to advance, thereby rendering the indexing function useless.

If preset hour digits are used to identify the field tapes, the time code generator should be operated only in the record-run mode. Because it is common practice to pause between recorded shots, a 30- or even a 60-minute cassette seldom is filled in that amount of clock time. Indeed, 30 to 60 minutes of actual recording may well represent a day's work. In the free-run mode, on the other hand, a shooting session that lasts more than an hour will wipe out the preset digit, even if that session produced less than an hour of recorded information.

Displaying the Time Code

Because time code is recorded as electronic information, it is invisible when it is recorded onto a videotape. This is true both for longitudinal time code recorded in one of the audio channels and for vertical interval time code. To use the time code to make editing decisions, you need to be able to see it. Two options—a time code reader and a time code character generator-inserter—are available.

A **time code counter** is a device that displays the time code as a visual digital readout in hours, minutes, seconds, and frames. On time-code-capable VCRs and edit control units, the tape counter functions as a built-in time code counter when the counter display switch is set to the time code mode. Or, the time code counter may be a piece of rack-mounted equipment that is positioned near the VCR providing the time code being read. If the time code output of the VCR is connected to a time code counter, the counter displays the time code information as the tape is played.

A **time code character generator-inserter** works like the time code counter in that it displays the time code as a digital readout. It also goes one step further by converting the readout into video information that can then be inserted into the picture on a monitor or rerecorded with the video information on another videotape. The character generator-inserter makes the time code numbers appear in a black window within the picture. Character generator-inserters can vary the size of both the window and time code numbers, and the position of their placement within the frame. Time code is often displayed at the bottom of the frame as editing decisions are being made. It is visible to the editor, who needs it to make editing decisions, but it does not interfere with the editor's view of the principal picture information in the frame (see Figure 10.6).

Figure 10.6
Video Frame with
Time Code Inserted

Window Dubs

A common step in the process of editing with time code involves making a window dub. A time code **window dub** is a copy of the original unedited videotape that is made by using the time code character generator-inserter to insert the time code into the picture. Making a window dub leaves you with two videotapes: (1) the original, with the time code information invisibly recorded as audio information in either the vertical interval, cue, or address tracks or one of the audio channels; and (2) a copy of the original tape, with the time code window visually inserted into the picture (see Figure 10.7).

Making Editing Decisions

With a window dub of all your unedited material, all editing decisions can easily be made with the use of a simple playback VCR and a monitor. As you view the window dub, the time code numbers will be displayed on the

Figure 10.7   Window Dub Schematic

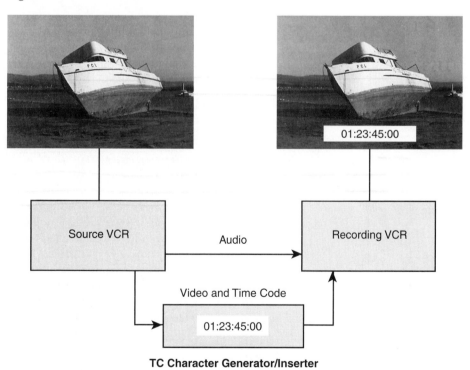

305

screen along with the picture. When an edit point is found, place the VCR in the pause/still mode. This freezes the frame and gives you a still picture along with a still-frame display of the time code for that precise frame of video information. You can then write down the time code numbers and prepare an **edit decision list,** or **EDL,** for the entire program, without tying up the editing system itself. Specify the in and out points for each shot in terms of their time code numbers on your list (see Figure 10.8). This information can then be entered into the editing system via the keyboard or numeric keypad.

If you are using a digital nonlinear editing system, the time code list will identify the beginning and end of each shot that needs to be digitized from the source tapes. Time code improves the process of digitizing field footage, because shots can be found faster and with more accuracy than on tapes without time code.

Not only does SMPTE time code allow you to specify the precise frame at which an edit is to begin and/or end, thus simplifying the process of editing, but also it speeds up the process of finding specific shots within

Figure 10.8
Edit List with
Time Code

Edit#	Tape Reel	Audio/Video	Cut/Dissolve	Transition Length	Source In	Source Out	Record In	Record Out	Time Code	Type
001	AX	V12	C		00:00:00:00	00:01:00:00	01:31:00:00	01:32:00:00	NN	R
002	AX	V	C		00:00:00:00	00:00:13:04	01:32:15:00	01:32:28:04	NN	R
003	01	A1	C		00:00:28:10	00:01:58:20	01:32:26:20	01:33:57:00	NN	R
004	BL	V	C		00:00:00:00	00:00:00:00	01:32:27:00	01:32:27:00	NN	R
004	02	V	D	075	00:04:01:27	00:04:08:21	01:32:27:00	01:32:33:24	DN	
005	02	V	C		00:04:04:17	00:04:04:17	01:32:29:28	01:32:29:28	NN	R
005	01	V	D	090	00:08:19:02	00:08:33:08	01:32:29:28	01:32:44:04	DN	
006	01	V	C		00:08:29:14	00:08:29:14	01:32:40:10	01:32:40:10	DN	R
006	02	V	D	065	00:03:59:13	00:04:22:24	01:32:40:10	01:33:03:21	NN	
007	03	V	C		00:01:52:16	00:02:01:04	01:32:52:28	01:33:01:16	NN	R
008	03	V	C		00:01:52:02	00:01:59:23	01:32:52:28	01:33:00:19	NN	R
009	03	V	C		00:01:52:15	00:02:02:22	01:32:52:13	01:33:02:20	NN	R
010	02	V	C		00:04:18:21	00:04:18:21	01:32:59:18	01:32:59:18	NN	R
011	03	V	C		00:47:08:00	00:47:20:11	01:32:59:18	01:33:11:29	NN	
012	02	V	C		00:04:18:21	00:04:18:21	01:32:59:18	01:32:59:18	NN	
013	03	V	C		00:47:08:00	00:47:20:11	01:32:59:18	01:33:11:29	NN	
014	03	V	C		00:47:12:10	00:47:12:10	01:33:03:28	01:33:03:28	NN	R
015	02	V	C		00:07:25:28	00:07:34:24	01:33:03:28	01:33:12:24	NN	
016	01	A1	C		00:00:28:10	00:01:16:09	01:32:26:20	01:33:14:19	NN	R
017	BL	A1	C		00:00:00:00	00:00:46:11	01:33:14:05	01:34:00:16	NN	R
018	02	V2	C		00:07:32:13	00:07:32:29	01:33:10:13	01:33:10:29	NN	R
018	03	V2	D	040	01:50:02:09	01:50:31:17	01:33:10:29	01:33:40:07	NN	
019	01	V	C		00:46:22:07	00:46:26:07	01:33:16:03	01:33:20:03	DN	
020	02	V	C		00:01:15:03	00:01:21:08	01:33:19:25	01:33:26:00	NN	R
021	01	V	C		00:47:35:16	00:47:49:16	01:33:24:22	01:33:38:22	DN	R
022	01	V	C		00:50:57:25	00:51:07:06	01:33:35:19	01:33:44:28	DN	R

a tape. The precise time code numbers for a particular video frame can be entered into the control unit, and the VCR will then fast-forward or rewind to the precise frame number specified in the command. This eliminates a time-consuming visual search for information with the search controls.

The edit list using time code numbers makes editing easier and more precise than control track editing. If a program needs to be re-edited, new time code numbers reflecting the changes to be made are entered into the system (or edited within the system). Many systems have the capability to **ripple** changes throughout an edit decision list. For example, a change in a shot early in a program (lengthening, shortening, or deleting) will affect the entry and exit points of all subsequent edits on the edit master tape. In a computer-aided time code system, such changes in the edit list are easily made by the computer by adding or subtracting the appropriate number of frames to each of the subsequent shots in the list. In a control track editing system, no such edit list exists. A change in one edit means that you will have to redo all other edits by finding the appropriate cues for each shot: dialogue, visuals, and so on. In addition, because some of even the simplest SMPTE edit control units allow an edit list to be entered, the video-tape editor can push a *perform edit* control or an *automatic assemble* button and leave the editing room as the machines automatically make each of the edits. In a control track system, the videotape editor has to manually relocate and perform each edit.

8mm Time Code

Some 8mm- and Hi8-format VCRs and camcorders include their own time code systems, called *8mm time code* on industrial/professional equipment or *RC* (*rewritable consumer*) *time code* on consumer-quality equipment. These time code systems are incompatible with each other but allow for precise editing on those editing systems that are capable of reading them.

The higher-quality 8mm time code functions in much the same way as the SMPTE time code: it can be transferred from one tape format to another; it can be added to a tape after it has been recorded; it can be used to generate window dubs; and, with the addition of the appropriate accessory interface, it can be converted into SMPTE time code when 8mm tapes are dubbed to another format.

Time Code
Edit Control Units

The feature that distinguishes a time code edit control unit from a control track edit control unit is the keyboard (see Figure 10.9). All time code control units contain a *numerical keyboard* into which the time code numbers

Figure 10.9
Time Code Editing
Controller

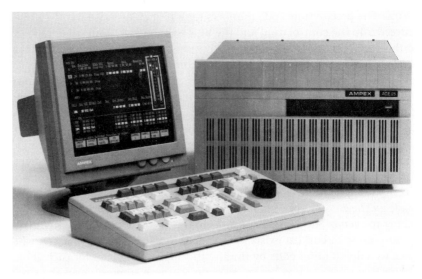

Ampex ACE 25 Video Editing System

for edit points are entered. Depending on the complexity of the control unit, it may accept the edits one at a time or it may be capable of storing an edit list and then executing the edits automatically when the list has been made final. Computer-controlled time code editing systems often have extensive memory for edit lists and often can accept, remember, and execute hundreds of edit decisions.

A number of different kinds of time code editing systems are in use. The simplest system is a cuts-only system, in which the time code controller can control one playback machine and one recorder. This system provides time code accuracy at a very simple level of operation. The next level of complexity is found in the controllers that can control two source machines simultaneously with the recorder. Multiple-source machines are necessary if any kind of transition other than a cut is desired. For example, a dissolve or a wipe requires the use of two playback machines. One tape is dissolved to the other, and the transition is recorded onto the editing VCR. Some edit controllers in this group achieve the special-effect transition within the control unit itself. Others require that the two VCRs be run through a special-effects generator in a video switcher and that the transition (wipe, dissolve, and so on) be manually made in the switcher (see Figure 10.10).

The most complex type of time code editing system has several playback machines, a recorder, and a switcher, which are all controlled by a computer. With this type of system, all edit commands are entered into

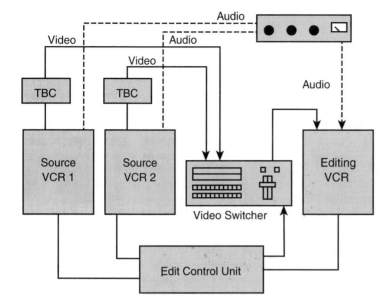

Figure 10.10 Video Switcher/
Editing System Schematic

the computer. The computer then cues up the playback machines and the recorder, rolls the tapes, and controls the execution of any special-effect transitions that have been programmed into the system.

On-Line and Off-Line Editing

Two terms frequently used to describe editing that have not yet been discussed are *on-line* and *off-line*. These terms primarily describe two different stages of the editing process.

Editing that is done **on-line** refers to editing the final program, usually on high-quality VCRs or a digital nonlinear editing system. Because rental costs for on-line editing time are fairly high, most producers make all of their editing decisions on paper before they go into the editing suite. In many cases, a rough cut of a program will be made from the window dubs on a cuts-only editing system, often using VHS-format tapes and machines. Or, if the program has a lot of visual effects and transitions, a nonlinear editing system may be used to create the preliminary off-line edited version of the program. This **off-line** editing is considerably cheaper than experimenting with edits on-line, and gives the production personnel the opportunity to see what the program will basically look like. When all the

309

final editing decisions have been made, the edit list and the original tapes can then be taken to the on-line editing system. There, the final program assembly is done (see Figure 10.1).

 ## The Video Switcher

The **video switcher** is a production device that allows editors working with linear tape-editing systems to combine or manipulate different video sources (see Figure 10.11). Its function parallels that of an audio mixer. A number of different video sources can be fed into the switcher, and the editor can select the source or combination of sources that will be fed out of the switcher to the recorder.

In postproduction, video switchers are used to perform transitions like fades, dissolves, and wipes; to key titles over tape; and to construct matte and chroma-key effects. (Keys, mattes, and chroma keys are discussed in detail in the next chapter.)

Each video source fed into the switcher (VCR, character generator, and so on) is assigned to a button on the switcher. These buttons are

Figure 10.11 Postproduction Video Switcher

Wipe Patterns

Joystick

Auto Transition Rate

Downstream Keyer

Fader Bar

Key, Program, and Preview Busses

Grass Valley 110

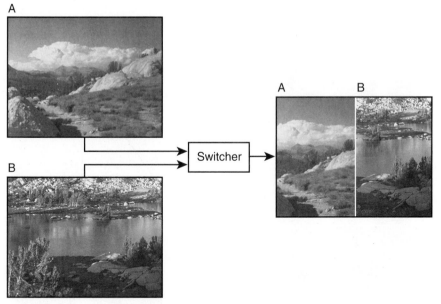

Figure 10.12
Split-Screen Wipe

arranged across the switcher in rows called busses. Each **buss** performs different key, effect, and transition functions.

Fader bars are used to manually control the speed at which transitions take place, and a **joystick,** or *wipe positioner,* is used to move the wipe patterns up, down, and around on the screen. In switchers having an *automatic transition rate control,* the speed of the transitions can be automatically controlled by programming the length of the transition into the switcher in terms of its frame rate (a one-second dissolve lasts for 30 frames, and so on).

Wipes are performed by presetting the wipe pattern and then selecting the wipe sources. Most switchers have a number of wipe patterns—how many depends on how complex the switcher is (see Figure 10.11). Wipes are frequently used to achieve a **split-screen** effect. A split screen is simply a horizontal wipe that has been stopped at the halfway point (see Figure 10.12). The definition of the edge of the wipe can also be controlled. Most switchers allow the operator to select either a *hard-edge* wipe or a *soft-edge* wipe.

Most modern postproduction switchers include a downstream keyer, which introduces matte or key effects over the output of the switcher, leaving the production busses free to perform other effects (see Figure 10.13). In computer-controlled editing systems that have a switcher interface, switcher functions are performed automatically when the switcher is given the command by the computer.

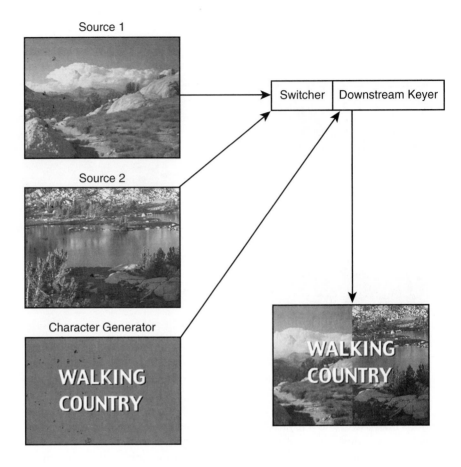

Figure 10.13
Split-Screen Wipe
with Downstream
Key

In digital nonlinear editing systems, transitions, keys, and composite effects are created with software that is part of the editing program, or with software plug-ins that are added to the editing program to give it more functionality.

 **Signal Processing**

Whenever a video signal is recorded, a certain amount of signal degradation takes place. Both the stability and the quality of the signal (how the picture looks) may be affected. For these and other reasons, several different kinds of signal-processing devices are routinely used during postproduction. The most common types of signal-processing units include time base correctors, video-processing amplifiers, and dropout compensators.

Time Base Correctors

A **time base corrector (TBC)** is used to correct timing errors in the signal that is played back from the videotape recorder. All VCRs introduce errors into the time base of recorded material. The *time base* refers to the rate at which individual lines, fields, and frames of video information are reproduced. As you know from the earlier discussion, each of these components of the video signal should take place in a precise amount of time: A line lasts 63.4 microseconds, a field has a duration of $^1/_{60}$ of a second, and a frame lasts $^1/_{30}$ of a second. Deviations from this model are called deviations in the time base of the signal. Portable VCRs are notorious for producing a video signal that deviates from the standard.

The function of the time base corrector is to correct the video signal with respect to timing. The VCR's output is fed into the time base corrector, where it is digitized, analyzed, and corrected. The time base corrector's output is a broadcast-quality signal in terms of its timing.

A time base corrector must be used in conjunction with any VCR if you plan to broadcast a tape. Similarly, if you want to transfer the material from one tape format to another, the VCR output should first be processed through a time base corrector to guarantee the ultimate stability of the dub. A time base corrector must also be used if the output from a VCR is going to be connected to a video switcher or if several VCRs are going to be used in an A/B-roll editing system.

The time base corrector stabilizes the video signal from the VCR(s) and synchronizes it with the other video sources in the system. This is done by routing the VCR's output signal into the time base corrector, which converts it into a digital signal and stores it line by line. Then, the time base corrector compares the horizontal sync pulses from the sync generator with the sync pulses on the tape. It brings the tape into sync with the standard established by the sync generator by reading out each line of information at the correct time. This ensures that each line of video coming from the VCR through the time base corrector begins and ends in time with the horizontal sync pulses supplied by the sync generator (see Figure 10.14).

Time base correctors are often described with respect to their *window,* which indicates how much information a time base corrector is able to store at a given time. Most modern time base correctors can store a full frame of information. They are called full-frame time base correctors, or **frame synchronizers.**

Figure 10.14   Signal Timing Corrected by a Time Base Corrector

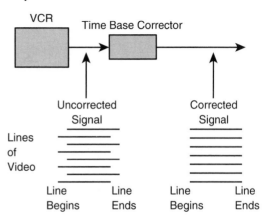

Processing Amplifiers

Time base correctors are commonly used to improve playback signal stability; improvements in signal quality are made with a video **processing amplifier,** or **proc amp.** Proc amps, or *color correctors* as they are sometimes called, are used to correct both the quality of the color in the signal and the quality of the sync and color burst signals. With a proc amp, adjustments can be made in the overall video level (gain) and setup level (pedestal), as well as in the quality of the color itself in terms of luminance, hue, and saturation.

As with time base correctors, there are limits to the amount of color correction possible with a proc amp. If the signal was originally recorded with gross errors resulting from camera malfunction or some other severe problems, the proc amp may not help.

Dropout Compensators

Another common type of signal processing equipment is the **dropout compensator (DOC).** The dropout compensator is used to correct signal-quality problems caused by the loss of particles of the magnetic coating from the surface of the tape. When dropouts are detected in a line of video information, information from the previous line is repeated to fill in the hole. Dropout compensators are frequently built into other video components. For example, time base correctors frequently have built-in dropout compensators, as do many VCRs.

Digital Nonlinear Video Editing

Although videotape remains the recording medium of choice for field acquisition, the use of linear videotape editing systems is being supplanted by a new generation of digital disc-based nonlinear editing systems (see Figure 11.1). This chapter focuses on desktop video production and digital nonlinear editing.

Desktop Video Production

In no area in the field of video production have more dramatic changes recently been made than in the emergence of the personal computer (PC) as a video production tool. Of course, computers have long been used in

Figure 11.1
Digital Nonlinear
Video Editing System

315

video production. The advanced linear time code editing systems discussed in the previous chapter use a computer to log edit decisions and to control VCRs and other production equipment during on-line editing sessions. Word-processing software packages designed to emulate standard video script formats have long been available, and the computer has widely been used by video producers for a number of ancillary production organization tasks such as budgeting, tape logging, facilities and equipment scheduling, and so on.

Recently, however, a number of software packages and hardware accessories have been developed that enable the personal computer to be used more extensively in video production. **Software** is a computer program, usually available for purchase on magnetic floppy disks or CD-ROMs, that contains a set of commands for the computer that allow it to perform a specified set of tasks, such as word processing, generation of video graphics for titles and graphs, video editing, and so on. Computer hardware and software manufacturers have now begun to refer to their systems as "video workstations" and "video production suites." The convergence of the computer with video production has given rise to a new term that describes the fusion of these two technologies: **desktop video (DTV)** (see Figure 11.1).

Today's desktop video production systems can be used to perform a number of functions that previously could be done only on very expensive pieces of single-function video production hardware.

Video Switching

The computer can function as a video switcher with separate inputs for various video sources. A full range of transitions (cut, fade, dissolve, wipe) are typically available (see Figure 11.2).

Keying

In combination with graphics software, text can be keyed over video. Chroma-key and luminance key systems are available.

Digital Video Effects

A full range of digital effects are available.

Still Store

This feature is used to create freeze-frames of video in the computer, which can then be manipulated with special effects.

Figure 11.2   Desktop Computer
Running a Video Switcher Program

Video Graphics

A wide range of graphics programs are available, including character generation, two- and three-dimensional graphics and animation, and video
paint systems that allow the graphic artist to modify or "paint" video images. These are described in more detail in the next chapter.

Audio Production

Hardware and software are available to allow the computer to function as a
multiple-input audio mixer. They can be used to do audio mixing independent from video production or in conjunction with video editing software.

Video Editing

The computer can be used in a variety of editing operations, such as off-
line editing, on-line edit controlling, and digital nonlinear editing.

Digital Nonlinear
Video Editing

The process through which audio and video are edited in computer-based video editing systems that provide random access to the video and audio information during the editing process, and in which edits are made with a "cut-and-paste" process similar to the way text is edited in a word-processing program, is referred to as **nonlinear editing (NLE).** Today's digital nonlinear video editing systems (DNLEs) take advantage of the computer's ability to record and play back pictures and sound, and exhibit a number of other significant characteristics that differentiate them from linear editing systems.

Digital versus Analog Signals

Nonlinear video editing systems work with a digital video signal, as opposed to the conventional analog signal. Videotape that has been shot in the field in one of the analog acquisition formats (e.g., Hi8, VHS/S-VHS, Betacam SP) is digitized as it is transferred into the computer. Analog footage is typically digitized in real time; that is, digitized time is equivalent to the length of the clip.

Figure 11.3
Panasonic DV Edit
System

If the field footage was acquired using a digital videotape format (e.g., DV, Digital S, Betacam SX), it may be possible to transfer the footage directly into the computer as a digital signal. Some digital editing systems—particularly those designed specifically for news editing—allow the digital clips to be input into the computer at faster-than-normal playing speed, thereby speeding up the editing process. (See Figure 11.3.)

Nonlinear versus Linear Editing

Videotape editing systems are linear by nature: shots on the source tapes are recorded in a linear sequence, and they can be accessed only by fast-forwarding or rewinding the source VCR. Edits are made on the editing VCR in sequential, linear fashion.

Nonlinear editing systems provide random access to source footage. The unedited field footage is converted into digital information and stored within the computer on hard-disk drives. Shots can be accessed immediately in any order—in much the same way that a compact disc (CD) player can go to any song on a CD almost instantly. In addition to providing random access to the video and audio information once it has been digitized, nonlinear systems allow the user to assemble and change shot sequences easily.

Nondestructive versus Destructive Editing

Digital nonlinear editing is *nondestructive* of the original field footage. Like linear video editing, nonlinear editing does not damage or change the original field footage. Editing is performed on the digitized copy of the original footage. However, nonlinear editing is also nondestructive of the shots in the editing time line.

In nonlinear editing, when in and out points are marked on a shot, the parts that have been trimmed are not erased. The in and out markers merely tell the computer which parts of the original clip to play back in the time line, and the unedited original clip remains in the computer's memory. A shot in the time line can be lengthened or shortened simply by moving the position of the in or out marker. This is different from linear editing, which actually trims each shot as it is edited into the program.

Insert and Overlay Edits

In nonlinear editing systems, even after a sequence of shots has been placed in the time line, a new shot can be inserted between them. This is called an **insert edit.** The finished shot sequence is equal to the total

319

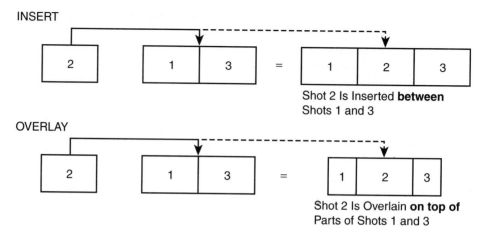

Figure 11.4 Nonlinear Insert and Overlay Edits

length of all of the clips. (See Figure 11.4.) There is no easy way to place a new shot between two shots that have already been recorded in a linear tape system. The ability to insert new material between shots or sequences is one of the great advantages of nonlinear editing over linear editing.

A shot that is used to replace and/or cover up a shot in the time line is called an **overlay edit.** An overlay does not increase the length of a shot sequence. (See Figure 11.4.) An overlay edit performed in a nonlinear system is equivalent to what has previously been defined as an insert edit performed on a linear tape system.

Editing Model

Digital nonlinear editing systems are organized around an editing model that incorporates clips and bins, edit windows, a time line, and transitions. (See Figures 11.5 and CP-7.)

Clips and Bins.   Clips are digital copies of the source material that is to be edited. Field video footage, audio sources, and graphics are all stored as clips. It is typical for the first frame of each clip to be displayed in a bin on the computer screen. This frame is sometimes called a *picture icon,* or *picon.* (See Figures 11.6 and CP-7.)

Individual clips are saved in a **bin.** Depending on the numbers and kinds of clips in the program, they may all be saved in one bin or they may be organized in a number of different bins (e.g., video in one bin, audio in another bin, graphics and effects in another, and so on). Bins can be named and color-coded to aid in the organization of the program's unedited raw material.

320

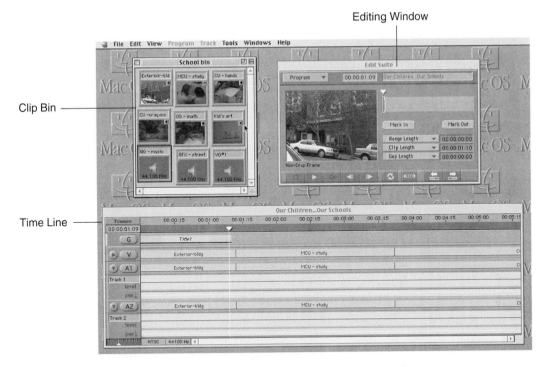

Figure 11.5 Nonlinear Video Editing Full-Screen Display

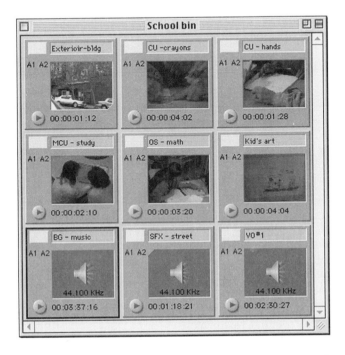

Figure 11.6
Clips in a Bin

Editing Window. Clips are trimmed in an **editing window.** Entry and exit points can be selected by eye or ear (look and listen to find the beginning and end of each clip), by time code numbers, or by selecting either an in or an out point and then specifying the length of the clip. (See Figure 11.7.)

Time Line. Once clips have been trimmed, they are placed into the program's time line. The **time line** is a graphical linear representation of the program. Each of the various program tracks (video, audio, graphics) appears in a vertical stack on the screen. The elements in each of the time line tracks can be manipulated independently or in conjunction with each

Figure 11.7
Editing Window

Figure 11.8   Time Line

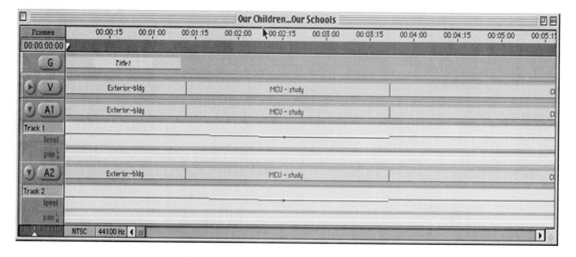

other (for example, if an audio track is synched with video, the audio clip will move along with the video to wherever it is placed in the time line). (See Figure 11.8.)

Transitions.   Once individual clips have been arranged in the proper sequence in the time line, transitions such as dissolves, wipes, and digital video effects can be added between the clips.

User Interface

Each nonlinear editing system is built around its own proprietary user interface. The *user interface* describes the visual elements of the editing program that appear on the computer screen (e.g., clips, bins, editing window, time line) and the steps through which editing is accomplished. Interfaces whose elements are easy for learners to grasp are referred to as *simple* or *intuitive interfaces*.

Three Types of Nonlinear Editing Systems

Off-Line Systems

Some nonlinear editing systems are used for off-line editing. Field footage, audio clips, and graphics are imported into the computer where editing decisions are made, taking advantage of the random-access and cut-and-paste features of the editing software. Rough cuts of the program, including transitions, titles, and digital video effects can be completed. Once editing decisions have been made and the edit decision list has been finalized, the EDL can be transferred to a floppy disk and the final program can be finished in an editing suite elsewhere.

Hybrid Systems

Hybrid systems combine elements of nonlinear and linear editing. In a hybrid nonlinear editing system, editing decisions are made in the computer program's time line, taking advantage of the nonlinear and random-access strengths of the system, but when all of the editing decisions have been made, the computer is used as an edit controller to control source and editing VCRs to finish the program on videotape. (See Figure 11.9.)

323

Figure 11.9 Hybrid Editing System: Videomedia OZ Video Editing System Screen Display

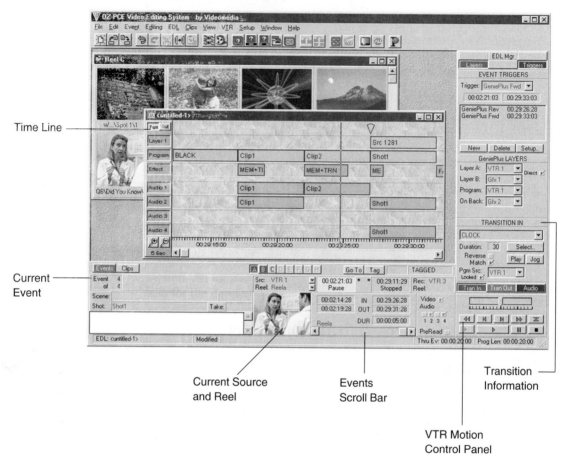

Time Line

Current Event

Current Source and Reel

Events Scroll Bar

Transition Information

VTR Motion Control Panel

On-Line Systems

The most sophisticated nonlinear editing systems are capable of producing a finished product, which is then *printed to tape.* All the picture and sound edits, graphics, transitions, and digital effects are completed within the computer and then output to a high-quality VCR, where they are recorded on videotape. Or, as is increasingly the case with nonlinear editing systems used to edit broadcast news, the final edited story may be transferred in digital form to a **video server**, where it resides until it is called up by the master control computer and replayed directly on air within the news program's broadcast.

As is the case with other kinds of video production equipment, non-linear editing systems vary widely in quality and cost. Some systems are designed for consumer and prosumer users, whereas others are targeted at the professional and broadcast production markets.

Components of a Nonlinear Video Editing System

The principal components of a nonlinear video editing system (see Figure 11.10) include:

1. A computer equipped with a central processing unit (CPU) fast enough to process video information
2. Nonlinear editing software to perform video editing
3. A sufficient amount of storage capacity for the computer, usually in the form of hard-drive disk arrays. Not only does editing require a lot of storage capacity, but also the system must be able to move the data through at a fast rate.

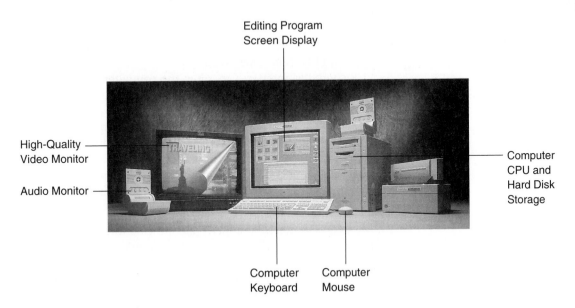

Figure 11.10   Nonlinear Video Editing System Components
(Media 100)

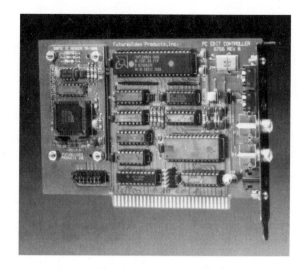

Figure 11.11 Computer Plug-In Card (Future Video Edit Controller and Time Code Reader)

4. Video hardware, including (a) a VCR to send the field footage into the computer and to record the finished product when the program is complete; (b) a time base corrector (TBC) to stabilize the signal of the playback VCR (once available only as an expensive piece of hardware, plug-in time base corrector cards are available for many computers at a fraction of what they used to cost [see Figure 11.11]); and (c) a time code reader board capable of reading VITC and LTC time code.
5. VCR/computer interfaces to allow the computer to control the playback and recording functions of one or more source and record VCRs.
6. A video input/output board to move the video signal into and out of the computer, unless the computer has direct audio and video inputs or a FireWire connector for digital video.
7. High-quality video and audio monitors so that image and sound quality can be monitored during the editing process.

For the system to function properly, all of the hardware and software components of the system must be compatible. In order to resolve the inevitable problems that occur when systems are assembled from components supplied by different manufacturers, some nonlinear editing systems are available in which all of the system components are supplied by one company. These complete systems are called **turnkey systems** because, theoretically, all the system operator needs to do is turn on the system and begin to edit.

The Process of Nonlinear Editing

In general, the process of nonlinear video editing involves the following four main steps: 1. log your field footage; 2. digitize your best takes; 3. edit your digitized material; and 4. print to tape.

Step 1. Log Your Analog or Digital Field Footage

Before you can begin to edit, you need to have a thorough and accurate record of your field footage and other source material.

Step 2. Digitize Your Best Takes

Select the Footage to Be Digitized.   The next step in the editing process is to convert videotape field footage to digital form in the nonlinear system's computer hard disk storage system. While it is generally true that videotape is cheap, computer hard drives are not. Although the cost is coming down rapidly, minute for minute, computer hard-drive storage is still more expensive than videotape, and the amount of storage is limited by the capacity of the system available. Therefore, you must make some preliminary choices about which shots you plan to use in your final project before you begin to digitize your material, as it is seldom possible to digitize everything that has been shot (unless, of course, you are working on a short project).

Select a Video Compression Rate.   When video is converted from analog to digital form, it is compressed. **Compression** allows the computer to reduce the amount of information that is stored in digital form. By varying the image quality (resolution, color versus black and white), frame rate, audio quality, and size of the video window ($1/4$ screen, $1/2$ screen, full screen), a given amount of footage will take more or less storage space. A high-resolution, color, full-screen image stored at 30 frames per second requires maximum storage capacity. The same material stored as a low-resolution, black-and-white, partial-screen image at a slower frame rate requires less storage capacity.

Digitize Shot by Shot.   Most systems allow the digitizer to mark an in and out point for each clip that is being digitized. This typically can be done in reference to SMPTE time code, or it can be done on the fly. Allow each shot to begin early and run long. This will be useful later on if you want to use a transition other than a cut to come into or out of the shot. Import additional elements, such as music and sound effects from compact discs and drawings, graphs, photos, and animations from illustration and animation programs.

Remember that, in most systems, digitizing takes place in real time. It can be thought of as dubbing your footage, shot by shot, into the digital domain. Digitizing can be a time-consuming part of the nonlinear editing process, particularly when a large amount of footage is involved.

Step 3. Edit Your Digitized Material

Trim Each Digitized Clip to its Actual In and Out Points.

Use the Time Line to Arrange Shots in the Proper Sequence.
With the computer's mouse, you can "drag and drop" shots into the time line at the appropriate place, and you can easily move them elsewhere if you decide to change the sequence. This is one of the most powerful advantages of nonlinear editing systems. The order of shots can be changed without re-editing the entire piece.

Add Transitions between Shots If They Are Not Cuts.   Most editing software systems allow you to choose from an extensive array of special-effect transitions.

Add Graphics.   Program titles, keyed titles, and other graphics can be created electronically within the editing program and incorporated into the project.

Add Music and Sound Effects.   As you are editing the picture, the sound attached to the picture will be assembled into the time line as well. In many cases, the initial definition of shots or clips may be driven by what is said, rather than by what is seen. All high-quality nonlinear systems allow for the addition of several other tracks of audio as well, and most projects will use four or more tracks (voice, natural sound, stereo music, sound effects, and so on).

Allow the System Time to Render the Special Effects and Transitions.   Rendering is a process through which the computer creates special effects and transitions frame by frame, or in some cases, field by field. Some systems are capable of replaying the edited sequence with its special effects and transitions in real time; other systems need time (sometimes a significant amount of time) to render each effect and transition. Depending on the complexity of the effects and transitions involved, the process may take hours to complete.

View the Edited Project in Real Time with High-Quality Video and Audio Monitoring in Order to Judge Its Effectiveness and Acceptability.

Make Changes as Necessary.   The general ease by which sequences can be rearranged or new material integrated into the time line is the principal advantage of nonlinear editing over linear editing.

Step 4. Print to Tape

If the nonlinear editing system is being used as an off-line editing tool, you can now generate an EDL, copied electronically onto a computer floppy disk, to take to the on-line editing room in order to assemble the project from the original field tape material. If the nonlinear system is a high-quality finishing system, you will be able to **print to tape.** Unless the production facility is equipped with a digital VCR, the edited program material will be reconverted to an analog signal and recorded onto a conventional analog VCR. This then becomes the program master tape.

Some Additional Things to Think About

Computers Crash.   Several years ago I was in the audience at the National Association of Broadcasters annual convention when the introductory demonstration of a new nonlinear editing system had to be aborted because the computer operating the system kept crashing. The presenter sagely observed: "If television crashed as often as computers, there would be riots in the streets."

Every Technology Has Its Weak Spot.   The old linear tape editing systems often mishandled tape during editing, reducing it to a pile of useless, wrinkled mylar. Computer-based nonlinear editing systems frequently crash because they don't have enough memory or processing speed to handle the demands of editing video or because of software conflicts within the computer. An occasional computer crash is to be expected when working with nonlinear editing. However, frequent system failures are often the result of a hardware or software problem that needs to be diagnosed and corrected if editing is to be completed in a timely manner.

Save Your Work Often.   Because computers crash with frequency, experienced editors save their work often. Many editing programs have an "auto-save" feature built into them that automatically saves complete

329

work at specified time intervals (e.g., 15 minutes, 30 minutes). Whether or not your system has this feature, get into the habit of saving your work regularly.

Pay Attention to Time Code.   SMPTE time code is an important tool in production and postproduction. It can make your work easier or harder, depending on how you manage it. When you shoot field footage, try not to leave gaps in the time code on the field tapes. Most nonlinear editing systems need continuous, ascending time code on field tapes to find and cue footage to be digitized. Also remember that the (minimum) five-second preroll time applies to footage shot with time code just as it applies to footage shot with control track. Machines need time to read the time code, cue the tape, and get up to speed. And additional footage at the head and tail of shots (with time code on it) may be important if you need to lengthen a shot later on, or if you want to add transitions in place of a cut.

Label Clearly.   Name and label your field tapes, give each shot a unique name when you digitize it, and name your program and its constituent parts clearly so that you can find your work on the hard drive of the computer on which you are editing.

Make Backups.   Make backup copies of your work if you do not finish in a single editing session, and make a backup copy of complete projects in case you decide to reedit them at some future time.

Budget Your Editing Time Well.   In many ways nonlinear editing seems to be "better" than linear editing because of its drag-and-drop editing and the ease with which edits can be made and/or changed. However, nonlinear editing is not necessarily faster than linear editing. Digitizing each clip takes time that linear editing does not require, and because it is possible to try different editing decisions before committing to them, it is not unusual for projects edited on nonlinear systems to take more time to complete than projects edited on linear systems.

12 Graphics and Design

The graphic materials selected or created for use on video convey important information to the viewer. The term **graphic materials** describes a spectrum of visual materials ranging from whole settings, in which action is staged, to the simplest of captions identifying a speaker. (See Figure 12.1.) Their content and their style—the manner in which they present that content—each contribute to the viewer's understanding of the message.

Figure 12.1
Generating Video Graphics with a Computer

 # Guiding
Principles

A relatively simple set of principles is central to the creation of effective graphics, regardless of how they are created. Of paramount importance are the principles of unity, clarity, and style.

Unity

For a program to be effective, all graphic materials must act together in support of the major theme or purpose of the program. Each element must be coordinated with the others if **unity** of effect is to be achieved. Failure to coordinate elements results in a distraction—the worst sin the graphic artist can commit—that causes the viewer to focus on some unique quality of the graphic, rather than on achieving the goal of viewing the program. The following series of numbers, for example, obviously lacks unity of expression:

one, two, three, IV, *fünf,* six, 7, *ocho*

Use of these numbers to identify points made in a public health meeting or a corporation's marketing goals would be dysfunctional. In a comedy program, however, it might provide effective visual support to the proceedings.

Unity of expression includes control of all aesthetic and expositional factors that enrich the presentation of the message, story, or personality around which the program is designed. Camera angles, lighting, editing techniques, and sound (each considered in separate chapters) also contribute to this overall expression and must be considered if unity is to be achieved.

Clarity

The concept of *clarity* involves both simplicity of expression and the visibility of the graphic elements or characters themselves. Obviously, the display of a full page of newsprint on a video screen means that each word will be too small to be legible. While the news stories may be selected on the basis of their importance to the program, their graphic presentation in a single shot is incompetent. The principle of clarity has been violated. Functional and practical factors in the preparation of television graphics must be considered if clarity is to be preserved.

Style

Video producers use program graphics to attract attention, establish a mood, generate interest, and inform viewers. Keeping all elements stylistically similar creates a visual harmony that supports the general theme or tone of the presentation in a systematic way. The style of a video presentation can take many forms. It may be realistic (as is the case for most news and documentary programs), expressive (e.g., music video), or abstract (e.g., experimental drama and dance).

Once the question of basic style is answered for the program, attention can be given to the design and preparation of graphic elements that will reinforce its expression. Graphics should be compatible with settings and costumes. For example, the lettering of graphics for a program set in a modern hospital should reinforce elements of that setting (e.g., modern, antiseptic, scientific). Use of an Old English alphabet to identify modern surgical procedures would distract the audience. All lettering, regardless of source, must match the other visual elements of the production.

Functional and Practical Factors

When designing graphic materials for television and video, special consideration needs to be given to a set of functional and practical factors that will determine their effectiveness. These factors include the aspect ratio, size of and essential area of the video screen, and the intelligibility and color and brightness of the graphics themselves.

Aspect Ratio

Graphic materials designed specifically for use in television and video are always designed with the aspect ratio of the screen in mind. Regardless of its size, the screen is a rectangle with an aspect ratio of 4 units wide by 3 units tall (NTSC) or 16 units wide by 9 units tall (HDTV). Graphic materials meant to fill the screen must maintain the appropriate proportions. (See Figure 12.2.)

Graphic materials recorded on location (e.g., street signs, company logos, plaques, or monuments) can ori-

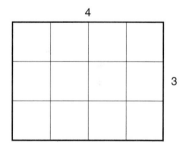

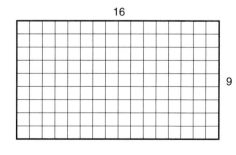

Figure 12.2 TV/Video Screen Aspect Ratios

ent the viewer to the location, but they may present problems if they are out of the correct screen aspect ratio. Objects may need to be reframed to conform to the aspect ratio of the video screen. (See Figure 3.7.)

Size of Screen

The major problem related to size is the tendency to put more information on the screen than the viewer can see clearly at a normal distance. This concept of audience distance from the screen is very important.

Computer users sit very close to the screen and are accustomed to looking at screens with a large amount of textual information. Television and video viewing presents a different situation, because the audience sits much farther away from the screen and cannot see small detail as well. For example, the home viewer sits 6 to 8 feet from the screen, whereas the student in a classroom might be more than 30 feet from the screen and forced to view the screen from less than an optimum angle. For this reason, try planning for graphics on a 2″ scratch pad. There is no room on such a small piece of paper to include more than the viewer can see on the television screen. Though not absolutely necessary, this technique encourages consideration of strong, simple expressions both in text and symbols.

Many field production clients request graphics based on apparent experience with magazine illustrations. Full-page advertisements seem to be about the size of the television screen (or much smaller), but, unlike television, they are viewed from a distance of 18 inches! Most often, the one-page illustration contains too much information for effective presentation on the screen. (See Figure 12.3.)

Figure 12.3   Printed Page-
to-Video Problem

The introduction of lightweight, portable television cameras and recorders changed the face of television news. Most local television stations, as well as the major broadcast networks, made the transition from film to portable video for electronic news gathering in the mid-1970s. The availability of reliable ³⁄₄″ portable VCRs and editing systems made large-scale commitment to ENG possible among local broadcasters.

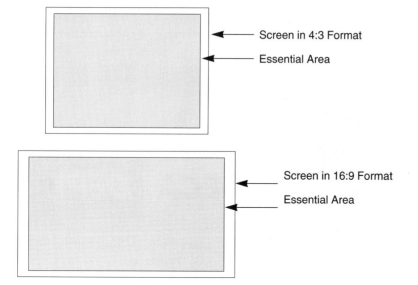

Screen in 4:3 Format

Essential Area

Screen in 16:9 Format

Essential Area

Figure 12.4   Screen
Essential Area

Essential Area of Screen

When preparing graphics for video, it is important to leave a margin around the edges of the screen. Due to edge distortion aggravated by the production and transmission processes, about 10 percent of the horizontal dimension of the screen must be left clear at each side, and 10 percent of the vertical dimension must remain vacant at the top and the bottom of the screen. The remaining space on the screen is termed the **essential area.** By the time the picture reaches the viewer, this area will fill the screen (see Figure 12.4). In most field production situations, the videographer can adjust the field of view to preserve the pictorial material for the viewer.

Another term for essential area is **safe-title area.** Some camera viewfinders display a safe-title area template superimposed over the image the camera sees as an aid to framing. Similarly, many computer-based video graphics programs used in the design of titles and animation contain safe-title templates as well.

Lower Third Titles.   A special situation arises when individuals who appear in a program need to be identified visually on screen. The conventional treatment is to superimpose or key the person's name and brief identifying information in the lower third of the frame. (See Figure 12.5.) Care must be taken to keep the bottom edge of the graphic, as well as its left and right sides, within the safe-title area. To improve readability, the title can be constructed within an opaque or transparent horizontal bar of color

335

Figure 12.5 Lower Third Titles

Keep Lower Third Titles within
the Safe Title Area

Lower Third Letters against
Contrasting Background

that will provide a background for the lettering and set it apart from the picture beneath it. Make sure the lettering remains on screen long enough to be read (five to eight seconds is usually sufficient for a simple identifying graphic). Also, pay attention to the placement of the graphic over the background picture. Lower-third titles work best over medium close-up shots. Avoid lower third titles when the background picture is a close-up or tight-close up—it is distracting to see a title appear over someone's mouth as he or she is speaking.

Intelligibility

Bold, simple arrangements communicate more directly and effectively than chaotic, cluttered, and overly verbal displays. Regarding **intelligibility**, the readability of textual materials, the most effective letters are no less than $1/10$ of the total screen in height and spaced so that the words formed are clear. If appropriate, letters and words may be designed to express something of their meaning by their very shape (see Figure 12.6). As with most novelties, this technique should be used sparingly and saved for special emphasis. Again, keep the lines forming the letters thick enough to be seen easily. The resolution limitations of the television system destroy illustrations crafted with too fine a line. This means that letters composed of very thin lines or decorated with serifs are often unsuitable for use in video graphics even though they are attractive in print. (See Figure 12.7.)

HDTV systems provide significantly better image resolution and picture detail. However, keep in mind that until the current stock of NTSC

Figure 12.6 Expressive Lettering

Figure 12.7
Intelligibility/Readability

home television receivers is replaced with HDTV receivers, the majority of home viewers will use set-top converters to display the HDTV picture on their NTSC receivers. When the signal is down-converted from digital HDTV to an analog NTSC signal, the 16:9 picture aspect ratio will be retained, but the improved resolution and picture detail of the HDTV signal will be lost.

Foreground and background detail must also be coordinated. The more detail in the background, the simpler the foreground graphic materials must be. The more detail in the foreground, the simpler (or more out of focus) the background must be (see Figure 12.8).

Figure 12.8 Relationship between Foreground Lettering and Background Detail

Color and Brightness

Much attention has been given to the choice of *colors* in graphic materials, especially with those associated with theater, advertising, and marketing. A trip through the supermarket confirms the popular notion that certain colors are linked with definable emotional responses. Reds and yellows are considered warm, greens and blues are cool, and dark colors are somber. Audiences know this code and generate expectations accordingly.

The visibility of objects and lettering is most often improved through the use of contrasting colors. For example, yellow letters against a dark blue background will be easier to read than light blue letters against the same dark blue background. (See Figures 12.9 and CP-8.) In addition, attention must be given to the relative brightness of those colors. This is particularly important if the video will be viewed on a black-and-white receiver. Many **gray scale** charts (a sequence of tints and tones ranging from white at one extreme to black at the other) are available to the producer, and arguments abound over just how many shades of gray (levels of brightness) can be identified on the screen (see Figure 12.10). As a rule of thumb, reduce the scale to 10 shades and maintain at least a 2-shade separation be-

Figure 12.9   Visibility and Contrasting Colors

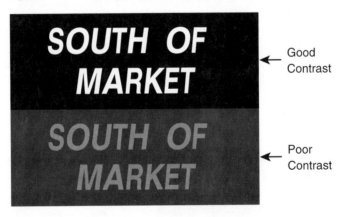

Good
Contrast

Poor
Contrast

Figure 12.10   Gray Scale

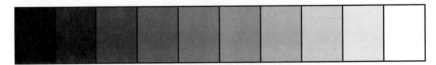

tween adjacent objects. Objects and graphics thus treated are visible because they are differentiated by both color and brightness. Adding texture and focus contrasts heightens the effect.

Sources of Graphics for Video

Graphic materials for video productions can come from a variety of sources, including camera cards, scanned images, and slides and film, or they may be created electronically.

Camera Cards

Before electronic graphics systems were developed, **camera cards**, also called **art cards**, were used extensively to create graphic materials for television and video. Line art, graphs and charts, and program titles were typically designed on pieces of 14″ × 11″ poster board. Why 14″ × 11″? That size represents an efficient division of the readily available poster materials (28″ × 22″). Because 14″ × 11″ is not exactly a 4:3 ratio, care must be taken to use only that portion that fits in the 4:3 rectangle. During the era of poster-board camera cards, graphic artists worked in a "real-size" environment, because the home television screens were about the same size as the cards. In the present electronic era, graphics can be viewed on screen instantly to assess their effectiveness.

Today, electronic graphics have replaced most of the traditional forms of card-mounted graphics, with one exception: photographs. Camera cards are still widely used to mount still photographs so they can be recorded onto videotape with a camcorder. If you plan to use card-mounted photographs in a production, you should be aware of two of the principal problems associated with their use: surface reflection and keystoning.

Surface Reflection.   The *surface texture* of camera cards may cause production problems. Glossy photographs provide the best example of materials requiring special treatment to avoid creating distracting glare. The solution involves arranging the card, camera, and illumination source so that light reflected from the shiny surface of the photograph is not reflected directly into the lens. The photograph must be flat for this technique to work properly. An animation stand or similar construct holding both the camera and all photographs in a constant relationship to each

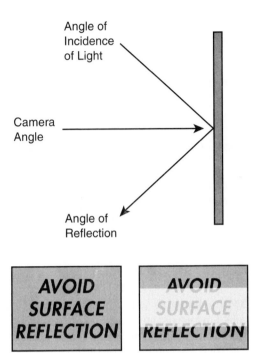

Figure 12.11 Avoiding Surface Reflection

Angle of Incidence of Light

Camera Angle

Angle of Reflection

AVOID SURFACE REFLECTION

AVOID SURFACE REFLECTION

Figure 12.12 Keystoning

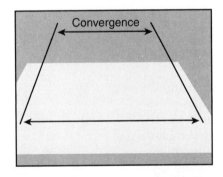

Convergence

This Sign Is Keystoned When Photographed from Below.

other is essential to the production of programs such as historical documentaries that rely heavily on still photographs for their visual content. The same reflection-avoidance principle applies when shooting through a glass door (see Figure 12.11).

Keystoning. If the camera card or photograph is not displayed perpendicular to the camera axis, another complication may arise: **keystoning.** This form of visual distortion is caused by placing one edge of the graphic closer to the camera than the opposite edge. The closer edge then appears to be larger because it fills a greater portion of the camera's field of view. This is especially troublesome when printed material is involved, unless, of course, distortion is desired for reasons of a specific story (see Figure 12.12).

Keystoning is often a problem when shooting signs and other graphic material on location. Signs mounted high above the ground improve readability for passersby, but they will appear to be keystoned on screen if they are shot from the typical camera position below the sign. (See Figure 12.12.)

Scanned Images

Problems with keystoning and surface reflection can be eliminated if the photograph or other graphic material can be electronically scanned, rather than photographed with the camcorder. **Flatbed scanners** are widely used to capture photos and other flat artwork. The image is stored as a digital file in a computer, which can later be transferred to video when the program is being edited. Most nonlinear video editing systems are capable of importing a variety of different still-image digital file formats.

Slides and Film

Still slides in 35mm format and motion picture film provide another source of graphic materials. Both need to be transferred to video in order to integrate them into a production. However, as is the case with art cards and photographs, 35mm slides can also be electronically scanned to create a digital file, which can then be imported into a nonlinear editing system or graphics program.

Electronically Generated Graphics

Most graphics used in television and video today are generated electronically with the use of a character generator or a computer based-graphics program.

Character Generators.   Largely through the use of titles generated by electronic character generators, most viewers have become conditioned to the appearance of titles within television programs. We see them at every significant point of a program. For example, titles appear at the beginning of every program, often superimposed over the background visuals. The name of a significant person within a program is commonly superimposed over the person during the program. At the end of each program, the familiar credit roll appears.

In linear tape-based editing systems, the character generator is typically a dedicated piece of hardware designed exclusively to generate lettering and titles, or a computer equipped with character-generating software. Most nonlinear editing systems contain character-generation software integrated within the editing program.

Character-generator systems contain three parts: a keyboard, a screen, and a memory system. (See Figure 12.13.) The character-generator

Ampex ALEX Character Generator System

Figure 12.13   Electronic
Character Generators

Generating Titles with a Character Generator for
a Video Production

keyboard is a standard typewriter keyboard, offering the full range of alphabetical and numerical symbols. Information typed in appears on the screen. The keyboard contains a number of controls that affect the lettering display. Sophisticated character generators contain a number of lettering styles or fonts. (See Figure 12.14.) In addition, they can vary character sizes from extremely small to rather large. The color of the background on which the letters appear can be adjusted, as well as the color and edges or borders of the letters themselves. Character generators produce white-,

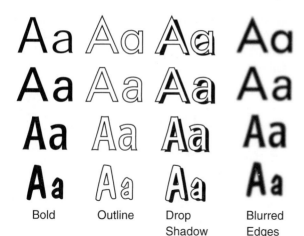

| Bold | Outline | Drop Shadow | Blurred Edges | **Figure 12.14** Typical Fonts |

black-, or colored-edged letters in hard, soft, outline, or shadow modes. The choices are mind boggling.

The keyboard also contains controls for positioning and displaying the letters. Centering is a common function, as is flashing. In the flashing mode, individual letters, words, or lines of information can be programmed to flash on and off. Some keyboards also provide control over the movement of the lettering: they can be programmed to *roll* (move vertically through the frame) or to *crawl* (move horizontally across the frame).

The information that is typed into the character generator is stored in its memory system. Simple systems store a few pages of information in internal memory. These memory systems tend to be *volatile;* that is, they are erased when the power is turned off. More sophisticated systems store information on magnetic floppy disks—small flexible disks like those used to store information from personal computers. *Magnetic floppy disk systems* are the most versatile, offering a large amount of storage with fast access for text editing.

Titling in the Camera.   Many consumer camcorders have simple character generators built into them. These devices generate titles within the camera at the moment of recording. There are a number of problems with these systems. First, the size, font style, and color of the letters may not be what is wanted. Second, a very limited amount of information can be generated and keyed over the picture, usually only several lines of a dozen or so characters each. Finally, once the titles are recorded, there is no way to remove them. Overall, the disadvantages outweigh the advantages associated with the use of these systems.

Computer-Based Video Graphics Systems.   When graphic elements more complex than simple character-generated titles are needed, computer-based video graphics systems are used to create them. These systems are described in detail next.

Computer-Based Video Graphics Systems

Most graphics used in video productions today are produced in computer-based video graphics systems. (See Figure 12.15.) Many of the components of these systems are similar to the components of the nonlinear editing systems discussed in the previous chapter. For this reason, sophisticated video graphics software programs are often bundled with nonlinear editing systems.

The basic element of the system is the computer, with ever-expanding capacity to accommodate increasingly sophisticated and technically demanding software. Computers used in graphics applications need to have a fast central processing unit (CPU)—particularly when moving video images and motion effects are involved—and a large amount of random-access memory (RAM).

The graphics system for video production must also contain substantial hard-drive capacity, video accelerator cards, a video monitor (20″ is good), a video capture board appropriate to the digital compression system

Figure 12.15   Quantel
Paintbox Express Video
Graphics System

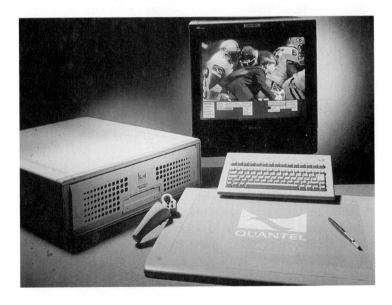

used, a time base corrector for the synchronization of inputs, and a digital audio card if visual effects are to be coordinated with sound.

With the addition of a video camera and a digitizing unit, camera-generated video images can be input into the computer and manipulated with the appropriate software programs. Similar manipulation of frames of information on videotape can be accomplished with the use of a frame grabber. A flatbed scanner can be used to digitize photographs and other pieces of flat artwork.

Computer-based video graphics systems are widely used to produce a variety of electronic graphics and effects. Typical graphics applications include character generation, two- and three-dimensional drawing and painting programs, animation, effects, and compositing.

Character Generation

Character-generator software programs enable the personal computer to provide a range of styles, sizes, and colors of letters and numbers out of which titles and credits are created.

Two-Dimensional Graphics

Advances in 2-D (two-dimensional) software make drawing, painting, and simple animation effects available to the low-budget videographer. (See Figure 12.16.) *Drawing systems* use pressure-sensitive "pens," which approach the expressive qualities of brushes in regard to line width, darkness, and edge hardness or softness. These electronic pens provide the video artist with freedom to compose beyond standard geometrical forms. This 2-D software also includes *painting systems,* which provide scores of pre-designed textures and multiple layers of images that can be manipulated in

Figure 12.16 Images Created in a 2-D Drawing and Painting Program

| Figure Outline Created in a Drawing Program | Shading and Texture Added with Electronic Painting Tools |

varying degrees of translucence. Elements of these composite images can be programmed to move horizontally, vertically, or diagonally on the screen with the use of simple animation effects.

Three-Dimensional Graphics

Advances in 3-D (three-dimensional) graphics are even more spectacular. Some systems provide hundreds of predesigned images that can appear to be illuminated from any angle ("light" control), can be seen from any angle ("camera" control), and can be made to rotate and move from foreground to background (size control). This is in addition to the texturing provided by the paint operation. More expensive 3-D systems allow the artist to create unique designs capable of photorealism in the manipulation of line, color, brightness, image layering, reflections, shadows, morphing, and animation (see Figure 12.17).

Animation

Many graphics used within programs are still images—they don't move. Others do move. One way of adding motion is with the use of animation software. In these systems a graphic is created using the system software, or it is imported into the animation program from a different source. **Keyframes** are then used to identify the starting, intermediate, and ending

Figure 12.17
Image Created in
3-D Animation
Program

points of the motion path of the graphic in the frame, and the animation software then interpolates the image data between each of the specified points to create the motion effect.

Effects

Because the video signal in the computer is digital, a wide range of two- and three-dimensional effects can easily be created. Two-dimensional digital video effects allow the image to be flipped, spun, tumbled, and rotated in the frame. The image appears to be flat, like a postcard. (See Figure 12.18.) The image can also be compressed (made smaller) or expanded (made larger). Three-dimensional effects like waves and ripples give the

Figure 12.18 Digital Video Effects

Full-Frame Image

Compressed Image

Full-Frame Image

Page Peel

347

image more depth and volume. The page peel is a very popular 3-D transition effect. (See Figure 12.18.) Other effects include image morphing and mapping flat images onto three-dimensional shapes like cubes and spheres.

Compositing

Compositing programs allow multiple layers of video to be manipulated. Character-generation software is an example of a simple compositing program—a layer of letters is combined with a background layer of video. More sophisticated programs allow the graphic artist or video editor to manipulate the images in multiple layers of video with varying degrees of transparency or opacity. (See Figure 12.19.)

Figure 12.19
Composited Image

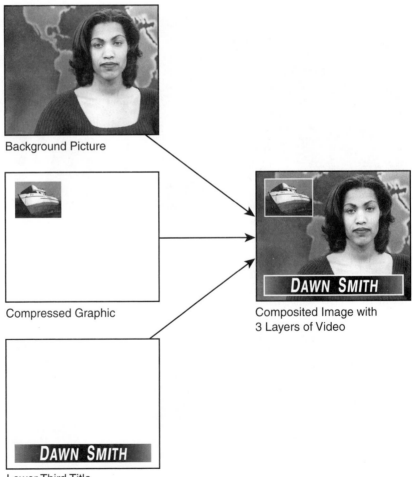

Background Picture

Compressed Graphic

Lower Third Title

Composited Image with
3 Layers of Video

Integrating Graphics and Effects Into a Video Production

Titling through a Video Switcher

In linear tape-based editing systems, a video switcher is often used to insert titles over the tape during editing. Two video sources—typically a character generator with the titles and a VCR with the background picture—are fed into the switcher and are combined there. The switcher output is recorded, and what you see at that point is the desired titling effect. (See Figure 12.20.) Two common methods of inserting titles with a switcher use keys and mattes.

Figure 12.20 Titling through a Video Switcher

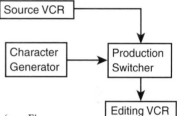

Keys

A **key** is an electronic switch from one video source to another (see Figure 12.21). Through keying, the lettering can be electronically cut into the background picture. The **clipper**, a small control on the switcher, regulates the point at which the electronic insertion of the lettering takes place. You can adjust the clipper so that the brightest frequencies of light trigger the electronic switch and the dark background of the source with the lettering

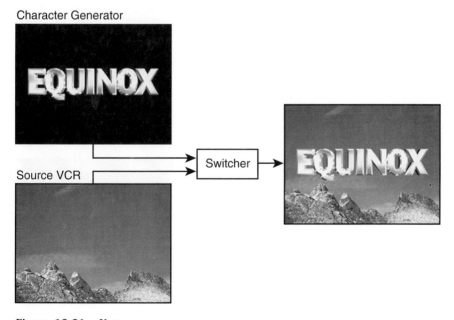

Figure 12.21 Key

is completely eliminated. Only the letters will then appear over the other picture. For this reason, lettering to be keyed in over a background is usually composed of bright letters on a dark background. The letters are cut into the other picture, and the background behind the letters disappears. Because the key is triggered by the brightness of the letters, this type of key is also called a *luminance key*.

Mattes

Another effect commonly used for titling is the **matte**, sometimes referred to as a *matte key*. A matte involves the use of three separate video sources: lettering, background picture, and another source to fill in the letters. (See

Figure 12.22   Matte

Letters Are Electronically Cut
into the Background.

A Fill Pattern Is Created.

Letters Are Filled with the Pattern.

Figure 12.22.) Typically the letters are first cut into the background using the clipper to adjust the clarity of the key. Then the letters are filled in with another source. Although any video source could be used, the source used most often is the **colorizer** or a color background generator. The colorizer simply generates a color video signal. By adjusting the hue, saturation, and luminance controls (found on either the colorizer or the switcher as part of the matte controls), the letters can be filled in with any color the colorizer can generate.

Matting in color is a simple way to make lettering more visible; sometimes white letters are not visible if they are keyed in over a white or very bright background. The addition of color can make the lettering stand out from the background source.

Chroma Keys

Another special effect that is part of the key and matte family of effects is the **chroma key**, also called a *chroma key matte*. Actually, a chroma key is more a matte than a key. As with a key and a matte, one video source is used to cut an outline into a background source. Then, like a matte, the outline is filled in with a third source.

A chroma key differs from a luminance key in the way in which the background is subtracted from the source to be keyed. In a chroma key, the background is subtracted by eliminating a particular color. In a simple key or matte, it is subtracted on the basis of brightness. The typical chroma key background color is blue or green, although other colors can be used. Place a newscaster in front of a blue or green background, engage the chroma-key effect, and the color background disappears. The newscaster can then be made to appear over any desired background (see Figure 12.23).

Chroma keys are frequently used in television newscasts during the presentation of weather information. In one typical application, a remote video camera is positioned outside the station to provide a live or taped view of a particular locale. The weathercaster remains in the studio and stands in front of the chroma-key background. When the two sources are combined, the weathercaster appears to be standing in front of the image produced by the background camera or tape source. Another very common application of chroma key in the presentation of weather data electronically places the weathercaster in front of a computer-generated map or perhaps even a video image gathered from a weather satellite.

Chroma keys can just as easily be applied to lettering. Generate white (or any other color) letters on a blue background with a character generator. Use the chroma keyer to subtract the blue background, and the letter will appear over the video source of your choice.

Figure 12.23   Chroma Key

Foreground Subject Is Recorded against
a Blue or Green Background.

Background Image Is Recorded
Separately.

Blue or Green Background Is Subtracted
and Foreground Image Is Combined with
Background Image.

As with a matte, a chroma key also gives you control over how the keyed source will be filled in. When the newscaster is chroma-keyed over a background, the camera shooting the newscaster is typically used to fill in the picture. One could just as easily fill in the outline of the newscaster with another source: color from a background generator, video supplied by a different camera, or a videotape. This would, however, make for a most unusual newscast.

Keying Titles without a Video Switcher

If you do not have access to an editing system with a video switcher, there are several other ways to produce professional-looking keyed graphics. Some automatic edit control units, for example, are capable of accepting the output from a character generator as a key source and can add the keyed title during the editing process. In addition, some character generators are able to **gen-lock** to an incoming video signal; that is, they can synchronize the video signal produced by the character generator with the incoming signal from the VCR. The video output from a VCR is fed into the character generator. The video output of the character generator (which now is a combination of both sources with the lettering from the character generator in the foreground and the picture information from the VCR in the background) can then be fed to another VCR to record the combined signal, or it can be fed to an editing VCR and edited directly into a program as it is being assembled. The technique of gen-locking a graphics generator to an incoming video signal from a VCR has been widely adopted by video producers who use inexpensive personal computers with graphics capabilities to generate video images and/or modify recorded video images with their computers. If a production switcher and character generator are not available, and if the titles and credits need not be keyed or superimposed over program video, a separate videotape of titles and credits recorded by a camera from cards or a computer printer can be inserted like any other video.

Titling in a Nonlinear Video Editing System

Nonlinear video editing systems provide a simpler and more direct method of integrating graphics into the final program. In addition to one or more video tracks and multiple audio tracks in the editing software's time line, a graphics or title track is also typically available. (See Figure 12.24.) Program titles, credits, and name keys can be created by using the built-in character-

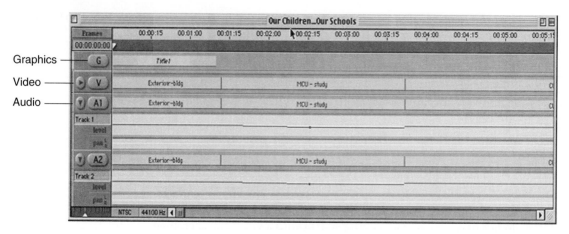

Figure 12.24 Graphics Track in Nonlinear Video Editing Time Line

generation software or by importing graphics created in appropriate software applications elsewhere. The beginning and end points of the graphic are identified on the time line, and the graphic is inserted over the background video.

13 Production Planning

Without a doubt, the key to success in field production lies in adequate production planning. The remote producer is at the mercy of the location and the people in the production and does not have the same kind of controlled situation as the studio video producer. Therefore, it is imperative that all elements of the production be as carefully planned as possible. This is not to suggest that such planning ensures that the production will go off without a hitch. If there is one thing that can be guaranteed in field production, it is that the unexpected will happen—and you must be able to cope with it.

Nevertheless, producers who carefully plan out the course of their productions undoubtedly have greater success in the field than do those who do not plan. In fact, the planning part of the production often involves more time and energy than does the actual production time in the field.

Stages and Types of Production

Three Stages of Production

All productions can be broken down into three stages: preproduction, production, and postproduction. The **preproduction** stage is crucial to a production's success because it is in this stage that the initial idea for the subject is developed and the production mechanism put into motion. Thorough preproduction planning ensures that the actual production phase goes smoothly. The **production** phase of a field production is the actual shooting time for the program. Finally, the **postproduction** phase involves the editing and packaging of the production. Once again, anticipating and solving problems through thorough planning in the preproduction and production stages will make the postproduction process easier.

355

When producers encounter unanticipated problems in the field, they may be inclined to say, "Don't worry, we'll fix it in postproduction." While this is sometimes possible, more often than not major problems that are not corrected in preproduction or production will haunt a production. Some problems can be solved, others cannot. The place to anticipate and solve problems is in preproduction, not postproduction.

Adequate planning is an important part of all three production stages. A comprehensive map of the program plan must be communicated clearly to all members of the production group for the overall program design and production to be executed efficiently and smoothly. This is in large part accomplished through production planning. All major decisions about a production should be made on paper before the camera is uncapped and the tape rolled.

Independent versus Client-Based Production

The production planning process is influenced by the nature of the production. An *independent production* is one in which the producer is responsible for the development of the program idea and does not have to report to another agency or individual for consultation or approval. This type of production operates somewhat differently from a *client-based production*—one in which the producer has been hired to carry out someone else's program idea.

Video producers find themselves in many different production situations. In the commercial arena, the producer most often executes production ideas developed by others. In the area of independent documentary production, the producer most often develops an idea and carries it through the production process. However, in many cases, the producer must report to a grant-giving agency to obtain the funds necessary for the production. The in-house corporate video producer may have to report to an executive producer or department head to win approval for production projects but may then be given significant autonomy to develop and execute the production idea.

Preproduction Planning

Getting and Developing a Program Idea

Whether a video program is developed to communicate an idea about a political issue, to attempt to persuade the audience to buy a particular brand of deodorant, to convey information about changes in corporate policy to employees, or to entertain through the presentation of a dramatic, comedic, or musical extravaganza, the program idea is at the heart of the production. No program can proceed without a basic idea governing its organization and production. Both the media experimentalist, who breaks narrative and aesthetic conventions of media structure in order to challenge the audience to focus on new relations between visual and aural images, and the instructional video producer, who uses the medium to clearly and unambiguously teach a subject to a target audience, make a series of initial decisions about the design of their respective programs.

In the early stages of program development, the program idea contains at least several components. Central to the idea is the concept of the program's subject. What does the program producer want to communicate? Evaluating the target audience gives the producer important information about the medium best suited for transmitting the idea, and the way in which the subject can best be treated in that medium to communicate the program idea effectively to the audience. So, in the initial planning stages of a program, we come full circle to concerns that were raised in the first chapter of this book: The idea for a program can be moved to effective actualization only through thorough consideration of the elements of subject, medium, treatment, and audience.

For the independent producer or the student who is required to complete a program for a video production course, getting the idea may be the hardest part of the production process. For the in-house producer or educational media specialist, ideas may be generated by resource people with expertise in particular content areas. The producer's role, then, is to adapt the content to the particular requirements of the medium and audience by applying the proper treatment to its development.

Program Conceptualization and Design

No matter what the source of the idea for a program or program segment, the video field producer should follow a method for the development and execution of the program idea. At least four areas should be addressed in the initial stages of program design and conceptualization: subject, treatment, visual potential, and feasibility.

Subject

Preliminary planning should consider the subject from at least two perspectives: content and structure. Analysis of the content of the subject identifies the important information to be conveyed in the piece—what is to be communicated and why this information is important and/or appealing to the audience.

357

Information about the subject and audience can be gathered by conducting basic research on the subject and audience. For many years, U.S. broadcasters were required to ascertain the needs of their communities through systematic research and interviews with community leaders and then to broadcast programming designed to meet those needs. The staffs of many ongoing program series include one or more researchers whose job it is to identify subjects of interest to their audiences. In news operations, assignment editors determine which of the day's stories have the greatest importance and/or potential interest to the viewing audience and then assign their production to the various ENG production teams.

Initial program planning should also consider the structure of the presentation. At the very least, you should make some preliminary plans as to the organization of the material. Aristotle's observation that all drama contains a beginning, a middle, and an end is just as useful to video producers as it is to theatrical dramatists. Indeed, concepts of dramatic structure are as indispensable to the producers of television news, documentaries, and commercials as they are to the producers of televised drama.

Program Format/Treatment of the Subject

Once the subject has been identified, a decision needs to be made about how the program idea will be presented. Not only does a program format have to be identified but also decisions need to be made about the way in which the subject will be treated within the chosen format. For example, concern about the negative consequences of tobacco use might lead one producer to produce a documentary on the medical consequences of smoking, while another producer might develop a campaign of public-service announcements (PSAs) to be distributed to local television stations.

The documentary approach can rely on the testimony of experts, focus on victims or survivors of smoking-related illnesses, or combine the two. The public-service announcements can focus on one issue or many, perhaps using so-called commercial production techniques.

Visual Potential

While developing a production idea, some thought must be given to the visual potential of the subject. In many ways, this is a two-edged sword. Concern with those subjects having greater visual potential over those with less visual potential has led to some serious, justified criticism of television. Subjects with more visual potential often seem to be those that receive coverage, while those with less visual potential are ignored.

In evaluating the visual potential of the subject, the producer should consider not only whether one subject has more visual potential than another but also how the visual potential of any subject can be maximized. On the surface, a discussion of the failing economy might seem to have less visual potential than a magazine segment on trained chimpanzees who parachute from airplanes on skis and slalom down a mountain ski course. But this may be only because the producer has not thought out the visual potential of the piece on economics. At the very least, discussion of economic theory could be supplemented with visual material on the subject: computer-generated graphics or perhaps three-dimensional models to convey information about various concepts or to support the discussion. Interviews or profiles of real people suffering the consequences of the economic problems can be integrated into the program. For example, a discussion of rising interest rates need not focus only on the statements of a mortgage banker sitting in an office. It might also include shots of construction sites and lumber mills to provide external visual information about the issues being discussed.

Even if additional visual material is not going to be used in the story, the visual potential of the basic interview with the banker should be considered. The interview location, camera position, shot selection, and lighting can all be manipulated to maximize the visual potential of the interview.

Feasibility

No program proposal is worth developing if it is not feasible. A documentary based on the lifestyle of the members of the local Zen Buddhist bakery might seem intriguing, but the likelihood of ever producing such a piece is slim if the local Buddhists are cloistered, have taken a vow of silence, refuse to allow interviews, and prohibit cameras from entering their premises. Preliminary decisions about the feasibility of the program should focus on the field producer's ability to get access to the subject as well as on the availability of resources to support the production. Production resources include *financial support* (an adequate budget to pay for the production), *personnel* (paid or unpaid production personnel to execute the production), and *equipment and facilities*.

Formal Program Proposal and Shooting Schedule

Once the preproduction planning has been completed, you will be able to develop a formal program proposal. The amount of detail contained in the proposal will vary, depending on your production situation. A proposal for submittal to an agency as part of an application for a development or production grant will be more detailed than one developed for an in-house production or an independent production not dependent on outside funds. Depending on your particular situation, your formal program proposal will contain some combination (and perhaps all) of the following elements.

Treatment.   A narrative description of the idea for the project should be presented to convey the essential idea behind the project, as well as its importance and need.

Outline of Major Elements.   This section should present an outline of the major elements of the program. If your proposal is for an entertainment or documentary program, this section identifies the program's most important parts. If you are producing an educational program, this section will outline your major goals or objectives, perhaps in the form of a list of what is to be learned from the program.

List of Locations and Setups.   A list of locations and setups is extremely important because it will give you an idea of how you will need to budget your production time. A *location* is a general area where shooting will take place, whereas the *setup* describes specific shooting areas at the more general location. For example, one might schedule a location shoot at the local airport. At that location, specific setups might be needed at the ticket area, baggage area, and maintenance area.

Outline of Proposed Shooting Schedule.   The shooting schedule outline presents a realistic estimate of how each production day will be spent. The outline should include a breakdown of the amount of time each segment is expected to take to shoot, as well as the more mundane elements such as time for travel, equipment setup, and breaks for the crew.

Figure 13.1 presents a proposal for a remote segment from the PBS series *Over Easy*. Notice how the four elements just listed are developed and presented in this proposal.

Comments on Technical Feasibility.   You should address any questions about access to the location, crowd control, or access to power and/or adequate light. If a remote survey has been completed, this can provide answers to the most important questions about the use of the proposed remote locations.

Script.   A script is an important part of any production. If your program will be completely scripted, a copy of the script or an excerpt from it should be included in the proposal. If your program is a documentary or is based on interviews, you will not have a complete script. Instead, present an outline of the major components of the program. (Scripts are discussed in greater detail later in this chapter.)

Evaluation.   Programs produced with particular goals in mind need to be evaluated for effectiveness. The proposal form, therefore, should contain a description of the method that you plan to use to evaluate the effectiveness of the program. Evaluation of program effectiveness can take many forms. You can simply propose to report the number of copies of the tape that you sell, provide an estimate of the number of people who see the program, or provide the number of broadcast stations or cable systems that carry it. If your program has specific learning objectives as its goal, you may want to test your audience to see how much of the information conveyed by the program they retain. Again, the extent to which this element is contained within the formal program proposal depends on the goals of the program itself.

Budget.   Many program proposals include an estimate of the budget for the program. The budget should be a realistic estimate of all the costs associated with the production. Video producers find themselves in a variety of production situations with respect to budgeting. For example, a home video producer or a student in a university production course may find that the only cost associated with a production is the cost of videotape. The independent producer, on the other hand, may have to rent a considerable amount of equipment for the field shoot, and facilities for postproduction editing. The field producer working within a television station might not have any responsibility at all for developing budgets, since all production costs may be carried as part of the normal operating expenses of the station.

How, then, does one go about developing a budget? Because the budget should present a realistic assessment of the costs associated with the production, developing the budget depends on your particular production situation. The cost of producing an hour of prime-time dramatic television for distribution on one of the commercial networks may exceed $1 million. Although only a few video producers work in this budget range, even nonbroadcast productions produced to professional specifications may be relatively expensive. For example, professionally produced programs for corporate and institutional clients may cost from $1,000 to $2,000 per minute of finished program.

Many producers of small-scale productions find that their budget needs are significantly more modest than those just described. A 30-minute independent documentary, a tape documenting the accomplishments of a community organization, or an edited videotape of a wedding ceremony can often be produced on a shoestring budget and delivered for a few thousand dollars or less.

Figure 13.1 *Over Easy* Segment Proposal

KQED, INC.
500 EIGHTH ST.
SAN FRANCISCO, CA 94103

Wednesday, August 2   Jim Langton
                             Disneyland   Al Miller—contact
                                                 (213) 555-8805 or
                                                 (714) 555-4456

6:30 AM	Call
6:30–7:30	Travel
7:30–8:30	Set Up Interview w/ Jim (Streetcar in Town Square)
8:30–8:45	Break
8:45–9:30	Shoot Interview with Jim
9:30–10:00	Shoot from Inside Trolley
10:00–11:00	Shoot off Trolley
	1. Scene with Gary
	2. Jim Changing Horses
	3. Jim Enters Main Street & Greets Ralph
	4. LS Trolley Car Drives Off
11:00–11:30	Lunch
11:30–12:00	Set-up for Parade (Town Square)
12:00–1:00	Shoot Mickey Mouse Parade
1:00–1:30	Set Up Exterior Disneyland (Entrance to Park)
1:30–1:45	Shoot Exterior Disneyland
1:45–3:00	Wrap and Travel

Four Set-Ups

1. Jim Interview in Town Square by train
2. Main Street
3. Parade in Town Square
4. Disneyland Entrance

Figure 13.1   Continued

Jim Langton
(213) 555-1196
Disneyland

Jim Langton at 62 is a rough and tough rodeo cowboy who for the last 15 years has worked as a driver of a horse-drawn streetcar on "Main Street, USA," in Disneyland. Although Jim still ropes calves in small rodeo contests on the weekends, his full-time job is at Disneyland. For Jim the job puts him in contact with two of his favorite things: horses and people. Jim talks about the older people who come to Disneyland, and what it's like to relate to them as well as the younger ones. Sometimes the job can be difficult—"It's like being a P.R. man all day long," he says. Jim enjoys being around the younger employees and adds, "I'm not exactly a spring chicken no more." Seven months ago Jim lost his thumb in a calf-roping accident and was in the hospital for the first time in his life. Several years ago he divorced his wife, who was also a rodeo cowgirl, and moved to California. Two years ago she committed suicide when she found out she had cancer. Today, Jim lives alone but retains a close relationship with his daughter and 95-year-old former father-in-law. Jim has lived an active life and is just reaching the stage of realizing that he too is growing old. He is just beginning to face the fact that he's got to prepare for his old age.

Elements
1. Second career
2. Living alone
3. Divorced late in life
4. Intergenerational relationships

Focus
1. How he feels about his job at Disneyland—the stress and the joy
2. His interrelations with the other younger employees and the tourists, young and old
3. His marriage and divorce
4. How he feels about living alone and preparing for his old age

Figure 13.2 shows the actual production costs for a small-scale production that resulted in the completion of a five-minute music video, produced with a professional S-VHS camcorder and edited on a digital non-linear editing system. The principal production equipment (camcorder, editing system, lights, microphones, etc.) was supplied by the university department in which the student who produced the program was enrolled. Members of the production crew were not paid for their time, thereby eliminating personnel expenses completely. Additional expenses included audio- and videotape, rental charges for a music recording studio, and miscellaneous supplies. The total cost of the production was $1,835.

Scripts

Because the types of programs that video field producers work with are quite varied, a number of different script formats and scripting strategies are used.

Story Outline Script.   In most electronic news gathering (ENG) situations, and in many other production situations as well (such as television magazine segments), a formal script probably will not be developed. Because time is of the essence in such productions, it is more likely that a story outline will be developed. The **story outline script** is a list of the major elements that will be used in the story. Usually, it specifies the locations to be used, the essential visual material to be recorded at the various locations, and the subjects of any interview segments. Occasionally, specific recommendations for shots, particularly transition shots and opening or closing shots, are specified (see Figure 13.3).

Sometimes the story outline is not written but is instead presented orally by the segment producer to the production crew. This type of production planning (or lack of it) is not recommended for the beginning producer. Professional crews are able to utilize this shorthand method of production planning principally because they are used to working together as a team and, most importantly, because they understand the conventions of television. That is, they all know what they need to get onto videotape in order to gather enough material for the story to hold together. Without even having a script, the camera operator knows what needs to be shot and may even stage multiple takes of a particular shot or sequence that will be important to the overall story. The producer may have a list of questions or an outline of subject matter to be treated in an interview.

In the ENG situation, an on-camera stand-up introduction and close are usually recorded on location. In other kinds of EFPs, such introductory and summary statements are most often added to the production later as a voice-over by the principal talent. In both types of productions, the video editor has responsibility for viewing the tape and making the primary

Figure 13.2   Small-Scale Production Budget

Music Video Production Budget

Shooting Days : 6
Length : 04:52

CASH FLOW

	Qty	Unit	Cost	Total	Nov	Dec	Jan	Feb	Mar	April	May	Jun
PRE-PRODUCTION												
Story development	1		15	**15**	15		50	30				
Music production (food+rent studio)	1		130	**130**	50							
Audio req (dat+cass+dubs)	1		38.9	**38.9**				38.9				
Location scanning (pictures+gas+permission)	1		50	**50**		25	25					
Sub-total				**233.9**								
PRODUCTION												
Talent	0		0	**0**								
Production personnel	0		0	**0**								
Production expenses												
Catering	1		110	**110**					110			
Make-up	0		0	**0**								
Props & Costumes	1		50	**50**					50			
Misc. Expenses	1		100	**100**				50	50			
Set				**249**					249			
Location/gas	1		50	**50**					50			
Field Equipment												
S-VHS GYX2	6	Day	0	**0**					0			
Camera supplies	2	Day	0	**0**					0			
Lighting	6	Day	0	**0**								
Playback machine	3	Day	0	**0**								
Tapes												
Dat tapes	0	tapes	15	**0**								
S-VHS tapes	16	tapes	14	**224**					224			
Film (stills) rolls	1	rolls	57.7	**57.7**				57.7				
Film development				**200**					200			
Sub-total				**1040.7**								
POST-PRODUCTION												
Photo-CD	2		180	**180**					180			
Videotape stock	2		50	**100**						100		
Jaz disks	1		80	**80**					80			
Rendering process	0		0	**0**								
Final editing	0		0	**0**								
Other expenses	1		50	**50**							15	
Video dubs	100		1.5	**150**							150	
Sub-total				**560**								
TOTAL				**183**	65	25	75	176.6	1193	100	200	0

Figure 13.3 *Evening Magazine* Story Outline

WESTINGHOUSE BROADCASTING COMPANY ☐ 855 BATTERY STREET ☐ SAN FRANCISCO, CA 94111 ☐ (415) 765-8832

OUTLINE FOR FALL FASHION

OPEN: Vis of Japan from the old stories that we did lasting about (:10) seconds before going to the V/O. The vis after that should follow the copy.

V/O #1 —   To find this year's hot fashion look we'll have to direct our sights to the east, to Japan—a land where art and beauty merge with life and a country determined enough to ride to world dominance atop a transistor. This year fashion is TURNING JAPANESE! (:15)

TRANSITION: To hot fashion show vis and music for (:10).

V/O #2 —   Fashion is all about what's new, and the Japanese look is certainly that. From the one-size-fits-all concept to exotic textiles, what some have come to call the BAG LADY look is this fall's hot fashion ticket. It is a blend of working-class cottons and the Japanese ethic of form and function. (:15)

BITE: (Beth Trier #3 4:23) "Right now they are what is hot, the trend. Therefore stores, retailers are picking up on it and making a lot of fuss about it . . . can comprehend it, we're not sure." (:15)

VIS: For Beth's I.D. use a shot of her from the fashion show.

V/O #3 —   Beth Trier of the *San Francisco Chronicle* doesn't feel that the Japanese look is just another trend, but rather an influence on fashion that will have an impact. (:08)

BITE: (Beth Trier #3 5:00) "The whole concept of dressing according to the Japanese . . . Taking a garment shaped like a box . . . fabric taken away from everyday concepts." (:30 cut down if it drags)

TRANSITION: To the art museum and vis of Issey Miyake . . . walking around. (:10)

V/O #4 —   One of the most influential of the Japanese designers is Issey Miyake—not a household word and probably will never be one, but his fashions adorn the likes of David Bowie, Grace Jones and Diana Ross. In design circles Miyake is equally noted for his art along with his fashion designs. (:10)

Figure 13.3   Continued

WESTINGHOUSE BROADCASTING COMPANY □ 855 BATTERY STREET □ SAN FRANCISCO, CA 94111 □ (415) 765-8832

BITE: (Issey #1 13:25) "When I see all the beautiful tradition . . . that is probably living inside me." (:30)

V/O #5 —   What has brought Miyake to San Francisco is an exhibition of his art called "Bodyworks," which is a computerized environmental show that highlights many of his art-to-wear pieces. But what people are waiting to see are the clothes. (:10)

TRANSITION: To the rehearsal music montage with the models and action. (:10)

TRT: 2:55

V/O #6 —   Tonight the hottest ticket in town is the Issey Miyake fashion show, and it's a packed house at I. Magnin. The show begins with a display of his ready-to-wear fashions called Plantation. To model these garments Miyake chose real people, and it's interesting to note the designs only come in one size. (:15)

VIS: Music up and pictures for about (:30).

V/O #7 —   Then it was time for Miyake to reveal his Fall Fashions to a waiting crowd. (:03)

VIS: Of the fashion show for as long as it'll hold up (:40)?

V/O #8 —   (This is the end my friend) Now think what you may, all I know is they were all shocked and amused by the mini-skirt. And the leisure suit was universally hated, but both are still around. Even though you may not rush out and buy a Miyake, one thing Beth Trier did say was the most lasting impact of Japanese clothes will be their creative use of natural fabrics. (:20)

O/C: (Rich #2 8:40) "Wool, silk, linen all-natural fibers for an all-natural guy." (Freeze video)

THE END!

editorial decisions about which shots to use, what order to use them in, and how much of the primary interview material to include in the segment. Figure 13.3 presents an example of a story outline written by a field producer for the video editor.

Storyboard. A **storyboard** is a visualization of the principal visual material in a film or television production. In developing a storyboard, the principal frames of visual information that correspond to the written script are drawn and arranged in sequence with the script. Storyboards have long been used in the production of television commercials and spot announcements. Because these announcements are short, the visual parts of the program can be drawn in considerable detail. Storyboards are also used extensively in feature-film production; they allow the director to see what the film will look like before it is shot. In some cases, directors even make preliminary decisions about shot choices and the arrangement of visual sequences on the basis of the still frames in the storyboards. Storyboards are also used extensively in the development stages of animated features.

The treatment of the content of a program is reflected in the storyboard. Producers are expected to present such storyboards to clients or potential backers as the primary means of "pitching" the proposed production. Often, commercial clients expect to consider several treatments before commissioning a production. The storyboard need not include each shot that will be used in the final product, but it must include the major visual elements that establish the scope and tone of the production. The storyboard is arranged in proper sequence so that the progression of the narrative is clear and the integration of sound and picture can be considered in practical terms.

The storyboard is a working document subject to change as the production design evolves. It reflects the vision and discipline of the producer and often allows the production crew to anticipate problems and prepare solutions before shooting begins.

The development of a full script and storyboard is probably the best exercise the beginning video producer can undertake to plan out a production's visual sequences. You can use a number of different storyboard formats. In the professional arena, storyboards such as the ones shown in Figures 13.4 and 13.5 are common. The individual frames of the storyboard are arranged across the page, with the principal audio information written below. For producers who feel they don't know how to draw well enough to construct a storyboard, computer programs with predrawn characters, locations, and properties are available at minimal cost (see Figure 13.6).

Full Script. Many single-camera productions are shot from a full script. In many ways, the use of a full script (and storyboard) creates the best of all possible production situations. Preparation of the full script and story-

Figure 13.4 Public Service Announcement Storyboard

Americans for Fair Elections

:30 "Check-off"

This is Eric Sevaried. Since I began covering politics, campaign costs have skyrocketed. More and more people are wondering: does money talk louder than votes? It doesn't have to. There's something you can do:

Check this box on your tax return. That'll keep our presidential elections financed publicly and not by special interest groups.

It won't increase your tax or lower your refund. So it doesn't cost you a cent.

Remember, check the "yes" box for fair elections.

CHECK THE BOX for FAIR ELECTIONS

A Public Service of This Station and Americans for Fair Elections

:10 "Check-off"

I'm Eric Sevaried. If you think that in politics, money talks louder than votes.

Check this box on your tax return.

CHECK THE BOX for FAIR ELECTIONS

A Public Service of This Station and Americans for Fair Elections

It doesn't cost you a cent--and it buys fair elections.

Figure 13.5 Commercial Storyboard

U.S. NAVY

Public Service Advertising

Title: "This is David"
Comm'l No.: QUAQ-2013

Time: 30 Seconds
Commercial Produced by BBDO/NY

For additional info please contact: Navy Recruiting Command, 4015 Wilson Blvd., Arlington, VA 22203 (703) 696-4777

Music up and under throughout
AVO: This is David.

DAVID: Oh, hi.

AVO: This is what David's done.

David went to college.

Sorry, Annapolis.

David taught himself to play piano,

the sax,

even the bagpipes. Well, maybe not the bagpipes.

David was NBA Rookie-of-the-Year.

He's also been to the Olympics...twice!

David even became a Naval Officer.

David's sure done a lot. But do you know

one thing David's never done?
DAVID: Drugs.

AVO: David doesn't do drugs.

Maybe that's why he's done so much.
DAVID: Hmmmmmmm.

Courtesy of Navy Recruiting Command, Arlington, VA.

370

Figure 13.6
Storyboard Quick
Computer Program
with Predrawn
Characters and
Location

board saves a great deal of time in the production and postproduction stages. Any program that is prepared for a client should be fully scripted. All educational/instructional programs and dramatic programs are fully scripted. Even many interview-based documentaries utilize very detailed shooting scripts. Although you may not know exactly what the interviewees will say, you can predict their general point of view and roughly the way they will answer your questions. The script can therefore describe in detail the program's organization, the questions to be asked, and the predicted answers. This will serve as the initial shooting guide. Modifications in the script can be made after the field material has been shot to bring it into line with what was actually said in the interview.

Although there are a number of different kinds of full-script styles or formats in use, the two-column split-page format is one of the most widely used and one of the most useful to beginning video producers. In this script format, information about the program's video is contained in the left column and information about the program's audio is contained in the right column (see Figure 13.7).

The full script will contain sufficient detail to answer most production questions. Location and shot angle are specified. This, in turn, may

Figure 13.7 Full Script in Split-Script Format with Numbered Shots

VIDEO SCRIPT

Title: "BRANCH PRODUCTION MANAGEMENT CASE STUDY"
Draft: FINAL

Note: Throughout the program, we hear natural background sounds appropriate to the scene. When we are focusing on people, at times we hear them speak under the narrator's voice. We may understand a word or phrase here and there, but what they say is not important to the content of the program unless it is detailed in quotes.

VIDEO	AUDIO
Super Title: "Case Study: Part I: The Players"	
Fade Up On: 1. Exterior: Front of branch seen from street. Signage is clearly visible. We hear street sounds.	NARRATOR (Male Voice, VO): Welcome to the Longtree Branch of XXXXXXXXXXXX Bank. We're located in a medium-sized California suburb.
Dissolve to: 2. Interior: WS (wide shot) of lobby. We see customers in line.	We serve a mix of customers with a variety of banking needs. Everyone from seniors to college students, merchants to manufacturers, middle-class families to professionals.
Cut to Pan of: 3. A TELLER crossing the lobby and approaching EDITH FARNSWORTH at her desk on the platform. There are pictures of her grandchildren behind the desk. The TELLER has a question for EDIE.	Edith Farnsworth, or Edie as she likes to be called, is our Branch Manager. Edie's been with the bank for twenty years and is proud to have risen to the Branch Manager position.
4. Another angle of EDIE. She is distracted from her conversation by something she notices in the branch (we do not see what it is).	She likes to be aware of everything that is going on in the branch and is always very busy.
5. MS of DOROTHEA HALL. Pull back to reveal EDIE conferring with her over a piece of business. They are standing somewhere behind the teller windows. EDIE nods, smiles at Dorothea, then exits frame.	Dorothea Hall is our Customer Service Representative. She and Edie have worked together since they first came to the bank as tellers.

Figure 13.7 Continued

Cut to:

6. DOROTHEA on phone. Hangs up and goes back to working on the daily report.

   Dorothea handles customer concerns and problem phone calls referred by the tellers.

7. CU of DOROTHEA's face as she works.

   She also compiles detailed daily reports for Edie.

8. GEORGE BEALES at the merchant window. He greets an approaching customer as if they know each other well.

   George Beales, our Purchase Merchant Teller, knows his customers well and enjoys working with them. He has been with the bank for six years and aspires to the job of Branch Manager.

suggest lens focal length, depth of field, and light requirements of the shot. The audio associated with the shot is also included because it is important to the duration of the shot and, if music is identified, to the rhythm of the shot, and to the speed of camera movement or movement of objects within the frame.

The full script is central to the calculation of the production budget. The production calendar is generated from the full script, as are equipment, location, audio, light, costume, and property requirements. These, in turn, lead to rental, transportation, food, insurance, and salary calculations (and profit, too, for that matter).

The split-script format lends itself particularly well to the *script breakdown*. In the script breakdown, each shot is given a number (if this was not already done in writing the original version of the script), a shot list is compiled, and then—by considering the shot list and the availability of shooting locations and any actors/actresses (talent) who may be involved in the production—a daily shooting plan for the production is constructed. Figure 13.8 presents an example of a shot list, and Figure 13.9 presents the plan for one day's shooting schedule on this production.

Preinterview

An extremely important part of the preproduction planning process is the preinterview. The **preinterview** is simply an interview scheduled before the production date with the program's subject. Preinterviews are important to both the segment producer and the interviewee. From the producer's perspective, a preinterview establishes contact with a subject and gives the producer initial permission to actually produce the piece. In terms of program design, the preinterview is an important point at which to gain

Figure 13.8   Shot List

		SHOT LIST:	
		Drug Diversion Program	
Shot	**Camera Angle**	**Description**	**Location**
1	LS	Probation officer giving instructions with people in background	Conference Room
2	MS	Probation officer	
3	CU	Officer giving instructions	
4	MS	Probation officer talking/holding agreement	
4A	Zoom to CU	Zoom in to CU of agreement	
5	MS	Probation officer explains program to David	
6	MS	David paying fee	Front Office
7	MS	David turning in proof of completion	
8	MS	Probation officer talks about program	Probation Office
9	CU	Probation officer	
10	CU	Sign on courtroom doors	Courtroom
11	LS	Dolly into courtroom	
12	LS	Judge refers David to diversion program	
13	MS	Courtroom activity	
14	MS	Judge	
15	CU	Judge	
16	MS	David's reaction (over the shoulder)	
17	CU	David	

familiarity with the subject in terms of the person and the content of the piece. The preinterview may well tell you what is important about the topic being investigated. This serves at least three functions: it provides initial information about the structure and content of the piece; it suggests possibilities for visual material to be incorporated into the piece; and it may suggest possibilities for interviews with other people or visits to other sites to gather additional information relevant to the program.

Often, the people who are the subjects of video field productions have not been on television before. For example, a magazine program that focuses on unusual people or unique local characters is likely to identify as subjects for segments people who have little experience on camera. The preinterview serves an important function for such subjects in that it allows them to establish rapport with the producer and/or other production personnel. This puts them at ease for the interview, particularly if a rough outline of the interview topics is discussed.

Figure 13.9
Shooting Schedule

SHOOTING SCHEDULE:
City and County of San Francisco
Adult Probation Department
Drug Diversion Program

Date: Friday, April 7
Location: Hall of Justice
                 880 Bryant St., Room 200
Contacts: Christina Marina 555-1718
                 Jimmy Lee 555-5717

Time	Activity/Shot
8:00 AM	Arrive and set up—Conference Room

9:30   **Call: David and Probation Officer**
              Probation officer explains program procedure
              1   LS with people in background
              2   MS Probation officer giving instructions
              3   CU Giving instructions
              4   MS Probation officer talking/holding agreement
              4A   Zoom in to CU on agreement
              5   MS Probation officer explains program to David

11:30   Set up—Probation Office

12:00   **Call: David and Probation Officer**
              Probation officer explains the rules
              6   MS Probation officer talks about program
              7   CU Probation officer talks about program

12:45   Shot of paying cash (near office)
              8   MS David paying fee
              9   MS David turning in proof of completion

1:00   Lunch Break

2:00   Set up—Courtroom

3:00   **Call: David and Judge Gross**
              Dolly Shot
              10   LS Dolly into the courtroom

3:30   Shots in courtroom
              11   CU Sign outside courtroom
              12   LS Judge refers David to diversion program
              13   MS Courtroom activity
              14   MS Judge
              15   CU Judge
              16   MS David's reaction (over the shoulder)
              17   CU David

4:30   Strike equipment and leave

There is no set way to approach the preinterview. Some producers are content to make the initial preinterview contacts with the subject over the telephone, whereas others prefer an in-person visit. In either situation, it is essential that the producer take accurate notes on the discussion. Some producers prefer to use an unobtrusive audiocassette recorder to tape the preinterview discussion.

When deciding whether or not to conduct a preinterview, several factors should be taken into account. Because the preinterview often entails a visit to the remote location, preinterviews are somewhat time consuming. This illustrates a major advantage to the telephone preinterview—it eliminates travel time and may be more efficient for the producer who is pressed for time. However, the producer who travels to the interview site can also conduct an on-site remote survey to gather information about the location.

Perhaps the greatest danger in the preinterview is that it may cause a loss of spontaneity in the actual interview. Few news producers who are conducting an investigative report would want their subjects to have the opportunity to rehearse their answers. Similarly, even in noninvestigative reports, subjects who appear to be reciting rehearsed answers to questions often lose credibility or destroy the credibility of the segment itself. The remote producer, then, must walk a careful line in conducting the preinterview. Important information about the subject should be gathered, and the subject should be put at ease, but this should not destroy the spontaneity of the interview, its personal nature, or the sense of discovery that makes an on-camera interview come alive.

Remote Surveys

Video producers working in the controlled environment of the studio know that they will always have adequate light for the production, adequate power for the equipment, and an acoustic environment that is insulated from unwanted, exterior noise. The video field producer has no such guarantees. Location production presents the production crew with an incredible array of variables that seldom concern the studio producer.

Every location is unique, so field producers adopt one of two strategies to deal with the peculiarities of different locations. You can bring along every piece of remote equipment imaginable, so that any production situation can be dealt with, or you can visit the remote location in advance of the production date to determine the location's characteristics and the production strategies and equipment needed to shoot in that location. If you are fortunate enough to have a production van equipped with a wide array of power, audio, and lighting equipment, you are operating at a considerable advantage over the field producer who must order and budget each piece of equipment individually. Most field producers rely heavily on the **remote survey**—a technical and aesthetic assessment of a remote location—to provide important information about the location in which the shoot will take place.

Technical Factors.   Any remote survey should gather data on at least three important technical factors: lighting, power, and sound. The available light in a location setting is extremely important. The remote survey should indicate what the nature of the available light is and whether there is enough of it to meet the camera's baselight requirements. If the light is not adequate, then external lights or reflectors will be needed. If external lights are used, then the availability of power may be critical. Not only will it be needed for the camcorder but also it may be needed to run the lights if adequate batteries are not available.

The location should also be assessed for sound characteristics. You need to know what kinds of microphones and how many of each are necessary.

Legal and Safety Factors.   Of primary importance with respect to the remote survey are certain legal and safety factors. The production crew should be able to operate safely in the remote location. The remote survey, therefore, should carefully identify any potential hazards on the location and determine whether the presence of the remote crew will create hazards. For example, consider a sequence that is to be shot on the floor of a warehouse where there is significant activity by forklifts moving pallets of merchandise within the production area. This should be duly noted in the remote survey. Will the crew be in the area in which the machines are operating? What will you do about the AC power lines? Will they interfere with the movement of the equipment?

Perhaps you plan to shoot a segment inside an elevator. How will you ensure that the elevator remains on the floor on which you are shooting? Will this present a problem to people in other parts of the building who might need the elevator to get from one part of the building to another?

Particularly in large buildings or industrial locations, it is always advisable to discuss the nature of the production with the maintenance or plant supervisor or the building supervisor. The supervisor will know about potential dangers that exist on the location and safety regulations that are in effect and may be able to help you solve technical problems with the location.

Aesthetic Factors.   The remote survey should also note any relevant aesthetic factors apparent at the location. For example, the technical survey may indicate that sufficient light exists on location, but if it comes from a variety of sources with different color temperatures (e.g., a mix of daylight and fluorescent light), it may be difficult to set the camera white balance properly.

Similarly, notes on the visual character of the remote location may identify important architectural features that should be included (or excluded) from the production. Particular attention should also be paid to the sound environment. An interview scheduled in a house that is near the runway of a large, busy airport presents a challenging, if not impossible, situation for the audio person. A house next to a school playground may have appeared to be a suitable location for an interview if the remote survey was conducted while all the children were in class. However, if several hundred children are loudly playing in the playground during the remote shoot, it will be difficult to obtain a good audio recording.

Access to the Location.   Your remote survey should also include information about access to the location. A primary concern is to obtain permission to shoot on the proposed location. If the property is private, permission from the owner should be obtained, preferably in writing. If the property is publicly owned, you will need to obtain permission from the appropriate agency. For example, in San Francisco, New York, and other large cities, permission must be obtained from the municipal government to shoot anywhere within the city. If you set up a camera and a tripod on a sidewalk, you must have the approval of the city agency that regulates these matters. If you are shooting a profit-making production, you may have to pay for the right to shoot and obtain an insurance policy that protects the city from damage suits in the event someone is injured during the production. If your project is nonprofit, the use fee and insurance requirements may be waived (see Appendix 4). Appendix 4 presents an example of a shooting permit required in San Francisco.

Permission to shoot in local, state, or national parks usually involves submitting the appropriate application. Similarly, if you are shooting in a public facility, you will need to obtain the permission from the appropriate agency. To shoot in the local airport or railway station, or on a city-owned bus, permission must first be granted by the supervising agency.

Conducting the Remote Survey

It is never possible to anticipate all the problems that may arise on a location shoot. However, it is certainly better to conduct a remote survey and anticipate some of them than to skip the survey and go to the location totally unaware. Several guidelines can be used to help you conduct a good remote survey.

Survey When Conditions Are Similar to the Shoot.   Try to survey the location at the same time of day and day of the week that you plan to do the actual shoot. If you plan to shoot on a weekend morning, survey the site on a weekend morning. This is primarily important in providing accurate information about the available light, but it is also important for other reasons. Traffic patterns and people patterns differ significantly from day to day (and certainly from weekday to weekend day) in many locations.

Bring a Viewer, Tape Measure, and Remote Survey Form.

Bring a viewer or Polaroid® camera, a tape measure, and a remote survey form with you (see Figure 13.10). Director's viewers, which enable you to see a location the way the camera will see it, are available from equipment supply houses. The viewer lets you look at the site and determine how it will look on camera. Also consider bringing along an instant camera. While the field of view produced by a Polaroid camera may not be equivalent to the field of view produced by your video camera, it will nevertheless show you the location in a frame. It is also extremely useful in providing a photographic record of the location.

Figure 13.10
Remote Survey Form

REMOTE SURVEY FORM

Production Title _____ Length _____

Location _____

Contact at Location _____ Phone # _____

Survey Day and Date _____ Time _____

Production Day and Date _____ Time _____

Producer _____ Director _____

Camera _____ Production Assistant _____

Other Crew _____

Remote Survey Equipment:
- ☐ Incident Light Meter   ☐ Paper and Pencils
- ☐ Tape Measure   ☐ Polaroid Camera

NOTES

Interior	Exterior
Lighting	Audio
AC power	Legal

A tape measure is particularly useful. Measure the dimensions of any rooms that you expect to shoot in. Measure the distance between rows of objects that are important to the shoot. For example, you may want to dolly the camera between rows of bottles of aging wine in a winery, but you will be able to do this only if the distance between the rows of bottles is greater than the spread of the tripod dolly.

Make Parking Arrangements. Where will you park? If you are transporting a significant amount of equipment, you will need to be able to park your vehicle near the remote location. Is parking readily available? Will you need special permission to park near the shooting site?

Consider Crowd Control. If you are shooting outside, how will you control the inevitable crowd of onlookers who will appear as soon as you set up the camera and lights? Even in the smallest amateur, nonprofit production, the appearance of a camera is sure to draw comments from passersby. Anticipate this and take steps to control the situation. For example, field producers who shoot in the skid row section of San Francisco have worked out an uneasy truce with local inhabitants. The production budgets usually contain a small fund used to pay off bystanders. A dollar or so will buy assurance that no one will jump in front of the camera when the tape is rolling.

Arrange for Food for Cast and Crew. You will need to provide food if your shoot lasts more than a few hours. The need for your cast and crew to eat should be seen as an essential part of the production and production planning rather than as a sign of weakness among crew members and cast. Is food readily available at the location, or will other arrangements need to be made?

Arrange for Bathroom Facilities. Consideration of the need for adequate bathroom facilities may seem to be far from the lofty ideals embodied in your program, but they are nonetheless essential.

Releases and Related Legal Issues

The video producer working for a television station or production house often has access to the legal department of the station or production center. However, many independent producers often work without the benefit of such readily available legal advice. Amateur, student, and independent producers may find that legal advice on production matters is available free or at low cost from their local media arts or community-access organization. In any event, there are a number of areas of legal concern that are of extreme importance to all video field producers.

Talent Releases.   Perhaps the most important factor to be considered is the need for the field producer to obtain releases from those individuals who appear on videotape or from those individuals whose voices are used in a tape. To use someone's image or voice in a production, you must obtain a **talent release**, which is a standard agreement signed by the subject giving permission for such use to the program producer or production agency (see Figure 13.11).

In documentary productions and other nonfiction programs or program segments (for example, magazine segments), talent releases are obtained from anyone who is interviewed as well as from anyone who can readily be identified in the picture, even if he or she does not speak. On remote locations, it is a good idea to warn people when videotaping begins so that they can get out of the camera's field of view if they don't want to be recorded.

For a fully scripted program using paid (or unpaid) actors and actresses, you should secure the appropriate talent releases well in advance of the production date. If the actors and actresses are paid for their services and sign contracts, the allowable uses of the performance will be specified in the contract. For unpaid talent, particularly in documentary programs or interview-based magazine segments, the talent release is usually obtained on the day of the taping. It is usually the responsibility of the producer to obtain the signed release.

Professional actors and actresses are familiar with contracts and releases. Nonprofessionals, who are frequently the people featured in student productions, are usually completely unfamiliar with releases. Therefore, it is extremely important that the producer, or someone else on the production staff, clearly explain what rights are conveyed to the production group when the release is signed.

There is little agreement as to whether it is better to obtain the release before an interview is recorded or after it. Obtaining the release prior to recording the interview is certainly preferable from the production team's standpoint. Why waste time recording an interview only to be refused permission to use it in the end? On the other hand, many interviewees are extremely nervous about granting the interview, and being confronted with a decision about signing a release before the taping may cause them to refuse to participate. For such subjects, it may be better to wait until after the taping is finished and then obtain the signed release.

Many subjects are nervous about how their images and voices will be used. Most producers and editors are ethical people who want to use the best of what was obtained in an interview, not the worst. A simple assurance from the producer about the intention to use the good material will

Figure 13.11   Talent Release

KTVU / FOX

Cox Broadcasting

KTVU RELEASE FORM

Date: _____

I _____

residing at

_____
　　　　　　　Street　　　　　　City　　　　　State　　　Zip

hereby consent to the photographing, recording, filming and use of my voice
or person, live or recorded, for broadcasting and exhibition as part of the
television special produced by students of San Francisco State University's
Broadcast and Electronic Communication Arts Department in conjunction
with KTVU/Fox television. The program will be aired as part of KTVU's
Family 2 Family educational series.

Further, I hereby release and otherwise agree to hold you harmless and to
indemnify you, your licensees and/or assigns, from any and all claims arising
out of, or resulting from, my appearance and my statements in the above
production.

Signature:　　　　　　　　　　　　**Parental Signature** (Needed if
　　　　　　　　　　　　　　　　　　child is under the age of 18)

_____　　_____

Print Name:　　　　　　　　　　　　**Print (Parent's) Name:**

_____　　_____

Telephone Number:　　　　　　　　**Date of Birth:**

_____　　_____

San Francisco Oakland, Two Jack London Sq., P.O. Box 22222, Oakland, CA 94623 (510) 834-1212 often put a subject at ease with respect to signing the release. If your production is noncommercial or educational in nature, this should also be stressed when asking the subject to sign the release.

Shooting in public places presents a unique situation with respect to obtaining releases from individuals in a crowd. Generally, the producer in such a situation is protected by the public nature of the area. However, it is always a good idea to make an announcement that the area is about to be videotaped or, if possible, to post signs with a similar announcement, so that anyone who doesn't want to appear in the production will have the opportunity to get out of the camera's field of view.

Video producers should also be aware of the special conditions that apply to the use of members of the American Federation of Television and Radio Actors (AFTRA) or the Screen Actors' Guild (SAG) in their productions. AFTRA and SAG members are bound by the contracts of their respective unions, and if such union members are used in productions, specific rules apply to their working conditions and salaries. If you are working on a low-budget, nonprofit production, the unions will often grant waivers that allow you to use union members without paying the standard union wages. Waiver forms are available from the local office of the appropriate union.

Location Releases.   As discussed earlier, location releases are sometimes necessary. Releases are often needed to shoot on city streets; in city, state, and national parks; and in public buildings such as government buildings, airports, and so on. The need for such location releases almost always extends to student producers, just as it applies to broadcast television producers. In many situations, however, the student producer can obtain a waiver of the use fee usually associated with the release.

Location Safety.   Field producers should also pay particular attention to the safety requirements in effect at any remote location. Depending on your location, a number of different state or local safety codes may apply. The Occupational Safety and Health Act (OSHA) is a federal law that requires the states to set up safety regulations for employee protection. You should be familiar with local OSHA requirements and abide by them. If you are shooting in a factory, mine, or other industrial area, the plant supervisor can usually give you information about any OSHA requirements that apply.

Use of Copyrighted Music, Film, or Tape.   Just as a release must be obtained from each person who appears in your production, so must permission be obtained if you plan to use any copyrighted material in your production. Violation of copyright with respect to music is very common but, nevertheless, illegal. Recorded music may *not* be used in a production unless permission is obtained from the copyright holder for its use. Similarly, any material that is broadcast or cablecast is almost always protected by copyright. It is illegal to tape something off the air and then incorporate it into your program. Permission must first be granted by the copyright holder. Troublesome and expensive legal hassles can be avoided if permission to use copyrighted material is granted before you use it in your program.

Stock Footage, Sound Effects, and Music.

There are numerous sound and visual image (tape and film) libraries that supply material to producers for a fee. Stock tape and film footage are typically available, as are sound effects and music. For example, old newsreel footage is available for a fee from Movie-Tone News in Los Angeles. The National Geographic Society in Washington, D.C., has an extensive collection of stock footage of wildlife, which is also available for a fee. The National Archives in Washington, D.C., has millions of feet of old newsreels and government film, all of which is in the public domain. No royalties have to be paid to use this film, but the Archives charges a minimal fee to search for and transfer the material to videotape.

Access to sources of stock footage and music has increased markedly for producers in recent years. Most of the professional video trade publications carry advertisements for companies that provide stock footage and music. Many producers buy libraries of music on compact discs or subscribe to services that provide them with music on a regular basis.

Perhaps one of the most interesting and efficient ways to gain access to music and stock footage libraries is through the World Wide Web. A video producer who has a personal computer linked to the World Wide Web can search a wide variety of stock footage and music catalogs on-line. In many cases, it is possible to preview sound and video clips on your desktop computer. One service, FOOTAGE.net, claims to provide access to nearly every stock footage library in the world through its on-line catalog service. (See Figure 13.12.)

If you are looking for a particular type of stock footage or sound, chances are good that you will be able to locate it and that rights to the material can be bought for a modest fee, depending on your intended use. The rights to copyrighted material cost more if you plan to use it in a widely distributed commercial production than if you plan to use it in a noncommercial program with a much smaller target audience.

Obtaining Original Music

One way to avoid the problems associated with obtaining permission to use copyrighted music in your production is to have someone compose original music for you. At first, it may seem more difficult to obtain origi-

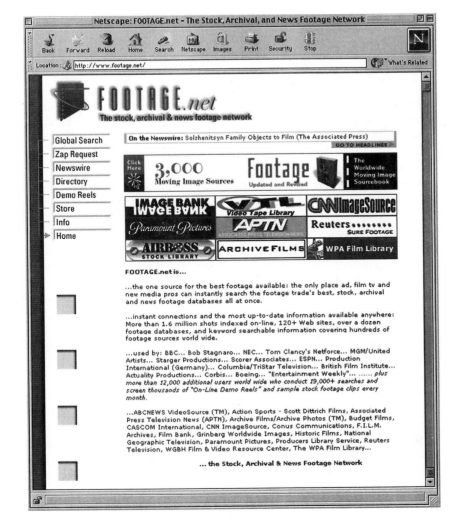

Figure 13.12
FOOTAGE.net
Home Page

nal music than to write for permission to use already-written music. In reality, this is not always the case.

Many professional and semiprofessional musicians, as well as many music students, will jump at the chance to write an original musical score, particularly if it is going to be used in a program that will be shown to a large audience. In most cases, music composed specifically for a program will work better than already-written music. Make sure that you obtain a release to use the music in your program, just as you would obtain a release for the appearance of talent in your program.

Production Planning

In many respects, while the actual process of shooting in the field is the focal point of the production, it is a rather insignificant part of the production process. This may seem like a paradox, given the amount of time we have spent describing production techniques, yet there is an element of truth to the statement. Preproduction planning and postproduction almost always take more time and energy than the time and energy spent on production itself. Weeks of preproduction planning may precede a one- or two-day shoot, and the material recorded during those two days may take another week or two to edit. Story or program conceptualization and development, script preparation, design of the storyboard, and coordination of all the preproduction elements require a considerable investment of time and creative energy. Alfred Hitchcock, the great film director, once commented that for him the most creative part of making a film was in visualizing the story and planning how he would shoot it. The actual process of filming the story was a technical exercise in which he merely tried to capture on film what he had already committed to paper.[1]

Admittedly, very few producers and directors possess Hitchcock's skill in transferring to film or tape the ideas that have been planned out on paper. Indeed, if there is one given in visual production, it is that the finished product will differ from the planned product. Production in general, and the process of field production in particular, has a unique dynamic in which things that appear to work on paper often do not work in production, and things that do not look good on paper sometimes seem to come alive in the actual production. Nevertheless, the initial planning and visualization of the production process are indispensable to the completion of the project.

From the standpoint of production planning and organization, three critical factors emerge during field production itself:

1. Equipment needs for a shoot must be identified and satisfied.
2. Crew assignments must be clearly delineated, and responsibility must be delegated to the appropriate crew members.
3. The material that is shot must conform to the script or script outline, and the shoot must proceed efficiently.

Equipment Needs

The remote survey will tell a field producer precisely how much equipment is needed for a shoot. If a remote survey has not been conducted, then it is always wise to bring a little more equipment than you think you might need, particularly with respect to peripheral production equipment such as lights, microphones, cables, and so on.

In any case, a remote production equipment checklist serves as a guide to your available equipment and should be filled out when the remote survey has been completed. Figure 13.13 presents a typical checklist that should suffice for most producers involved in simple- to intermediate-level shoots.

Figure 13.13
Remote Production
Equipment
Checklist

REMOTE PRODUCTION
EQUIPMENT CHECKLIST

VIDEO
- ☐ Camcorder
- ☐ Videotape
- ☐ Tripod
- ☐ Tripod Dolly
- ☐ Lens Filters
- ☐ Shoulder Brace
- ☐ Monopod

LIGHTING
- ☐ Light Meter
- ☐ Spotlights
- ☐ Broadlights
- ☐ Softlights
- ☐ Light Stands
- ☐ Replacement Lamps
- ☐ Barn Doors
- ☐ Scrims
- ☐ Dichroic Filter
- ☐ Gels
- ☐ Lighting Kit

LEGAL
- ☐ Talent Release Forms
- ☐ Location Permits

MONITORING
- ☐ Color Video Monitor
- ☐ Headphones
- ☐ Audio Cables
- ☐ Video Cables

AUDIO
- ☐ Microphones
- ☐ Microphone Connectors/Adapters
- ☐ Wind Screens
- ☐ Audio Cables
- ☐ Audio Mixers
- ☐ Headphones
- ☐ Microphone Batteries

POWER
- ☐ Batteries
      Camcorder
      Monitor
- ☐ AC Adapters
- ☐ 2-Prong to 3-Prong Adapter
- ☐ Extension Cords
- ☐ 15 Amp Fuses

OTHER
- ☐ Pocket Knife
- ☐ Gaffer's Tape
- ☐ Black Tape (Electrician's)
- ☐ Face Powder
- ☐ Props
- ☐ Set Dressing
- ☐ Clothing and Costumes
- ☐ _____
- ☐ _____
- ☐ _____

NOTES:

Production Title _____

Production Date and Time _____

Crew Assignments

The size of the crew and the responsibilities of the crew members vary with the type of production. An ENG crew, for example, may very well consist of two people: the camera operator and the on-camera talent. The camera operator, or shooter, has responsibility for operating the camcorder and thus principal responsibility for recording acceptable picture and sound. The on-camera talent, usually the segment or story producer, has responsibility for conveying the details of the story outline to the shooter, suggesting needed visuals, conducting required interviews, providing the on-camera stand-up introduction (or *intro*) and summary (or *extro*), and writing and delivering any additional voice-over narration. A more elaborate ENG crew might include an additional crew person who takes responsibility for sound recording.

In simple EFP shoots, characterized by those in which magazine segments are built out of on-location interview material, a three-person crew is often used. The producer has responsibility for story design and execution. The camera operator has responsibility for shooting the segments and for making sure that enough material is recorded to facilitate editing of the piece. The shooter, therefore, must make decisions about camera position, lens angle, zoom activity, and retakes of significant material. Although the field producer has the ultimate responsibility for planning the segment, the shooter has significant autonomy in shooting the visual material. A good shooter must be flexible, alert, and have a good eye for the visual potential of the scene and must also keep in mind the requirements of the editor and the editing process. This is necessary to obtain material that will make the piece visually interesting and coherent.

The production assistant (PA) in an EFP shoot serves a number of important functions. The PA takes responsibility for setting up any needed lighting instruments and microphones, functions as sound recordist (particularly if a fishpole-type microphone is used), and labels tapes as they are shot. The PA is often called on to set up and strike equipment and to make sure that an adequate supply of charged batteries is available. In addition, he or she is often responsible for driving the crew to and from the location. If the producer has primary responsibility for story design and the shooter primary responsibility for visualization, the PA has the responsibility for making sure that the shoot goes smoothly in a technical sense.

Many, if not most, EFP crews that shoot magazine-type material also use on-camera talent. Most often this is *not* the segment producer, and in this regard, magazine EFP differs significantly from ENG shooting. The questions the on-camera talent asks are developed through consultation with the producer, who has significant responsibility for directing the questions and producing the actual content of the piece.

These two types of production situations are fairly simple ones. In some production situations, the field production crew can be extremely large. For example, in the production of a dramatic script (whether it is artistic, theatrical, or instructional in orientation), the crew will most likely consist of a producer, director, camera operator, lighting director and assistants, audio director and assistants, talent, make-up crew, set designers and/or properties coordinators, and maybe even a stuntperson or two. In these full-scale productions, the director becomes the field production person with primary responsibility for coordinating all elements of the production. The director is responsible for visualizing the script and blocking (staging) the action and for communicating these decisions to the appropriate cast and crew members.

Regardless of whether the production has a designated director or whether the producer or camera operator acts as the director, the director's role in the field is an important one. The director must delegate responsibility for performing production tasks to the various crew members, must have a clear idea of how the individual shots in the production will look, and must communicate that idea to the camera operator. The director must also analyze the shooting situation in order to direct the sequence in which shots or segments are recorded.

With respect to the last point, the goal is to make certain that the most important things are shot first. The ENG crew covering a disaster in progress has to make quick decisions in the field with respect to what to shoot and in which order to shoot it. The magazine EFP producer has to decide on the order in which interviews and supplementary visual material will be recorded and how much time to allocate to shooting each element. The director of the dramatic script needs to break down the script into its component parts and decide how best to make use of the actors, actresses, and various locations.

Labeling Tapes
in the Field

Just as thorough preproduction planning creates a record or plan of what is supposed to happen during production, tape labeling and logging create a record of what happens during production. The importance of identifying individual tapes and their content is critical, particularly when you consider that a 30-minute program shot in 1/2" S-VHS-C format with a 10:1 **shooting ratio** (in which 10 times as much tape is shot as is finally used in the program) produces at least 15 mini-cassettes of material (300 minutes of unedited footage = 15 cassettes of 20 minutes each). Some way needs to be found to label and identify material. These suggestions should help you keep track of the content of your field tapes.

Label Field Tapes As They Are Shot.   Each tape should be labeled in the field as it is used. This is usually the duty of the PA. The most common method of labeling is simply to affix an adhesive label to the cassette box with the tape number and a brief description of the content, such as tape 1—parachuting chimps. If an adequate number of tapes are available, you might want to record different interviews or shots from different locations on separate tapes. Each segment can then be clearly identified when it is time to edit the piece. This also eliminates the danger of accidentally recording over and erasing a segment. Also, if a field tape should be lost or destroyed, only one segment of material will be lost rather than a number of segments. As field tapes are recorded and labeled, the record safety device should be removed or engaged to prevent accidental erasure.

Slate the Tapes.   It is common practice to slate the head of each tape for identification purposes. The **slate** simply records onto the tape information about the content of the upcoming material. This is extremely useful, particularly if the tape and its box should become separated.

If the content of the tape will be an interview, it is good practice simply to ask the person who is the subject of the interview to face the camera and state his or her name and occupation (or other relevant data). This will then serve to identify the person on the tape to the production personnel (and the editor, in particular). Another advantage of this type of identification is that it provides you with the correct pronunciation of the subject's name. Because the narration that will be added to a piece may well contain a reference to the name of the subject, correct pronunciation is essential.

Another method of slating involves the use of a formal production slate that is held in front of the camera at the beginning of the tape and at the beginning of each shot. An example of a production slate is shown in Figure 13.14. The slate should contain the essential information about the production. It is common to include the title of the production and names of the director, producer, and camera operator; the date; the shot and take number; and any other relevant notes. This kind of formal slate is typically used only when the production being videotaped is fully scripted. Because individual shots with-

Figure 13.14   Production Slate

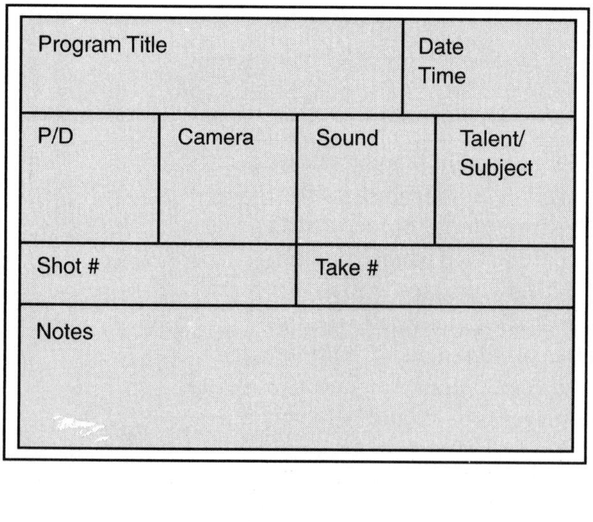

Program Title			Date Time
P/D	Camera	Sound	Talent/ Subject
Shot #		Take #	
Notes			

in the script need to be staged and recorded, the slate serves as a simple and consistent way to identify the shots on tape. If multiple takes of a particular shot are recorded, the good take can be identified from the bad takes by referring to the take number.

Postproduction Planning

Logging the Tapes

A **tape log** or field footage log is a list and description of every shot on the tape. When a program is fully scripted, tapes are usually logged in the field as they are recorded. This provides an instant record of what was shot and which takes were good and bad. At the end of the day, the director can compare the log with the script and check to see that all the necessary material was recorded.

In many types of field production, including most ENG and interview-based EFP productions, the tape log is not done in the field. Rather, tape logging is done in postproduction by the videotape editor. The editor must look at all the videotape anyway, and the process of tape logging therefore serves two functions: First, it allows the editor to see all the material shot in the field and to create a log. Second, it allows the editor to make initial judgments about the material in terms of what is good and bad, or what works and doesn't work. The process of logging, then, is often the initial step taken by the video editor in determining the basic structure and content of the edited program (see Figure 13.15).

Logging is more easily and accurately completed for videotapes that are encoded with SMPTE time code. However, tape logs can also be prepared for programs without time code. Make sure the counter on the VCR is set to zero and the tape is rewound to the beginning. Then simply note the reel number of the tape and the counter numbers for each shot or sequence on the tape. A more accurate log can be prepared by using a stopwatch to time the length of each segment.

If time permits, it is a good idea to type the videotape logs. This is particularly important if the tapes contain lengthy interviews and if decisions are to be made jointly by the production crew about what to include in or exclude from the program. Typed transcripts of interviews and tape logs make all the basic program information available to all members of the production crew.

An increasing number of personal computer software programs for tape logging are also available. Individual shots are logged by shot and take numbers, time code (in and out), shot angle (CU, LS, MC, etc.), and a brief narrative description. (See Figure 13.16.) Many of these software programs allow the video producer to take advantage of the database management capabilities of the computer. In some systems, the user can ask the computer to identify all the shots in the list that were taken from a similar angle (all CUs, for example) or all shots in which a particular word or character's name appears in the description (all shots of Jane, all shots of the giant pumpkin, etc.). Separate lists of these shots can be compiled and saved. If the editor needs a close-up, a shot of Jane, or a shot of the giant pumpkin, the available choices can be easily reviewed from the newly composed lists.

Figure 13.15   Tape Log (Field Footage Log)

Boy Meets Girl
Raw Footage Log

From	To	Shot	Description	Quality	Use?
Shoot # one — dream sequence					
0:00:00	0:00:31	LS & Pan	Alex walks up the street toward cafe. Walks inside.	Fair	
0:00:34	0:00:58	LS & Pan	Alex walking to cafe door. Stops briefly to look over at sign. Does not enter cafe.	Fair	
0:01:06	0:01:30	LS & Pan	Alex walking into cafe.	Fair	
0:01:33	0:01:43	MS	Writing on cafe window: "Kaffe Kreuzberg"	Good	
0:02:01	0:02:26	LS & Pan	Alex walking into cafe.	Good	
0:02:52	0:03:19	LS & Pan	From inside cafe. Alex walks through door and takes a seat.	Fair	
0:03:19	0:03:43	LS & Pan	Same as above.	Good	
0:03:54	0:04:18	LS & Pan	Same as above. Shot on auto iris—no detail in face.	Poor	
0:04:31	0:04:42	LS	Carol walks into cafe looking at camera and walks past camera.	Fair	
0:05:02	0:05:13	LS	Same as above, but Carol walks slower.	Good	
0:05:16	0:05:23	MCU	Carol standing inside cafe door. She then walks toward camera looking at camera.	Good	
0:05:24	0:05:38	MCU	Same as above, except Carol smiles.	Good	
0:05:39	0:06:02	LS	Lori standing inside cafe door. She's looking away then looks directly at camera. (Then discussion to clarify her movements for next shot.)	Good	
0:06:10	0:06:17	LS	Lori walks into cafe, looks at the camera with disdain, then walks toward it and past it.	Good	
0:06:20	0:06:28	CU	Lori looks at camera dryly then walks out of the frame.	Fair	
0:06:37	0:06:39	CU	Lori looks at camera, rolls her eyes, then walks out of the frame.	Good	
0:06:42	0:06:52	LS	Jerry walks into cafe, looks at camera, stops, smiles, then walks out of the frame.	Fair	
0:06:56	0:07:05	LS	Same as above.	Fair	
0:07:06	0:07:14	LS	Same as above.	Fair	
0:07:15	0:07:26	CU	Jerry looking straight at the camera. He smiles and winks.	Fair	

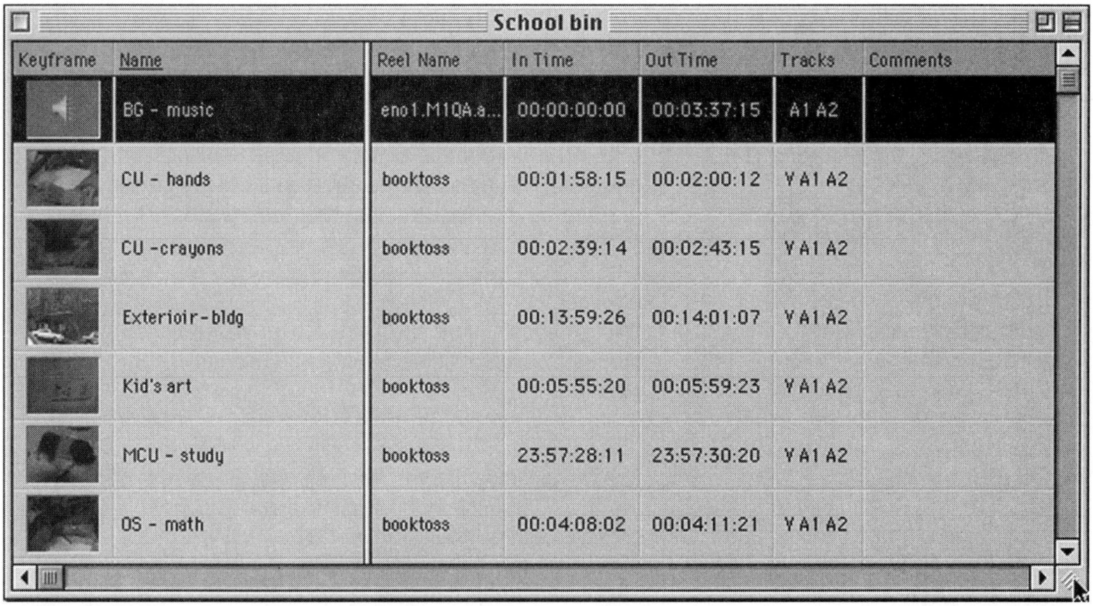

Keyframe	Name	Reel Name	In Time	Out Time	Tracks	Comments
	BG – music	eno1.M1QA.a...	00:00:00:00	00:03:37:15	A1 A2	
	CU – hands	booktoss	00:01:58:15	00:02:00:12	V A1 A2	
	CU –crayons	booktoss	00:02:39:14	00:02:43:15	V A1 A2	
	Exterioir–bldg	booktoss	00:13:59:26	00:14:01:07	V A1 A2	
	Kid's art	booktoss	00:05:55:20	00:05:59:23	V A1 A2	
	MCU – study	booktoss	23:57:28:11	23:57:30:20	V A1 A2	
	OS – math	booktoss	00:04:08:02	00:04:11:21	V A1 A2	

Figure 13.16 Computerized Shot Log

The Rough Cut

Once all the tape has been logged, the editing process can begin. The first step in the process is to develop a preliminary editing script. An **editing script** is a written plan for editing a production and consists of a list of all of the shots to be used, a brief description of each one, and a notation of the in and out points (the beginning and end) of each shot.

Particularly in programs built around interviews, the first edit is usually cut to match the audio segment of the interviews, because that conveys the meaning of the piece. If montages are used to introduce the piece or bridge segments, they should be identified in the script as well. The preliminary editing script, then, provides a rough guide to what the final program will look like. The edit of the program that is made from the preliminary editing script is called the **rough cut.** It provides a rough template of the final program. If your production was fully scripted to begin with, you may be able to write the editing information (shot number, in and out points) directly onto your script. (See Figure 13.17.) If your program was unscripted or semi-scripted, you may find that a standardized edit worksheet is a handy way to keep track of your editing information (see Figure 13.18).

Figure 13.17 Preliminary Editing Script with Time Code Edit Points

(01:04:06:00) Fade up, busy wide shot of deconstructing the Intel set at ITN (01:07:49:00) Callarman carrying away glass block	(natural sound full at first and fading under first VO) **It is mid-July in Studio 3 at ITN, an independent San Francisco production facility. A small crew of technicians and production assistants begin to clear the studio in preparation for constructing the *PetLine* set.**
(01:08:31:00) James carrying flat away (01:16:58:00) KW/CC hoisting up bookshelf	(Weimer VO, 03:25:43:00) "We're switching from an Intel set to a *PetLine* set, so we brought down all the flats for Intel and brought in all the flats for *PetLine*. . . .
(03:27:00:00) Chris Weimer OC *Lower 3rd: "Kris Weimer, Camera & Lighting"*	"We had a lot of background lights that were for the Intel shoot that we don't need for the *PetLine* shoot, so we're taking them down. . . . Doing glass block lights for the *PetLine* set—just changing all the lighting around."
(01:09:22:00) KW removing light (02:16:28:00) CC installing spud	**Two crews are prominent in the *PetLine* studio during this preproduction phase—the camera and lighting crew and the set construction crew.**
(02:13:05:00) Aaron & assistant drilling (02:20:00:00) CU Aaron drilling, pull to reveal Aaron & CC	**Alternately working together or in their individual areas, these specialists are pushing toward a seemingly unrealistic deadline—to establish the broadcast-ready look of *PetLine* . . .** **in a single day.**

When making a rough cut of an interview-based program, don't worry about bad edits or jump cuts from one audio segment to another. Edit to achieve sense in what is said. The rough cut can then be viewed to see whether it conveys the essential meaning that is desired and whether it adheres to your time limitations. The position of various sequences can then be considered. You may want to cut out some and add others or lengthen some and shorten others.

You will also want to make a preliminary judgment about the pace of the program or program segment. Does it flow? Does it drag along? If it seems slow, then you will need to find ways to pick up the pace. Perhaps sequences can be shortened or bridges built between sequences. Perhaps music can be added under certain segments, or long interview segments

Figure 13.18   Edit Worksheet

Edit List
Show Title: Love Makes a Family

Edit #	Tape #	Time In	Time Out	Video/ Audio	Description
1.	5	05:29:30:10	05:32:27:05	Audio	MUSIC
2.	CG #1	1 sec fade up; hold 4 sec; 1 sec dissolve to next shot.			
3.	1	01:17:30:13	01:17:43:15	V&A	audio lead in: dissolve from CG at 01:17:31:21
4.	1	01:23:55:10	01:24:00:00	V&A	2-shot white women
5.	3	03:26:18:20	03:26:27:21	V&A	MCU black woman
6.	3	03:29:28:02	03:29:38:15	V&A	MS Asian man
7.	3	03:20:03:21	03:20:15:29	V&A	CU single mom
8.	4	04:30:50:16	04:31:04:19	V&A	MCU Cara

FADE TO BLACK
MUSIC UP

Edit #	Tape #	Time In	Time Out	Video/ Audio	Description
9.	CG "Love Makes a Family" FADE UP OVER BLACK, then FADE TO BLACK				
10.	2	02:14:09:26	02:14:15:03	Audio	Marisa's VO
11.	10	10:38:41:03	10:38:46:05	Video	photo, FADE UP over previous audio cut FROM BLACK then FADE TO BLACK
12.	CG "Co-Parenting" FADE UP FROM BLACK, then FADE TO BLACK, FADE MUSIC OUT				
13.	2	02:17:37:00	02:18:29:21	V&A (split)	audio under CG video in at 02:17:39:13

can be replaced with tighter voice-over narration by the announcer. Through decisions such as these, the rough cut will be modified and the final editing script produced.

The Final Edit

The final editing script will incorporate the changes suggested after watching the rough cut and modifying the preliminary editing script. The final edited version of the program should fulfill the goals set out in the initial program treatment. The essential meaning of the piece should be efficiently and effectively conveyed through the medium of video. Particular attention should be paid to visualization and sound. Finally, the program should conform to the limits placed on its length. If you plan to distribute your program through traditional broadcast channels, it should conform to broadcast standards for length. A 32-minute documentary will not be aired uncut, even if it reveals the ultimate truth about the meaning of existence. At the very least, it will need to be trimmed to 28:30, and if commercials are to be inserted, it will have to be cut even further.

Client Consultation

If your production was produced for a client, you may need client approval of the final cut. In such situations, the client will probably have been involved throughout the production process, and most certainly should see the rough cut so that you can receive some feedback at that time.

Copyright

Copyright has been discussed earlier with respect to obtaining permission to use material that has been copyrighted by someone else. However, as a producer of a complete program, you may decide that you want to protect your rights to the program you have produced. This is particularly important if you believe that your program has commercial potential or if you want to control its distribution and display.

A video program automatically gains copyright protection as soon as it is created and "fixed" in a copy; that is, when it exists in recorded form. However, to protect against copyright infringement of your work, the U.S. Copyright Office recommends that the copyrighted work display a copyright notice including the word *Copyright* or its symbol (©) or abbreviation (Copr.) as well as the name of the author of the work and the date of its first publication; for example, © R. Compesi, 2000.

The U.S. Copyright Office registers claims to copyright and issues certificates of registration. To obtain a copy of the form used for programs produced on videotape—Form PA (for works of the performing arts; see Appendix 5)—contact the Register of Copyrights, Library of Congress, Washington, D.C. 20559. You can also obtain a copy of the form on-line at: http://lcweb.loc.gov/copyright. Then send the completed form, the filing fee, and a copy of your videotape to the Register of Copyrights at the address provided above.

Generally, if you produced your program independently, you will be considered the author and owner of the program. If you produced it for your employer, then the program is a work made for hire and your employer will own the copyright. If the program is a specially commissioned work, it will be owned by your client if you sign a "work made for-hire" agreement. If you are a student at a college or university, you should check your institution's policy with regard to copyright. Many schools stipulate that they be named the copyright owner for any programs produced using their facilities.

The length of time that the copyright remains in effect depends on the status of the owner. If you are the program's author, the copyright term is for the length of your life and 70 years after your death. If your program is a work made for hire, the copyright will protect it for 95 years after its first publication.

Distribution

No discussion of production planning is complete without at least some mention of the area of distribution. For the home video producer or the student working on a class project, the issue of distribution is relatively simple: you assemble a captive audience (friends, family, classmates, or instructor), put the videotape into a playback VCR, and then observe their response. Similarly, the employee of a broadcast or cable station is usually not overly concerned about distribution—the program or segment is completed and then aired as part of an individual program or series.

For the independent producer, however, the area of distribution is critical. We all make video programs to be seen, and in many cases we hope that they will be seen by rather large audiences. The problem of distribution, then, is one of maximizing the exposure of the program to its target audience.

In recent years, the opportunities for distribution of visual materials have opened up somewhat. Whereas only a few years ago the options were limited, the proliferation of VCRs in education and industry, the expansion of the cable television industry, and access to public broadcasting and public-access cable television have given independent producers a number of realistic alternatives for distribution. In addition, the large number of video festivals and competitions throughout the country also provide a significant number of outlets for visual materials.

The type of distribution you desire depends quite clearly on the program's content and target audience. Producers of educational materials might find a receptive market among public broadcasters or any one of the educational program distribution services. Documentary producers have traditionally had a rough time earning back the cost of their investment but nonetheless have a number of distribution options. Video festivals, public broadcasting, subscription cable systems, and individual sales to libraries and other organizations all provide potential outlets and sources of revenue. A program on cancer, for example, might be attractive not only to a number of broadcast or cable outlets but also to local (or national) cancer societies or other health agencies. Individual hospitals might be interested in the program if it could be used for counseling or providing basic information to patients.

Clearly, you need to accurately assess the market potential of your program in its initial stages of development. If a widespread sales campaign is contemplated, then promotional material and a list of potential buyers should be developed. An independent producer can rent out or sell tapes and can distribute them independently (through self-distribution) or through an established distribution service.

Ethics and Video Production

Although this text has concentrated primarily on the technical and aesthetic elements of video production, no discussion of video production is complete without a consideration of the topic of ethics, particularly as they apply to media producers.

Codes of Ethics

One of the marks of a profession is the presence of a code of ethics for members of the group. Physicians and attorneys are bound by codes of conduct that identify standards of behavior that they are expected to embrace. In the field of electronic media, the Radio and Television News Directors Association and the Society of Professional Journalists have published codes of conduct. Although the focus of these codes is on encouraging good journalistic practice, some of their principal tenets are useful for the nonjournalist to consider as well. Among the values held in common by the two codes are honesty and fairness, respect for subjects and colleagues, avoidance of conflicts of interest, and accountability to audiences and to fellow members of the profession.

A comprehensive code of ethics for Canandian electronic media professionals has been developed by the Canadian Association of Broadcasters. The CAB code of ethics urges its members to provide programming that addresses the range of tastes in the audience; to respect human rights and avoid discriminatory program material; to reflect the moral and ethical standards of Canadian society in developing prosocial programming for children; to develop educational program material; to treat controversial public issues fairly; to ensure that advertising is in good taste, truthful, and believable; to avoid the use of subliminal devices in program material; and to avoid programming that relies on stereotypical sex-role images. The code also encourages member broadcast stations to seek out the highest-quality employees possible and to make service in the broadcasting industry an attractive and permanent career.

How far removed from the current reality of broadcasting and electronic media in the United States this seems! Ironically, the principal trade organization for broadcasting and cable in the United States, the National Association of Broadcasters, has not had a published code of ethics since 1978, when it abandoned its code in the face of a U.S. Justice Department challenge to several of the code's provisions.

Public-Interest Obligations of Digital Television Broadcasters

As this book goes to press, in part as a result of public pressure to encourage responsible performance among those broadcasters who have received free allocations of spectrum space for digital broadcasting, the President's Advisory Committee on Public-Interest Obligations of Digital Television Broadcasters has recommended a set of public-interest standards that all digital television stations should be required to meet. Among the committee's recommendations are requirements for digital broadcasters to ascertain community needs and to broadcast programming to meet those needs; to air public-service announcements throughout the broadcast day; and to provide public-affairs programs with an emphasis on local issues. In addition, the committee recommends reinstitution of the NAB code.

Implicit in these proposed recommendations is the understanding that with access to electronic media comes a responsibility to consider the needs of the audience, as well as the needs of shareholders who own for-profit media entities. And this concern with the audience brings the present discussion full circle to where it began in the first chapter—not only with an understanding of the technical and aesthetic dimensions of television and video, but also with an awareness that the programs that you produce will be seen by audiences and may well have a significant impact on them.

Your Role as a Producer

As a media producer you will have many choices to make—about the kinds of programs you will produce, about the way you will treat individuals who appear in your programs, about the way you will interact with the people with whom you work, and about the way you will think about your audience. An ethical producer should consider each of these factors and act accordingly, keeping in mind the principles of honesty, fairness, and respect, among others.

As you move forward in your career in the electronic media with the new skills you have gained in part by reading this book, consider the following statement about television, made by former CBS newscaster Edward R. Murrow more than 50 years ago: "This instrument can teach, it can illuminate, yes, and it can even inspire. But it can only do so to the extent that humans are determined to use it to those ends. Otherwise it is merely lights and wires in a box."

NOTES

1. Crawley, Budge; Markle, Fletcher; and Pratley, Gerald, "I Wish I Didn't Have to Shoot the Picture: An Interview with Alfred Hitchcock," in LaValley, Albert H. (ed.), *Focus on Hitchcock*, Englewood Cliffs, NJ: Prentice Hall, 1972, pp. 22–27.
2. Murrow, Edward R. Speech at the Radio and Television News Directors (RTNDA) Annual Conference, 1958. Quoted in Willard D. Rowland, Jr. and Michael Tracey, "Global Politics of Public Service Broadcasting in the Early 1990s," paper presented to the International Communication Association, Miami, FL, May 23, 1992.

Production Projects

This appendix includes eight production projects designed to sharpen your production skills. The projects are arranged by type and complexity and focus on a range of production styles. Purposeful writing, careful attention to light, camera, and microphone problems, and crisp editing are important to each project; the tasks become more complex as you work down the list. The first three projects can be relatively simple sound-and-picture statements; the second group, "News" and "Instructional," can require more attention to crafting a message to be used by an intended audience in a specific way; the final group, "Magazine Feature," "Historic Minute," and "Music Video," demand the most sophisticated control of the tools of production.

As you work on each of these projects, you should follow the guidelines for production planning and development that were discussed in Chapter 13 and collect the following material:

1. Production log. Keep a log of all time spent on the project. Make daily entries to update the log while your project is in progress. Include all your planning material in your log. Also keep track of important phone numbers, names of contacts, meeting dates and times, and so on.

2. Script and storyboard

3. Remote survey form

4. Tape logs

5. Editing scripts

6. Release forms

Use a notebook or looseleaf binder to organize all the planning materials for your project.

PROJECT 1
Personal Statement

Video has often been characterized as a personal medium. Your first project is to write and record a 60-second personal video statement. Write a script and draw a storyboard for your statement so that someone else can act as camera operator and you can deliver the on-camera statement. Consider the following guidelines as you develop your project.

Subject. Make a statement about something that is important to you. This can be something that has affected you personally or an issue about which you have strong personal feelings. For example, one extremely effective personal video statement was made by a young man with severe speech anxiety. Whenever he was asked to give a speech or make a presentation, he became so nervous that he could barely talk. In his personal video statement, he described his speech anxiety and how nervous he was making the presentation! As the camera slowly zoomed in to a close-up, his nervousness became apparent. However, after viewing the tape himself, he felt much more confident about his oral presentation style. Although he had been nervous, his presentation was nevertheless quite effective.

Structure. Deliver your statement without interruption. Your personal statement should be recorded in a single 60-second session. Do not plan to edit your statement. Try to use the camera effectively with respect to composition, zooming, panning, and so on.

Audience. Identify the projected audience for this statement. The message can be aimed at friends, family, or a general audience.

Length. 60 seconds.

Editing. None.

PROJECT 2
Video Postcard

All too often, the medium of television is reduced to "radio with pictures." This project is calculated to reverse that trend in that emphasis is on capturing the essence of a place in one continuing picture. Music, sound effects, dialogue, or narration should augment the video, not dominate it. In addition, video editing is limited to the provision of a clean opening from and closing to black.

By effective placement and movement of the camera, control of focus, and field of view, you will convey the frantic pace of traffic on a city street, the authority of a public building, the serenity of a pond at sunrise, the chill of winter on the plains, or whatever gives your part of the world its character. You will establish a mood in which many messages or stories could be set.

Subject.   Design a video statement that describes the central character of a place in or near your community.

Structure.   Design your statement as a single continuing shot.

Audience.   Identify a specific target audience appropriate to the mood and style of your visual statement.

Length.   20 to 30 seconds.

Editing.   None, except to provide black at the opening and closing of the statement.

PROJECT 3
Public-Service Announcement

Public-service announcements (PSAs) are a standard feature of commercial broadcast schedules. A PSA is

> any announcement (including network) for which no charge is made and which promotes programs, activities, or services of federal, state, or local governments (e.g., recruiting, sales of bonds, etc.) and other announcements regarded as serving community interests, excluding time signals, routine weather announcements, and promotional announcements.[1]

Although many PSAs are noncontroversial, some organizations use the PSA format to develop short spot messages on controversial issues of public importance.

Subject.   Design a PSA on a topic of your choice. You can produce a PSA for a local organization or you can design one that is issue oriented.

Structure.   Design your PSA with editing in mind. You may want to include shots of a spokesperson for an organization, people involved with a particular group, or other visuals that identify the organization or issue to which your message is directed. Remember that most PSAs attempt to mobilize people to action—they provide an address or phone number that viewers can contact for more information. Therefore, you should include a graphic that provides an address or phone number that viewers can contact to get more information about the organization or issue featured in your PSA.

Audience.   Adults in your community.

Length.   30 or 60 seconds.

Editing.   Continuity and dynamic.

PROJECT 4
News

The on-the-scene field news report is a staple of television news. Design and produce a self-contained news report—one that is complete in itself.

Subject.   News report of a local event, issue, or person.

Structure.   The report should contain an introduction and close delivered by the reporter. These may be given on-camera or off-camera as a voice-over. Consider including the following elements in the news story:

1. On-camera stand-up delivered by the news reporter
2. Sound-on-tape interview with the subject of the story, an expert on the topic, a witness to the event, and so on
3. Visuals of the event, issue, or person
4. Voice-over narration over the visuals. Try to achieve a good mix between the level of the voice-over and the natural sound that accompanies the visuals.

Audience.   Most news programs are targeted at adult audiences. You can produce your news spot for an adult audience, or you might want to try to produce one aimed at children or adolescents. In any event, specify the characteristics of your target audience.

Length.   Approximately two minutes.

Editing.   Continuity.

PROJECT 5
Instructional

An instructional program is designed to teach someone something. Is there something that you know about or know how to do that would make an interesting subject for an instructional segment? Perhaps you are an excellent cook or a good mechanic. Consider teaching someone how to make a pizza or how to change the oil in an automobile. A demonstration of a mechanical device is often a good subject for an instructional segment because it has great visual potential.

Subject.   An instructional program segment that will teach the audience something new.

Structure.   You may want to appear on camera as the expert or the teacher, or you may want to present the bulk of the spoken part of the program with an off-camera voice-over. If you choose the latter option, remember to record and maintain the natural sound on the visuals.

Audience.   Identify a specific target audience for your tape. This is very important because you must structure your instructional program to appeal to your audience.

Length.   Two minutes.

Editing.   Continuity.

PROJECT 6
Magazine Feature

The television magazine feature has gained immense popularity in recent years. Magazine features differ somewhat from traditional news field reports. Their subject matter is usually considered softer than that of news pieces—that is, they tend to be a mix of information and entertainment. Magazine features are also usually longer than typical news stories and often attempt to enhance the presentation of information with interesting editing and music. Their purpose is to tell a story in an interesting manner.

Subject.   Focus your magazine feature on an interesting person in your community or on someone who has an interesting job or hobby. If you decide to profile an interesting place or event, try to identify a spokesperson whom you can interview.

Structure.   Magazine features usually include segments of interviews with the subject of the piece, off-camera voice-overs from the segment reporter or host, generous amounts of music (for mood, pace, and transitions), and innovative editing. Try to build at least one transition segment into your magazine piece that is an edited montage of music and pictures.

Audience.   General adult.

Length.   Five minutes.

Editing.   Continuity and dynamic.

PROJECT 7
Historic Minute

Using appropriate graphic materials and sound support, describe a person or an event of special significance to your community. Focus on the contribution your subject made to the progress of our society or on the progress of which it is a measure.

Subject.   Person or event of historic importance.

Structure.   Strong narrative supported by an edited montage of photos, graphic materials, videotaped action scenes, sound effects, and music, as appropriate.

Audience.   General adult.

Length.   One minute.

Editing.   Continuity and dynamic.

PROJECT 8
Music Video

Music video segments representing a range of musical styles and target audiences are visible at almost any time of day on most cable television systems in the United States. MTV (Music Television), VH-1 (Video Hits 1), the Disney Channel, and the Nashville Network (TNN) are four cable television channels that regularly feature music video segments. Many music videos are produced as promotional pieces for new musical artists or new songs recorded by established performers. Some music videos—particularly those targeted at children and featured on the Disney Channel or as segments within the PBS television series *Sesame Street*—are designed to teach something to their audiences as well as to entertain them.

Subject.   Identify a local band or performer (singer or musician) to serve as the performing talent for your music video.

Structure.   All music videos combine a soundtrack of the musical performance with appropriate visual images. Some music videos focus exclusively on the musical artist(s) in performance of their work, other music videos dramatize the narrative found in the lyrics of the song, and still others combine elements of the musical performance with images dramatizing the song. Determine which approach best suits the performer and performance you have chosen to present.

Audience.   Identify the specific target audience for your tape. This may be determined by the type of music represented in the selected performance.

Length. Approximately three minutes. Music video production can be fairly complex. You will do best to limit the length of your music video segment.

Editing. Continuity and dynamic.

NOTE

1. *Code of Federal Regulations 73.18101*, Washington, D.C.: U.S. Government Printing Office, 1983, pp. 355–56.

Development of Videotape Recording

The Magnetic Recording Process

The development of a practical means of electronically recording the video signal was a goal of many small and large companies in the 1940s and 1950s. The principles applied in audiotape recorders acted as a model for these potential inventors. Successful audiotape recording systems had been developed in which the audio signal was fed to an audio head and then transferred to a piece of magnetic tape. The **head** was a small electromagnet, and the strength of the magnetic field produced by the head varied in proportion to the variations in the current—the audio signal—fed into it. The signal could be stored on magnetic tape because the variations in the magnetic field produced by the head were recorded by the particles embedded in the tape.

Engineers found that the quality of a recording could be improved by varying two factors: the gap in the head and the speed of the tape. The gap in the head is a microscopic space between the two sides of the electromagnet. The smaller this gap, the higher the frequency of signal it is capable of recording. Similarly, as the speed of the tape increases, so does its frequency response. For example, audiotape moving at 15 **inches per second** can record a greater range of frequencies than can tape moving at $7^1/_2''$ per second. This occurs because when the tape moves past the heads at a faster speed, more magnetic particles on the tape are available to store the signal, because more of them come in contact with the heads at the higher speed. A tape moving at 15″ per second can store more information than can tape moving at $7^1/_2''$ per second. As a result, the 15″-per-second recording sounds and looks better than the recording made at a slower speed. This is one reason why the quality of recordings produced on professional audio-tape recorders operating at 15″ per second is significantly better than what you are able to achieve on your home audiocassette deck, which operates at $1\frac{7}{8}$″ per second.

Early Attempts at Videotape Recording

Recording the video signal presented a major problem to video engineers because it is so much more complex than the audio signal. The video signal contains not only the picture and sound information but all the signal synchronizing information as well. In addition, the range of frequencies necessary to create the video image is considerably wider than the range of frequencies found in audio. In audio recording, the frequency range of the recorded signal falls between 15 Htz (or cycles per second) and 20,000 Hz, for a range of about 20,000 cycles per second. But the range of frequencies in the NTSC video signal varies from about 30 Hz to 4.5 million Hz—a range of nearly 4.5 million cycles per second.

Nevertheless, video engineers reasoned that they could successfully record the video image if they could figure out a way to manipulate the same variables (head gap and tape speed) that had been successfully manipulated to achieve audio recording. In one of the early recording attempts, Bing Crosby Productions actually modified an audiotape recorder so that it would accept a video signal. Rather than use only 1 head, they arranged 11 recording heads across a tape. Even with these 11 heads, the Bing Crosby team was not able to achieve an acceptable recording until it increased the tape speed. The system they finally developed used 11 stationary video heads and a tape that moved at 100″ per second.[1] RCA also attempted to develop a recording system at this time; like the Bing Crosby team, RCA's efforts centered on moving the tape extremely fast across a stationary head assembly. In the RCA system, only one video head was used, but to make a satisfactory recording, the tape had to move at 360″ per second.

The BBC (British Broadcasting Corporation) was also involved in early VTR development experiments and in 1955 began broadcasting with a system called VERA (vision electronic recording apparatus).[2] However, it suffered from the same problem as the U.S. systems. With a recording speed of 200″ per second, a 30-minute program required approximately 30,000 feet of videotape on a reel five feet in diameter. Thus, while these systems were capable of recording and playing back the video signal on videotape, they simply were not practical because they required huge amounts of tape.

Solution to the Problem:
Moving Heads

At about the same time that these experiments were being conducted, Ampex Corporation, a small electronics company in Redwood City, California, hit on the idea that tape-to-head speed could be maximized not only by moving the tape past the heads but also by moving the heads themselves. Ampex developed a recorder that utilized four rotating heads mounted in a drum that spun as the tape moved across it at 15″ per second. Using this system, it was possible to record 60 minutes of material on a reel of tape 2,400 feet in length and about one foot in diameter.

The system invented by Ampex became the broadcast industry standard. The tape was 2″ wide, and the process of using four heads to record the signal was called **quadruplex** recording. Until the development of 1″ VTRs in the late 1970s, the term *2″ quad* was synonymous with the broadcast standard of recording.

NOTES

1. Robinson, Richard, *The Video Primer,* rev. ed., New York: Quick Fox, 1978, p. 248.
2. Kybett, Harry, *Video Tape Recorders,* 2nd ed., Indianapolis: Howard W. Sams & Co., 1978, p. 10.

411

APPENDIX THREE

Measurement of Light Intensity

The science of photometry, the measurement of the intensity of light, preceded the use of the electric light. An open flame was used in the early experiments; thus, light intensity is universally expressed in units of candlepower. Simply stated, a **foot-candle** represents the amount of light radiated from an **international candle** that reaches a point one foot from the theoretical center of the flame. The term *foot-candle* is used to describe the minimum light level required for camera operations as well as the power or intensity of light produced by lighting instruments.

Foot-candles can be expressed in terms of **lumens** per square foot. The amount of light generated by the candle flame is expressed in lumens (which means "light" in Latin). It is the accumulation of light radiated in *all* directions from the flame. A *sphere* with a radius of one foot represents all the points of light created by a flame in the center of that sphere. There are 12.57 square feet on the surface of a sphere with a radius of one foot (sphere surface = $4\pi r^2$), and each square foot receives the same amount of light from the flame. Hence, at a distance of one foot, the candle produces a total of 12.57 lumens—one for each square foot of surface area. This terminology is used to rate lamps (*lightbulbs* in common terms). The capacity of reflectors to capture a portion of the light produced by a lamp and focus it back through the center point toward the subject is also expressed in lumens.

Another term, **lux**, is used to indicate the basic illumination requirements of a camera. Simply stated, a lux substitutes *one meter* for the one foot used to calculate foot-candles. One lux equals one lumen per square meter; one foot-candle is one lumen per square foot. There are about 10 lux per foot-candle because of the inverse square law, which describes the amount that the intensity of light decreases as the distance from the light source increases. We can use the formula $4\pi r^2$ to see the increase in a sphere's surface area in relation to an increase in the radius of that sphere:

1′ radius = 12.57 square feet of surface
2′ radius = 50.27 square feet of surface
3′ radius = 113.10 square feet of surface

Therefore, the light reaching the surface of the sphere with a radius of two feet is spread over four times the area of that of a sphere with a radius of one foot. The light intensity at any point is one-fourth that of the sphere with one-half the radius.

A sphere with a three-foot radius contains nine times the surface area of a sphere with a one-foot radius. The light intensity at any point on that larger sphere is one-ninth that of the smaller sphere.

One meter equals about 3′ 3″; therefore, a lux is about one-tenth of a foot-candle.

Video producers rely on the inverse square law when they position lighting instruments relative to a person being videotaped. Because dimmers are seldom available in the field, the producer can move a light short distances toward or away from the subject to produce relatively significant increases or decreases in the intensity of the light falling on the subject. Doubling the distance reduces the intensity on the subject by one-fourth; halving the distance creates four times the light intensity.

Remember, the inverse square law applies only to light with a point source (the center of a candle flame or the filament in an incandescent lamp). There is no point source to calculate from a fluorescent tube close to and larger than an object illuminated by it, because the illumination literally comes from everywhere.

No discussion of the measurement of light intensity would be complete without consideration of the *cosine law of incident light*. This law concerns the intensity of light on a surface when all parts of that surface are *not* equidistant from the light source. The effect of this law is seen in film and video as shading on surfaces that are not perpendicular to the beam of light. This shading contributes to the illusion of a three-dimensional picture on your television screen. Briefly, just as the light produced by the candle in a sphere has to cover a greater area as the radius increases (and, consequently, illuminates any point within that expanded sphere to a lesser extent), the light from a point source is spread over a larger surface as that surface is tilted away from the perpendicular, and becomes less intense in direct

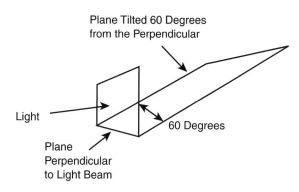

Figure A3.1 Cosine Law of Incident Light

ratio to the angle of tilt. Stated another way, the brightness of the perpendicular plane is multiplied by the cosine of the angle of tilt to determine the brightness of the tilted plane (see Figure A3.1).

At 60 degrees of tilt, the tilted plane is twice the size of the perpendicular plane. Therefore, the light energy radiated from the point source will have to cover twice the area and will appear less intense than it would on the smaller perpendicular plane. The ratio of intensities is found in the cosine of the angle of tilt; hence the term *cosine law of incident light*.[1]

NOTE

1. Sturrock, Walter, and Staley, K. A., *Fundamentals of Lights and Lighting*, General Electric Bulletin LD-2, January 1956, pp. 5–6.

Guidelines and Information for Filming in San Francisco

1. Filming in San Francisco will be arranged through the Film Office, which will make referrals to departments and other jurisdictions (Police Department, Recreation and Park Department, Muni Railway, Golden Gate National Recreation Area (G.G.N.R.A.), Airport, Bridges, Department of Public Works, the Presidio, Coast Guard, Fire Department, etc.) in order to arrange orderly filming in compliance with the law.

2. A certificate of insurance will be filed in the Film Office prior to filming, endorsed to the City and County of San Francisco (see Use Agreement for detailed information).

3. A permit fee to the San Francisco Film Office of $100 to $300 for each day of filming will be expected from each film company, except for nonprofit and student productions.

$100.00	Video, Travel, Documentary, Still Photography, Industrial, Other
$200.00	Commercials
$300.00	Television series and movies/Feature films

4. Uniformed police officers, working voluntary duty on an overtime basis only, will be assigned to motion picture details when the Office of the Chief deems it advisable for public safety and convenience. The number of officers assigned will be determined by the Police Department Coordinating Unit, depending on the extent of filming and other factors. A deposit for police services will be required in advance.

5. San Francisco Police Department vehicles, uniforms, insignia, and equipment will not be made available for use by film companies. Filming on departmental property must have express written approval of the Chief of Police.

6. San Francisco streets must be posted for parking or filming 24 hours prior to call time. See Police Department guidelines or contact Film Office for further information.

7. Residential areas can be used for filming only between the hours of 7 A.M. and 10 P.M. Night shooting between the hours of 10 P.M. and 7 A.M. is restricted without the prior express joint written approval of the Film Office and the Police Department. Commercial areas may be restricted between the hours of 6:30 and 9:30 A.M. and 3:30 and 6:30 P.M., due to rush hour traffic. Otherwise, commercial areas are available for filming. Industrial areas can be used for filming 24 hours a day, with care given not to affect the work activities in the area.

8. Companies are requested to provide the Film Office and the Police Department with copies of shooting scripts and location schedules so that potential traffic and parking problems can be anticipated and avoided.

9. A film company, **no later** than 24 hours before shooting in a residential neighborhood, must notify in writing the residents in the area as to the company, shooting times, and the name, address, and phone numbers of the companies' local office or representative. Prior to filming, the Film Office must be notified that this information has been distributed.

10. Meals shall not be eaten on public rights-of-way.

11. All production vehicles shall be visibly identified (including equipment rental vehicles) with the name of the production company. Such identification is to be placed in the windshield of each vehicle while on location.

12. The production company shall not interfere with the normal activities of a neighborhood. Filming crews and equipment should not interfere with street sweeping or refuse collection. No littering is permitted and must be cleaned up completely when leaving the location. The public must not be deprived egress or ingress to private or public property.

U.S. Copyright Office Short Form PA

FEE CHANGES

Registration filing fees are effective through June 30, 1999. For information on the fee changes, write the Copyright Office, check http://www.loc.gov/copyright, or call (202) 707-3000. Beginning as early as January 1, 2000, the Copyright Office may impose a service charge when insufficient fees are received.

FORM PA

For a Work of the Performing Arts
UNITED STATES COPYRIGHT OFFICE

REGISTRATION NUMBER

PA   PAU

EFFECTIVE DATE OF REGISTRATION

_____ _____ _____
Month   Day   Year

DO NOT WRITE ABOVE THIS LINE. IF YOU NEED MORE SPACE, USE A SEPARATE CONTINUATION SHEET.

1

TITLE OF THIS WORK ▼

PREVIOUS OR ALTERNATIVE TITLES ▼

NATURE OF THIS WORK ▼ See instructions

2   **a**

NAME OF AUTHOR ▼

DATES OF BIRTH AND DEATH
Year Born ▼   Year Died ▼

Was this contribution to the work a "work made for hire"?
☐ Yes
☐ No

AUTHOR'S NATIONALITY OR DOMICILE
Name of Country
OR { Citizen of ▶ _____
Domiciled in▶ _____

WAS THIS AUTHOR'S CONTRIBUTION TO THE WORK
Anonymous? ☐ Yes ☐ No
Pseudonymous? ☐ Yes ☐ No

If the answer to either of these questions is "Yes," see detailed instructions.

NATURE OF AUTHORSHIP Briefly describe nature of material created by this author in which copyright is claimed. ▼

NOTE

Under the law, the "author" of a "work made for hire" is generally the employer, not the employee (see instructions). For any part of this work that was "made for hire" check "Yes" in the space provided, give the employer (or other person for whom the work was prepared) as "Author" of that part, and leave the space for dates of birth and death blank.

b

NAME OF AUTHOR ▼

DATES OF BIRTH AND DEATH
Year Born ▼   Year Died ▼

Was this contribution to the work a "work made for hire"?
☐ Yes
☐ No

AUTHOR'S NATIONALITY OR DOMICILE
Name of Country
OR { Citizen of ▶ _____
Domiciled in▶ _____

WAS THIS AUTHOR'S CONTRIBUTION TO THE WORK
Anonymous? ☐ Yes ☐ No
Pseudonymous? ☐ Yes ☐ No

If the answer to either of these questions is "Yes," see detailed instructions.

NATURE OF AUTHORSHIP Briefly describe nature of material created by this author in which copyright is claimed. ▼

c

NAME OF AUTHOR ▼

DATES OF BIRTH AND DEATH
Year Born ▼   Year Died ▼

Was this contribution to the work a "work made for hire"?
☐ Yes
☐ No

AUTHOR'S NATIONALITY OR DOMICILE
Name of Country
OR { Citizen of ▶ _____
Domiciled in▶ _____

WAS THIS AUTHOR'S CONTRIBUTION TO THE WORK
Anonymous? ☐ Yes ☐ No
Pseudonymous? ☐ Yes ☐ No

If the answer to either of these questions is "Yes," see detailed instructions.

NATURE OF AUTHORSHIP Briefly describe nature of material created by this author in which copyright is claimed. ▼

3   **a**

YEAR IN WHICH CREATION OF THIS WORK WAS COMPLETED This information must be given ◀Year in all cases.

b **DATE AND NATION OF FIRST PUBLICATION OF THIS PARTICULAR WORK**
Complete this information ONLY if this work has been published.
Month▶ _____ Day▶ _____ Year▶ _____
◀ Nation

4

See instructions before completing this space.

COPYRIGHT CLAIMANT(S) Name and address must be given even if the claimant is the same as the author given in space 2. ▼

TRANSFER If the claimant(s) named here in space 4 is (are) different from the author(s) named in space 2, give a brief statement of how the claimant(s) obtained ownership of the copyright. ▼

APPLICATION RECEIVED

ONE DEPOSIT RECEIVED

TWO DEPOSITS RECEIVED

FUNDS RECEIVED

DO NOT WRITE HERE
OFFICE USE ONLY

MORE ON BACK ▶ • Complete all applicable spaces (numbers 5-9) on the reverse side of this page.
• See detailed instructions.   • Sign the form at line 8.

DO NOT WRITE HERE
Page 1 of _____ pages

418

DO NOT WRITE ABOVE THIS LINE. IF YOU NEED MORE SPACE, USE A SEPARATE CONTINUATION SHEET.

PREVIOUS REGISTRATION Has registration for this work, or for an earlier version of this work, already been made in the Copyright Office?

☐ **Yes** ☐ **No** If your answer is "Yes," why is another registration being sought? (Check appropriate box.) ▼

a. ☐ This is the first published edition of a work previously registered in unpublished form.

b. ☐ This is the first application submitted by this author as copyright claimant.

c. ☐ This is a changed version of the work, as shown by space 6 on this application.

If your answer is "Yes," give: **Previous Registration Number** ▼   **Year of Registration** ▼

5

DERIVATIVE WORK OR COMPILATION Complete both space 6a and 6b for a derivative work; complete only 6b for a compilation.

Preexisting Material Identify any preexisting work or works that this work is based on or incorporates. ▼

a

6

See instructions before completing this space.

Material Added to This Work Give a brief, general statement of the material that has been added to this work and in which copyright is claimed. ▼

b

DEPOSIT ACCOUNT If the registration fee is to be charged to a Deposit Account established in the Copyright Office, give name and number of Account.

Name ▼   **Account Number** ▼

7

CORRESPONDENCE Give name and address to which correspondence about this application should be sent.   Name/Address/Apt/City/State/ZIP ▼

Area code and daytime telephone number ▶ (   )   Fax number ▶ (   )

Email ▶

CERTIFICATION* I, the undersigned, hereby certify that I am the (check only one) ▼

☐ author

☐ other copyright claimant

☐ owner of exclusive right(s)

☐ authorized agent of _____

Name of author or other copyright claimant, or owner of exclusive right(s) ▲

of the work identified in this application and that the statements made by me in this application are correct to the best of my knowledge.

8

Typed or printed name and date ▼ If this application gives a date of publication in space 3, do not sign and submit it before that date.

Date ▶

Handwritten signature (X) ▼

x _____

419

Digital Information and the Metric System

With the proliferation of computers in audio and video production, familiarity with some of the basic terminology of digital computing and the metric system is necessary.

Computers process information in binary digital form. The smallest unit of measure is a **bit**, which is an abbreviation for *bi*nary dig*it*. Each bit has two possible values: 0 (off) and 1 (on). A **byte** is 8 bits, or 2^8 and contains 256 discrete values:

$$2^8 = 2 \times 2 \times 2 \times 2 \times 2 \times 2 \times 2 \times 2 = 256$$

The metric number system is used for counting, because it easily deals with very large numbers. The metric system uses the following prefixes:

kilo (k) = 1,000 (thousand)
mega (M) = 1,000,000 (million)
giga (G) = 1,000,000,000 (billion)
tera (T) = 1,000,000,000,000 (trillion)

This system makes it easier to describe large phenomena. For example, the bandwidth of broadcast television is 6 MHz (six megahertz). This is a more economical way to describe 6,000,000 Hz (six million hertz).

Because the metric system is built on a base of 10 and computers count with binary numbers, values in the computer world differ slightly from the pure metric numbers above. As a result,

1 kilobyte = 2^{10} bytes = $2 \times 2 \times 2 \times 2 \times 2 \times 2 \times 2 \times 2 \times 2 \times 2$
= 1,024 bytes (not 1,000)

Consequently,

1 megabyte = 1,024 kilobytes
1 gigabyte = 1,024 megabytes
1 terabyte = 1,024 gigabytes

Glossary

Above-Eye-Level Camera Position: The camera is placed higher than the subject and shoots down at it.

A/B-Roll Editing: Technique of rolling two source VCRs (the A machine and B machine) simultaneously while editing in order to perform special audio or video effects.

AC Adapter: A device used to convert alternating current (AC) to direct current (DC). Most portable video equipment requires the use of an AC adapter to convert regular household current to DC.

Additive Primary Colors: Red, green, and blue are the additive primary colors of light. A color separation system based on these primary colors operates in all color video cameras.

Aesthetic Factors: Production variables and the ways in which they can be manipulated to affect audience response to the video message.

Alternating Current (AC): The type of electrical power supplied to households in the United States and Canada.

Ambient Noise: Unwanted background sound that interferes with the principal audio.

Amplitude: The height of a wave. With respect to sound, amplitude determines the intensity or loudness of the sound.

Analog Signal: A signal that is continuously proportional or analogous to the input.

Aperture: The size of the iris opening of the lens, usually calibrated in f-stops.

Aperture Ring: A device that controls the size of the iris opening (aperture) of the lens.

Arc: Semicircular movement of the camera and its support around a scene.

Aspect Ratio: The relationship of the width of the television screen to its height, expressed as a ratio of 4:3 or 16:9.

Aspect Ratio Converter: Switch on a camera lens that selects the aspect ratio of the image produced as either 4:3 or 16:9.

Assemble Editing: (1) Editing in which new control track and audio and video information are recorded onto the tape in the editing VCR. (2) The process of adding new information to a tape shot by shot, or scene by scene, in sequence.

At-Eye-Level Camera Position: Camera and subject are at the same height; the camera does not look up or down at the subject.

ATSC (Advanced Television System Committee) Standard: Standard for United States digital television set by the ATSC and adopted by the FCC in December 1996.

Audio: The sound portion of a video program.

Audiocassette: An audiotape packaged in a cassette housing.

Audio In: Line-level audio input; place where the audio signal is fed into a piece of equipment.

Audio Mixer: Equipment that combines a number of independent audio inputs into one output signal.

Audio Out: Line-level audio output; place where the audio signal comes out of a piece of equipment.

Audio Track Chart: A log of sound sources arranged along a time line indicating where they occur in a video program.

Automatic Aperture: Electronic device that automatically sets the lens iris for correct exposure in the available light.

Automatic Aperture Lock: Locks in an aperture setting after it has been calculated by the automatic aperture control.

Automatic Backspace Editing: Automatic feature on many camcorders that produces clean transitions from one shot to the next when VCR record trigger is pushed.

Automatic Focus (Auto-Focus): Automatic focusing device on some cameras; operates by emitting a beam of infrared light or ultrasound.

Automatic Gain Control (AGC): Electronic device that automatically adjusts the amplification of an audio or video signal. See also *Manual Gain Control.*

Automatic Track Finding (ATF): Signal that automatically adjusts tracking on some VCRs, eliminating the need for manual tracking controls.

Azimuth Recording: Recording process in which the gap of the video head is angled several degrees off the perpendicular line in the video track. This eliminates the need for guard bands, thus allowing more video information to be recorded onto the tape.

Background Light: Light that falls on the background of a scene, often used to create mood or indicate time of day.

Backlight: Hard, focused light above and behind the subject used to separate the subject from the background by outlining the subject with a thin line of bright light.

Backspacing: Rewinding a videotape several seconds from the edit point in order to allow the machine to reach stable playing speed in time for the edit. Also called *backtiming, prerolling,* or *cuing.*

Backtiming: See *Backspacing.*

Balance: The distribution of the mass created by people or objects in the frame. This mass may be distributed evenly (symmetrical balance) or unevenly (asymmetrical balance).

Balanced Line: Professional-quality audio cable or connector with two signal leads and a shield that protects the signal from outside interference.

Barn Door: Metal flap that can be attached to a spotlight to control the way in which the light is thrown onto a scene.

Base Illumination: Omnidirectional (or nondirectional) baselight that illuminates without creating shadows.

Baselight: The amount, or intensity, of light required to make a scene visible to the camera.

Battery Meter: Camcorder viewfinder display that monitors the amount of power remaining in the battery.

Bayonet Connector: See *BNC Connector.*

Bayonet Mount: Type of lens connector on professional video cameras in which the end of the lens is inserted into the opening in the camera head and turned until it locks into place.

Below-Eye-Level Camera Position: The camera is placed lower than the subject and shoots up at it.

Beta (Betamax): Once-popular $1/_2$″ consumer videocassette format developed by Sony Corporation.

Betacam/Betacam SP: Professional-quality $1/_2$″ videotape recording format developed by Sony Corporation.

Bidirectional: A microphone pickup pattern that is sensitive to sound coming in from the front or back of the microphone but not the sides. Characteristic of ribbon, or velocity, microphones.

Bin: Window in which audio, graphics, and video clips are stored in the nonlinear editing model.

Bit: Abbreviation for binary digit; a number that can have a value of either 0 (off) or 1 (on). Eight bits equal one byte.

Black Balance: Adjustment of the camera's black level or pedestal level, usually set at 7.5 IRE.

Blanking Pulse: The signal at the end of each line (horizontal blanking) and field (vertical blanking) of the video signal that turns off the picture information.

Blast Filter: Filter built into some microphones. Protects against sound distortion caused by strong blasts of breath when a microphone is placed too close to the subject's mouth. Also called a *pop filter.*

Blocking Diagram: A plan that indicates the position and movement of people and equipment in a production.

BNC Connector: A bayonet-type twist-lock connector used as a video connector on almost all professional equipment.

Body Pack: Wireless microphone system transmitting unit manufactured as a unit separate from the microphone, typically hidden on the body of the person who is the source of the sound.

Boom: An extendable pole on a tripod base, sometimes wheeled, by which the microphone is suspended close to the action.

Both Edit: An edit that simultaneously affects both audio and video.

Bounce Light: Illumination of an object indirectly by reflecting light onto the object from a wall, floor, or ceiling.

Brightness: The range of values from black to white in the television picture. In color television, brightness is called *luminance.*

Broadcast: Transmission of radio and television signals through the air. Video and/or audio signals are transmitted from an antenna through the use of a carrier signal.

Broadcast Quality: (1) Technical standards set by the Federal Communications Commission for broadcast television signals. (2) Program content and production values of broadcastable material.

B-Roll: Visual, cutaway video footage used to cover voice-over or narration.

Bulk Eraser: A powerful electromagnet used to erase video- or audiotapes.

Burn-in: Damage to the photoconductive surface of a camera pickup tube due to overexposure to extremely bright light.

Buss: A row of buttons corresponding to different video inputs on a video switcher.

Byte: A group of binary data consisting of eight bits.

Cablecast: Transmission of radio and television signals via a wire or cable. Receivers must be connected to the cable to receive the signal.

Camcorder: A one-piece video recording system in which the camera and videocassette recorder are combined into one easily carried unit.

Camera Control Unit (CCU): Electronic circuitry that regulates the way in which the camera produces the video signal.

Camera Light: A battery-powered light mounted directly onto a video camera.

Camera Microphone: A microphone built into or attached to a portable video camera.

Camera Setup: Adjustment of the electronic parameters of the camera to provide accurate recording, including registration, white balance, black balance, and gain.

Capstan: A rotating shaft driven by the motor of the videotape or audiotape recorder that pulls the tape through the machine.

Capstan Servo: A servomechanism that adjusts the playback speed of a videotape by reading the control track pulses on the tape.

Cardioid: A heart-shaped microphone pickup pattern characterized by sensitivity to sound in the front but less sensitivity to the sides and rear.

Cassette: A plastic device that holds videotape or audiotape. The tape moves from the feed reel to the take-up reel inside the cassette when playing or recording. Cassette systems are self-threading, eliminating the need to manually thread the tape around the record and playback heads.

CD-ROM: Compact disc read-only memory. A small disc used to store computer data or digital audio or video data in compressed form.

Center of Interest: The most important part of a picture in terms of the visual interest it generates.

Character Generator: Electronic device used to generate electronic lettering for use in video productions. Usually contains a keyboard, screen, and memory system for information storage.

Charge-Coupled Device (CCD): A camera pickup device that uses silicon chips to generate the video signal.

Chroma Key: A special matte effect in which a particular colored area is eliminated from one shot and filled in with new video information from another source.

Chrominance: The color part of the color signal, composed of hue and saturation. The three chrominance channels in the color signal are red, green, and blue.

Click Stop: F-stop lens setting that clicks into place.

Clip: Digital copy of audio, graphics, and video source material in a nonlinear editing system.

Clipper: A control on a video switcher used to adjust the level of a key.

Close-up (CU): A tight shot that fills the screen with an object or the head of a subject.

Color Bars: Standard display of yellow, cyan, green, magenta, red, and blue bars used as a color reference by video engineers.

Color Burst: A 3.58 megahertz control pulse that controls the phasing of the color signal and ensures that the color information is kept in proper synchronization.

Color Encoder: Electronic component within a video camera that combines the individual chrominance and luminance channels into the color signal.

Color Temperature: Variations in the quality of what appears to be white light, measured in degrees Kelvin (°K). Standard television lights operate at 3,200°K. Light with a higher color temperature appears bluish; light with a lower color temperature appears reddish.

Colorizer: Electronic component of a video switcher used to generate color, often for the purpose of coloring letters. Also called a *color background generator*.

Comet Tail: A type of lag caused when a camera pickup tube is overstimulated by a light or a point of reflected light, creating an effect that looks like the tail of a comet trailing behind a bright point of light.

Compact Disc (CD): High-quality audio storage medium in which recorded information is read and reproduced via a laser beam.

Compatibility: The capability of a particular VCR to play back a particular videotape. Compatibility is determined by the size and the format of the videotape recording and the size and the format of the playback machine.

Complementary Angle: A shooting technique in which the eyeline of one person looking to one side of the screen is balanced by the converging eyeline of another person. Each person becomes the target object of the other's eyeline.

Component Recording: High-quality video recording process in which luminance and chrominance information is recorded in separate tracks on the videotape.

Composite Signal: A video signal that includes both video information and sync.

Composited Image: A multilayered image.

Compression: Video data-recording technique that reduces the amount of information that is stored in digital form as it is being converted from an analog signal.

Condenser Microphone: A high-quality microphone that uses an electric capacitor to generate the audio signal. Requires battery or phantom power to operate.

Confidence Heads: Video playback heads positioned immediately behind the principal recording heads that allow the recording to be monitored through a playback monitor as it is being recorded. Used to check the quality of a recording while the production is in progress.

Contact Microphone: A microphone attached directly to an object for sound pickup.

Continuity Editing: Editing of dialogue or action without discontinuous jumps in time or place.

Contrast Range: The range or ratio between the darkest and brightest part of an image. Most portable color video cameras function within a maximum contrast range of 30:1 or 40:1. Also called *contrast ratio.*

Control Track: A series of electronic impulses recorded directly onto the videotape in their own track that regulate the playback timing of the system. Helical scan systems have 30 control track pulses per second.

Control Track Editor: An automatic edit control unit that backtimes the videotape and executes edits by counting control track pulses on the tape.

Convertible Camera: A video camera designed to be used either in the studio or in the field.

Creative Editor: An individual with significant responsibility for making and executing editing decisions. Understands the aesthetic principles of editing as well as how to operate the video editing equipment.

Crossfade: A sound transition similar to a visual dissolve. As one sound fades out, the next one fades in, with slight overlap of the two sounds during the transition.

Cross-Keying: Use of two key lights to illuminate two subjects from reverse angles.

Crystal Black: See *Video Black.*

Cuing: See *Backspacing.*

Cut: A straight edit from one audio or video source to another, resulting in an instantaneous change. The most common transition in video and film editing.

Cutaway: A cut to a shot that is related to the main action or separate from it. In an interview, cutaways include reaction shots of the interviewer and shots of people, places, or things referred to in the interview.

Cut-In: A cut to a close-up detail of a shot or scene.

Cut-Out: A cut to a wide or establishing shot after a close-up.

Cuts-Only Editing System: A linear video-tape editing system in which the only transition possible between shots is a cut.

Cutting on Action: The technique of using action as the motivation for a cut from one shot to another.

Cycles per Second (CPS): See *Hertz (Hz)*.

Cyclorama (Cyc): Background curtain typically suspended on a curved metal track around the perimeter of a video studio.

Decibel (dB): A standard unit, or ratio, of measure for gauging the relative intensity of a sound.

Dedicated Time Code: Individual time code produced by a time code generator that is assigned to one VCR. Can be stopped and started. Also called *zero-start time code*.

Degrees Kelvin (°K): A measure of the quality of light or the degree of whiteness of light. The hotter the filament, the whiter the light radiated from it.

Depth of Field: The portion of a scene in front of the camera that is in focus. Measured from the point in focus closest to the camera to the point in focus farthest from the camera.

Desk Stand: Small microphone mount used to support a microphone on a desk or table in front of someone who is speaking.

Desktop Video (DTV): Video production that utilizes personal computers to generate video images and/or modify or edit recorded video images.

Dew Lamp: Warning light to indicate when moisture or condensation has formed on the head drum.

Dialogue: Conversation between two or more people.

Dichroic Filter: Filter that allows only certain frequencies of light to pass. Used in camera prisms and to adjust the color temperature of light sources.

Diffuser: See *Scrim*.

Digital Audio Workstation (DAW): Computer equipped with appropriate hardware and software for the manipulation and editing of sound.

Digital Nonlinear Editing System (DNLE): See *Nonlinear Editing*.

Digital Signal: A signal in which the input is converted into bits of information that can be stored as numerical data.

Digital Video Effect (DVE): Special effects made possible by signal processing equipment that digitizes and processes the video signal. Image compression and expansion are common types of digital effects.

Digital Videocassette (DV): A 6.35mm ($1/4''$) videocassette recording format that records digital audio and digital component video signals. Three format variants differ in terms of the width of the recorded video tracks: the consumer- and prosumer-level DV utilizes a 10-micron-wide track, Sony's professional DVCAM features a 15-micron track, and the professional-quality DVCPRO (Panasonic and others) features an 18-micron track.

Digitizing: Conversion of an analog signal into a digital signal.

Dimmer: A device that changes the intensity of a light by varying the voltage supplied to the lighting instrument.

DIN Connector: A type of connector often used to connect an external battery to a VCR. Abbreviation for *Deutsche-Industrie-Norm*.

Direct Current (DC): The type of current supplied by batteries. Most portable video systems require a 12-volt DC power source.

Directional Continuity: Characters or objects that are moving in one shot continue to move in the same general direction in a subsequent shot. An element of continuity editing.

Directional Light: Focused light coming from a particular direction, creating areas of light and shadow on the subject.

Dissolve: A gradual transition in which one visual source slowly fades out while another slowly fades in and the two sources overlap during the transition.

Dolly (In or Out): Actual movement of the camera and its support toward or away from the scene.

Downstream Keyer: A device on a video switcher that introduces a key or matte over the line output, leaving the mix/effects busses free to perform other effects.

Drop-Frame Time Code: Type of SMPTE time code that drops (skips) two frames per minute except the tenth minute of each hour. See also *Non-Drop-Frame Time Code.*

Dropout: Loss of particles of magnetic coating from the surface of a videotape. Adversely affects picture quality and stability.

Dropout Compensator (DOC): An electronic device that detects the loss of information on a videotape caused by oxide dropouts and corrects the problem by replacing the lost information with information from the line that immediately preceded it.

Dub: (1) A copy of a video- or audiotape. (2) To transfer video or audio information from one tape to another.

DVD (Digital Versatile Disc): High-density compact disc used to store data, text, and large audio or video files.

Dynamic Editing: Editing technique that utilizes visual material to create an impact rather than simply to convey literal meaning or achieve continuity of action. More affective and complex than continuity editing. Also called *complexity editing.*

Dynamic Microphone: A rugged, professional-quality microphone widely used in field production.

Ear Shot: Any medium close-up or close-up shot that shows the subject in profile, rather than from the front, and in which the ear is in the center of the picture.

Earphone: A small device that fits into an ear. Used to monitor audio.

Earspeaker: Small audio speaker built into the side of a camcorder that allows the camera operator to hear the sound input directly without the use of headphones or an earphone.

Edit Decision List (EDL): A list of all the edits for a program. Specifies all the edit in points and out points, often with reference to SMPTE time code. Also called *edit list.*

Edit Master Tape: The videotape onto which editing will be done.

Editing: The process of arranging individual shots or sequences into an appropriate order.

Editing Script: A written plan for editing a program. Consists of a brief description of each shot, including its in (entry) and out (exit) points.

Editing to Music: Editing that is motivated by a melodic or rhythmic element (the beat) in a piece of music.

Editing VCR: Videocassette recorder equipped with special electronic circuitry that enables it to edit the video signal. Can record and play back videotapes.

Editing Window: Window in which clips are trimmed in a nonlinear editing system.

Editor: See *Video Editor.*

Electret Condenser: Small battery-powered condenser microphone.

Electron Gun: (1) In a camera pickup tube, a device located at the rear of the tube that emits a stream of electrons, which scans the target. (2) In a television monitor or receiver, a device that emits a beam of electrons, which hits the phosphorescent surface of the picture tube and makes the video image visible.

Electronic Editing: A process of rerecording video information into a new sequence by using one or more playback (source) VCRs and one editing (record) VCR.

Electronic Field Production (EFP): Video production that takes place in a location outside a television studio. Usually refers to single-camera productions shot to be edited in postproduction.

Electronic News Gathering (ENG): The use of electronic video equipment for reporting news from field locations. Also called *electronic journalism.*

Electronic Viewfinder: A small monitor mounted on a video camera that reproduces the scene the camera is shooting. The camera operator looks at the electronic viewfinder to cover the action.

Encoded Color Signal: The full color video signal, including chrominance, luminance, and synchronizing information.

EP: See *SLP/EP.*

Equalizer: Audio component that allows the level of various ranges of frequencies within the signal to be manipulated in order to shape the overall quality of the sound.

Erase Head: A head that erases information from a tape so that new information can be recorded in its place.

Essential Area: The central, usable area of a video screen.

Establishing Shot: An overall wide-angle view of a scene, usually a long shot. Shows the relationship of the parts to each other and to the scene as a whole.

E-to-E: Electronics-to-electronics. Method of monitoring a signal that is being fed into a VCR.

External Microphone: Any microphone not built into or mounted onto the field camera.

External Sync: Sync pulses generated by a source other than the camera, usually a sync generator.

Extreme Close-Up (ECU): The tightest shot possible on a person or object. Also called a *tight close-up* (*TCU*).

Extreme Long Shot (XLS): A very-wide-angle, panoramic shot of the elements of a scene.

Eyeline: A line created by the eyes when someone looks at a target object. Eyelines and the position of the target object are very important in creating continuity through editing.

Eyepiece Viewfinder: The most common type of viewfinder found on portable video cameras. Allows the camera operator's (videographer's) eye to be placed firmly against the camera.

Eyeroom: See *Noseroom.*

Fade: A gradual transition from black to an image or sound (fade-up) or from an image or sound to black (fade-down or fade-out).

Fader Bar: Device on a video switcher that controls the output of the mix/effects buss. Used to perform fades, dissolves, and wipes.

F-Connector: A video connector frequently used on coaxial cables carrying an RF signal, such as a cable TV connection, or the RF output from a VCR.

Feedback: (1) Electronic distortion caused when a live microphone is placed near a speaker that is reproducing its output, or when a video camera shoots into its own monitor. Audio feedback is audible as a loud screech; video feedback appears as an undulating pattern of light and color. (2) That part of the communication process in which audience responses to the production are transmitted to the producers.

Field: One-half of a video frame (262.5 lines in NTSC).

428

Field Production: See *Electronic Field Production (EFP)*.

Fill Light: (1) Nondirectional light, set at one-half to three-fourths of the intensity of the key and positioned opposite it. Used to fill in, but not eliminate completely, the shadows created on the subject by the key light. (2) Any light used to fill in shadows.

Film-Style Lighting: Lighting technique in which the lighting setup is changed each time the camera position is changed. Lighting done shot by shot. Also called *single-camera lighting*.

Filter: A device used to eliminate certain frequencies of light or sound.

Filter Wheel: A component built into a video camera that is used to correct the color temperature of incoming light.

FireWire: A high-speed digital interconnect standard (IEEE 1394) that allows digital video and audio to be moved directly into and out of a computer.

Fishpole: A handheld telescoping metal rod widely used as a microphone support in field production.

Flag: An opaque card with a handle that is used to control the way in which light falls on a scene.

Flashback: Insertion into a sequence of a shot or scene that took place in the past, prior to the main action.

Flashforward: Insertion into a sequence of a shot or scene that takes place in the future, after the main action.

Flatbed Scanner: Device used to convert photographs and flat artwork into a digital file.

Floodlight: Light that produces a wide beam of relatively soft, unfocused light. Also called *broadlight*.

Floor Stand: Telescoping stand used to support a light or microphone.

Fluorescent Lamp: Gas-filled glass tube coated on the inside with chemicals that glow when electrical power is applied to the lamp.

Fluid Head: High-quality tripod head that allows extremely smooth camera movement (panning and tilting).

Flying Erase Head: An erase head positioned in front of the video record head that allows precise frames of information to be erased. Makes insert editing possible.

Focal Length: The distance from the optical center of the lens to the point where the image is in focus (the face of the CCD). The angle of view of a lens is determined by its focal length.

Focus: Sharp detail in the important parts of the image. Pictures may be in focus or out of focus.

Focus Ring: A device that controls the distance between lens elements, thereby allowing the lens to focus on objects at different distances from the camera. Located at the far end of the lens on portable video cameras.

Foot-candle (FC): A measure of the intensity of light.

Format: See *Tape Formats*.

Frame: One of the basic units of the video signal. There are 29.97 frames per second in the American NTSC system.

Frame Accuracy: The ability of an editing system to make an edit exactly on the planned frame. Most control track editing systems are *not* frame accurate.

Frame Synchronizer: A time base corrector that is capable of storing a full frame of video information. Often used to synchronize nonsynchronous remote signals to other synchronous signals in a television station or video production house. Also widely used to produce video graphics.

Framing: The placement of people or objects within the video frame.

Free-Run: Operating mode of a time code generator in which time code is continuously produced while generator's power is on.

Frequency: The number of times a wave repeats itself in one second. Usually measured in Hertz (Hz). The frequency of a sound wave determines its pitch.

Frequency Response: The ability of any video or audio component to accurately reproduce a wide range of frequencies.

Friction Head: Inexpensive tripod head that gives fair control over camera movement.

F-Stop: A standard calibration of the size of the aperture opening of a lens.

Gain: Control of the amplification or level of an audio or video signal. May be automatic or manual.

Gain Boost: Special switch on some cameras that boosts the amplification of the video signal. Used most often in low-light situations to improve color reproduction. May make the picture look noisy.

Gamma: A measure of the camera's ability to reproduce the tonal gradations of a scene.

Gap: The small space between the two sides of a video recording and playback head.

Gel: Plastic or polyester filter, sometimes called *color media*, used to change the color or color temperature of a light source. Short for *gelatin*.

Generation: The relationship of a dubbed copy of a tape to the original. The original is a first-generation tape; the first copy made from the original is a second-generation tape; and so on. Signal quality decreases with each new generation.

Gen-Lock: Synchronization of one piece of video equipment to an incoming video signal from another piece of equipment.

Glitch: A momentary problem in the video signal. Often caused by a loss of stability or dropouts in the tape.

Graphic Material: Visual materials for video. Ranges from whole settings in which action is staged to simple captions identifying speakers.

Graphics: Printed, drawn, photographed, or electronically generated graphic material incorporated into a production.

Gray Scale: A test pattern of 7 to 10 shades of gray, which correspond to the brightness range that the video system is capable of reproducing.

Guard Band: Blank area between tracks of video or audio information on tape.

Halogen-Metal-Iodide (HMI) Light: A highly efficient professional light instrument that produces light matching the color temperature of daylight.

Hanging Microphone: A microphone hung above a scene for sound pickup.

Hard Disk: Magnetic storage system for a computer.

Head: A small electromagnet used to record a video or audio signal onto magnetic tape or to play back the signal from tape.

Head Clog: Clogging of the gap in the video or audio head caused by excessive oxide dropouts from the tape.

Head Drum: Metal cylinder inside a VCR around which the tape is wrapped to bring it into contact with the video heads.

Head Drum Servo: A servomechanism that adjusts the position of the video heads spinning in the head drum so that they rotate in phase with the tracks of video information on the videotape.

Headphones: Device used for monitoring audio. Consists of two small speakers attached to a flexible band that is worn on the head, positioning the speakers over the listener's ears.

Headroom: The distance within the television frame between the top of the subject's head and the top edge of the frame.

Helical Scan: Tracks of video information laid down at an angle on the tape. Characteristic of all modern VCRs. Also called *slant-track recording*.

Hertz (Hz): Standard unit of measure of the frequency of a wave in cycles per second.

High-Definition Television (HDTV): Digital video recording and transmission system that features improved resolution resulting from an increase in the number of horizontal scanning lines and a wider aspect ratio (16:9 versus conventional 4:3) than the traditional NTSC broadcast standards.

High-Impedance: Equipment rated up to 20,000 ohms. Also called *high-Z*.

Horizontal Resolution: See *Resolution*.

Hot Spot: Overexposed portion of a picture; bright, glowing spot in which color and detail are lost.

House Sync: Sync supplied by a sync generator to all the video equipment in a given facility.

Hue: A recognizable color: red, blue, green, or the like.

Image Compression: Digital video effect that squeezes the horizontal and/or vertical dimensions of the picture, thereby reducing it in size within the frame.

Image Expansion: Digital video effect that stretches the horizontal and/or vertical dimensions of the picture, causing it to grow larger within the frame.

Impedance (Z): The amount of resistance in a circuit, measured in ohms (Ω). Audio equipment may be high-impedance or low-impedance.

Incandescent Lamp: Lightbulb that is similar in construction to a common household bulb. Has a tungsten filament within an evacuated glass bulb.

Inches per Second (ips): Measure of the speed at which video- and audiotape move.

Incident Light: The light radiating directly from a source or sources that falls on an object or scene.

Input Overload Distortion: Distortion of the audio signal caused by placing the microphone too close to the sound source. Characteristic of condenser microphones.

Insert and Track Information (ITI): A data track in Digital Video Cassette (DV) tape formats.

Insert Edit: An edit in which new audio or video information is recorded onto the tape in the editing VCR, leaving the control track undisturbed.

Insert Editing: The process of inserting a shot or sequence into a preexisting sequence.

Interformat Editing: Videotape editing in which the source tape is edited onto a master tape of a different format.

Interlaced Scanning: The process by which the odd and even lines of a video picture are scanned. First one field of odd lines is scanned, then one field of even lines is scanned. Also called *2:1 interlaced scanning*.

Internal Sync: Sync pulses generated within a camera.

International Candle: The light given off by the flame of a sperm candle $7/_8$" in diameter burning at the rate of 7.776 grams per hour, or its equivalent.

Inverse Square Rule: A method of calculating the intensity of light falling on a scene from a given instrument. Reducing the distance between the source instrument and the scene by one half produces four times as much light on the scene.

Iris: A circular diaphragm composed of overlapping leaves that can be manipulated to create a hole of variable size in its center which controls the amount of light passing through the lens. May be controlled manually or automatically.

Jack: Female receptacle for a pin-type audio connector.

Joystick: A stick-like control on an edit control unit that can be used to move the tapes forward or backward in a number of different modes: frame by frame, slow motion, normal motion, or fast motion. Performs the same function as a search dial. On a video switcher, a joystick is often used as the wipe positioner, which allows selected wipe patterns to be moved up or down on the screen.

JPEG (Joint Photographic Experts Group) Compression: Digital compression standard for still or moving images.

Jump Cut: A discontinuous transition from one shot to another caused by a difference in the size and position of the subject in the two shots. Jump cuts often occur when the middle of a shot is removed and the two remaining pieces are joined together, as in editing dialogue.

Kelvin (°K): See *Degrees Kelvin (°K)*.

Kelvinometer: A color temperature meter, used to measure the color temperature of light.

Key: Special effect used in titling in which one video source (usually the keyed graphics) appears as opaque letters over the background video.

Key Light: The brightest light on the scene. Establishes the form of the subject by providing bright illumination and producing shadows on the subject.

Keyframe: In animation programs, identifies the beginning, intermediate and ending points of the motion path of the image.

Keystoning: Distortion of visual material caused when a graphic (or object) is not displayed perpendicular to the camera axis.

Kinescope: Archival film recording of a television broadcast made by focusing a film camera on a television screen.

Lag: A smearing effect visible in the picture when the camera or subject moves. Often caused by improper or inadequate lighting.

Large-Format: Video equipment that is large and not portable. Tape width is 2″ or 1″; VTRs and cameras are very large.

Lavaliere Microphone: A small microphone pinned onto someone or hung around the subject's neck with a string.

Laying Down Tracks: The process of recording music, voice, or sound effects onto the audio channel of a videocassette so they can later be edited onto the edit master tape.

Leader Sequence: Information that identifies a program, usually recorded at the beginning of a videotape.

Lens: The optical component of a camera. Collects incoming light and focuses it on the camera image sensor.

Lens Cap: A protective cap that can be attached to the end of the lens barrel when the camera is not in operation.

Lens Flare: Optical distortion of a picture caused when a light shines directly into the camera lens. Can be prevented by changing the position of the light or camera, or by shielding the lens with a lens hood.

Lens Hood: A rubber extension at the front of a lens that works like a visor to prevent unwanted light from hitting the lens and causing lens flare.

Level: The strength of an audio or video signal.

Light Meter: A device used to measure the light on a scene. Incident light meters measure the amount of light falling on the scene; reflected light meters measure the amount of light reflected off the scene.

Lighting Plot: A plan that indicates the type and position of each of the lighting instruments in a scene or shot.

Line: In the NTSC system, each television frame is composed of 525 lines of information. ATSC formats include 480-, 720- and 1,080-line variants.

Linear Videotape Editing: Videotape editing system in which edits are made in sequential fashion, one after the other, starting at the beginning of the program or segment and working to the end.

Line-Level Audio Signal: An amplified audio signal considerably stronger than a microphone-level signal. A line-level audio signal is one volt.

Longitudinal Time Code (LTC): SMPTE time code recorded in a linear audio or address track of a videotape or audiotape. Compare with *vertical interval time code (VITC)*.

Long Shot (LS): A shot from a wide angle that shows the relationship between actors or actresses and their setting. Often used as an establishing shot.

Low-Cut Filter: An audio filter that eliminates low-frequency sounds from the audio signal.

Low-Impedance: Equipment rated at 600 ohms or below. Characteristic of most professional microphones. Also called *low-Z*.

LP: Long-play (four-hour) mode on VHS machines.

Lumen: A unit of measure of the flow of light.

Luminance: See *Brightness*.

Lux: A unit of illumination.

M-II: Professional-quality $1/2''$ videotape recording format developed by Matsushita Corporation.

Macro Lens: A lens used for extreme close-ups. Many portable video cameras have a built-in macro lens that is activated by a macro lever.

Macro Lever: Lever on the barrel of the lens that activates the macro lens.

Manual Gain Control: Manual control of the amplification of an audio or video signal. See also *Automatic Gain Control*.

Matched Cut: A cut from one shot to a shot that is too similar in terms of angle of view and camera position. Similar to a jump cut.

Matched Frame Edit: An edit between two adjacent frames of video information in the same shot.

Matte: Special video effect that combines three separate sources. Often used to add color to titles in a video production.

Medium Close-Up (MCU): A head-and-shoulders shot that ends at the chest of the subject. One of the most frequently used shots in television.

Medium Shot (MS): A shot from a medium angle of view, often used to show the relationship between people in a shot or scene.

Microphone: A transducer that changes sound waves into electrical energy.

Microphone In (Mic In): Input jack used to connect a microphone to a piece of electronic equipment.

Microphone-Level Signal: Unamplified output of a microphone; a very weak signal usually measured in millivolts.

Microphone Proximity Effect: Tendency of a microphone to overemphasize the reproduction of low frequencies in relation to higher frequencies as the distance between the sound source and microphone decreases.

Mini-Cassette: A videocassette in a small tape housing designed to be used in a portable camcorder.

Mini-Plug: A small single-pin, unbalanced plug frequently used as a microphone and earphone connector.

Mix: The technique of combining several simultaneous sound sources in such a way that their relative volume matches their importance.

Modeling: Creating the illusion of three-dimensional subjects and objects on the two-dimensional video screen through lighting.

Moiré: A herringbone-like pattern of video noise, frequently caused by radio frequency interference or high-contrast patterns on the subject being videotaped.

Monitor: (1) To check the audio or visual quality of a recording by listening to it or looking at it. (2) A device used to display an audio or video signal. (3) A video set not capable of receiving a broadcast signal.

Monopod: A single telescoping support tube attached to the base of a camera. Often inserted into a belt pouch and used on portable cameras with rear-mounted eyepiece viewfinders.

MPEG (Motion Picture Experts Group) Compression: Digital compression standard for CD-ROMs (MPEG-1) and broadcast television (MPEG-2).

Multimedia: Computer program that incorporates animation, sound, text, illustrations, and video, frequently produced for distribution on CD-ROM.

Narration: Description of a visual scene provided by a narrator, frequently as a voice-over (VO).

Natural Sound (Nat Sound): Sound naturally present on a location that is organically connected to the visual action taking place.

Neutral-Density Filter: A filter that reduces the amount of light hitting the camera CCD without affecting its color temperature.

Noise: (1) Unintended sound. (2) Unwanted electrical interference. Video noise, or snow, makes the picture look grainy; audio noise is audible as static or hiss.

Noncomposite Signal: A video signal that includes only the video (picture) information, but not horizontal and vertical sync.

Non-Drop-Frame Time Code: SMPTE time code generated at the rate of 30 frames per second. Because the actual frame rate of NTSC video is 29.97 frames per second, non-drop-frame time code does not provide an accurate measure of real elapsed time. See also *Drop-Frame Time Code.*

Nonlinear Editing: Type of video editing made possible by magnetic-disk-based editing systems that allow random access to the audio and video information stored on the disc. Differs from the sequential linear editing characterized by videotape-based editing systems.

Noseroom: The distance within the television frame between the edge of the subject's nose, seen in profile, and the edge of the frame. Also called *eyeroom.*

Notch Filter: A special audio filter that eliminates a particular range of frequencies within the signal.

NTSC (National Television System Committee) Standard: Early technical standard for U.S. television line and frame scanning rates, as well as the system for television color.

Objective Camera: The camera acts as an unseen observer of the action and presents a neutral-perspective view from outside the scene.

Off-Line: Preliminary stage in video editing process in which a rough cut (or edit) of a program is made, frequently using window dubs of field footage with SMPTE time code.

Ohm (Ω): A measure of electrical resistance.

Omnidirectional: A microphone pickup pattern that is sensitive to sound coming in from all directions.

180-Degree Rule: See *Principal Action Axis.*

On-Line: (1) In video editing, refers to editing the final version of the program or program segment, usually on a high-quality editing system. (2) When using a video switcher, refers to the source that is going out as part of the program that is being broadcast or recorded.

Open Reel: A metal or plastic device that holds videotape or audiotape. Open-reel tapes must be threaded through the playback and record heads and then fastened to the take-up reel for normal operation. Both 2″ and 1″ videotape recorders use open-reel tape.

Operating Light Level: The amount of light, measured in foot-candles, that a camera needs to produce a picture. The optimum light level is the recommended amount; the minimum light level is the smallest amount of light the camera must have, but usually results in an inferior picture.

Optical-Video Transducer: In a video camera, the CCD image sensor that changes incoming light into an electrical video signal.

Overlapping: Shooting technique in which dialogue or action at the end of one shot is repeated at the beginning of the next shot. Makes editing easier.

Overlapping Edit: The process in which the end of one shot is erased and recorded over by the beginning of the next shot during the process of editing.

Overlay Edit: In nonlinear editing systems, a shot that is used to replace and/or cover up a shot of similar length in the time line.

Over-the-Shoulder Shot: Camera shot, usually of two people. Person in foreground has back to the camera; second person is slightly in the background and faces the camera.

Page Pull or Page Push: Digital video effect in which the picture appears to be pushed or pulled off the screen.

Page Turn: Digital video effect in which the picture appears to turn like the page of a book, revealing a new picture (or page).

Paint: Adjustment of camera color reproduction to achieve a particular mood or effect.

Pan: Horizontal movement of the camera head only. Short for *panorama*.

Parallel Cutting: Cutting between two actions that are happening at the same time in different locations or between events happening at different points in time. A type of dynamic editing.

Patching: Connecting audio and video inputs and outputs with a cable.

Peak Limiter: An electronic device that prevents the audio signal from exceeding 100 percent (0 dB) on the volume unit meter scale. Also called an *audio limiter*.

Peak Program Meter (PPM): Audio meter that monitors loudness peaks in an audio signal.

Peak White: The highest part of the video waveform, equivalent to the brightest part of the scene being shot. Should not exceed 100 percent on the waveform.

Pedestal: Black level; control over the reproduction of the deepest shades of black reproduced by the camera. Usually set at 7.5 percent on the waveform monitor.

Persistence of Vision: Perceptual phenomenon that creates the illusion of motion in a movie.

Phone Plug: A large, unbalanced single-pin plug used as a headphone or microphone connector.

Pickup Pattern: The pattern of directions in which a microphone is sensitive to incoming sound.

Pickup Tube: Vacuum tube inside a video camera that changes light into an electrical video signal, made obsolete by the CCD.

Ping-Pong: To rerecord time code and audio on different channels on a videotape by making a dub of the original material.

Pistol Grip: A small handle attached to a shotgun microphone.

Pitch: The high or low quality of a particular sound; results from differences in the frequency of sound waves.

Pixels: Literally picture elements. Extremely small silicon semiconductors arranged in precise horizontal and vertical rows on a CCD chip that change incoming light into electrical energy.

Point of View (POV): See *Subjective Camera*.

Pop Filter: See *Blast Filter*.

Portable VCR: Lightweight, battery-powered videocassette recorder designed for remote field production.

Portapak: Early term used to describe a small portable camera and VCR recording system.

Postproduction: State of production after field production is complete. Principal component is usually editing.

Poststriping: Adding time code to a videotape that was originally recorded without it.

Potentiometer (Pot): Used to increase or decrease the gain amplification of an electronic signal.

Preinterview: An interview with the potential subject of a program or program segment that takes place before the actual production date. Used to gain familiarity with the subject and to put novice subjects at ease before they appear on camera.

Preproduction: Production planning before the production begins.

Prerolling: See *Backspacing*.

Pressure Zone Microphone (PZM): Registered trade name of Crown International, for its boundary microphone with a hemispheric pickup pattern.

Principal Action Axis: In staging for continuity, the camera stays within an imaginary 180-degree semicircle created by the line formed by the principal action in a scene and thus stays on one side of the action. Also called the *principal vector line* or the *180-degree rule*.

Principal Vector Line: See *Principal Action Axis*.

Printing to Tape: Recording onto videotape a finished program or segment that was first edited in a computer-based digital nonlinear editing system.

Prism Block: A glass prism in high-quality video cameras that breaks incoming light into its red, green, and blue components.

Processing Amplifier (Proc Amp): A device to correct color quality as well as sync and color burst in the video signal.

Producer: The member of the production team who is responsible for the overall organization of a production.

Production: (1) The shooting stage of the video production process. See also *Preproduction* and *Postproduction*. (2) The video program itself.

Production Assistant (PA): The member of the field production team who serves as a general assistant. Often has responsibility for setting up audio, helping with lighting, carrying equipment, and logging tapes.

Progressive Scanning: Scanning each of the lines in the video frame in successive order. Scanning begins at the top of the frame and continues to the bottom.

Pulse Code Modulation (PCM): High-quality digital-audio recording process utilized in some portable VCRs.

Quadruplex: Large-format system of videotape recording in which four video heads rotating at high speed scan a 2″ videotape. For many years the broadcast standard; now obsolete.

Quantizing: Process of sampling an analog waveform and converting it into digital information.

Question Re-Ask: Technique frequently used in single-camera production; questions asked by an interviewer are recorded onto videotape after interview has been completed.

Quick-Release Plate: Mounting system used on a camcorder and tripod head to allow for fast mounting and release of the camcorder on the tripod.

Radio Frequency (RF): The range of electromagnetic frequencies used to transmit broadcast or cablecast signals. Different frequencies correspond with different channels of reception.

Range Extender: Optical device attached to the end of a lens or built into the lens itself that increases the magnifying power of the lens. A 2:1 range extender doubles the focal length of the lens.

RCA/Phono Connector: A small unbalanced audio connector often used for line-level audio inputs and outputs. Also used as a video connector in home video equipment.

Reaction Shot: A cut, usually to a close-up of a person, that shows a reaction to what was just seen or said.

Receiver: A television capable of picking up an RF-modulated video signal.

Record-Run: Operating mode of a time code generator in which time code is produced only when the VCR is in the record mode.

Record Safety: A safety device built into a videocassette to prevent accidental erasure of the tape. A red button on $3/4''$ cassettes; a small plastic tab or switch on $1/2''$, 6.35mm, and 8mm cassettes.

Record VCR: In an editing system, the editing VCR. Also refers to any VCR capable of making a recording from a camera or line input, from another VCR, or off the air.

Reference White: Brightest possible point a video system will reproduce. Should not exceed 100 percent on the waveform.

Reflected Light: The light reaching the camera from the scene.

Reflector: Any opaque substance, usually bright metal or treated fabric, designed to redirect light back onto a scene. An important part of standard lighting instruments.

Remote Production: Any video production that takes place outside a studio. It may be as simple as a single-camera production or as complicated as large-scale coverage of a sports event.

Remote Survey: A survey to gather technical and aesthetic information about a remote location in which a program will be shot.

Rendering: Time-consuming process through which a computer creates special effects, transitions, and animation frame by frame, or in some cases, field by field.

Resolution: A measure of the amount of detail in a picture.

Retrace: The time during blanking that it takes the beam in a cathode ray tube (CRT) to move from the end of one line to the beginning of the next (horizontal retrace) or from the bottom of one field to the top of the next (vertical retrace).

Reverse Angle: Complementary angle of videotaping people so that their eyelines converge when the individual shots are edited together.

RF Interference: Audio or video noise caused by proximity to an RF transmitter.

RF Modulator: A device that converts standard electrical audio and video signals into a radio frequency signal that can be displayed on a conventional television receiver.

RGB Signal: Unencoded red, green, and blue video signals.

Ribbon Microphone: High-quality voice microphone designed originally for use in radio. Also called a *velocity microphone*.

Ripple: Computer update of an edit list. When a change in an edit affects the entry and exit points of all subsequent edits, corrections on the edit list ripple through the editing system.

Room Tone: Ambient sound present on location. Sometimes recorded and dubbed back onto an audio track during editing to preserve sound continuity.

Rough Cut: A preliminary edited version of a program.

Safe Track: The audio track on a videotape that is located in the interior of the tape, away from the outside edge, which is subject to damage in use and storage.

Safe-Title Area: Essential area; the central, usable area of the video screen where titles and graphics should be placed to be legible.

Sampling: See *Quantizing*.

Sampling Rate: In audio and video recording, describes how often the elements of the analog signal are converted into packets of digital information. See *Quantizing*.

Saturation: The intensity or vividness of a color. For example, pink is a lightly saturated red, whereas deep red is highly saturated.

Scrim: A type of light diffuser used to reduce the amount of light and make it softer.

Search Dial: A circular control on a VCR or edit control unit used to move a videotape forward or backward at various speeds.

Segue: A transition from one sound to another in which one sound source fades or cuts out completely and then the next source fades or cuts in. There is no overlap of the two sounds.

Selective Focus: The technique of keeping some parts of the picture in focus while others are out of focus. Emphasizes depth and draws the viewer's attention to particular elements in a shot.

Servo-Lock Indicator: Warning light on a VCR that indicates when the machine has reached the proper play or recording speed and the picture has stabilized.

Servomechanism (Servo): A variable-speed motor used to control various mechanical systems in video equipment.

Shock Mount: A rubber cradle used to attach a shotgun microphone to a boom and insulate it from noise.

Shooter: In video field production, the camera operator. Also called the *videographer*.

Shooting Ratio: Ratio of amount of tape shot to amount actually used in the final production. If 20 minutes of tape is shot to produce a one-minute production, the shooting ratio is 20:1.

Shotgun Microphone: Microphone with an extremely directional pickup pattern, often used to pick up sound at a distance.

Shoulder Mount: A contoured brace attached to the bottom of a portable video camera; allows the camera to be carried on the camera operator's shoulder.

Signal-to-Noise Ratio (S/N): Ratio of electronic noise to the total signal, expressed in decibels (dB). Measures how much higher the signal level is than the noise.

Silk: A giant cloth diffuser used to control light intensity and color temperature in outdoor productions.

Slant-Track: Helical scan recording.

Slate: Audio or video information used to identify the material that will immediately follow on a videotape.

SLP/EP: Standard long-play/extended-play (six-hour) mode on VHS machines.

Small Computer System Interface (SCSI): Rectangular connector used to attach peripheral devices to a personal computer. SCSI is pronounced "scuzzy."

Small-Format: Portable video equipment characterized by its small size. Tape width is 6.35mm, 8mm, $1/2''$, or $3/4''$; camera image sensors are $1/3''$, $1/2''$, or $2/3''$.

Smear: Unique type of CCD image distortion, visible as a bright vertical band running through the image, caused by a very bright point of illumination in the scene.

SMPTE Time Code: Society of Motion Picture and Television Engineers time code. A binary electronic signal that is recorded onto videotape. Identifies each frame in terms of hours, minutes, seconds, and frames; aids in computer editing. Two main types of time code are longitudinal time code (LTC) and vertical interval time code (VITC).

Soft Light: A floodlight with an aluminized cloth reflector stretched over a frame; produces a bright, shadow-free light.

Software: (1) A computer program that contains a set of commands that allow a computer to perform various tasks, such as word processing, video graphics generation, etc. (2) A video program or program segment; as opposed to video equipment, which is called *hardware.*

Sound: (1) A pattern in the vibration or movement of molecules of air. (2) Any aural component of a program that is intentionally present.

Sound Bite: (1) Voice segment of the subject of an interview. (2) A sound-on-tape (video and audio) segment of a person speaking on camera. (3) Any sound-on-tape or voice-over use of an individual's voice within an edited program.

Sound Effects (SFX): Prerecorded or live sounds that are added to a production, often to reinforce the visuals or to convey a sense of place.

Sound on Tape (SOT): Picture and synchronous sound recorded onto videotape.

Sound Perspective: The matching of loud sound with close objects and quiet sound with faraway objects so that sound and picture seem to be the same distance away.

Sound Presence: Characteristic of the quality of a close sound that distinguishes it from a faraway sound; can be created by placing the microphone very close to the sound source.

Source VCR: In a linear editing system, the playback VCR.

SP: Standard-play (two-hour) mode on VHS and S-VHS machines.

Split Edit: An edit in which sound and picture are edited individually rather than simultaneously. Two separate edits are made on the same shot—one on audio, the other on picture—and one follows the other in time. Also called *L edits* or *L cuts.*

Split Screen: Special effect in which two images are simultaneously displayed on the television screen. Usually activated by stopping a horizontal wipe at the halfway point.

Spotlight: Lighting instrument that produces a narrow beam of hard, focused light. May have a variable or fixed beam.

Standard-Definition Television (SDTV): Video pictures with 480 active scanning lines in either 4:3 or 16:9 aspect ratio.

Standby Switch: Switch found on many video cameras that reduces the camera's power consumption. Allows the camera electronics and image sensor to warm up, but does not cause the image sensor to produce an image.

Stand-up: Sound-on-tape segment in which the reporter is seen on camera and talks directly into the camera. Commonly used in electronic news gathering.

Steadicam®: Camera mounting system that allows a camera operator to carry a camera and achieve extremely smooth camera movement. Registered trademark of Cinema Products.

439

Sticks: A wooden tripod.

Story Outline Script: Script format used for magazine-style production. Often includes a description of the story, a list of locations to be used, essential visual material to be recorded at the various locations, and the names of individuals who will appear in interview segments.

Storyboard: A script that contains illustrations of the principal visual elements of a production.

Stripe Filter: Color separation device found on the face of the image sensor in single-CCD cameras; breaks incoming light into its red, blue, green, and luminance components.

Subjective Camera: The camera acts as a participant in the scene. The perspective presented is that of a participant rather than an observer. Also called *point of view* (*POV*).

Subtractive Color: Color theory concerned with mixing pigments, paints, and dyes. Subtractive primary colors are magenta, cyan, and yellow.

Supercardioid: A very directional microphone pickup pattern that is sensitive to sound in a very narrow angle in front of the microphone. Characteristic of shotgun microphones.

Superimposition: Special effect in which two video sources are combined through the use of a video switcher. Both sources appear on the screen simultaneously and are somewhat transparent because neither is at full strength. Formerly used to superimpose titles; most title graphics are now keyed over the background video.

S-VHS: Super-VHS. A $1/2$″ video recording format with greatly improved luminance- and chrominance-recording capabilities in comparison with conventional VHS format.

S-Video Connector: Video input/output connection on monitors and VCRs used in conjunction with Hi8 and S-VHS systems in which luminance (Y) and chrominance (C) signals are processed separately. Such systems yield better color purity and image detail than conventional signal processing and display.

Sync Generator: A device that generates horizontal and vertical sync pulses. Typically used when several cameras are used simultaneously in conjunction with a video switcher; it synchronizes them with all the other equipment used in the production.

Sync Pulse: The synchronizing signal that controls the scanning of individual lines of information (horizontal sync) and individual fields of video information (vertical sync).

Talent Release: A standard agreement signed by an individual who appears in a video production. Gives the program producer or production agency permission to use the subject's image and/or voice.

Tape Format: Describes differences in the width and physical configuration of a videotape, the location of audio, video, control track, and time code information on the tape, as well as the type of recording process employed. Popular portable videotape formats include: 8mm/Hi8, VHS/S-VHS, DV, and Betacam SP.

Tape Log: A list and description of every shot on a particular videotape.

Tape Speed: The speed at which the tape is pulled through the VCR.

Tape Transport Controls: Buttons that control the movement of a videotape within a VCR. Typical controls include PLAY, STOP, FAST FORWARD, SEARCH, REWIND, RECORD, and PAUSE.

Target Object: The end point of an eyeline. The object or person that someone is looking at.

Technical Editor: Usually a production subordinate who executes the editing decisions that have been made by someone else. More concerned with the operation of the editing system from a technical standpoint than with making creative editing decisions.

Technical Factors: Principles of video equipment operation; understanding how the components of the video field production system function and interrelate.

Telephoto Lens: A lens with a long focal length and a narrow angle of view. Magnifies a scene by making distant objects appear to be large and close.

Three-Point Lighting: Traditional lighting technique that utilizes a key light to establish the form, a backlight to separate the object from its background, and a fill light (or lights) to reduce the intensity of the shadows created by the key.

Tight Close-Up (TCU): Very close framing of the subject. See *Extreme Close-Up*.

Tilt: Vertical (up-and-down) movement of the camera head similar to the movement of the head when a person looks up or down.

Time Base Corrector (TBC): Electronic device used to correct timing errors in the video signal on a videotape as it is played back.

Time Code: Electronic information recorded onto videotape that identifies each video frame in terms of hours, minutes, seconds, and frame number. The two principal types of time code are SMPTE/EBU time code and 8mm time code.

Time Code Character Generator-Inserter: Converts time code readout into video information that can then be inserted into the picture on a monitor or rerecorded with the video information on another videotape.

Time Code Counter: Displays time code as a visual digital readout in hours, minutes, seconds, and frames.

Time Code Generator: Electronic component that produces time code.

Timed Cut: Editing technique in which shot length is determined by time rather than by content. A cut or series of cuts, each of a certain duration.

Time-of-Day Time Code: Time code generator that is referenced to a 24-hour clock and runs continuously day and night. Typically found in large production houses where one time code generator feeds time code simultaneously to all the VCRs in the facility.

Time Line: Graphical linear representation of a program in a nonlinear editing system.

Tone Generator: An audio oscillator that generates an electronic tone used to set the levels on audio equipment.

Track: (1) An area of video, audio, or control track information on a tape. (2) Music, voice, or sound effects that are recorded onto the audio channel of a videocassette so that they can later be edited into the edit master tape.

Track Pitch: The width of the track of video information on a videotape. Track pitch is affected by the width of the video head and the speed at which the tape moves through the machine.

Tracking: Adjustment that controls the way in which the video heads line up with the tracks of video information on a tape. The video heads must be precisely aligned with the video tracks to produce a clear and stable playback picture.

Tracking Control: A device that adjusts the position of the video heads in relation to the tracks of video information on the tape. Used to optimize the level of the playback signal.

Tracking Meter: Meter that displays the strength of the video signal in playback. Maximum meter display indicates that the heads are tracking correctly over the tracks of video information.

Tracking Shot: Moving camera effect typically created by rolling a wheeled camera dolly, often mounted on a set of rigid tracks, in front of the scene being photographed.

Transverse Scan: Tracks of video information laid down in vertical lines on the tape. Characteristic of 2″ quadruplex recording.

Trim: To add or subtract frames from an edit point after it has been entered into the control unit.

Tripod: A three-legged device used to support a camera. Tripods contain legs (which may telescope) and a head (where the camera is attached), and may include wheels (a dolly) to allow easy movement. Also called *sticks*.

Truck (Left or Right): Horizontal movement of the camera and its support in front of a scene. Also called *tracking*.

Tungsten-Halogen Lamp: Lighting instrument in which a quartz bulb is filled with halogen. The filament is tungsten. These bulbs burn at a constant color temperature of 3,200°K and are the industry standard for professional lighting equipment.

Umbrella: Special fabric device used to soften and diffuse the quality of light produced by open-faced spotlights and floodlights.

Unbalanced Line: Inexpensive audio cable or connector widely used on portable audio and video equipment; susceptible to electrical and RF interference.

Unity: Principle of graphic material design in which all materials act together in support of the major theme or purpose of the program.

VCR: See *Videocassette Recorder* (*VCR*).

VCR Trigger: Button on camcorder lens assembly that stops and starts the camcorder recording process.

Vectorscope: Special oscilloscope used to monitor the color video signal.

Velocity Microphone: See *Ribbon Microphone*.

Vertical Interval Time Code (VITC): SMPTE time code inserted in the vertical blanking area of the video signal. Compare with *longitudinal time code* (*LTC*).

VHS: Video home system. The most popular $1/2$″ consumer videocassette format.

Video: The picture portion of the television signal; an electronic signal used to record or transmit television images.

Video Black: A black video signal that contains horizontal and vertical sync pulses along with color burst. Also called *crystal black*.

Video Editor: The member of the video production team who is responsible for editing the field video footage into its finished form.

Video Field Production: Video production that takes place in a location outside a television/video production studio. Usually refers to single-camera productions shot to be edited in postproduction.

Video In: Line-level video input; place where the video signal feeds into a piece of equipment.

Video Insert: See *Insert Edit*.

Video Out: Line-level video output; place where the video signal comes out of a piece of equipment.

Video Player: A playback-only VCR that does not contain recording circuitry.

Video Player-Recorder: A VCR that has the capability to play back and record a videotape.

Video Server: Computer equipped with a hard disk storage system used to record and play back video, often in a configuration in which it is connected to other computer workstations.

Video Signal: An unmodulated electrical signal containing the synchronizing and picture information that forms the video picture.

Video Switcher: Production device that allows several video sources to be mixed and manipulated. Used to perform dissolves, wipes, and other special effects.

Videocassette: A videotape that has been packaged in a cassette housing.

Videocassette Recorder (VCR): Videotape recorder that records the video and audio signals onto a videocassette.

Videographer: In video field production, the camera operator. Also called the *shooter*.

Videotape: Oxide- or metal-particle-coated plastic (polyester or mylar) used to record video and audio signals.

Viewfinder: A small video monitor attached to the camera. Used by the camera operator to frame the scene being shot. Also called *electronic viewfinder*.

Virtual Set: An electronically generated image of a scene that is used instead of an actual setting as the background for a subject.

Voice-over (VO): Narration that is delivered from off camera. The voice of the narrator is heard over background visuals, but the narrator is not seen.

Volume: Relative intensity or loudness of sound.

Volume Unit (VU) Meter: A meter indicating audio levels in a standard calibration of signal strength.

VTR: Videotape recorder. See also *Videocassette Recorder* (*VCR*).

Watt: A unit of electrical power. Watts = amps × volts.

Waveform: The form of a video signal when it is displayed on a waveform monitor, a special oscilloscope designed to display the video signal.

White Balance: Adjustment of the relative intensity of the chrominance channels in a color video camera to allow the camera to produce an accurate white picture in the light available on location. Compensates for differences in the color temperature of light.

Wide-Angle Lens: A lens with a short focal length and a wide angle of view.

Window Dub: A copy of a videotape that includes the time code display in a black box, or window, keyed into the picture information.

Windscreen: Foam cover placed over a microphone to eliminate wind noise. Also called a *wind filter*.

Wipe: A transition in which one screen image is replaced by another. The second image cuts a preselected hard- or soft-edged pattern (such as a circle, square, diagonal, or diamond) into the frame as the transition takes place. Accomplished with the use of a video switcher or special effects software.

Wired Microphone: Any microphone connected to an input via a cable.

Wireless Microphone: A microphone that sends its signal to a receiver via RF transmission rather than through a cable. Also called a *radio microphone*.

Writing Speed: The speed at which the video heads hit the videotape, determined by the rotation speed of the heads, the speed at which the tape is pulled through the VCR, and the size of the head drum. In general, the higher the writing speed, the better the recording quality.

Wrong Field Edit: An edit that does not correctly join together the fields of information from two different frames of video, resulting in a curved black line that appears for an instant at the top of the frame.

XLR Connector: A three-pin connector used on professional-quality equipment for audio inputs and outputs. Also called a *Cannon connector.*

Y/C Signal Processing: A set of video signals with separate luminance (Y) and chrominance (C). Color purity and image detail are higher quality than composite recording. Also called S-Video.

Z-Axis: The dimension toward and away from the camera; the imaginary line from the camera passing through the object.

Zebra-Stripe: Type of camera viewfinder video level indicator.

Zoom: Apparent motion created by moving the lens elements in or out. Brings the scene closer to, or moves it farther away from, the viewer.

Zoom Lens: A variable-focal-length lens.

Zoom Ratio: The ratio of the wide-angle and narrow-angle focal lengths on a zoom lens. A zoom lens with a wide-angle focal length of 8mm and a narrow-angle focal length of 80mm has a zoom ratio of 10:1. Also called *zoom range.*

Zoom Ring: A device that controls the focal length adjustment on a zoom lens. May be automatic or manual.

Bibliography

Books

Alkin, Glyn. *Sound Techniques for Video and TV*. 2nd ed. London: Focal Press, 1989.

Alten, Stanley R. *Audio in Media*. 5th ed. Belmont, CA: Wadsworth, 1999.

Apple Computer. *Demystifying Multimedia*. San Francisco: Vivid, 1993.

Armer, Alan A. *Directing Television and Film*. 2nd ed. Belmont, CA: Wadsworth, 1993.

Berger, Arthur Asa. *Scripts: Writing for Radio and Television*. Newbury Park, CA: Sage, 1990.

Breyer, Richard; Moller, Peter; and Schoonmaker, Michael. *Making Television Programs: A Professional Approach*. 2nd ed. Prospect Heights, IL: Waveland Press, 1991.

Brown, Blain. *Motion Picture and Video Lighting*. Rev. ed. Boston: Focal Press, 1995.

Browne, Steven E. *Videotape Editing: A Post-production Primer*. 3rd ed. Boston: Focal Press, 1996.

Burrows, Thomas D.; Wood, Donald J.; and Gross, Lynne. *Television Production: Disciplines and Techniques*. 6th ed. Dubuque, IA: Wm. C. Brown, 1994.

Davis, Steve. *SPARS Time Code Primer*. Lake Worth, FL: Society of Professional Audio Recording Services, 1997.

DiZazzo, Ray. *Corporate Scriptwriting*. Boston: Focal Press, 1992.

Eargle, John. *Handbook of Recording Engineering*. 2nd ed. New York: Van Nostrand Reinhold, 1991.

Gaskill, Arthur L., and Englander, David A. *How to Shoot a Movie and Video Story*. 4th ed. Dobbs Ferry, NY: Morgan and Morgan, 1985.

Bibliography

Gayeski, Diane. *Corporate and Instructional Video.* 2nd ed. Englewood Cliffs, NJ: Prentice Hall, 1991.

Hartwig, Robert L. *Basic TV Technology.* Boston: Focal Press, 1990.

Hausman, Carl. *Institutional Video.* Belmont, CA: Wadsworth, 1991.

Hausman, Carl, and Palombo, Philip J. *Modern Video Production: Tools, Techniques, Applications.* New York: HarperCollins, 1993.

Hewitt, John N. *Air Words: Writing for Broadcast News.* 2nd ed. Mountain View, CA: Mayfield, 1995.

———. *Sequences: Strategies for Shooting News in the Real World.* Mountain View, CA: Mayfield, 1988.

Hilliard, Robert L. *Writing for Television and Radio.* 6th ed. Belmont, CA: Wadsworth, 1996.

Holsinger, Erik. *MacWEEK Guide to Desktop Video.* Emeryville, CA: Ziff-Davis Press, 1993.

Huber, David M. *Audio Production Techniques for Video.* Boston: Focal Press, 1992.

Hyde, Stuart. *Television and Radio Announcing.* 8th ed. Boston: Houghton Mifflin, 1998.

Jacobs, Bob. *How to Be an Independent Video Producer.* White Plains, NY: Knowledge Industries, 1986.

Kenney, Ritch, and Groome, Kevin. *Television Camera Operation.* Burbank, CA: Tellem Publications, 1987.

Lewis, Colby, and Green, Tom. *The TV Director/Interpreter.* Rev. ed. New York: Hastings House, 1990.

Lyver, Des. *Basics of Video Sound.* Oxford: Focal Press, 1998.

Mathias, Harry, and Patterson, Richard. *Electronic Cinematography.* Belmont, CA: Wadsworth, 1985.

Medoff, Norman, and Tanquary, Tom. *Portable Video: ENG and EFP.* 3rd ed. White Plains, NY: Knowledge Industries, 1997.

Merrill, Joan. *Camcorder Video: Shooting and Editing Techniques.* Englewood Cliffs, NJ: Prentice Hall, 1992.

Miller, Philip. *Media Law for Producers.* 3rd ed. Boston: Focal Press, 1998.

Millerson, Gerald. *The Technique of Lighting for Television and Film.* 3rd ed. Boston: Focal Press, 1991.

———. *The Technique of Television Production.* 12th ed. New York: Hastings House, 1990.

———. *Video Production Handbook.* 2nd ed. London: Focal Press, 1992.

Murch, Walter. *In the Blink of an Eye: A Perspective on Film Editing.* Beverly Hills, CA: Silman-James, 1995.

Nisbett, Alec. *The Use of Microphones.* 3rd ed. London: Focal Press, 1989.

Ohanian, Thomas A. *Digital Nonlinear Editing.* 2nd ed. Boston: Focal Press, 1998.

Orlik, Peter B. *Broadcast-Cable Copywriting.* 6th ed. Boston: Allyn and Bacon, 1997.

Pank, Bob (ed.). *The Digital Fact Book.* 8th ed. Darien, CT: Quantel, 1996.

Richards, Ron. *A Director's Method for Film and Television.* Boston: Focal Press, 1992.

Ritsko, Alan J. *Lighting for Location Motion Pictures.* New York: Van Nostrand Reinhold, 1979.

446

Roth, Cliff. *The Real Facts about Desktop Video Editing.* Aliso Viejo, CA: Future Video Products, 1992.

Rubin, Michael. *Nonlinear: A Guide to Digital Film and Video Editing.* 3rd ed. Gainesville, FL: Triad, 1995.

Seel, Peter B., and Grant, August E. (eds.). *Broadcast Technology Update.* Boston: Focal Press, 1997.

Shook, Frederick. *Television Field Production and Reporting.* 2nd ed. New York: Longman, 1996.

Shyles, Leonard. *Video Production Handbook.* Boston: Houghton Mifflin, 1998.

Smith, David L. *Video Communication.* Belmont, CA: Wadsworth, 1991.

Thompson, Roy. *Grammar of the Edit.* Oxford: Focal Press, 1998.

Utz, Peter. *Today's Video: Equipment, Setup, and Production.* 2nd ed. Englewood Cliffs, NJ: Prentice Hall, 1992.

Walters, Roger L. *Broadcast Writing: Principles and Practices.* New York: McGraw-Hill, 1994.

Watkinson, John. *An Introduction to Digital Audio.* Oxford: Focal Press, 1994.

Watts, Harris. *Directing on Camera.* London: Aavo Media, 1992.

Whittaker, Ron. *Video Field Production.* 2nd ed. Mountain View, CA: Mayfield, 1996.

Wiese, Michael. *Film and Video Budgets.* 2nd ed. Westport, CT: Michael Wiese Film Productions, 1995.

———. *The Independent Film and Videomaker's Guide.* 2nd ed. Boston: Focal Press, 1998.

Wurtzel, Alan, and Rosenbaum, John. *Television Production.* 4th ed. New York: McGraw-Hill, 1995.

Yager, Tom. *The Multimedia Production Handbook for the PC, Macintosh, and Amiga.* Boston: Academic Press Professional, 1993.

Zaza, Tony. *Audio Design: Sound Recording Techniques for Film and Video.* Englewood Cliffs, NJ: Prentice Hall, 1991.

Zettl, Herbert. *Sight Sound Motion: Applied Media Aesthetics.* 3rd ed. Belmont, CA: Wadsworth, 1999.

———. *Television Production Handbook.* 7th ed. Belmont, CA: Wadsworth, 2000.

———. *Video Basics 2.* Belmont, CA: Wadsworth, 1998.

Periodicals

AV Video. White Plains, NY: Montage Publishing.

Digital Video Magazine. San Francisco: Miller-Freeman.

TV Technology. Falls Church, VA: IMAS Publishing (USA).

Video Systems. Overland Park, KS: Intertec Publishing.

Videography. New York: PSN Publications.

Videomaker. Chico, CA: Videomaker.

Index

Credits

Color Plates (CP)

CP-4, Ronald J. Compesi; CP-5 a, b, c, Andrew Tsonis; CP-6, Paul Costa; CP-7, Grass Valley Group; CP-9 and CP-10, Tektronix

Chapter 1

Page 5, Figure 1.1, Paul Costa; page 9, Figure 1.2, Ronald J. Compesi; page 11, Figure 1.3, National Aeronautics and Space Administration (NASA); page 13, Figure 1.4, Ronald J. Compesi; page 14, Figure 1.5 a, Sony Electronics, Inc.; b, JVC Professional Products Company; c, Panasonic Broadcast and Digital Systems Company

Chapter 2

Page 21, Figure 2.1, Ikegami Electronics (U.S.A.), Inc.; page 25, Figure 2.3, Ronald J. Compesi; page 38, Figure 2.9, Ronald J. Compesi; page 41, Figure 2.10, Ikegami Electronics (U.S.A.), Inc.; page 42, Figure 2.11, Sharp Electronics Corp.; page 43, Figure 2.12, Panasonic Broadcast and Digital Systems Company; page 43, Figure 2.13, Ronald J. Compesi

Chapter 3

Page 48, Figure 3.1, Ronald J. Compesi; page 56, Figure 3.4, Ronald J. Compesi; page 58, Figure 3.5, Ronald E. Sherriffs; page 59, Figure 3.6, Ronald J. Compesi; page 64, Figure 3.7 , Ronald J. Compesi; page 65, Figure 3.8, Ronald J. Compesi; page 67, Figure 3.9, Ronald J. Compesi; page 68, Figure 3.10, Ronald J. Compesi; page, 69, Figure 3.11, Ronald J. Compesi; page 70, Figure 3.12, Ronald J. Compesi; page 71, 3.13,

Ronald J. Compesi; page 72, Ronald J. Compesi; page 80, Figure 3.15, Ronald J. Compesi; page 85, Figure 3.17, Ronald J. Compesi; page 85, Figure 3.18, Ronald J. Compesi; page 86, Figure 3.19, Ronald J. Compesi; page 87, Figure 3.20, Ronald J. Compesi

Chapter 4

Page 98, Figure 4.6, Ronald J. Compesi; page 107, Figure 4.9 a, Sony Electronics, Inc.; b, Panasonic Broadcast & Digital Systems Company; c, Sony Electronics, Inc.; page 108, Figure 4.10 a, b, Panasonic Broadcast & Digital Systems Company; c, d, Sony Electronics, Inc.; page 109, Figure 4.11, Panasonic Broadcast & Digital Systems Company; page 114, Figure 4.12, Ronald J. Compesi; page 115, Figure 4.13, Ronald J. Compesi; page 119, Figure 4.15, Ikegami Electronics,(U.S.A), Inc.; page 120, Figure 4.16, Sony Electronics, Inc.

Chapter 5

Page 121, Figure 5.1, Ronald J. Compesi; page 122, Figure 5.2 a, c Sony Electronics, Inc., b, Panasonic Broadcast & Digital Systems Company; page 123, Figure 5.3 a, Panasonic Broadcast & Digital Systems Company; b, Sony Electronics, Inc.; page 124 Figure 5.4, Ronald J. Compesi; page 129, Figure 5.5, Ronald J. Compesi; page 134, Figure 5.6, Ronald J. Compesi; page 139, Figure 5.8, Ronald J. Compesi; page 140, Figure 5.9, Ronald J. Compesi; page 142, Figure 5.10, Ronald J. Compesi; page 145, Figure 5.11, Ronald J. Compesi; page 147, Figure 5.12, Cinema Products Corp.

Chapter 6

Page 150 Figure 6.1, Ronald J. Compesi; page 152, Figure 6.3, Ronald J. Compesi; page 158, Figure 6.6, Ronald J. Compesi; page 160, Figure 6.7, Ronald J. Compesi; page 161, Figure 68, Ronald J. Compesi; page 162-163, Figure 6.9 a, b, c, d, Lowell Light Manufacturing, Inc.; e, Paul Costa; f, De Sisti Lighting; page 165, Figure 6.11, Ronald J. Compesi; page 166, Figure 6.12 a, Josh Haworth, b, Eric Crapo, c, Ronald J. Compesi; page 167, Figure 6.13, Kino Flo, Inc.; page 6.14 a, b, Kino Flo, Inc.; page 168, Figure 6.15 a, b, Ronald J. Compesi; page 170, Figure 6.16, Sony Electronics, Inc.; page 178, Figure 6.20, Ronald J. Compesi; 182, Figure 6.23, Ronald J. Compesi; page 185, Figure 6.24, Ronald J. Compesi; page 190, Figure 6.28, Paul Costa

Chapter 7

Page 203, Figure 7.6 a, Ronald J. Compesi, b, JVC Professional Products Company; page 205, Figure 7.7, Ronald J. Compesi; page 206, Figure 7.8, Ronald J. Compesi; page 208, Figure 7.9, Andre Chow; page 211, Figure 7.11,

Shure Brothers, Inc.; page 216, Figure 7.13, Ronald J. Compesi; page 218, Shure Brothers, Inc.; page 231, Figure 7.18 a, Sony Electronics, Inc., b, Ronald J. Compesi; page 232, Figure 7.19, Digidesign, a division of Avid Technology, Inc.

Chapter 8

Page 247, Figure 8.1, Ronald J. Compesi; page 248, Figure 8.2 , Ronald J. Compesi; page 249, Figure 8.3, Ronald J. Compesi; page 249, Figure 8.4, Ronald J. Compesi; page 250, Figure 8.5, Ronald J. Compesi; page, 251, Figure 8.6, Ronald J. Compesi; page 252, Figure 8.7, Ronald J. Compesi; page 253, Figure 257, Ronald J. Compesi

Chapter 9

Page 264, Figure 9.1, JVC Professional Products Company; page 267, Figure 9.4 a, Sony Electronics, Inc.; b, Ronald J. Compesi; c, JVC Professional Products Company; page 286, Figure 9.10, Ronald J. Compesi; page 293, Figure 9.12, Mackie Designs, Inc.

Chapter 10

Page 295, Figure 10.1, Grass Valley Group; page 297, Figure 10.3 a, Sony Electronics, Inc.; b, Videonics, Inc.; page 302, Figure 10.5 a, Future Video; b, c, Ronald J. Compesi; page 304, Figure 10.6, Ronald J. Compesi; page 305, Figure 10.7, Ronald J. Compesi; page 308, Figure 10.9, Ampex Corporation; page 310, Figure 10.11, Grass Valley Group; page 311, Figure 10.12, Larry Whitney; page 312, Figure 10.13, Larry Whitney

Chapter 11

Page 315, Figure 11.1, Grass Valley Group; page 317, Figure 11.2, Ronald J. Compesi; page 318, Figure 11.3, Panasonic Broadcast and Digital Systems, Inc.; pages 321-322, Figures 11.5-11.8, Larry Whitney; page 324, Figure 11.9, Videomedia, Inc.; page 325, Figure 11.10, Grass Valley Group; page 326, Figure 11.11, Future Video

Chapter 12

Page 331, Figure 12.1, Ronald J. Compesi; page 334, Figure 12.3, Ronald J. Compesi; page 336, Figure 12.5, Ronald J. Compesi; page 337, Figure 12.8, Ronald J. Compesi; page 340, Figure 12.12, Ronald J. Compesi; page 342, Figure 12.13 a, Ampex Corporation; b, Ronald J. Compesi; page 344, Figure 12.15, Quantel, Inc.; page 346, Figure 12.17, Marshall Hash; page 348, Figure 12.19, Ronald J. Compesi; page, 349, Figure 12.21, Larry Whitney; page 352, Figure 12.23, Andrew Tsonis; page 354, Figure 12.24, Larry Whitney

Chapter 13

Pages 362-363, Figure 13.1, KQED/Power Rector; pages 366-367, Figure 13.3, Matt Chan/KPIX; page 369, Figure 13.4, Public Media Center; page 370, Figure 13.5, Navy Recruiting Command; page 371, Figure 13.6, Power Production Software; pages 372-373, Figure 13.7, Fargo Bank; page 385, Figure 13.12, FOOTAGE.net; page 393, Figure 13.16, Larry Whitney

Appendix 4

Lorrae Rominger, San Francisco Film and Video Arts Commission

Appendix 5

United States Copyright Office (in public domain)